CW00393261

The Independent Methodists

A History

John Dolan

Foreword by
David Bebbington

©

James Clarke & Co

James Clarke & Co
P.O. Box 60
Cambridge
CB1 2NT

www.jamesclarke.co.uk
publishing@jamesclarke.co.uk

First Published in 2005

ISBN (10): 0 227 67983 0
ISBN (13): 978 0 227 67983 8

British Library Cataloguing in Publication Data
A catalogue record is available from the British Library

Copyright © John Dolan, 2005

All rights reserved. No part of this edition may be reproduced,
stored in a retrieval system, or transmitted in any form or by any means,
electronic, mechanical, photocopying, recording or otherwise,
without the prior permission in writing from the Publisher.

CONTENTS

Foreword   5

Acknowledgements   7

Abbreviations   9

Introduction: Methodism at the end of the Eighteenth Century   12

THE FIRST PHASE, 1796-1860

Chapter 1: Methodist Lay Revivalist Sects 1796-1815   15

Chapter 2: Social and Political Factors 1815-60   42

Chapter 3: The Shaping of the Movement 1815-60   74

THE SECOND PHASE 1860-1927

Chapter 4: From Sect to Denomination 1860-1927   117

Chapter 5: The Wider Interface: Independent Methodism in its Contemporary Context 1860-1927   166

THE THIRD PHASE 1927-2005

Chapter 6: An Established Denomination 1927-1960   200

Chapter 7: Adapting to a Post-Christian Culture 1960-2005   234

Conclusions   267

Appendices 273

1. An Address to the Independent Methodist Churches, 1815
2. Rules of the Independent Methodist Missionary Society, 1825
3. The Testimony and Principles of Union, 1855
4. Methodist Union, An Independent Methodist Response, 1903
5. Temperance Policy 1900
6. Statement of Faith and Practice 1927
7. Statement of Faith 1984
8. Statement of Practice 2000
9. Missionaries sent out during 1826
10. Primitive Methodist groups defecting to Free Gospelism 1830-55
11. Independent Methodist Day Schools
12. Statistics 1871-2001

Bibliography 299

Index 312

Foreword

Within the diverse mosaic of Evangelical Nonconformity, Independent Methodists have been particularly marked by internal variety. Their chapels had different origins, often through schism from other denominations, and held contrasting attitudes on a range of issues. Displaying much of the sturdy individualism of the North of England, where most of their congregations were planted, they were often few in number but strong in conviction. The members of the Bolton church, formed early in 1820, reported to the annual meeting later the same year that they were already making solid progress. 'Our beginning was but small, only ten in number, but we are now increased threefold; may we be like a threefold cord, not to be easily broken by either men or devils.'[1] The Independent Methodists of Bolton were certainly not broken, creating one of the most flourishing causes in the connexion. Their comment, however, has an application to the whole body, for Independent Methodism was woven from three strands.

First, it was intensely Methodist. The movement was ablaze with the evangelistic fire of the Wesleyans. Its doctrines were those taught by John Wesley and expressed in the hymnody of his brother Charles. Independent Methodists were Arminian in theology, believing that all might be saved, and long upheld the possibility of attaining entire sanctification on earth. They possessed the distinctive features of Methodist organisation. There were class meetings, lovefeasts and preachers' plans; there were circuits, districts and a conference, usually called the annual meeting. Developments during the nineteenth century generally reflected those in the larger Methodist denominations whose ethos they shared – a broadening of theology, an endorsement of temperance and an identification with political Liberalism.

Secondly, however, members of the connexion differed from other Methodists in their system of church government. They were resolutely independent, insisting that each congregation was solely in charge of its own affairs. Adhesion to a circuit was a voluntary act; no external authority might interfere in the internal life of a congregation. In 1815 they declared that each church was 'independent of any canon laws, or of any Conference, or any other Church whatever of the same persuasion'.[2] This characteristic made them close to the Congregationalists and Baptists, who both maintained the same principle of local ecclesiastical autonomy. It was towards the Baptists that they gravitated when, at the opening of the twenty-first century, they decided to forge a fresh denominational identity. They were called 'Independent' for good reason.

In the third place, Independent Methodists repudiated any payment for preachers. This practice was often the fruit of acute poverty, for the movement originally recruited heavily among the dispossessed. The policy of giving no salaries, however, was part of a broader principle that, since every believer was called to ministry, there should be no clerical distinction among them. The rejection of a 'hireling ministry' aligned them with the Brethren and Churches of Christ, but it was also associated with convictions that approximated to those of the Quakers. Since nobody was excluded from ministry, women as well as men had access to all church offices. Other Quaker-like features such as a strong strain of pacifism made for easy co-operation with the Society of Friends, particularly in overseas missions. The earliest society, which arose at Warrington in about 1796, was at first known as the Quaker Methodists.

For over two centuries Independent Methodists have maintained their distinctive threefold standpoint. John Dolan, one of their number, has written a comprehensive study of the movement, bringing the story down to the present day. It has entailed tracking down the primary sources, published and unpublished, for a host of autonomous chapels, many of them extinct, and making a sustained analysis of the developing trends in their corporate life. The task has been pursued with an acute awareness of the changing social and religious climate they inhabited. The resulting account is thorough, persuasive and illuminating. One of the most fascinating pieces in the Evangelical Nonconformist mosaic has now received its due.

David Bebbington
April 2005
University of Stirling

1. Stephen Rothwell, *Memorials of the Independent Methodist Chapel, Folds Road, Bolton* (Bolton: G. Winterburn, 1887), 10.
2. 'An Address to the Independent Methodist Churches', 1815, see Appendix 1, 273.

Acknowledgements

As honorary archivist for the Independent Methodists, I have been privileged to have ready access to the primary source material which provided the basis and inspiration for this book. Initially, it took the form of a research degree thesis, under the title, *Methodist Lay Sectarianism. The Independent Methodists 1796-1927*. This was then extended to cover the period from 1927 to the time of writing.

In acknowledging the help which I received while writing my thesis, I must first mention my supervisor, Rev. Dr. Herbert McGonigle who, at the time, was Principal of the Nazarene Theological College, Manchester, where my research was conducted. His ready availability and perceptive comments helped to give shape and balance to the final thesis and checked my enthusiasm to include far more than was possible! I am also grateful to my external supervisor, Professor David Bebbington, whose comments on my first completed script proved immensely valuable and who pointed me to further helpful lines of research. He has also kindly written the Foreword.

At a more informal level, the Rev. Dr. Kenneth Lysons made many helpful suggestions, particularly on background reading, and proved a useful sounding board on a number of occasions, while several officers of the IM Connexion have read all or part of the finished work and commented on it from Independent Methodism's own perspective. Others offered information which I would otherwise not have unearthed and I would mention especially Dr. Douglas Harrison who made available to me the fruits of his own research into the Nottinghamshire Independent Primitive Methodists; Colin Dews and Dr. Gordon Terry, who supplied me with numerous pieces of information on the Yorkshire part of the story; Norma Virgoe for information on the former IM churches of Norfolk; and Rev. Dr. Stephen Hatcher for access to his thesis and the library of the Englesea Brook Museum of Primitive Methodism. Some family historians provided valuable and interesting information: Ron Naylor (Berresford family of

Macclesfield); Christine Crumblehulme (Crumblehulme family of Bolton); Marie Smith and David Denovan (Denovan family of Glasgow).

For the section of the book which goes beyond the years covered by the thesis, I have received valuable contributions and comments from various members of the Independent Methodist Churches past and present: Dennis Downing, Betty Stout, Hilda Rolfe, David Hill, Tony and Enid Headon, Jim Faulkner, Philip Lockley, Bill Burrows and Marjorie Berry. Some of them enlisted the help of others and I hope that those concerned will consider themselves included in these thanks. To these, I would add my colleague at the Independent Methodist Resource Centre, Andrew Rigby, who has helped with some of the practical aspects of storing materials and printing the later drafts of the work.

I have received help from several libraries and record offices and would like to record my thanks to their staff: the Methodist Archives (Manchester), the Wesley Studies Library (Oxford), the British Library, the Public Record Office, Lancashire Record Office, Cheshire Record Office, Bradford Record Office and Sheffield Archives. To these, I would add numerous public libraries, but most particularly those at Liverpool, Manchester, Glasgow, Gateshead, Sunderland, Newcastle-upon-Tyne, Bolton, Warrington, Preston, Sheffield, Wakefield, Halifax, Batley and the Oldham Local Studies Centre. St. Deniol's Library (Hawarden) and Dr. Williams's Library (London) provided not only books but also oases of calm for quiet, extended study.

Finally, I must record my debt of gratitude to the members at Stockton Heath Independent Methodist Church, Warrington, which I serve as minister, for their interest and encouragement, and also for their patience and understanding when I have needed to take 'time out' at various stages of the project.

John Dolan,
Warrington, 2005

Abbreviations

Used in the text

BLC	British Lessons Council	OM	Original Methodist
FCC	Free Church Council	PM	Primitive Methodist
IM	Independent Methodist	UMFC	United Methodist Free Churches
IPM	Independent Primitive Methodist	WM	Wesleyan Methodist
MNC	Methodist New Connexion	WMA	Wesleyan Methodist Association
NCC	Northern Counties Confederation	WPM	Wesleyan Protestant Methodist
NCEC	National Christian Education Council	WR	Wesleyan Reformers
NFCC	National Free Church Council	WRU	Wesleyan Reform Union
NSSU	National Sunday School Union		

Used in endnotes

CCMins — Connexional Committee Minutes

CRO — Chester Record Office

DMBI — *Dictionary of Methodism in Great Britain and Ireland* (London: Epworth, 2000)

ECMins — Evangelistic Committee Minutes

HMCGB — *History of the Methodist Church in Great Britain* (London: Epworth), Four vols. (1965-1988)

IMA — Independent Methodist Archives

IMMag — *The Independent Methodist Magazine* (also published as *Free Gospel Advocate, Free Gospel Magazine* or *Magazine of the United Free Gospel Churches)*

IMMins — Independent Methodist Minutes (later included in the Year Book)

IM(M)Mins — Minutes of Independent Methodist Minority Churches 1854-60.

IMYB — Independent Methodist Year Book

IQ — *Independent Quarterly*

MCA — Methodist Church Archives, Manchester

NHM — *New History of Methodism* (London: Hodder & Stoughton, 1909)

PMMag — Primitive Methodist Magazine

PMMins — Primitive Methodist Minutes

PWHS — Proceedings of the Wesley Historical Society

ZT — *Zion's Trumpet* (Magazine of Minority Churches 1854-60)

John Wesley

Introduction
Methodism at the End
of the Eighteenth Century

John Wesley died in 1791, at a time when political change was happening in mainland Europe and its impact was being felt in Britain. Revolution in France was matched, on the one hand, by a growing wish for political reform among British people and, on the other, by a growing fear among the ruling classes that the bloodshed in France could happen in Britain too. Moreover, Britain was experiencing unprecedented changes of its own as a predominantly agricultural nation rapidly changed into an industrial society where large numbers of working people migrated to growing towns and cities, especially in the north of England.

Against this backcloth, historians have analysed the factors leading to Methodism's gradual separation from the Church of England and its subsequent splintering process.[1] The actual status of Methodism was itself ambiguous; was it a party within the Church of England or was it a new form of dissent? Whatever the views of Methodists themselves, in the eyes of the government and the Anglican hierarchy, they were Dissenters.[2] This identification created a particular problem for them, since some of the Dissenters of the time welcomed the French Revolution and the democratic ideas associated with it. There was therefore widespread suspicion that that Methodists, as Dissenters, had Jacobin sympathies. Wishing to avoid such suspicions, the response of the Methodist Conference was to make statements reminding members of their obligations to loyally submit to the king and his government.[3]

However, the issue of democracy was not so easily dispelled and inevitably began to affect Methodism following Wesley's death, particularly through the relationship between preachers and people. While a general egalitarianism prevailed among the preachers themselves, the role of lay people remained confined to society and circuit rather than district and conference. This was not entirely exceptional, since the assumption that the preachers represented the laity was consistent with the pattern of national government embodied in the unreformed House of Commons.[4] However, in an age when democratic ideas were gaining ground, it was unsurprising that the matter of lay representation would raise its head in Methodism during the 1790s.

But there were theological as well as political factors in the trend towards religious democracy. Robert Currie saw this trend as an antithesis to Wesley's doctrine of Christian Perfection or Scriptural Holiness.[5] The promotion of Christian Perfection, he argued, required an authoritarian regime which inevitably conflicted with the desire of people to have greater control of their affairs at local level. Conversely, Bernard Semmel argued that the pursuit of personal sanctification gave people of all social classes a greater sense of responsibility for their standing with God. By the same token, he reasoned that this made them realise that a lay ministry, with a high view of Christian holiness, could provide for their spiritual needs in a way which the professional ministry, in much of the country, was failing to do. He therefore saw Wesley's doctrine as the *source* of an incipient egalitarianism rather than an obstacle to it.[6]

To take Semmel's argument still further, some Methodist lay people had been stimulated to act even more independently by their attraction to individualistic forms of revivalism which went beyond Wesley's teaching on perfection, to the point at which they were in danger of becoming out of control.[7] Respected preachers such as Joseph Entwisle had serious doubts about some of the more extreme manifestations of revivalism, which looked more antinomian than genuinely pietistic.[8]

In the view of Julia Werner, the Wesleyan leadership became so absorbed with proving itself loyal to king and country that it failed to cope with either revivalism or the expression of lay opinion.[9] However, Methodism's leadership in the 1790s was not totally insensitive to the wishes of grass-roots members. For example, in an attempt to meet the wishes of both parties – 'Church' and separatists – the Conference of 1793 decided that each local society could choose, if it wished, to have a Methodist-supervised sacrament, provided that the members of the society were unanimous in this wish. Not surprisingly, finding that this gave the power of veto to any individual who chose to use it, this was amended a year later and put in more general terms. By 1795, the move towards separation was gathering momentum and Conference approved a Plan of Pacification, which entailed the agreement of people at local level on a wide range of issues. Then in 1797, power was devolved in even greater measure when further authority was transferred from Conference to Quarterly Meetings, with broader representation. The Conference reported, 'out of our great love for peace and union, and . . . to satisfy your minds, we have given up to you by far the greatest part of the Superintendent's authority.'[10] But the right of all nominations stayed with the Superintendent and no meetings were allowed without his presence.

When, eventually, it was clear that Methodism was separating from the Church of England, certain consequences inevitably followed for a body which had not previously defined itself as a church. Societies which had met in borrowed premises now needed registered places of worship – so chapels had to be built. The itinerant preachers became *de facto* pastors, as the people no longer looked to the incumbents of their local parish churches for pastoral care. Costs rose and these were passed on to the people. In areas where there was great poverty, this caused discontent and even resistance well into the next century. In some cases, the Conference had little alternative but to heed local reactions, as at Warrington in 1796 (then in the Northwich Circuit), when Conference decided that the town's Bank Street Chapel should have its own itinerant. The leaders wrote back, said that they were well enough served by their local preachers and, in any event, they were too poor to pay an itinerant. The matter was not raised again until 1812.[11]

Despite the Conference's moves towards greater democratisation, the itinerants still held great authority at local level, with power to decree what activities should or should not take place in the societies and also disciplinary powers in relation to members. This brought inevitable tension where local people were now used to having some degree of discretion and it proved the flashpoint which brought two of the earliest Independent Methodist groups into being, in Warrington and Manchester.[12]

Initially, neither radicalism nor revivalism succeeded in splitting Methodism, but in 1796 the former issue brought one of the itinerant preachers, Alexander Kilham, into conflict with the parent body. Kilham was concerned with what he saw as the social inequalities in Methodism. Arguing through speeches and pamphlets that all men were equal *spiritually*, he pressed for a social expression of that equality by according all believing members of Methodist societies a vote at every level.[13] Eventually, he was brought to trial on charges of disrupting Methodism and duly expelled. Kilham and those sympathetic to him subsequently banded together to form the Methodist New Connexion, the first of Methodism's post-Wesley schisms.[14] While the numbers involved were not great, the process of severance indicated the underlying stresses in Methodism.[15] As Hempton has commented, Kilham had 'struck raw nerves of anti-clericalism'[16] among artisan Methodists; those nerves would be exposed even more fully as the Independent Methodists emerged over the next 25 years.

However, worship in the New Connexion was indistinguishable from that in the Wesleyan chapels and, although lay people now had a greater say in the government of local societies and the Conference of the New

Connexion, order and discipline remained. Consequently, there were defections when some found that insubordination was not accepted;[17] others left to pursue a spirituality which was more overtly revivalist. Some of the defectors from the New Connexion became part of the embryonic Independent Methodist movement which appeared to offer them greater freedom.[18] Having made a major step in defecting from the main Methodist body to become New Connexionists, a second defection probably seemed less daunting. The mould had been broken and new shapes would take time to form.

Revivalism, local autonomy, fraternal equality and opportunities for lay leadership were some of the issues that would lead to Methodist fragmentation up to the middle of the nineteenth century. Each of the new groupings would emphasise some or all of these issues, but the Independent Methodists were probably the most radical of all of them, rejecting both connexional government and the Methodist concept of the pastoral office. The following chapters will show how they formed churches in different locations and eventually coalesced to become a new denomination.

Notes to Introduction

1. For example: J.M. Turner, *Conflict and Reconciliation* (London: Epworth, 1985), 9ff.; J. Walsh 'Methodism at the end of the Eighteenth Century' in R.E. Davies and G. Rupp (eds.), *A History of the Methodist Church in Great Britain* (4 vols.; London: Epworth, 1965) 1:277ff.
2. See Walsh, *HMCGB,* 1:303 for the varying views within Methodism on its status.
3. *Ibid,* 304; Turner, *Conflict and Reconciliation,* 118.
4. Walsh, *HMCGB,* 1:281.
5. R. Currie, *Methodism Divided* (London: Faber, 1968), 80f.
6. B. Semmel, *The Methodist Revolution,* (London: Heinemann, 1973) 112.
7. C. Dews, *Ranters, Revivalists, Radicals and Reformers* (Leeds Methodist District, 1996), 45. See also the account of the Bandroom Methodists of Manchester in Chapter 3.
8. *Memoir of the Rev. Joseph Entwistle by his son,* (Bristol, 1848), 212f.
9. J.S. Werner, *The Primitive Methodist Connexion: Its Background and Early History* (London: University of Wisconsin Press, 1984) 4.
10. *Methodist Conference Minutes,* 1797, 1. 377, 392, 394.
11. *IMMag* 1907, 27.
12. See Chapter 1.
13. Alexander Kilham, *The progress of liberty amongst the people called Methodists* (Alnwick, 1796), 35f.
14. J.T. Wilkinson, 'The Rise of Other Methodist Traditions', *HMCGB,* 2:286ff.
15. Turner, *Conflict and Reconciliation,* 119.
16. D. Hempton *Methodism and Politics in British Society 1750-1850.* (London: Hutchinson & Co. 1984), 71.
17. Wilkinson, *HMCGB,* 2:290.
18. See Chapter 1.

Chapter 1
Methodist Lay Revivalist Sects, 1796-1815

Independent Methodism did not result from a single event or issue, nor did it emanate from the initiative of a single leader. In the two decades that straddled the turn of the eighteenth and nineteenth centuries, the turbulence in Methodism and the nation threw up various localised sectarian groups which sprang from either disciplinary measures or other causes of disaffection. The story of the Independent Methodists is not, therefore, so much one of expansion from a single starting point as the sewing together of a patchwork quilt of groups which emerged under different names and in different locations.

Churches of autonomous character, sometimes referred to as 'independent', had branched from Methodism earlier in the eighteenth century, notably under the leadership of John Bennett in Lancashire[1] and Thomas Bryant in Sheffield[2], but none resulted from conflict over lay rights. By contrast, each of the local sects and societies which eventually formed the Independent Methodist denomination was entirely a lay people's movement.

1. Origins

1.1. The Quaker Methodists of Warrington

The story behind the Quaker Methodists who broke from Wesleyan Methodism c.1796, is known only from their founders' verbal accounts which were not put into writing until nearly 60 years later.[3] There is no corresponding record from the Wesleyan Methodist perspective.

The Bank Street Methodist society in Warrington was in the Northwich Circuit; at one point the Conference planned to station an itinerant preacher in Warrington, but this was abandoned in the face of local opposition. However, for pastoral supervision, the society still came under the Northwich itinerant whose visits were infrequent,[4] with the result that it was largely led by its local preachers. Some of them held cottage meetings (a common enough Methodist practice) which were popular with the members. However, one particular itinerant, John Booth,[5] decided to terminate them and required all meetings to take place on the church premises and under his supervision.[6] Four local preachers felt in conscience that they could not accept Booth's ruling, withdrew from the Methodists, took rented premises and began to meet with others who shared their convictions. What appeared to them as unwarranted authoritarianism resulted in a reaction against Methodist itinerancy and in favour of local autonomy. Later, the dissident Wesleyans were joined by some disaffected Quakers and became, effectively, a hybrid of two disciplines. They took the name 'Quaker Methodists',[7] retained Methodist doctrine, class meetings, lovefeasts, preaching and hymnsinging, but adopted Quaker speech and dress, times of silent waiting upon God and eschewed the sacraments.

The blending of two seemingly incompatible strands of spirituality and ecclesiology warrants examination. The Society of Friends was well established in the Warrington area, with three meetinghouses, but their records offer no direct insights into the reasons for the defection of members in the 1790s. However, during the eighteenth century most Quaker groups had retreated into either quietism or latitudinarianism[8] and their numbers had fallen. The emergence in Warrington of a non-clerical, egalitarian society would have a ready appeal to Quakers who wanted spiritual vitality without compromising their basic principles. Moreover, the levelling, experiential nature of Methodist-style class and band meetings would sit well with the historic Quaker belief in the direct revelation of God to the individual believer. At first, the refusal of the Quaker Methodists to countenance paid ministry may have been due to the poverty of the former Bank Street Methodists, who had said that they were too poor to pay an itinerant, but eventually this became a matter of principle, due, at least in part, to the influence of Quaker ideology.[9]

The fusion of the two ideologies was also largely influenced through Peter Phillips (1778-1853), an early leader who went on to become the patriarch not only of his own church, but also of the eventual denomination. Phillips was fostered by a Quaker couple in his childhood, but followed his brother into Bank Street Chapel, where he had a conversion experience and also met his future wife, Hannah Peacock.[10] Undoubtedly, his strong personal influence served to promote Quaker values and practices in the new society. But Phillips' contribution was by no means unique; in the decade which followed the establishment of the new group, other voices from the Quaker world would influence them. These included Quaker evangelists of revivalist character, such as Dr. Paul Johnson of Dublin[11] and Dorothy Ripley of Whitby,[12] who visited Warrington during the first few years of the nineteenth century and found a ready welcome among the Quaker Methodists.

Peter Phillips (1778-1853) and Hannah Phillips (1780-1858)

The first chapel in Warrington was built in 1802 and named after its location at Friars Green, on the site of the former Augustinian friary. This church's early registers show its founders to be predominantly artisan: William Maginnis (glass cutter), George Brimelow (weaver), Peter Phillips and his brother Joshua (chairmakers). Other occupations noted in the first two decades of the nineteenth century included shoemakers, farmers, a hat manufacturer and a spade maker. The majority of members appear to have been artisans rather than unskilled labourers, but there were also literate men such as schoolmasters and excise officers.[13] The Quaker Methodists of Warrington existed alone until 1806, apparently without outside contact, but extending their activities through cottage meetings over a radius of several miles. Some of these eventually led to the formation of additional churches.[14]

1.2. Dissent from the Methodist New Connexion

An entirely different set of circumstances led to the formation of sectarian groups of similar character in three other North-West towns between 1799 and 1802 and a later one in Yorkshire. In each case, they had at least partial origins from Alexander Kilham's Methodist New Connexion, still in its own infancy.

Gamaliel Swindells (1767-1833), a hatter by trade, was a Methodist class leader at the age of 16 and avidly studied the works of Wesley and John Fletcher of Madeley. In 1798 he became a founding member and trustee of the Stockport New Connexion society, which first met in his warehouse. He was appointed leader of the society's first class meeting and it quickly acquired a revivalist character.[15] However, once the society opened its chapel (Mount Tabor), the relationship between Swindells and others in the society went sour. It represented, as Julia Werner put it, 'the radicalism of unenfranchised merchants, millowners and professional men,'[16] rather than the poor and dispossessed, who must have hoped that it would give them a real stake in an egalitarian form of Methodism. Unfortunately, their hopes were disappointed and their revivalist leanings also apparently went unsatisfied. Swindells' biographer commented:

> had he found their great professions of liberality sincere, he might
> have lived and died in connection with them, but finding that the
> greatest difference lay betwixt the words 'Old Connexion' and
> 'New Connexion', except that what power had been conceded by
> the preachers of the New Connexion in favour of the people was
> only in favour of the rich members who were nearly always
> appointed the lay delegates to the conference, together with some
> shuffling relative to the appointment of trustees for Mount Tabor
> Chapel, and the introduction of an organ, against the will of the
> people, together with other matters of similar import. . . .'[17]

This says much about the sensitivity of the poorer members of the society who evidently felt marginalised in a church which they had helped to establish. But at Stockport there was no evidence of the Quaker influences which were at work in Warrington. Swindells' followers became known simply as 'revivalists'. They rented premises in the Royal Oak Yard on High Street[18] and by 1808 had established preaching places in four villages around the town.[19] Hugh Bourne described how 'a number of poor but very pious people', living at Stockport, called 'revivalists',[20] were the means of bringing him and some others into the experience of entire sanctification. This led to a time of revival at Harriseahead and Tunstall in the North Staffordshire Potteries. If those mentioned by Bourne were members of Swindells' group, it anchors their theology firmly in the Wesleyan tradition and also puts them in the wider context of the revivalism which proved such a driving force in the development of both Primitive and Independent Methodism.

In Macclesfield, some Wesleyan Methodists withdrew from their society in 1798 to form a New Connexion Church. This church recorded 97 members in 1801,[21] after which it vanished from New Connexion records. Vickers noted, 'They shared to the full Kilham's desire for freedom, but the organisation shaped by him, though having democratic features, did not satisfy their zeal for revivalism, with its moods and methods swayed by the Spirit.'[22] Thus, according to Vickers, the New Connexion members became Independent Methodists. However, the source of his information is not indicated and no primary records from either denomination survive to explain what happened. The picture is further complicated by the emergence in 1802 of a split in one of the Wesleyan societies in Macclesfield. Jabez Bunting, later to become the most powerful figure in Wesleyan Methodism, was stationed in Macclesfield at the time and noted:

> The remnant of the Lower Eyres Society, headed by Gregory, Nightingale, Beresford, etc. have formed themselves into a regular Independent Church. They assume the modest title of 'Christian Revivalists'.[23]

That this group was the eventual Independent Methodist society of Macclesfield is confirmed by the fact that Beresford presided at the Annual Meeting of 1810[24] and Gregory acted as secretary in 1808.[25] How the erstwhile New Connexion society fits into the picture remains a mystery, but the coincidence of its apparent demise after 1801 and the emergence of the Independent Methodists in the following year may suggest that these two groups came together as a single society, but this cannot be confirmed with certainty.

Thomas Gregory had been a local preacher with the Wesleyan Methodists.[26] Joseph Nightingale, a local pamphleteer, was a man of unstable character who soon left and became one of the most ardent critics of revivalism, turning later to Unitarianism, then to deism.[27] John Beresford (c1754-1816),[28] cotton master and merchant of Hurdsfield Mills, became a great friend to Hugh Bourne and Peter Phillips, was the church's most prominent leader and remained so until his death. He was one of the prime movers in 1806 for the building of Providence Chapel in Parsonage Street, the deeds for which stated that it was to be used by 'persons of the Independent Interest dissenting from the established Church of England upon the old Methodistical principles and called the Christian Revivalists.'[29] This description shows how the two concepts of *Independence* (in the sense used by the 'Independents' of early dissent) and *Methodism* were coming together before the name itself was coined or the denomination was formed. Additionally, it shows that some of the early groups which eventually linked to the Independent Methodists placed an emphasis on their revivalist character to the point of reflecting this in their chosen title.

Bunting's contempt for the revivalists of Macclesfield was made abundantly clear when he posted a copy of their rules to two of the other preachers for their amusement.[30] An extract from the rules survives in quotation form only, but it gives a useful insight into an important aspect of the revivalists' character:

> Let us walk by the same rule – We may truly pronounce those churches happy, however plain and poor, in which
>   'No simony or sinecure is known,

Where works the bee – no honey for the drone.'
In the primitive church, profession of faith in Christ accredited
by a holy life, was accounted a sufficient title to membership.[31]

This is one of the earliest references to what would become the
Independent Methodists' negative perception of paid preachers who, in their
view, lived off the members of their churches. Like the societies at
Warrington and Stockport, this group also catered for the poor.

The departure of the Macclesfield group of churches from the Independent
Methodist fraternity was as sudden as its arrival. Due to host the conference
of the churches in 1814, it defected before the date and was received as a
circuit at the 1814 Methodist New Connexion Conference instead.[32] No reason
was recorded at the time; Vickers, writing over a century later, stated that
Macclesfield 'ran well for a time, but eventually yielded to the attractions of a
settled ministry.'[33] This is probably correct as short-term experiments in free
gospelism were not uncommon; those groups which found the experiment
unsatisfactory or unsuccessful simply abandoned it.

In Preston, the Wesleyan Methodists in Back Lane Chapel suffered loss
in 1801/2 when about 165 members withdrew and formed a New Connexion
Church in Lord Street. Among its members was one George Smith, who
subsequently joined (or led) a further splinter group, this time along free
gospel lines, similar to the ones at Stockport and Macclesfield. A weaver
by trade, Smith began life in great poverty which continued into his early
years of married life. After an unsuccessful spell as a shopkeeper, he
returned to weaving and went on to become a substantial manufacturer and
property owner.[34] The new church seems to have been very much under his
direction and possibly dependent on his benevolence.

In 1806, Lorenzo Dow visited Preston where he attended the lovefeast
of this group, which he identified with other revivalist and Quaker
Methodist groups, describing them as 'free gospellers'.[35] However, Preston
did not link with the other churches until 1810 when it was recorded, for
the first known time, in the Annual Meeting Minutes. In 1814 George Smith
built Vauxhall Road Chapel as a Quaker Methodist Church, but in 1817 he
was reconciled with the Wesleyans and returned to their fold. The cause
was wound up and the chapel passed into other hands. Smith, however, was
to prove a dissident yet again, joining the Protestant Methodists in 1829
during another upheaval.[36]

Of all the groups which left the New Connexion to join the Independent
Methodists, the last and largest was at Sheffield, when a group of members
left Scotland Street, a church with a long independent tradition. Founded by
Thomas Bryant in 1765 as an 'independent' Methodist Church, it had joined
the New Connexion after Bryant's death and Alexander Kilham briefly served

as its minister.[37] This church included in its ranks people who were active in radical politics.[38] Now, several years on, it would only require an assertion of authority to bring out again the latent independence of spirit which this society had long experienced. This, it seems, was what happened.

> It was early in the year 1814 that some differences took place between the preachers and people at Scotland Street Chapel, when in consequence of much domineering conduct of the former, a good number of the friends took themselves away and begun [*sic*] to turn themselves into an Independent Methodist Church.[39]

Once established and linked with the Independent Methodists, the new church appointed honorary pastors from among its membership.[40] Mission churches were successfully established and in 1821 a chapel was built in Bow Street.[41] By 1824, the membership of Bow Street and its branches was 483.[42] It fulfilled an important role in the development of the Independent Methodists throughout the 1820s.[43]

1.3. The Band Room Methodists of Manchester

A draper named John Broadhurst was converted around 1790 and joined the Methodist Chapel in Oldham Street, Manchester, where he soon became an ardent worker.[44] Along with others he established a number of meeting places in the city,[45] including a 'Band Room' in North Street.[46] It became the scene of large numbers of conversions, which, in the view of James Sigston, meant that it 'had been eminently owned of God',[47] but official Methodism was less complimentary, describing Broadhurst and his associates as 'more zealous than wise'.[48] The conduct of their meetings, which were notable for unrestricted participation and highly charged emotionalism, raised understandable concerns on the part of the itinerant preachers. However, though they were organised and attended by Methodist members, they were not held on Methodist premises and the organisers resisted circuit discipline.

Some time before the Band Room leaders came into open conflict with successive itinerant preachers, an incident occurred which foreshadowed the eventual polarisation of organised revivalism from the central leadership of Methodism. An eyewitness account told the story of what happened at a Band Room service one day in 1798:

> In the pulpit stood a very slim, timid-looking boy, who gave out the preparatory hymn in peace. Then, Sister Broadhurst and Brother Dowley insisted on praying and both were gratified. But when a brother of name unknown sought to exercise in prayer for the third time, the wrath of honest John Burkenhead . . . was

kindled and he shouted, 'It's time for the young man to begin.'
So the service proceeded without further interruption.[49]

The young man in question was Jabez Bunting, nineteen years old, in
the Band Room by appointment to deliver his trial sermon. Bunting never
forgot his experience and was to prove a formidable opponent to the
activities of the revivalists, particularly during his later stationings in
Macclesfield and Manchester, both centres of Methodist revivalism.[50]

Five years after Bunting's memorable debut at the Band Room, William
Jenkins, then superintendent, felt that he had to do something. On 17 June
1803, he wrote to John Broadhurst, on behalf of himself and his colleagues,
Robert Lomas and Charles Atmore, expressing his concern. On the conduct
of meetings, he commented, 'I cannot but think it offensive to God, who
has declared himself the God of order, not of confusion: For what is it but
mere human passions mixing themselves, to say the least, with the pure
flame of love and devotion which is ascending to God?'[51] Turning to the
subject of the supervision of meetings, he offered no objection to the use
of private rooms, but said that they should be under the direction of the
church; otherwise they would be sources of schism. He then addressed the
contentious matter of the Sunday afternoon meetings at the Band Room
when non-members were allowed to testify openly. This was contrary to
Methodist discipline, which required class and band meetings to be limited
to members only. Finally, he drew attention to Friday evening meetings at
the Band Room when a group of members came together to appoint one
another to different places during the following week. Again, this was
contrary to Methodist discipline which gave the responsibility for all
appointments to the Superintendent. The Band Room practice, Jenkins
stressed, made it in effect 'a kingdom within a kingdom, or two supreme
authorities in one community.'[52] The letter concluded with a request to
meet with Broadhurst and discuss matters further.

The outcome was a 'Plan of Reconciliation' to which Broadhurst and
his friends agreed. This was not, apparently, committed to writing, but
William Jenkins later recalled the two main stipulations:

> 1st. No one should be admitted into the Band (so called) without
> producing a society ticket or note from an itinerant preacher. (It
> was stated particularly that the meeting with respect to admission,
> should be on the same footing as our lovefeasts.) 2ndly. That an
> itinerant preacher should attend and preside and direct the
> Meetings as often as we could make it convenient.[53]

It was added that these regulations should be introduced gradually.
Broadhurst would stand at the door for two or three Sundays and exclude

those he thought proper. He would give notice of the regulations and thereafter enforce them. The Conference that year approved of these decisions and everyone hoped that the matter had been resolved.[54] In the event, the new regulations were ignored and the Band Room went on in much the same way as before. Gradually, the preachers gave up on it and left its members to their own devices in the hope that the group would wither away. However, the Band Room leaders continued to attend Leaders' Meetings at Oldham Street. This situation must have caused considerable tension over the following two and a half years, during which time the preachers made sure that any newly appointed leaders were not Band Room attenders.

Finally, it was the failure of the Band Room people to conform to a decision of the Oldham Street Leaders' Meeting that brought matters to a head. It was agreed that a shared Watchnight and Covenant service should be held at Oldham Street on the first Sunday in the New Year of 1806 and that the other places of worship, including the North Street Band Room, should close for the occasion. However, North Street remained open and its usual attenders were absent from Oldham Street, thereby not sharing in the renewal of the Covenant.

Jabez Bunting was now back in Manchester as a fully fledged but relatively junior itinerant preacher, ready to do battle with this group of revivalists whose activities were well known to him. He and the other preachers and leaders were now determined to take Broadhurst and his supporters to task, demanding conformity on two issues: the closure of the North Street room when Covenant or Lovefeast services were held at any of the other places, and the authorisation of the Superintendent or Leaders' Meeting for individuals to attend the Sunday afternoon 'experience' meetings. After some delay, the North Street leaders replied to say that their only concession to the requirements of the leaders was that they would appoint door keepers to check who was admitted to the meetings and they would take steps to prevent unsuitable people from speaking or praying openly.

This response was, of course, unsatisfactory to the preachers and leaders, so a meeting was held with seven North Street leaders to discuss matters further. Bunting had, by this time, armed himself with the facts of the 1803 agreement[55] and, at this meeting, he and the other preachers, John Reynolds and William Leach, turned the screw even tighter by adding a further demand – that, where possible, they should conduct the meetings at North Street themselves. This was, in essence, no more than the stipulations made in 1803, but there was an obviously stronger intention to enforce them.

Challenged by this assertion of authority, the North Street leaders refused to submit to the Leaders' Meeting or even to allow any travelling preacher to conduct the meeting in North Street. What followed was an ultimatum sent to John Broadhurst, stating that they would either have to accede to the rulings given or cease to be Methodists. The reply was sent on the same day, indicating that they had chosen the latter course.[56] A week later, they had constituted themselves as the 'Methodist Independent Church.'[57] They immediately resolved not to unite with any other church on matters of government or finance.[58] This resolution would later have a bearing on the type of union adopted by the Independent Methodists.

The departure of the North Street meeting from the Wesleyan fold did not end the matter. Bunting had not finished with his attempts to undo what he saw as the damage caused by the Band Room revivalists and succeeded in regaining the allegiance of several of Broadhurst's apprentices, although Broadhurst took with him about 250 members.[59] One of the most significant effects of this conflict was the production of a pamphlet (already cited) entitled, *A Statement of Facts and Observations relative to the late Separation from the Society in Manchester, affectionately addressed to the members of that body by their Preachers and Leaders*. This was a reasoned account of the line taken by the preachers and leaders towards Broadhurst and his associates. Its author is not named, but its sentiments are certainly consistent with those expressed by Bunting in subsequent years. His part in this document and the decisive action taken in relation to the Band Room was a significant step in the process which would see him become the dominant figure in Methodism for the next fifty years and the scourge of further dissidents.

The *Statement of Facts* has been described as 'the earliest exposition of the Wesleyan doctrine of the Pastoral Office.'[60] As this was still only fifteen years after Wesley's death, and Wesleyan Methodism had gone through constitutional turmoil on the road to becoming a denomination, it is hardly surprising that the transition of role from preacher to minister was still incomplete. So if the Band Room controversy had achieved nothing else, it served to focus the minds of the Wesleyans on the kind of church and ministry they would establish during the years ahead.

By the same token, the exercise of firm discipline set the Methodist Independents of Manchester on a course which would take them still further from their Methodist roots at least in matters of church government. It also 'hastened rather than delayed the threat of union amongst revivalists which had emerged at Macclesfield in 1803.'[61] The Band Room duly forged links with the other groups which have already been identified.[62]

1.4. Oldham: a Parish Church Rift

About 1806, a number of worshippers at St Peter's Church, Oldham, had 'been brought to see the necessity and importance of inward religion, to the enjoyment of pardon and, being justified by faith, had peace with God and rejoiced because the love of God was shed abroad in their hearts.'[63] Under the leadership of Joseph Matley, this group held a weekly meeting for Bible reading and Christian fellowship. At one such meeting, a group member, John Nield, took a text and used it as the basis for an exhortation. Matley, a staunch churchman, disapproved, believing that this was the prerogative of the clergyman alone. Some of the group supported Nield and they began to hold meetings in an upper room, later transferring to an old disused mill in Whitehead Square. The incumbent of St Peter's called upon them to discontinue their meetings but, rather than do so, they separated from the church altogether.[64]

The dissidents took for themselves the title 'Independent Methodist' – and became the first church to use the name which the denomination eventually adopted. In this instance, neither rampant revivalism nor Quaker stillness appears to have been a defining characteristic. By taking the word 'Independent' from the world of old Dissent and linking it with 'Methodist' which reflected their spiritual experience, the Oldham people captured better than any of the other formative groups the essence of the movement that was yet to be. Their departing action illustrated the increasing readiness of working people to assert their rights to self-determination and to meet their own spiritual needs, despite the apparent price of sectarian isolation. This would be repeated in numerous towns and villages in the decades ahead. In 1816 the Oldham Independent Methodists built a chapel in George Street and, from this, other churches came in due course and extended their activities into other parts of the town.[65]

1.5. The Sigstonians

In Leeds, some 300 revivalist Methodists, under the leadership of James Sigston, a schoolmaster, left their circuit in 1805 and formed an independent society, known as the Sigstonians or Kirkgate Screamers. The evidence suggests that this society was represented at the first Independent Methodist Annual Meeting in 1806, but not afterwards.[66] The Sigstonians remained in existence until 1807 when there was a reconciliation and they were re-instated in the Old Connexion. However, this reunion would lead to further problems two decades later when Sigston played a major part in the Protestant Methodist schism.[67]

2. Corporate Formation

The first attempt to unify these unconnected lay sectarian groups occurred in 1803 on the initiative of William Bramwell, an itinerant Methodist preacher, then based in Leeds. Bramwell had served in the Leeds Circuit for two years and was highly successful as an evangelist, but his revivalist methods met with some disapproval and opposition as a result of the disorder and indiscipline which followed in their wake. Pressure on him within the circuit grew and he fled to Manchester without telling his colleagues in the circuit where he had gone.[68] This matter was raised at the District Meeting on 6 July 1803, but as he had not been traced by this date, it was referred to the ensuing Conference. Bramwell's choice of destination was determined by his plan to link John Broadhurst's Bandroom Methodists, the Christian Revivalists in Macclesfield and his own supporters in Leeds to form a new division of Methodists. Broadhurst was willing to secede but evidently his members were not and the scheme collapsed. Bramwell was subsequently received back into the Conference fold[69] and promptly stationed in the rural backwater of Wetherby. The prospective new denomination was stillborn.

Bramwell's scheme was motivated by a desire to take Methodism back to its early roots and was based on the perception that something of its revivalist ethos was being lost as it moved increasingly to formalised religion. Lorenzo Dow (reflecting revivalist views) lamented Bramwell's submission:

> From what I could collect [sic], it appears to me that William Bramwell ought to have launched out as a champion for God, but unbelief to trust God with his family etc., caused him apparently to shrink. . . . It appears that he saw the formality and danger into which the English Connexion were exposed and sinking: he came out for a space and God began to open his way, but through unbelief, the reasoning of Satan, and the solicitations of his brethren, he was prevailed upon to shrink, recant in part and return; in consequence of which some pious ones who requested Christian liberty to pray with mourners, etc. and united with him to dissent, were left in a dilemma here.[70]

Had Bramwell's attempt been successful, the story of reformed Methodism would have been different, as Mounfield observed a century later;[71] a unified, revivalist denomination would have pre-empted the later emergence of both Primitive and Independent Methodism as separate denominations, though differences over the payment of preachers could have caused later internal schism. Two years after Bramwell's departure from the field, Lorenzo Dow himself (1777-1834) arrived on the scene. Born at Coventry, Connecticut, his roots lay in Methodism, but his ministry was largely freelance and was based on the frontier-style revivalism of camp meetings which gained renown, if not notoriety, for bizarre happenings. Camp Meetings were four– or five-day gatherings, usually in wilderness clearings, designed for the benefit of people who lived in remote settlements and who had little contact with an organised church. Strange phenomena accompanied them: falling to the ground, uncontrollable laughter and even animal noises.[72] Operating on a freelance basis, Dow travelled widely and eventually visited Ireland during the years 1799-1801. Nicholas Smethen, a Methodist preacher who bitterly opposed him, wrote to his friend Matthias Joyce in Dublin, forewarning him of the evangelist's impending visit:

Lorenzo Dow (1777-1834)

> His manners have been clownish in the extreme, his habit and appearance more filthy than a savage Indian; his public discourses as mere rhapsody, the substance often an insult upon the gospel. . . . He has affected a recognizance of the secrets of men' hearts and lives, and even assumed the awful prerogative of prescience . . . pretending to foretell . . . the deaths or calamities of persons, etc.[73]

Nevertheless, Dow preached widely in Ireland and developed a firm friendship with the Quaker preacher, Dr Paul Johnson. In 1805, with his wife, Peggy, he crossed the Atlantic again, this time for England. His arrival in Liverpool coincided with a business visit to the city by Peter Phillips, the leader of the Warrington Quaker Methodists. Phillips attended a meeting at which Dow was speaking, was impressed by what he heard, and immediately invited him to Warrington, where he was well received by the society members.[74] The home of Peter and Hannah Phillips thereafter became Dow's base throughout his stay in England. From there he moved from place to place in Lancashire, Cheshire and West Yorkshire, finding a hearing wherever he could and then moving on. Normally he left church planting to others, but two IM societies in the Warrington area trace their beginnings to his ministry.[75]

English Methodism's leaders would have nothing to do with the persistent American who turned up on their doorsteps and even at the Conference, uninvited.[76] However, at Leigh and Northwich he was readily accepted in Wesleyan pulpits and, after a tussle with the trustees, Joseph Bradford invited him to preach at Macclesfield where his preaching had already made a mark in the town through his visits to the revivalists.[77] Sometimes he found openings in New Connexion societies, but the revivalist sects received him more readily than any others and the Warrington leaders wrote a letter of commendation for him before he left England.[78] Dow identified with their characteristics, particularly the freedoms they allowed in worship, ministry and evangelism. Bracketing the groups together, he commented 'they call themselves the Christian Revivalists, some call them the Free Gospellers; they are of the third division (the Kilhamites being the second,) [sic] somewhat similar to the Quaker Methodists, and of the spirit of the Methodists in America.'[79]

At some point, between May and July 1806, the churches which would form the embryonic Union of IM Churches met together for the first time, but neither date nor venue are known.[80] The sole record of this meeting lies in Dow's comment on 23 July that 'they called a conference some weeks ago to know each other's minds and see how near they could come towards the outlines of a general union.'[81] He then described a tour which he made of the participating churches a few weeks later, starting from Warrington and going in turn to Macclesfield, Stockport, Manchester, Oldham and Leeds. Thereafter, the Independent Methodists met every year at Whitsuntide by invitation of various churches in turn. The title Annual (or Yearly) Meeting reflected the Quakerism of the Warrington group and also avoided the term 'Conference', which held for them a connotation of central direction and authority.

1807 saw both the departure of Lorenzo Dow and a convergence of three strands of revivalist activity: the Independent/Quaker Methodists, the 'Magic' Methodists and the embryonic Camp Meeting Methodists of the Potteries. The Magic Methodists' key figure was James Crawfoot (1758-1839), a Methodist local preacher living in Delamere Forest, Cheshire, where he had helped to establish a society at Brinn in the Northwich Circuit. He also held meetings at his home on the last Saturday evening of each month, when anyone who felt led by the Spirit to speak was free to do so. During the meetings, people sometimes fell into trances and claimed to see visions. Crawfoot, himself a visionary and mystic, exercised the 'gift' of the laying on of hands, which was believed to convey divine power. This intense focus on the spirit world and the strange phenomena experienced in his meetings earned them the description 'Magic Methodists'.[82] As Crawfoot's preaching duties took him to the Warrington area, he was well acquainted with the Quaker Methodists and had some sympathy with them.

Crawfoot's activities in Delamere were contemporaneous with those of Hugh Bourne (1772-1852), a North Staffordshire carpenter and a Methodist local preacher, who had been involved in a revival movement in his own area from 1801.[83] This movement, initially cottage-based and lay-led, took root at Harriseahead, which, like Warrington, was effectively on the fringe of Methodist supervision, but Bourne put all his earliest societies into the care of the nearby Burslem Circuit. As with Peter Phillips at Warrington, his own spiritual experience owed much to a mixture of Methodist and Quaker influences.[84] In April, 1807, Bourne heard Dow preach at Harriseahead and bought from him two pamphlets on the subject of camp meetings.[85] A few weeks later, on 31 May, after Dow had returned to America, Bourne organised the first camp meeting in England at Mow Cop, a bleak hillside on the Staffordshire/Cheshire border. The Independent Methodists of Macclesfield, who had already heard Dow's advocacy of camp meetings, attended in considerable numbers and supplied some of the speakers.[86] In the following month, Bourne made the first of many visits to Crawfoot's meetings at Delamere. According to Herod, Crawfoot thereupon took him on a preaching journey which included the Warrington area and this led to his introduction to the Quaker Methodists.[87]

Bourne organised a second meeting at Mow Cop on 19 July, much to the displeasure of the itinerant preachers at Burslem who duly took the matter to Methodist Conference, meeting at Liverpool, where a resolution was passed:

> It is our judgement, that even supposing such meetings to be allowable in America, they are highly improper in England, and likely to be productive of much mischief. And we disclaim all connexion with them.[88]

Thus began a course of events which led, a year later, to Bourne's expulsion from Methodist membership on account of his persistent involvement in camp meetings. He continued to preach among societies that came within his orbit, now known as 'Camp Meeting Methodists', and began to make frequent visits to other revivalist groups, notably at Macclesfield and Warrington, which welcomed his ministry. He went on to exercise a strong pastoral interest in them, often for weeks at a time, preaching, visiting and exchanging views with the leaders, some of whom became his close personal friends.[89]

James Crawfoot also fell foul of Wesleyan Methodist discipline when he accepted a request to preach at the Warrington Quaker Methodists' chapel.[90] This came to the attention of his local circuit at Northwich, where the Quaker Methodist secession of 1796 would still be remembered with displeasure. Crawfoot was duly summoned to the Circuit meeting, the complaint against him being that he had undertaken this appointment without the Circuit's consent. He pleaded guilty and 'gave it as his opinion that it was neither scriptural nor reasonable for any section of the church of Jesus Christ to restrict to their particular sphere the labours of a preacher that was not paid by them for his services.' He then added: 'Mr. Chairman, if you have deviated from the old usages, I have not. I still remain a *primitive* Methodist.'[91] His parting shot provided an unwitting pointer to the birth of the Primitive Methodist Connexion, whose leaders were profoundly influenced by him in the early years of their preaching ministry.[92] He was always welcomed by the various Quaker Methodist meetings in the Warrington area, but his influence was more significant for his mystical spirituality than for any form of church polity.

The Independent Methodists' second Annual Meeting, held at Macclesfield in 1807[93], arranged an interchange of preachers 'to promote variety.'[94] The presence of Hugh Bourne at this meeting was a sign of the growing affinity between the Independent and Camp Meeting Methodists. The Annual Meeting of 1808 was again held at Macclesfield and was the first of which there are extant Minutes.[95] Again, Bourne attended and subsequently wrote his *Remarks on the Ministry of Women*. Five churches were represented, some of which also had mission stations. In addition to church reports, statistics were given, though this was not usually done until much later. They showed the strengths of the constituent churches as follows:

Manchester	493
Macclesfield	398
Warrington	187
Stockport	63
Oldham	78

The purpose of the Annual Meeting was stated as fourfold: 'To promote and maintain a spirit of unity – to enquire into the state of the different churches – to suggest plans of usefulness – and to promote the interest of the Redeemer's kingdom on the earth.'[96] Every church reported an increase, Manchester and Macclesfield showing additions of nearly 200 at each place since the previous year. The revivalist surge was evidently not abating, despite the hope of Bunting and others that it would eventually wither away.

Aside from the Annual Meetings, the revivalist nexus retained fraternal but unstructured links, irrespective of the peculiarities of its constituent elements. Some of the leaders of this group – Hugh Bourne,[97] Peter Phillips, Paul Johnson and James Sigston – met in 1808 in Warrington to promote the continuation of the revival begun by the work of Lorenzo Dow, Paul Johnson and extended by the Camp Meetings. The outcome was a decision to publish the autobiography of Benjamin Abbott, a popular American evangelist. This, according to Herod, was well received among working-class people and went on to become a standard publication of the Primitive Methodist Bookroom.[98]

The Independent Methodists, at this stage, were therefore involved with two forms of association – the formal association of their Annual Meetings and an informal fraternal of leaders, where the objects appear to have been solely spiritual. The informal association perhaps reflected more authentically than the IM Annual Meetings what was happening among the varied revivalist sects – a process that would see the emergence of churches that were often cottage-based, rooted in working-class culture and poverty, experiential in spirituality and Methodist in doctrine. The ensuing denominational structures simply became the channels through which these elements found expression.

For a time, it looked as though the Camp Meeting Methodists and Independent Methodists would become one.[99] Bourne himself was reluctant to break ranks with them, but realised that the non-payment principle was hindering the further expansion of his work. Describing events in 1811, when the leaders of the Camp Meeting group came together with the followers of William Clowes, another Potteries-based revivalist, to form the Primitive Methodists, he noted:

> Hitherto the temporal concerns had been borne chiefly by four individuals; but as these had to live by the labour of their hands, the work had begun to extend beyond their means; and the connexion could not properly exert its energies, nor extend its progress. It was also a general opinion that the weight ought no longer to be borne by a few individuals. The people, in general, wished to assist, but hitherto they had no opportunity of regularly subscribing to the support of the cause; and on this account some had refused to join.[100]

Thus the Primitive and Independent Methodists amicably went their separate ways, though personal contacts between Bourne and his friends at Warrington and Macclesfield continued. Once Primitive Methodism had embraced paid ministry and connexionalism,[101] it became the natural channel for the revivalist movement. Its itinerant preachers were able to expand the movement as they travelled around the country, whereas the Independent Methodists had no one who was in a position to take the movement into new areas, due to the constraints of secular employment.

While the events of these years occurred against the backdrop of issues of conviction, the behaviour of some of the characters concerned suggests that personality as well as principle played its part, as the preceding account of events has shown. This tendency was just as likely to lead churches out of the Independent Methodist grouping as into it. In the case of John Broadhurst, the Manchester draper, refusal to comply with Methodist discipline over a period of years led to the exodus of his Bandroom Methodists. James Sigston, the Leeds schoolmaster, and George Smith, the Preston cloth manufacturer, were both twice involved in ruptures from Wesleyan Methodism. In between those events, these two men were involved with the Independent Methodists whom they also left when it suited them. Beresford, the Macclesfield mill owner, broke with Wesleyan Methodism in 1802, only to break with the Independent Methodists twelve years later. The Sheffield IM congregation had defected from the Methodist New Connexion in 1814, but under the huge influence of its leader, Dr George Turton, transferred to the Protestant Methodists in 1830.[102] Thus, determined leaders – usually people of greater substance than their followers – could direct the allegiances of others, moving them in and out of different Methodist groupings almost at will.[103]

3. Influences which shaped the Independent Methodists

3.1. The Methodist Influence

The structures of Methodism helped define its new offshoot as an authentic child of Methodism. Class and outdoor meetings, preachers' plans, lovefeasts and the use of Charles Wesley's hymns all gave the IM societies an unmistakable Methodist flavour, but they were rooted most firmly in their Methodist heritage through their theology and spirituality.[104]

The early Independent Methodists were fully aligned with other forms of Methodism in their Arminian belief that salvation was possible for all and their adherence to John Wesley's teachings on holiness. This was later promulgated through the denominational magazine, proclaimed by the preachers and written into the early constitutions of some of the churches. The doctrines which they published in 1822 affirmed Wesley's teaching on new birth, entire sanctification and the 'necessity of holding faith fast unto death.'[105] An earlier publication by the Liverpool Church asserted that its doctrines were those 'contained in the Homilies of the Church of England . . . also the doctrines contained in the writings of the late Rev. John Wesley.'[106] This seems to have been a continued emphasis in the early decades of the nineteenth century, illustrated by an address to the churches in 1831 when the writers urged attention to John Wesley's axiom that where holiness of heart was pursued, the work of God prospered abundantly.[107]

Certainly up to this time, there is anecdotal evidence that early Independent Methodists pursued holiness as Wesley taught it. The obituary of William Ambler of Sheffield stated, 'his desire to grow in grace led him to see the need of a deeper work, even the sanctification of his nature, a deliverance from pride and every other indwelling evil. For this he prayed and obtained the blessing.'[108] Alice Shovelton of Leigh described how, in 1822, she had been convinced of her need for entire sanctification after hearing a sermon by a visiting IM preacher on 1 Corinthians 1:30. This was later corroborated when she heard Samuel Balmer, a Warrington IM preacher expound the subject from 1 John 1:9. She wrote, 'I was convinced by this discourse of the necessity of sanctification: from that time on I saw that the possession of a sanctified heart was attainable through Christ and incessantly set about the work.'[109]

Beyond the middle of the nineteenth century, as in other branches of Methodism, such testimonies appeared less frequently as perfectionist claims were regarded with increasing uncertainty.[110] By 1855, Independent Methodism had accepted a doctrinal statement which no longer made sanctification a separate experience from conversion but basically saw it as the fruit of a person's repentance and saving faith.[111]

3.2. The Revivalist Influence

But if the sober-minded pursuit of holiness within a disciplined society occupied the minds of some IM people, others looked for divine blessing in the heady revivalism which Wesleyan Methodism now shunned. The influence of Dow, followed by involvement with Crawfoot, Bourne and others, reflected the prevailing trend. Risley, near Warrington, a society founded by Dow, was a synonym for revivals and revival habits. Hugh Bourne wrote: 'We had a meeting at Risley: an exceedingly powerful time. I received new light on the ministry. Here each one does that which is right in his own eyes. They stand, sit, kneel, pray, exhort, etc, as they are moved. I was very fond of this way.'[112] However, his colleague, William Clowes, took a different view of the same meeting, noting, 'We went down to Risley and found a people very singular in their notions and manner of worship, *which we did not at all admire*, nevertheless the Lord made us very useful among them.'[113]

The Risley style of meeting was similar to that of the Manchester Band Room which had occasioned such despair to the Methodist authorities and personal affront to Jabez Bunting. Nowhere was revivalism denounced more vigorously than in the writings of Joseph Nightingale, himself a founder leader of the Christian Revivalists (Independent Methodists) of Macclesfield, later turned Unitarian, who wrote:

> The Revivalists are those Methodists who are more particularly partial to noisy meetings. – They claim, as a Christian privilege, a right to indulge their propensities to prayer and praise, at all times and on all occasions. This liberty they will take during [*sic*] the minister is engaged in preaching; and indeed at any other time they think themselves called upon by the motions of the Spirit of God. They are a simple, harmless and well-meaning body; but enthusiastical and ungovernable to an extraordinary degree.[114]

Elsewhere he noted,

> I have seen a preacher bite his lips with anguish and chagrin or gnash his teeth with just indignation, when he has found himself so completely overpowered by the obstreperousness of his audience that he has been forced to sit down with fatigue in the pulpit or to descend and wander from pew to pew, endeavouring to quell the tumult of which his own sermon has been the efficient cause.[115]

However, for all its shortcomings and evidence of emotional immaturity, revivalism contained in itself the seeds of the free gospelism which the Independent Methodists embraced and its roots lay in the pietism and experimental religion from which Methodism itself had sprung. By their nature, revivalist gatherings produced for participants a shared experience which had an enormous effect on the dynamics of their corporate faith, raising the hopes of many to engage, for instance, in preaching, once considered the sole preserve of the ordained clergyman.[116] This was evident enough in the development of Wesleyan Methodism in the eighteenth century and was taken further by the Independent Methodists.

3.3. The Quaker Influence

Revivalism and Quakerism sat well together as expressions of experimental religion, spontaneous worship and the worth of the individual believer. But Quakerism went beyond unstructured revivalism in its contribution to the IM view of ministry, on two counts.

Firstly, the Quakers rejected a paid ministry as a matter of principle. In 1651, George Fox publicly took a clergyman to task for preaching on 'Ho, every one that thirsteth, let him come freely, without money and without price.' On hearing his text announced, Fox challenged, 'Come down, thou deceiver and hireling, for dost thou bid people come freely and take the water of life freely, and yet thou takest three hundred pounds from them for preaching the Scriptures to them. . . . Did not Christ command his ministers, "Freely you have received, freely give"?'[117] The Independent Methodists adopted exactly the same principle of opposing payment for preaching; it became one of the characteristics which defined all their early churches and which brought them together.

Though early leaders such as Peter Phillips took a tolerant view of paid ministry as exercised by others, some of his successors, such as William Sanderson,[118] resorted to the rhetoric of Fox, dismissing Anglican clergy and Methodist itinerant preachers alike as 'hirelings'. It would become one of Independent Methodism's most overtly sectarian characteristics.

Secondly, Independent Methodists were debtors to the Quakers' interpretation of the priesthood of all believers, that '*all* the living members of a congregation are in the position of priests: all have the priestly privilege of direct access to God and of responsibility for the souls of others.'[119] In the Quaker mind, the separation of the people of God into two categories, clergy and lay, created a false distinction and denied the high calling of the individual Christian. By adopting exactly this view, Independent Methodism, like Quakerism, elevated the ordinary church member and gave each a higher standing before God than a distinctive clerical caste permitted.

4. Conclusion: The Position up to 1815

Apart from local planting efforts, the Independent Methodists experienced little expansion in their first decade. The only churches added during 1806-15 were Preston and Blackburn (1810), Wilmslow (1813) and Sheffield and Rastrick (1814), but Macclesfield left in 1814 and Manchester temporarily withdrew in the same year, returning by 1820.

While all the churches wanted some form of union, none wanted centralised direction. Hence, Annual Meetings were deliberative in nature and took few decisions. They were short in duration as most of the delegates would be working people, with limited scope for absence from work. Each church would send delegates and report on its current state of health. The names of the preachers attached to each church were read out and the minutes would confirm that they were of exemplary character. The meeting appointed a President and Secretary whose duties were purely limited to the meeting itself; no one remained in office between Annual Meetings and no funds were held. Much of the time was devoted to preaching, both at the host church, beginning at an early hour, and in the open air. Between Annual Meetings, the only contact seems to have consisted of the interchange of preachers and informal encounters at events such as Camp Meetings. Each church conducted its own affairs and left the others to do likewise, as the address to the churches at the 1815 Annual Meeting indicated:

> the sole reason for our assembling together once [a] year as Churches is that the real state of each church might be inquired into, and that they may be assisted if occasion require, that ministers may on proper occasions pay a friendly visit, from one church to another, and if anything can be suggested for the good of the whole, well; but yet every church is left to its own discretion, for none can say to another, why does thou so?[120]

As Figure 1 shows, this association of churches remained entirely regional.[121] However, the period from about 1818 onwards saw significant, if occasionally ephemeral expansion, as the next two chapters will show.

Figure 1
Distribution of Independent Methodist Churches, 1814

*Where there was more than one church in the vicinity of the towns
shown, the number of churches is indicated in brackets. The majority
of these churches were in homes or rented properties.
Few congregations had their own chapels.*

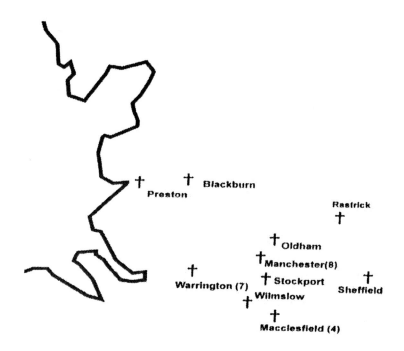

Notes to Chapter One

1. H. Rack, 'Survival, Revival: John Bennet, Methodism and the Old Dissent',
   *Studies in Church History 7: Protestant Evangelicalism: Britain, Ireland,
   Germany and America c.1750–c.1950* (Oxford: Published for the
   Ecclesiastical History Society by Basil Blackwell, 1990), 13ff.
2. J. Telford, *The Letters of the Reverend John Wesley, A.M.,* (8 vols.; London:
   Epworth, 1931), 4:252.
3. W. Brimelow, *A Free Church and a Free Ministry* (London: Elliot
   Stock:1883), 8ff.; A. Mounfield (Ed.). *A Short History of Independent
   Methodism,* (Independent Methodist Bookroom, 1905) 4ff.
4. This is, in itself, significant. Independent Methodism found fertile soil in areas
   which were at the fringe of Wesleyan activity. A comparable instance was at

Lowton Common, near Warrington, in 1819, where the Wesleyans stopped
sending preachers and the Independent Methodists filled the gap. Mounfield,
Short History, 66f.

5. Booth was stationed at Northwich from 1796-98. K.B. Garlick, *Mr. Wesley's Preachers* (London: World Methodist Historical Society, 1977), 10.

6. This would be consistent with a recent Conference ruling which was designed to check some of the more anarchic, revivalist tendencies of the time. A ruling given at the 1797 Conference declared: 'We allow that other formal meetings be held if they first receive the approbation of the superintendent and Leaders' or Quarterly Meeting; provided also that the Superintendent if he please, be present at every such meeting'. If this ruling was the basis of Booth's decision, it would probably date the breach which led to the formation of the new group as 1797, rather than the long-believed date of 1796.

7. This name was dropped during the middle of the nineteenth century.

8. R.M. Jones, *The Later Periods of Quakerism* (London: Macmillan & Co., 1929), 291.

9. See 3.3. The Quaker Influence for further examination of the influence of Quakerism on the Independent Methodist movement.

10. J.A. Dolan, *Peter's People* (Wigan, Independent Methodist Churches: 1996), 2ff.

11. Paul Johnson was friend and physician to Lorenzo Dow, whose journal is the main source of information about him. L. Dow, *The Dealings of God, Man and the Devil as experienced in the Life, Experience and Travels of Lorenzo Dow* (Norwich, Connecticut: William Faulkner, 1833), 83ff.

12. Dorothy Ripley was the daughter of William Ripley, a Methodist local preacher. She came under Quaker influence and travelled by faith on both sides of the Atlantic. She stood against slavery, received the support of Thomas Jefferson and addressed the U.S. Congress. A Mounfield, 'Dorothy Ripley' in *Proceedings of the Wesley Historical Society* Vol. 7, 31-33.

13. Register of Births and Namings 1806 onwards, Friars Green Independent Methodist Church, Warrington.

14. James Vickers, *History of Independent Methodism* (Wigan: Independent Methodist Bookroom, 1920), 28; Independent Methodist Minutes,1808; Independent Methodist Preachers' Plan, Warrington, 1824. (IMA)

15. W.H. Lockley, *The Story of the Stockport Circuit of the United Methodist Church*, 1909.

16. J.S. Werner, *The Primitive Methodist Connexion, Its Background and Early History* (London: University of Wisconsin Press, 1984), 24.

17. S. Peacock, *Memorials of Gamaliel Swindells, late of Stockport,* (Stockport: Samuel Dodge, 1833), 6.

18. Letter: W.J. Skillen to A. Dalby, 18 May 1973, referring to Stockport newspaper articles in the 1880s. (IMA)

19. IMMins. 1808.

20. H. Bourne, *History of the Primitive Methodists* (Bemersley, 1823), 7.

21. Minutes of the Methodist New Connexion, 1801.

22. Vickers, *History*, 11.

23. Letter: Jabez Bunting to Richard Reece, 11 June, 1803.

24. IMMins, 1810.

25. IMMins, 1808.
26. B. Smith, *History of Methodism in Macclesfield,* (London: Wesleyan Conference Office, 1875), 375.
27. G. Malmgreen, *Silk Town: Industry and Culture in Macclesfield 1750-1845* (Hull University Press, 1985), 152.
28. Extensive details in unpublished typescript by Ron Naylor of Sutton, Macclesfield, a descendant of John Beresford (IMA).
29. Deeds of Parsonage Street Chapel, Macclesfield, 1808 (Copy in IMA); C. Stella Davies, *History of Macclesfield* (Manchester University Press, 1961), 338f.
30. Bunting to Reece, 11 June. 1803.
31. J. Nightingale, *Portraiture of Methodism* (London, 1807), 489.
32. *Minutes of the Methodist New Connexion,* 1814.
33. Vickers, *History,* 11.
34. 'Memoir of George Smith' in *Wesleyan Methodist Association Magazine,* 1839, 282.
35. Dow, *Life and Experience,* 223.
36. *WMA Magazine,* 1839, 282.
37. *The Methodist New Connexion in Sheffield 1797-1879*, Local History Pamphlet Vol. 74. no. 7 (Sheffield Local History Library).
38. D. Hempton, *Methodism and Politics in British Society 1750-1850.* (London: Hutchinson & Co. 1984), 73.
39. IMMins. 1815, 15.
40. *Directory of Sheffield,* 1833, 94.
41. T. Ramsey, *The Picture of Sheffield* (1824), 154. Ramsey incorrectly states that the Independent Methodists seceded from the Wesleyan Methodists rather than from the New Connexion.
42. IMMins, 1824.
43. See Chapter 3.
44. 'Memoir of Francis Marris' in *Wesleyan Methodist Magazine* 1840, 625ff.
45. The Register of Dissenting Meeting Houses (CRO) contains meeting house licences for five properties, all of which bear Broadhurst's signature, dated between 1795 – 1798.
46. The 'Band Room' was a place where Methodist 'bands' (small groups) met for mutual edification.
47. J. Sigston, *A Brief Memoir of Joseph Woolstenholme* (London: WMA Bookroom, 1846), 3.
48. T.P. Bunting, *The Life of Jabez Bunting, D.D., with Notices of Contemporary Persons and Events* (4 vols.; London, 1859), 1:96.
49. *Ibid.*
50. Jabez Bunting was the architect of Wesleyan Methodism's development and its most dominant figure in the first half of the nineteenth century, serving as both President and Secretary of the Conference in his time. Autocratic in disposition, he figured in each of the major rifts in Methodism between 1828 and 1849. See John Kent, *Jabez Bunting, the Last Wesleyan* (London: Epworth, 1955).
51. Letter: William Jenkins to John Broadhurst, 17 June, 1803, quoted in *A Statement of Facts and Observations relative to the late Separation from the Society in Manchester, affectionately addressed to the members of that*

body by their Preachers and Leaders (Manchester: S. Russell, 1806), 27.
52. *Statement of Facts,* 30.
53. Letter: William Jenkins to Jabez Bunting, 29 January, 1806
54. *Statement of Facts,* 27.
55. Jenkins to Bunting, 29 January, 1806.
56. Letter: Holland Hoole to James Wood, 31 January, 1806, quoted in *Statement of Facts,* 11.
57. Title page of rule book, printed in *IMMag,* 1908, 196.
58. S. Rothwell, *Memorials of Folds Road Independent Methodist Chapel, Bolton* (2 vols.; Bolton: Independent Methodist Bookroom, 1887) i, 20.
59. D.A. Gowland, *Methodist Secessions* (Manchester: Chetham Society, 1979), 23.
60. J.C. Bowmer, *Pastor and People* (London: Epworth, 1975), 73.
61. W.R. Ward, *Religion and Society in England 1790-1850* (London: B.T. Batsford Ltd., 1972), 82. See 5 below.
62. IMMins.1808. The links were fairly informal; these Minutes provide the earliest extant proof of the union of the Bandroom Methodists with the other Independent Methodists.
63. 'Reminiscences of upwards of Fifty Years: Independent Methodism in Oldham', *IMMag.*1862, 186.
64. Mounfield, *Short History*, 95.
65. *IMMag.* 1862, 188.
66. See 2. Corporate Formation
67. D.C. Dews, 'Methodism in Leeds from 1791 to 1861', (University of Bradford M. Phil. thesis, 1984), 330ff.
68. Dews, 'Methodism in Leeds', 327.
69. Ward, *Religion and Society,* 81.
70. Dow, *Life and Experience,* 230.
71. Mounfield, *Short History,* 2.
72. Werner, *Primitive Methodist Connexion,* 46.
73. Quoted in C.C. Sellers, *Lorenzo Dow, The Bearer of the Word* (New York: Minton, Balch & Co, 1928), 105.
74. 'The Life and Labours of Peter Phillips', *Zion's Trumpet,* April 1855, 182.
75. Stockton Heath and Risley, which continue to the present day. Mounfield, *Short History,* 16ff.
76. Dow, *Life and Experience,* 221f.
77. *Ibid,* 245.
78. *Ibid,* 361.
79. *Ibid,* 229. However, in a later reference, Dow distinguished the Quaker Methodists from the Revivalists or Free Gospellers, suggesting that he saw a qualitative difference between them. Arthur Mounfield drew the same distinction early in the twentieth century. Dow, *Life and Experience,* 254; 'Short Historical Sketch' *in IMYB*, 1903, 9.
80. The term 'Connexion' was not used until a much later date.
81. Dow, *Experience and Travels,* 231.
82. H. Rack, *The Magic Methodists* (Methodist Church Chapel Aid Association Ltd., 2001), 2f.
83. Bourne, *History*, 5.

84. J. Walford, *Memoirs of the Life and Labours of the Late Venerable Hugh Bourne* (2 vols.; London: T. King and Burslem: R. Timmis, 1855), 1:38.
85. J. Petty, *The History of the Primitive Methodist Connexion* (London: Richard Davies, Conference Offices, 1860), 14.
86. H.B. Kendall, *The Origin and History of the Primitive Methodist Church* (2 vols.; London, Edwin Dalton, und.), 1:65.
87. G. Herod, *Historical and Biographical Sketches, Forming a Compendium of the History of the Primitive Methodist Connexion up to the Year 1823* (London, 1851), 259.
88. Minutes of the Methodist Conference, 1812 edn., ii (1807), 403. For a full account of the reasons behind these events, see Werner, 59ff; Petty, *History*, 12ff; and Kendall, *Origin and History*, 1:56ff.
89. J.A. Dolan, *From Barn to Chapel*, (Warrington, 1989), 21ff. This gives a detailed account of the friendship between Hugh Bourne and the Eaton family of Stockton Heath, based on Bourne's MS Journal.
90. Herod, *Biographical Sketches*, 252.
91. *Ibid*, 253.
92. However, it should not be construed that this was how Primitive Methodism came to be so called. See H. Rack, *How Primitive was Primitive Methodism?* (Englesea Brook: 6th Chapel Aid Lecture, 1996), 4.
93. The only known reference to this meeting comes in the Journal of Hugh Bourne who described it as their 'first conference', which suggests that the previous year's meeting was only an informal one.
94. Walford *Bourne*, 1:154.
95. IMMins. 1808
96. IMMins. 1808.
97. Bourne had been expelled from the Methodist Society of which he was a member on 27 June, shortly before this meeting took place. Petty, *History*, 25.
98. Herod, *Biographical Sketches*, 466f.
99. Kendall notes that, after his conversion, Bourne was undecided as to which church he should join: the Quakers or the Methodists, while the Quaker Methodists provided a possible *tertium quid*. Kendall, *Origin and History*, 1:15.
100. Bourne, *History*, 40.
101. Bourne, *History*, 41: Werner, *Primitive Methodist Connexion*, 75f.
102. See Chapter 3.
103. The Tent Methodists, who existed 1814-32, provided another example of a small Methodist sect which ministered to the needs of the poor, lacked coherence and was heavily dependent on leaders who eventually went into other denominations. J.K. Lander, *Itinerant Temples* (Carlisle: Paternoster Press, 2003), 162ff.
104. See W. Durant, *The Story of Friars Green Church* (Warrington, 1951), 22 and 'The Preachers' Plan, Manchester, August-November 1815' for examples of Methodist-style activity in the churches.
105. Doctrines, Church Government and Discipline considered by the Independant [*sic*] Methodists to be consitent [*sic*] with the Word of God (Sheffield, 1822) 4f.
106. The Doctrines and Rules of the Independent Methodist Church established

July 1818 in Liverpool,6.

107. 'An Address to all members connected with the Independent Methodist Churches', IMMins 1831, 21.

108. 'Memoir of William Ambler', IMMins 1815, 18.

109. 'A Brief Account of the Life of Alice Shovelton, the eldest daughter of John and Ann Shovelton of Bedford, Lancashire', *IMMag* 1828, 481.

110. D.W. Bebbington, 'Holiness in Nineteenth Century Methodism' in W.M. Jacob and N. Yates (eds.), *Crown and Mitre: Religion and Society in Northern Europe since the Reformation* (Woodbridge, Suffolk: Boydell Press, 1993), 162f.

111. See Appendix 3, Clause 13.

112. Walford, 1:207.

113. Quoted in Mounfield, *Short History*, 20.

114. Nightingale, *Portraiture,* 489.

115. *Ibid,* 218f.

116. Russell E. Richey, 'Revivalism : In search of a Definition', *Wesleyan Theological Journal* Vol. 28 (1993), 167.

117. J.L.Nickalls (Ed.) *The Journal of George Fox,* (Cambridge University Press, 1952), 76.

118. Vickers, *History*, 46.

119. Edward Grubb, *What is Quakerism?* (London: George Allen and Unwin Ltd. 1917), 61.

120. Full text in Appendix 1.

121. See Figure 1, p. 36.

Chapter 2
Social and Political Factors 1815-60

1. Poverty, Radical Politics and the Free Gospel

The Independent Methodists experienced a new influx of churches during the years 1818-24, firstly in Lancashire and subsequently on Tyneside. The factors common to them were poverty, radical politics or both. The end of the Napoleonic Wars in 1815 was followed by hardship on the domestic front. Town dwellers in particular suffered as a result of the passing of the Corn Law which raised the price of bread. Moreover, there was a glut on the labour market as men returned from the war to find peacetime employment.[1] Wages were pushed down accordingly and the gap between rich and poor widened. To some Methodists, the funding of ministers (and often chapels with mortgages) became an impossible financial burden, with the result that they embraced free gospelism for reasons of poverty rather than principle. Handloom cotton weavers were among those who suffered and who turned to radical politics, particularly during the years 1816-19.[2] The self-employed status of the weavers, whose work and domestic lives functioned closely together, gave them a natural affinity with the local autonomy offered by Independent Methodism.

In the second decade of the nineteenth century, the attention of the Wesleyan Methodist leadership in Liverpool was drawn to the substantial Welsh element in its membership and the needs of its Welsh-speaking society. Help was sought from the Conference in the provision of a Welsh-speaking preacher, but the lean post-war times caused the Conference to look for economies. Special provision for a minority group began to look like an unaffordable luxury, as Jonathan Crowther, a leading itinerant, wrote:

> it looks strange to me that Liverpool itself should claim £94 19s. 6d. for supporting a Welch [*sic*] preacher in that town. I think if our very large society of English Christians there, cannot supply their poor Welch townsmen with preaching, they ought to be without, at least till times grow better.[3]

Despite Crowther's misgivings, Conference continued to appoint a Welsh minister to Liverpool, but the relationship between English and Welsh, Conference and local society, was an uneasy one, and money was always a problem, the Welsh contingent proving disruptive and unwilling to pay full contributions to funds.[4] In 1818, matters came to a head in the Welsh Wesleyan Methodist Church at Benn's Gardens, when a new rule was framed whereby only those who had paid their weekly and quarterly contributions could benefit from the Poor Fund.

Thomas Jones (1785-1864), former slave ship sailor and now self-employed bookseller,[5] was the Poor Steward at the time and therefore responsible for enforcing the rule, which he regarded as unreasonable. On 7 May, he surrendered his class book at a Leaders' Meeting to the minister, Edward Jones, saying that he objected to taking as much as sixpence per week, from women who were old and poor, so that the minister and his colleagues could enjoy at least £200 per annum.[6] Uproar ensued and a further meeting failed to resolve the matter. Thomas Jones offered to meet with those who sympathised with him, upon which invitation the minister declared that anyone who attended would be expelled. A number of people took up the gauntlet and, according to Thomas Jones, their response led to the formation of the first Independent Methodist Church in Liverpool.

The comparison between the minister's stipend and the poverty of the poorest members inevitably carried great emotional weight. Jones's argument was, of course, somewhat specious, as payments into the Poor Fund had no bearing on the minister's income. Nevertheless, the timing of the new rule was bound to provoke a backlash, given the circumstances of the poor at the time. The Welsh societies in Liverpool suffered a drop of fifty-three in their membership between June and September 1818 and it is reasonable to assume that most of these were the people who joined Thomas Jones in his newly-formed Independent Methodist Church.[7]

The constitution of the new church reflected the views and sympathies held by Independent Methodists generally.[8] Its doctrines were uncompromisingly Wesleyan, but the polity was firmly congregational and ministry was gratuitous. The members described their church as one 'which acknowledges no head but Jesus Christ, for we consider ourselves all brethren; all enjoy the same equal rights and privileges as men and as Christians; no one member assuming a power to rule over the rest'.[9] The blame for the rift at Benn's Gardens, rightly or wrongly, was attributed to the perceived privileges of a paid ministry which was not accountable to the local congregation. Thomas Jones became a determined proselytiser for Independent Methodism, taking every opportunity to see it established in his native North Wales over the next twenty years.[10] As a businessman whose interests took him into the principality, he had the obvious freedom of movement which employed people lacked.

In 1819, the Wesleyan Methodist society at Lowton Common (Lancashire), where many members were weavers, was at low ebb and, for a number of weeks, no preachers were sent to it. Richard Eckersley, one of the leaders, complained about this to the circuit authorities and reportedly received the reply, 'You do not deserve any preaching; you send us no money.'[11] Thereafter, an approach was made to the Congregational Church in Leigh to take over responsibility for the chapel, but this was declined.[12] Next, Peter Phillips was contacted at Warrington. The outcome of his visit was that the Warrington Independent Methodists agreed to spend forty pounds on improvements and arranged for a supply of preachers. In this way the church became affiliated to the Independent Methodists.[13] Throughout the nineteenth century, it remained a strong village society and typified the kind of environment where Independent Methodism thrived.

The clash between members' poverty and the demands of the Wesleyan superintendent minister at Lancaster in 1824[14] provides a further illustration of this recurring problem, but it also shows that such clashes were sometimes influenced by specific, local issues, in this instance a trade depression in the town.[15] Despite this adverse economic situation, which affected most of his members, the Wesleyan superintendent minister was determined to enforce the rule which required them to pay weekly class pence and a shilling quarterly, threatening expulsion to those who failed to do so. Most of the leaders sympathised with their poorer members and resigned their offices and membership. Of 132 members recorded in the Wesleyan Society, only forty-one were still in membership three years later. Of those who were lost, fifty-five formed themselves into a new society, taking the name 'Methodist Independent', though a few later returned to the Wesleyans. The new society included three former Wesleyan class leaders – Richard Tomlinson, a chairmaker, Robert Burrow, a coal dealer, and James Furness, a shoemaker.[16] Once again, this would be a church led by tradesmen. The new body made contact with the Quaker Methodists at Warrington and was duly represented at the 1825 Annual Meeting when it was received into membership.[17]

The foregoing examples appear to have had little direct political involvement, but elsewhere the political leanings of some Methodists undoubtedly led to internal conflict and, ultimately, schism. Wesleyan Methodism's caution over radical politics dated back to the 1790s,[18] but more recent issues now focused its collective mind. In 1811, the Connexional solicitor, Thomas Allan, had successfully campaigned against the plans of the Home Secretary, Lord Sidmouth, to curb itinerant preaching. In the aftermath of this, he prepared an address to the Prime Minister, Spencer Perceval, pointing out that Methodism had been a means of keeping the working classes docile and that it had no wish to engage in politics, being thoroughly loyal to the government.[19]

A year after Sidmouth's Bill was lost, a new Toleration Act was passed on 29 July 1812, largely through Allan's influence, resulting in the repeal of the Five Mile Act and the Conventicle Act. Methodism and old Dissent alike benefited from the new legislation which now affirmed the rights of their ministers in law. However, the new status accorded to Methodists meant that they had to maintain loyalty to the crown and good order during a time of radical ferment.[20] A circular was issued in the wake of the new Toleration Act, urging all Methodists to 'Fear the Lord and their King and meddle not with them that are given to change.'[21] Nevertheless, the following years saw an increasing involvement of Methodist lay people in reform groups and activities. Members whose trades were adversely affected by changing social conditions and work practices found themselves forced to chose between their reformist convictions and calls to loyalty and submission by their ministers.

On 19 August 1819, a public meeting was held in St. Peter's Fields, Manchester, when people marched from various north-west towns to demonstrate peacefully in favour of parliamentary reform. Fearing a riot, the Manchester magistrates sent in armed soldiers to arrest the speakers and break up the gathering. In the chaos which ensued, several people were killed and many more injured. The 'Peterloo Massacre', as it became known, resulted in a huge public outcry. However, Methodism's response showed little sympathy to those who had suffered injury or bereavement. Its Committee on Religious Privileges, still concerned that government repression could fall on Methodism, wrote an open letter to the societies in November, denouncing 'tumultuous assemblies' and the 'wild and delusive political theories' which occasioned them. The letter called upon all Methodists to abstain from such meetings and warned them not to join 'private political associations privately organised.' Then came the ultimatum: 'Any person connected with our body persisting after due admonition in identifying himself with the factious and disloyal shall forthwith be expelled from the Society according to our established rules.' Finally, the poor were urged to 'bear their privations with patience and to seek relief not in schemes of agitation and crime, but in reliance on Divine Providence, and in continuous prayer for the blessing of God on our country and on themselves.'[22]

Among those present at Peterloo were some handloom weavers from Wingates (Westhoughton, Lancashire), members of the Methodist society at Rose Bank, where the minister, S. Sugden, took a dim view of their political interests and their backwardness in paying contributions. A late nineteenth-century chronicler, John Coop, told one side of the story which, by this time, had passed into local folk-lore:

He [Sugden] was unwilling to accept their pleas for poverty as a sufficient excuse for their laggard payments, and their politics were heinous indeed and aggravated matters. George Hodson frankly told Mr. Sugden that Wingates folk could preach and pray for themselves, as indeed they had to, since he only came for their money. Robert Bamber said 'his politics was a part of his religion, because in a state of political thraldom there could be no such thing as spiritual freedom.'[23]

There is no independent verification of Coop's version of events, but Peterloo appears to have brought about the final rift between the minister and the weavers. Bamber was present on the fateful day in Manchester and he and others later rented a cottage where they started holding meetings. Contact was made with Peter Phillips at Warrington and he came to them to explain the organisation and principles of the Independent Methodists, whom they duly joined.[24] As at Lowton Common, the egalitarian polity of the Independent Methodists suited the independent-minded weavers of Wingates who, by their own admission, were only too willing to 'preach and pray for themselves.' This church was born as much from political convictions as religious ones and it continued to be a force for social and political change in ensuing years.

Politics and poverty also raised their heads in nearby Bolton, where there was an awareness that the problem was not merely local:

The year 1819 was a period of much affliction and trial to the members of the Wesleyan connection [*sic*], on account of the frequent introduction of political matters into the pulpit, and the rigorous exactions made upon the poor for their contributions, many of whom were unable to support the preachers to that extent they required, and consequently they did not experience that kindness from them, which, in consideration of their privations, they stood so much in need of.

The writer went on to say that this was the case at Bridge Street Church, Bolton, where Thomas Hill was then the superintendent minister. He continued:

Mr. H[ill]'s conduct was exceedingly oppressive; taking names out of class papers when members could not pay; continually pressing upon them for money, both in the pulpit and in the classes; and also intermixing political matters with the preaching of the gospel.[25]

Although Wesleyan Methodism forbade the pursuance of radical politics, it allowed preachers to remind their congregations of the need for loyalty to the crown and to submit themselves to the ruling authorities. Reformist members resented this as a blatantly one-sided practice which amounted to 'intermixing political matters with the preaching of the gospel.'

Several of the Bolton members, most of them weavers, held radical views and admired the campaigner, Henry Hunt, who played a prominent part in the Peterloo demonstration, but Thomas Hill took a different view. Some of his members were accustomed to imitate Hunt by wearing white felt hats. On one occasion, they placed their hats on a table during a week-night meeting, whereupon Hill allegedly swept them off the table, remarking, 'Who do these belong to?' This was, reputedly, the last straw which broke the camel's back. The outraged Radicals duly decided that they could no longer stay where they were and resolved to make for themselves a new spiritual home.[26] Ten men left Bridge Street and in February 1820 formed a new church. According to William Fallows, who later left Bolton for America, all were Radicals.[27] John Fallows, in whose house the new church began, was committed to the Radical cause enough to name one of his children Henry Hunt Fallows after his hero.[28] Once again, Peter Phillips was contacted and the new church adopted an Independent Methodist identity.

When the Independent Methodists were strong enough to build their first chapel in Folds Road, it became known as 'the Radical Chapel'[29] though its leaders were at pains to point out that its political interests were secondary to its spiritual ones. 'We bless God for His gracious work amongst us,' they noted, 'that some have come to hear out of curiosity thinking to hear something of politics, but the ever-blessed Spirit has over-ruled their coming as the means of their conversion.'[30]

On the other side of the country, the anger and sense of injustice felt nationally at the events of Peterloo led to a public demonstration at Newcastle Town Moor, where some 50,000 people gathered on 11 October 1819. Among the speakers was William H. Stephenson, teacher at Burton Colliery and Methodist local preacher in the North Shields Circuit. Referring to the events at Manchester, he spoke of the 'barbarous and cruel yeomanry' and the 'cruel magistrates', argued that the offences committed warranted capital punishment, and concluded, with a rhetorical flourish, 'I would rather die with Pompey in the cause of liberty than be enthroned with Caesar on its ruins.'[31] His action in addressing a radical meeting precipitated a crisis which affected Methodism nationally. The North Shields superintendent, Robert Pilter, came under pressure to remove Stephenson from the plan and asked him to stand down voluntarily, but he refused.[32] Pilter was on the horns of a dilemma, pressurised on the one hand to remove Stephenson but realising that this could result in the loss of members and the resignation of some local preachers. There was no easy answer, so the matter was referred to the Methodist Committee on Religious Privileges which ruled that it was improper for a Methodist to speak at a reform meeting, that any local preacher or class leader who did do should be suspended and that expulsion would follow unless he promised not to do so again. This was followed by a further ruling which debarred members of private political associations from becoming members of Methodist societies.[33]

Stephenson refused to give an undertaking to refrain from attending further reform meetings, with the result that he was duly suspended from the plan and expelled from membership. Infuriated with the outcome, he wrote to Pilter and his colleague Robert Jackson. After complaining about his expulsion, he went on to attack the itinerancy on the grounds of what he saw as elitism and greed:

> The people are groaning under the pecuniary burdens which are imposed upon them from time to time. One collection follows another in rapid succession, and they never know where the misery will end. There are more than seventy collections every year, either public or private – was this always the case? We answer, It was not; a time was, when Methodist preachers had little more than fifty pounds per annum; their wants then were few, they laboured for souls, and success in their labours was to them a sufficient recompense. Superfine coats, water-proof hats, silk stockings and gold watches were never the object of their pursuits – Surely, Sir this cannot be said for the present race of Methodist Preachers.[34]

The picture Stephenson painted of Methodist preachers was hardly fair or accurate, but it created a caricature which passed into Independent Methodist folklore in the years ahead. It also gave him a form of martyrdom which attracted the sympathy of others.

While the Stephenson case was still *sub judice*, two preachers in the nearby Gateshead Circuit were also threatened with expulsion unless they renounced all connection with the reformers. This they refused to do and, unlike Stephenson, quietly withdrew their Methodist membership, along with about twenty other members.[35] A Methodist class leader was also (reputedly) expelled because his wife hung a red ribbon (Hunt's favour) at the door of their house while he was ill.[36] A new door opened for the Gateshead reformers when they heard of the Independent Methodists and obtained a copy of the rules of the church at Sheffield. They resolved to embrace Independent Methodist principles and, on 28 October 1819, their first place of worship opened at Gateshead Fell, where two men, Thomas Fletcher, a pitman, and Dennis Turnbull, a shoemaker, gave the use of their cottages. Four years later a chapel was built in the grounds of Fletcher's cottage.[37]

During the same week, a further two preachers in the North Shields Circuit withdrew and joined the Independent Methodists. One of them was Hugh Kelly, whose later account of the events provides a valuable picture of the movement's early attempt to establish itself in the Northeast.[38] The political factor in his choice was plain:

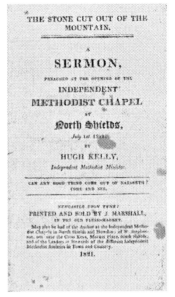

> He had long venerated the preachers for their piety and usefulness, and admired in them that penetration and discernment which seemed to characterise them: But, when the subject of *Reform* was agitated, the only antidote afforded by them against the dreaded spread of this spirit, was, *'Do not dip*

*Title page of a sermon
by Hugh Kelly*

> *too deep into politics.'* Now he could not help seeing that the grand principle of politics was founded on that saying of Jesus Christ, *as ye would that men should do to you, do ye even so to them; for this is the law and the prophets.* Hence his reasons for quitting the old connexion, may be found in the opposition of the preachers to the purest principles of morality.[39]

The Wesleyans expected the new movement to wither and die, dismissing its preachers as obscure and illiterate; the idea that the gospel could be preached and new churches planted without a paid ministry was regarded as impracticable. Countering this point, Kelly argued that some Methodist societies received a travelling preacher only once a quarter, so they effectively functioned on the voluntary system already.[40] Another allegation made against the Independent Methodists was that they taught politics, to which Kelly replied, predictably, that if it was wrong for a reformer to publish political sentiments from the pulpit, it was equally wrong for a Whig or Tory to do so. He insisted that the members of his new denomination were loyal to the king and government, industrious and honest, but that they had a right to petition against abuses.

In December 1819, further churches were started on Tyneside and a 'union' was established, with quarterly meetings. By July 1820, the impact on Wesleyan Methodism in the area was beginning to be felt. Pilter wrote to Bunting:

Stevenson [sic] and his radicals have done us hurt. A new chapel opened for Sunday evening service in the next street and occupied by an Independent youth said to equal the late Spence of Liverpool seriously affects our congregations.[41]

In May of the same year, the church at Gateshead reported by letter to the Independent Methodist Annual Meeting, held at Sheffield, but said that financial embarrassment prevented it from sending a delegate.[42] A year later, Stephenson attended the Annual Meeting, this time at Oldham. His report evidently aroused sympathy and interest among the delegates and he was given nine pounds to help the churches out of their current difficulties.

In 1822, the IM preachers went into Sunderland where they held a mass meeting on the Town Moor which led to the formation of another church.[43] A local benefactor donated a piece of ground and a public appeal was launched to fund the building of a chapel.[44] By 1824, the Gateshead and Shields Union, as it was then called, had seven churches, seven branches, 331 members and nineteen preachers.[45] The preachers were to be unpaid, but provision was allowed where a preacher was sent out to plant or visit churches: 'if the churches which he is visiting are not able to support him, the church which sends him forth shall give him wages to do them service.'[46] This was a greater concession than any other IM church would make at this time; for most of them, the very suggestion of 'wages' would have smacked of 'hirelingism.' However, weaknesses were beginning to show and Kelly frankly exposed them.

Having suffered verbal abuse from others, their pulpits were soon similarly 'desecrated by controversy and a strife of words.'[47] The publicity about the opening of the chapel at Newcastle was couched in such intemperate language that, as Kelly said, it 'caused it to be treated with well deserved contempt,'[48] while Stephenson also drew Kelly's personal criticism, after preaching and printing an inflammatory sermon on the coronation of George IV.[49] They also attempted to prove that they could plant churches without paid ministers and opened more places than they could manage, resulting in a shortage of preachers and financial embarrassment.[50] This was compounded by their attempts to attract people by telling them that they wanted no money, with the result that people gave none. As Kelly put it, 'They found now that it was much easier to destroy than to excite a spirit of Christian liberality.'[51] Finally, lack of experience in leadership led to stormy meetings and personality conflicts. Stephenson was at the centre of one particular squabble which ran on for two years, and he was finally expelled in 1823.[52]

The later history of this group of churches is lost in obscurity; after defecting to the Wesleyan Protestant Methodists in 1830,[53] little is known of them. They were perhaps more significant as a marker of Wesleyan Methodism's loss of influence among the working classes than for any lasting impact upon the Independent Methodist movement. The massive expansion of Primitive Methodism in the area during the next forty years was to bring a new revivalist impulse and a strong body of churches rooted in working class-culture.

2. Peter Phillips and the Pacifist Response

The involvement of Peter Phillips in the new Lancashire churches illustrates the extent to which he was regarded as the main focus of reference for the Independent Methodists at this time, though they accorded central authority to no one. Paradoxically, he shared none of the radicalism of the Wingates and Bolton people and positively eschewed the polemics of people like William Stephenson. His only extant sermon, written shortly after Peterloo, reflected a Quaker view of violence. Phillips announced in advance to his congregation that he would preach on the text, 'He that hath no sword let him sell his cloak and buy one.' In a town which had its fair share of insurgents, this was enough to attract widespread attention. A large congregation gathered, including officers of the law, while neighbours barricaded their windows in anticipation of a riot. However, the alarm proved to be unwarranted and Phillips, in the event, preached a pacifist sermon. He began:

> Can these words mean a weapon of destruction? I think not. From the character of Christ, which according to prophecy was that he should be called the Prince of Peace; that His government should be a government of peace; that in His kingdom (His holy mountain) they should neither hurt nor destroy; that the sword should be made into a ploughshare and the spear into a pruning-hook. And therefore, the angels sang when He was born, 'Glory to God in the highest, on earth peace.'

In conclusion, he said:

> Lastly, it cannot mean the sword for destruction of life, because He hath said, 'Thou shalt not kill' and 'Thou shalt do no murder.' And we know that when the apostles wanted to call for fire from heaven to destroy, Christ said, 'Ye know not what spirit we are of. The Son of Man came not to destroy men's lives but to save.'[54]

Through a timely announcement and a single sermon, Phillips had deflected official suspicion away from his own proletarian church.

The question inevitably remains: how did the pacifist preacher of Warrington not only attract the attention of dissident Methodists in radical communities, but also win their confidence? The answer may be twofold. Firstly, the loose nature of Independent Methodism made no requirement of member societies on questions of political allegiance. Each society could adopt its own standpoint, so long as it adhered to the two basic principles of a free church and an unpaid ministry. Secondly, Phillips had shown by example that a church run *by* working people *for* working people could not only survive but flourish and go on to plant other churches. This exactly matched the aspirations of the groups in question. Furthermore, his own background as a self-employed tradesman gave him an affinity with spinners and weavers which an increasingly professional Methodist clergy was ceasing to have. Beside these issues, his pacifism was of less significance to them and may even have tempered the views of those who would have gone to greater extremes in the pursuit of reform.

3. Persecution

Whatever their aspirations, one of the recurring themes among sectarian groups was that of persecution. They were not welcomed by the establishment, either civil or ecclesiastical, to whom they posed at best a nuisance and at worst a threat. To the more respectable, order was important and justified their opposition to undisciplined sectarian groups; to the sects themselves, disapproval appeared to be only a thin line apart from persecution. Verbal denunciation of their revivalist activities by a local vicar or even a Free Church minister was perceived as persecution; so was the termination of their tenancy of a chapel or meeting house, especially when this was influenced by squire or parson. The small society at Lane Delph, Hanley, was typically held in low regard.

> Independency is so contrary to the views of all other professing Christian sects here, that we are counted as the filth and offscourings of all things.[55]

Mob reaction to open air preaching and neighbourhood hostility to cottage meetings compounded a sense of social ostracism. In the early years of the nineteenth century, home meeting places were prone to physical attack. On one occasion at Roe Green, (Worsley, Lancashire) a slate was placed over the chimney of Joseph Okell's cottage to smoke the worshippers out, while on another occasion, the door was boarded from the outside to keep the Bible Class members in![56]

In 1811, James Ashton, whose house at Lowton, Lancashire, had been used by the Independent Methodists for preaching purposes since before 1806, was admonished as a 'refractory person' by the local Rector, John Pennington, and ordered to produce a meeting house licence. In fact, Ashton had taken out a licence five years previously in the mistaken hope that legality would bring security.

. . . a multitude of persecutors of the most bitter character surrounded his house whenever he and his brethren met for worship. Stones, sludge and brickbats were hurled at them, while their ears were saluted with the most awful and bitter language. These mobs were frequently headed by those who professed to be the friends of religion.[57]

This sense of religious persecution was undoubtedly compounded by sheer poverty, prompting comments such as that of the Manchester Church in 1827 that they were 'a poor and despised people'.[58] A low self-image would last for at least two generations before they became more prosperous and respectable.

4. Education

Early Sunday Schools aimed to provide elementary education for poor children, many of whom formed a cheap labour force during the week, working long hours and with only Sunday free for recreation or education. For millions of them, the Sunday School provided a route into literacy and, for many of them, out of poverty. It was, as W.R. Ward has said, 'the only religious institution which the nineteenth century public in the mass had any intention of using.'[59]

Sunday Schools were sometimes operated by town committees, sometimes by individuals and sometimes by churches, which included all the main Protestant denominations.[60] In the case of Wesleyan Methodism, the superintendent Minister had oversight of schools in his circuit and was expected to ensure that they conformed to Conference regulations.[61] By contrast, churches of an autonomous character, such as the Independent Methodists, could organise schools entirely in their own way. The address to the churches at the 1824 Annual Meeting reflected their growing recognition of the value of the institution:

> The instruction of youth requires and calls for your utmost exertions. To implant right sentiments in their minds, and good principles in their hearts, is the most important point of education; it tends frequently to the enjoyment of grace and peace here, and glory hereafter, thus producing those happy consequences and results that it is impossible fully to describe. It becomes, then, an imperious duty for you, as parents, to place in the hands of your children those books that are calculated to forward this object, and also to become advocates for, and assistants to, those useful seminaries of religious instruction, the Sabbath Schools.[62]

Only three IM churches are known to have started Sunday Schools before 1815. Some, such as Stockport and Macclesfield, made no attempt to do so, being located near to huge undenominational town schools, the one at Stockport being the largest in the world, catering for over 6,000 children.[63] However, during the 1820s, most Independent Methodists embraced Sunday School work enthusiastically; by lining themselves up with a national movement they were unwittingly moving away from separatism.

The first Independent Methodist Sunday School owed its origins to Peter Phillips, who, as a child, had benefited from the provision of an Anglican Sunday School near to his home in the 1780s and knew its value. By 1807, with a number of small cottage-based churches already under his care, he saw an opportunity to venture into this field himself. Stockton Heath, two miles from the centre of Warrington, was a community which lacked any place of education. Here he set about establishing a school in the same barn where the church met. An eyewitness account of the opening, written later by his son, tells the story:

> I was present at the opening and well remember the circumstance – it was a very humble beginning . . . there were only a very few books; a large sheet was posted behind the door, on which was printed the alphabet, and my father, surrounded by the boys, pointed with a stick to the letters, and the whole group with all their might, shouted A, B, C. . . .
>
> After the morning lessons were over, those of the children who came from a great distance ate the dinner which they had brought with them in the school-room. . . . The older boys and girls, when they knew my father had to preach in the afternoon, would be sure to wait for him, and if he happened to come before the time, they solicited him to sing with them the hymns and anthems which he had taught them. He used to draw a stave upon the door and teach them the elements of music: he was remarkably kind and affable with them, and became a great favourite.[64]

Sunday School was a full day affair and the Stockton Heath rules indicated that sessions began at 8.30.a.m. and 1.00.p.m.[65] By the early 1820s, it numbered over 300.[66] Sunday Schools were still few and far between, with the result that places at them were in great demand and children walked some distance to attend. Such was the success of the school at Stockton Heath that Peter Phillips went on to establish schools at Friars Green in 1810 and Brick Street in 1823. In the latter case, he was moved by the ragged appearance of children in the Cockhedge area of the town, where poverty was rife. With the object of providing secular instruction as well as Bible teaching, a school was built where adults as well as children found opportunity to learn.[67] Phillips' philanthropic outlook both reflected an IM response to poverty and helped to shape it.

The Oldham Independent Methodists also set about Sunday School work in earnest, beginning in 1816 with the building of their chapel and later hiring buildings as preaching places and schools in other parts of the town and surrounding villages. In total, they ran seven schools, totalling over 1000 scholars between 1824-1836, though some of these ran only for a few years.[68] Their degree of enterprise demonstrated the level of ability and commitment found in this church of (primarily) tradesmen and factory workers.

The Sunday School movement was not without areas of controversy. One of

STOCKTON HEATH
SUNDAY SCHOOL.

PARENTS are affectionately requested, as they desire either the usefulness or happiness of the Children who are taught at this School, to attend to the following Rules and to impress them all on the minds of their Children.

RULES.

1 On all occasions speak the truth.
2 Attend School constantly at half past eight o'clock in the morning and one in the afternoon.
3 Come to and go from School orderly.
4 Attend School with hands and face clean, hair combed, and shoes clean.
5 Be silent in School.
6 Behave with solemnity and reverence while reading the Holy Scriptures, and in all places of Public Worship.
7 Use no bad words, or ill names.
8 Never mock lame or deformed persons.
9 Avoid all bad company, and all quarrelling and contentions.
10 Be kind to all men and also to animals.
11 Be obedient at home to parents and friends.
12 Obey immediately the Rules and Orders of the School.
13 Remember that the eye of God is always upon you wherever you are; and that

There's not a sin that you commit,
Nor wicked word you say,
But in God's dreadful book 'tis writ
Against the Judgement day.

Rules of Stockton Heath Sunday School

these concerned the teaching of writing, which some regarded as an infringement of the Sabbath. William Hey, a Leeds surgeon and co-founder of the town's Sunday School movement, argued that writing did not promote the salvation of man and, unlike reading, did not prepare a person for knowing the will of God. Writing was, therefore, a secular activity and should not be practised on the Sabbath.[69] This was the view taken by many evangelical Christians at the time, including the Wesleyan Methodist leader, Jabez Bunting, who opposed Sunday writing in Methodist schools from 1808 and continued to fight against it throughout his life. At the Wesleyan Conferences between 1819 and 1827, he succeeded in carrying measures which effectively forbade the teaching of writing in Methodist schools.[70] Not all Methodists shared his views and the issue both served to sustain an internal conflict and also to drive children away from Methodist schools into others (including those of the Independent Methodists) where writing was taught.

A writer to the IM magazine was sharply critical of the Wesleyan position, drawing particular attention to the difference which writing made to children from poor homes. He concluded, 'So, because they learned to write at the Sabbath School they escape the misery of begging their bread, or being shut up in a parish workhouse.' In a pointed rebuff to Wesleyan sensitivities, he cited

Wesley's practice of writing part of his journal on a Sunday and the necessary task of recording the renewal of class tickets on Sundays as evidence that it was impossible to relegate writing purely to the realm of the secular.[71] His line of argument reflected the views of Independent Methodists generally.

Laqueur has distinguished between those who thought poverty was a station ordained by God and those who saw education as a means whereby the poor could elevate themselves by their own talents.[72] The Independent Methodists plainly fell into the latter category. They were acutely conscious of their poverty, but invariably looked for ways out of it and never regarded it as divinely ordained. Writing was such an exit route and was sometimes a key factor in a school's popularity. At Wigan, after an initial struggle, the introduction of writing attracted increased numbers to the IM Sunday School which went on to be a flourishing one.

A day's Sunday School programme at Bolton typified that in many places:

> About the year 1828, and long afterward, the arrangements were –
> opening at half past nine with singing and prayer; calling the scholars'
> names and recording their attendances; teaching in the classes; an
> address or reading from the desk; spelling in the classes; conclusion,
> by twelve o'clock, with singing and prayer; a similar course being
> followed in the afternoon from half-past one to four.[73]

By this time, Sunday Schools were following a pattern which had become established throughout the country, following the establishment of the Sunday School Union in 1803.[74] Many IM Sunday Schools affiliated to the Union, which gave them an early taste for interdenominational co-operation and provided a valuable counterbalance to their churches' continuing sectarian characteristics. Materials were produced for use in schools and each town had its own depot from which they could be obtained.

Those learning to read and write were not always children. Sometimes, children were the teachers and adults the learners. Even by 1923, there were people still living who remembered teaching middle-aged men and women to make strokes and pot-hooks.[75] While elementary education provided the motivation to attend Sunday Schools, those operated by churches invariably featured religious teaching also. This sometimes helped refute the allegations of some Anglican clergy that they were places of treason and sedition.[76] At Sunderland, where memories of vast working-class demonstrations were still fresh in the public mind in 1822, an appeal for support stressed the religious rather than the academic benefits of Sunday Schools:

> Sunday Schools stand recommended to the patronage of a Religious
> Public by this consideration chiefly, that in the instruction there
> imparted, *Religion* occupies the central place. The object of Teachers

is not so much to make *learned* as *good* men; and though the Annals
of Sunday Schools cannot boast of a Train of Philosophers, they are
enriched with the names of many who, through their instrumentality,
have been made 'wise unto salvation.'[77]

Having no denominational direction, IM Sunday Schools followed no
uniform pattern. Some were sufficiently independent of church control to
decide whether or not to allow the school to remain under the jurisdiction
of a particular church. At Charlestown, Ashton-under-Lyne (Lancashire),
the managing committee in 1824 discussed whether the teachers should
continue to run the school or whether they should give it up to the patronage
of one of the religious bodies in the town and, if so, which one.[78]

It has been a matter of debate among social historians whether Sunday
Schools usually sprang from working-class roots or were tools of employers
who used them as a mechanism of control and direction,[79] but there are few
examples of the latter in the case of Independent Methodist Sunday Schools
where wealthy employers were rarely found in their congregations. With the
possible exception of the patronage of the millowner Richard Clarke at Roe
Green (Worsley, Lancashire) and the prosperous draper John Broadhurst at
Manchester, small tradesmen initiated most of them, possibly with financial
support from local sympathisers. This was typified at Wingates which branched
into Sunday School work in 1820, with tradesmen and shopkeepers taking up
the role of teachers who 'taught reading and writing gratuitously'.[80]

Because maintenance and even provision of buildings often fell to the
school itself, the financial need was great, as exemplified by a Warrington
appeal in 1827:

> The managers and trustees of the Stockton Heath and Brick Street
> Schools respectfully inform their friends and the public that, in
> consequence of having recently erected the school in Brick Street
> and are now building one at Stockton Heath, the funds are more
> than exhausted; they again acknowledge their past liberality and
> solicit a share of public patronage.[81]

Where the premises were not owned, there would often be rent to pay,
together with heating costs and repairs. The purchase of teaching and pupils'
materials was a major item of expenditure, often entailing enough books,
pens and ink to supply several hundred children. One of the main sources
of income was the annual 'Charity Sermon', on which occasion a public
appeal would be made and the day's collections would be augmented by
donations from local people who saw the obvious benefit of the Sunday
School to the local community.[82]

As with other denominations, Independent Methodist Sunday Schools developed a culture of their own, with libraries, field days, sick and burial societies, clothing clubs and other means of provision for the social and material members of scholars and teachers. Sometimes a school's own funds would even be used to contribute to the funeral costs of teachers, including those who had left and who now went on an 'out' list.[83] The resulting micro welfare state created a sense of community interdependence which played a critical part in holding a Sunday School or its church together.

To address the obvious need for the teaching of writing, the 1827 Wesleyan Conference recommended that writing and arithmetic should be taught to older children on weekday evenings as a reward for regular attendance and good conduct on the Sabbath.[84] Bolton historian Stephen Rothwell highlighted the impracticality of this and accurately reflected the views of most Independent Methodists:

> the opportunities for the poor for obtaining education on week-days were scanty as compared with later times, and persons resisting what they deemed likely to abolish Sunday School tuition in writing would derive stimulus from the fact that all children employed in cotton mills ordinarily began the day's work at six o'clock in the morning and left off at half-past seven in the evening.[85]

Few children who had worked for thirteen and a half hours would be in any fit state to concentrate on writing in evenings. Laqueur argues that evening classes were a successful feature of the Wesleyans' policy, as they were attended by 10% of their Sunday School children, but by definition this meant that 90% did *not* attend and therefore did *not* learn to write in schools where Conference policy was observed.[86]

As Independent Methodist schools taught writing on Sundays, the need for evening classes was not as great, but some churches felt that these could meet a need, not for children, but for young men. They were particularly successful at Wigan in the late 1820s, where John Fell and Joseph Mercer rented a property and started a night school for miners who had received no elementary education.[87] This immediately met a need in the community.[88] Similarly, Thomas Eaton at Stockton Heath, agent for the Duke of Bridgewater's canal, used his office in the evenings to run classes for young men who worked on the farms or the canal boats.[89]

For children, the possibilities of evening education began to be more realistic following Lord Althorp's Factory Act of 1833, which set legal limits to the working hours of children and young people.[90] Charlestown Sunday School at Ashton-under-Lyne took advantage of this new opportunity and the managing committee agreed that Aaron Whitehead, the Sunday School Secretary, should teach reading, writing, arithmetic and other scientific learning on two nights a week for the scholars.[91]

Sometimes the opening of a chapel created the means to establish an educational facility. One radical reforming Independent Methodist had a curriculum mapped out, ready to be implemented as soon as the chapel at Gateshead Fell was opened:

> J. Hindmarch begs to announce to his friends, that he will in future teach in the above New Chapel, Reading, Writing, Arithmetic, Geometry, Mensuration, Gauging, Land Surveying and Book-Keeping.[92]

This was an example of an institution where the curriculum was entirely secular, even if it was motivated by Christian concern. Hindmarch, like others whose political and religious opinions stood closely together, was providing an establishment which would offer uneducated, labouring young men a chance to break out of the cycle of poverty by acquiring skills which could raise their opportunities for better employment and economic independence.

Free churches often entered the field of education years ahead of their Anglican neighbours, but some were unable to compete when the better-resourced Anglicans started schools of their own. In Wigan, the Independent Methodists had entered virgin territory in the late 1820s, but a decade later they faced a new challenge. Putting a brave face on it, they reported:

> Through the allurements of a temporal nature held out to our Sunday School scholars by the conductors of a large school near to our chapel erected by the Establishment, many of our children, as well as many from other schools in the town, have been enticed from us; but, on the whole, we are doing well in this department.[93]

Temporal allurements could, indeed, determine children's allegiance, and generally speaking, Independent Methodists were in no position to offer them, but a rare example of an Independent Methodist Sunday School upstaging its Anglican neighbour occurred at Roe Green, Worsley. A report on various Church of England Sunday Schools in the area, written in 1844, speaks of the Sunday School at nearby Beesley dropping from a hundred scholars in June 1834 to forty-one in August 1844, 'in consequence of a Wesleyan [*sic*] building a School near thereto, adjoining his house, and employing the youngsters in a power-loom mill, built by him.[94] The Wigan and Roe Green examples both illustrate how social and economic pressures could determine which Sunday School a child attended. Although the Sunday School movement blurred sectarianism through the schools' common purpose, the competitive element, particularly between Establishment and Nonconformity, prevented it from being altogether eradicated.

In their seminal work on the 1851 Religious Census, K.D.M. Snell and P.S. Ell have shown that denominations with the most proletarian adherence had a particularly weak association between Sunday School and church, citing the Primitive Methodists, Independent Methodists and Bible Christians as examples.[95] This may have reflected their inability to draw a full complement of teachers from within their own ranks and the need to use non-adherents for the purpose. But the same argument must lead to the conclusion that sectarian advancement was not a primary motive in the establishing of Sunday Schools by the denominations in question. In any event, this was a comparative rather than an absolute weakness. For most Independent Methodist Churches, the Sunday Schools often represented their most successful enterprises, giving them a stake in the local community and laying the foundations of faith for future church members. The action of the early Oldham Independent Methodists, for example, in establishing Sunday Schools in parts of their town such as Waterhead Mill where there was no educational provision indicated how a Sunday School could serve as a bridgehead for wider work in a new area.[96]

In the earlier part of the nineteenth century, education proved to be an area which highlighted the elements which Independent Methodists had in common with other free churches, rather than those which differentiated them. This common interest foreshadowed the major battles which the free churches would fight together on the educational front in the late nineteenth century.

5. Temperance

Alcohol abuse was a serious problem in the early nineteenth century, particularly among working class men whose wages were often paid – and later spent – in the public house nearest to their place of work.[97] The resultant poverty and suffering of their families became proverbial. However, there were widespread misconceptions about the nature of alcohol. The dangers of excessive spirit-drinking had long been recognised, but beer, the working man's drink, was regarded as having important food properties and its use was therefore regarded not so much as an indulgence as good dietary practice, so long as it did not lead to drunkenness.[98] As the records of a number of early Independent Methodist Churches show, it was common for visiting preachers to be supplied with beer or wine on arrival for an appointment and also afterwards. Beer for choir singers was also standard provision on special occasions.[99] One issue of the denominational magazine even included a recipe for parsnip wine.[100]

In 1830, the Beer Act, which was designed to allow free trade and end brewers' monopolies, made provision for the opening of unlicensed beerhouses which were not subject to the same constraints as public houses.

One of the arguments for the Act was that it would lessen spirit-drinking and so promote temperance. The outcome was very different; six years after the Act was passed, there were over 44,000 'Free Trade' beerhouses in existence and drunkenness increased dramatically.[101] Beer was now sold at bakers' and chandlers' shops, while regular drinking places were opened in cellars, back alleys in town slums, village sheds and even in woods. Opening hours and other regulations of Parliament were virtually ignored.[102]

The problem was exacerbated by problems of poverty and poor living conditions. The ready availability of cheap liquor in the close vicinities of people's homes caused a huge rise in beer consumption among the poorest people, for whom alcohol and its effects provided something of a release from the misery and squalor of their everyday lives. The 'jerry shops', as they were called, offered the same kind of superficial escape from the harsh realities of life that drugs brought in the late twentieth century.[103]

The escalating problem stimulated the formation of temperance societies which were based on pledges of abstinence. Like Sunday Schools, they were sometimes but not always connected to churches. The first societies were usually based on principles of either moderation or abstinence from spirits only, but one particular advocate of complete teetotalism, George Harrison Birkett, a Dublin Quaker, and founder of the National Temperance Society of Ireland, received support from Thomas Eaton, leader of the Independent Methodists of Stockton Heath, while staying in Warrington in March, 1830.[104] Eaton made his Chapel available for a meeting and on 4 April a Temperance Society was formed. The pledge formulated by Birkett stated:

> We whose names are subscribed, believing that Intemperance with its attendant evils is promoted by prevailing opinions and practices with respect to the use of intoxicating liquors, and that decided means of reformation are decidedly called for, resolve to abstain from the use of inebriating liquors ourselves, to dissuade others from using them and by all proper means to discountenance the causes and practices of intemperance.[105]

A later claim by Arthur Mounfield that the society was based on Birkett's total abstinence pledge has to be weighed against the fact that the first roll book of the society records a pledge against spirits only.[106] This was probably a *temperance* society in the terms understood at the time, rather than one based on full abstinence, but it represented an important step in the development of the movement in the Warrington area. Temperance meetings continued to be held in Warrington at the Mechanics' Institute. In 1834, having heard of the rise of societies on a total abstinence principle, a number of members expressed the wish to sign a teetotal pledge but were refused in the belief that beer was necessary to personal health.[107] Nevertheless, a meeting was held in the vestry at Friars Green IM Chapel in October, 1834, and the Warrington Total Abstinence Society began.

Two years' experience of the Beer Act spurred on the movement for abstinence from all forms of alcoholic drink. The greatest advocate of the movement, Joseph Livesey, a Preston cheesefactor, launched a campaign which soon gathered national momentum; this would become his life's work.[108] Although his was not specifically a religious movement, Independent Methodists in several towns proved to be some of his earliest supporters. Working as they did, among the poorest of people in urban areas of northern industrial towns, they experienced at first hand the effects of the 'jerry shops' on family life and the lost working hours of those whose drinking habits became completely out of control. One of the first places where Livesey's message of total abstinence was received with acclaim was Bolton, where the town's citizens heard him for the first time in Folds Road IM Chapel on 16 July 1833.[109] There was an existing sympathy for the movement which had become established in the town two years earlier, but Livesey's visit and his lecture in the chapel had the effect of revitalizing the movement and giving people the option of signing one of two pledges – a moderation one and an abstinence one.[110]

The Bolton New Temperance Society (as it became known) met in various locations, including the Town Hall, but members of Folds Road Chapel remained very much to the fore of its activities in the ensuing years. One of them, Thomas Entwistle, described how he and others went to great lengths to support reformed drunkards in their resolution:

> We have commenced a system of visitation; several of the members are appointed to go round every Sunday morning for the purpose of distributing temperance tracts and exhorting the members to adhere firmly to the resolution they have pledged themselves to, and I assure you the most happy results have been produced by this system.[111]

Entwistle's programme underlines the fact that it was one thing for a man with a drink problem to sign a pledge in the euphoria of the moment; it was another matter to keep it, and many who signed the pledge would afterwards lapse. Nevertheless, the temperance advocates saw visible improvement in those who kept to their pledge; thus rewarded, they resolutely persevered with their work.

By the late 1830s, the movement was gaining ground to such an extent that some Independent Methodists felt able to apply temperance principles to church disciplines. The first salvo was fired in 1838 by the church at Stockport, which proposed to the Annual Meeting that churches should only allow abstainers to occupy the pulpit – an audacious suggestion for a movement less than a decade old. In the event, delegates were unconvinced and the proposal was rejected on the grounds that it was coercive.[112] A different issue, that of the kind of wine used in the Lord's Supper, was tackled three years later, when a proposal was carried:

> That the different societies be earnestly requested to take into consideration the necessity and importance of receiving the Sacrament or Lord's Supper in the pure juice of the grape instead of fermented wine.[113]

This appeared, from the abstainers' viewpoint, to have marked a move forward, but in 1846 the same resolution was repeated – a clear indication that it may have been passed on the previous occasion, but not all churches had complied with it. The promotion of temperance ideas in churches did not always receive a favourable response. To a generation which had never considered the need for abstinence and for whom beer, in particular, was a staple drink, the whole subject was highly controversial. At Oldham, the matter led to open discord and closed minds, as the 1851 report showed:

> With some, matters that cannot be made tests of membership, or rules to measure a brother's stature in Christianity, have been urged so dogmatically as to become offensive, while those who have differed from them in opinion have obstinately refused to examine the principles of their brethren, or to seek for that information which is within their reach.[114]

The outcome was a schism which led to the formation of a new church which met first at Bank Top and later built a chapel in King Street.

On the wider front, the benefits of temperance were soon recognised – better home lives, reduced poverty, reduced crime, better workmanship and fewer working hours lost. Soon, those with a vested interest in seeing the progress of the movement took practical steps to advance it. In Warrington, several leading citizens of the town banded together in 1836 to form 'The Association for the Promotion of Useful Information in Connexion with Temperance.' Members of its founding committee included the town's leading wire and soap manufacturers, together with solicitor and historian, William Beamont, who later became the town's first mayor. They also included the Independent Methodists Peter Phillips, William Phillips, Thomas Eaton and Peter Longshaw – all of them (except Eaton, a canal agent) from a different social stratum, but already recognised for their pioneering work in the movement.[115]

A year earlier, Peter Phillips, with another Independent Methodist, John Nield of Oldham, became founding committee members of the British Temperance League.[116] The influence of these men, who were widely respected in their home areas and the wider Union of Churches, undoubtedly served to make Independent Methodism, in due course, a strongly teetotal denomination. As in other denominations such as the Primitive Methodists, teetotalism became the dominant aspect of an underlying Puritanism which equally frowned upon dancing, card-playing and other forms of popular pleasure. Where 'temperance chapels' played a strong part in community life, the temperance ethos often proved more widely pervasive. The Independent Methodists at Roe Green, Worsley, could proudly claim in 1908 that, thanks to their temperance activities over the previous seventy years, their village still had no public house.[117]

6. Chartism

Just as many Independent Methodists in the 1820s embraced the Radical Reform movement, so those from the late 1830s began to sympathise with the Chartist movement which provided a collective voice for the grievances of the poor. Some became active Chartists, such as Festus Fielden at Lees, near Oldham, leader of a small church where the members all knew the meaning of acute poverty. Fielden was well regarded both as a local preacher and a speaker at Chartist meetings.[118] Like the earlier Radical Reformers, he represented a strand within Independent Methodism which saw religion and politics as indivisible, the latter being a concrete expression of the former. More significant than Fielden was Ben Rushton of Ovenden, Halifax, a prominent Yorkshire Chartist. Once a preacher in the Methodist New Connexion, according to E.P. Thompson he either withdrew or was expelled.[119] Rushton was connected with the Independent Methodist causes at Rastrick and Halifax in the 1820s and later with the Gospel Pilgrims (an IM sect) in the Bradford area.[120] The Gospel Pilgrim chapels at Little Horton and Bradford were both used for Chartist meetings,[121] perhaps not surprisingly in the former case, as Horton was 'a very hot-bed of Chartism.'[122] At a Chartist Camp Meeting in 1839, Rushton indicated his aversion to paid ministry when he said that he had given nothing to the parsons since 1821 – probably a reference to his refusal to pay parish tithes or church rates.[123] By this time, he was estranged from church and chapel, but never abandoned the rhetoric of Christianity.[124] When he died, in 1853, it was reported that 'the wish of the departed patriot was that no paid priest should officiate at his funeral.'[125]

However, some Independent Methodists abhorred Chartist methods, which sometimes involved violence, and were more disposed to urge restraint. Adam Howarth at Westhoughton managed to persuade several of his neighbours against violent action by sending them bags of potatoes – a potent argument for hungry men.[126] Others, such as Peter Phillips at Warrington, would engage in peaceful demonstrations as occasion required, but held fast to their pacifist convictions. There were problems when a church's membership contained a mixture of views on Chartism. This happened at Leigh (Lancashire) where William Sanderson took the opening service of a chapel in 1841. He noted: 'The services were well attended, a Church was formed which promised well, but strong Chartist opinions being brought in, broke it up.'[127] While Chartism had political ideals which addressed the needs of the impoverished people who made up most of the IM Churches, its methods created for some of them a conflict of conscience. Social revolt and Quaker-like pacifism could not easily co-exist in a single chapel. Independent Methodist heterogeneity was both a strength and a weakness; it reflected the autonomy of the local church, but exposed its inability to speak with a single voice on any issues beyond its basic ecclesiology.

7. Two Modern Interpretations of the Independent Methodists: Valenze and Watts

Having outlined some aspects of Independent Methodism in its contemporary context, it is necessary at this juncture to consider what others have concluded from their studies of its development. The main modern interpreter of its history during this period, albeit from a sociological perspective, Deborah Valenze, gave a full chapter (and parts of other chapters) to the subject in *Prophetic Sons and Daughters,*[128] a work devoted to the study of female preaching and popular religion in industrial England. Valenze brought grassroots Independent Methodism to life as she depicted vividly the struggles of the people, whose faith was lived out in home-based believing communities untouched by professional clergy. Importantly, she also highlighted the role of women in ministry and leadership, a significant characteristic of Independent Methodism. Her description of Independent Methodism as a movement which evolved in mill towns as 'a theology of the dispossessed'[129] is borne out by the present chapter and the fact that Independent Methodist churches were usually established in the middle of the poorest communities. However, some of her other assertions are less supportable. She commented, 'Teetotalism, fasting and plain dress replaced customary behaviour, and preachers demonstrated commitment to sectarian values by following a strict code of personal asceticism and refusing all pay for their work.'[130] This interpretation seems to be based on a conflation of the IM principle of unpaid ministry and the actual poverty of many adherents. In reality, the only work for which they refused payment was preaching, in the belief that they should not be a burden on their congregations and that they should earn their own living in the secular world. While teetotalism was common practice, there is no evidence that fasting was widely adopted as a spiritual discipline. Many people lived with starvation-level poverty during the 'hungry forties'[131] and later during the Cotton Famine,[132] but this was hardly an asceticism of choice.

Of greater concern is Valenze's portrayal of the Independent Methodists as people whose 'faith was full of vengefulness and self-righteous anger'. In support of this assertion, she highlighted some of the imprecatory psalms which, she stated, were used at IM funerals; in fact the examples she used were from Weber's comments on the psalms in question and none featured (as she implied) in the IM obituaries cited in her footnotes.[133]

Finally, questions must remain over Valenze's main conclusion: 'At a time when working-class political movements were growing in importance and strength, Independent Methodists withdrew from such developments and focused their energies on supportive efforts of their own.' This withdrawal thesis is based largely on examples of disillusioned Chartists who became IM converts, but these men belonged in a brief time frame and she made no reference to Independent Methodists who were radical reformers in the 1820s (as noted earlier in this chapter) or Liberal politicians in the late nineteenth century.[134]

The comments of Michael Watts are incidental to his much wider study of the history of dissent, but they take into account political as well as domestic factors. Watts followed earlier writers in attributing Independent Methodism's origins to lay evangelistic activity, but he challenged Valenze's view that the growth of cottage-based churches was part of 'the struggle for domestic security in an increasingly uncertain world' and argued that a greater factor at this time was the integration of work and home – a relevant point for the handloom weavers whose homes were the bases of several early IM churches.[135] He further pointed out that not only Quakers but some Methodists felt strongly that ministers should earn their own livings and not live off the contributions of their members.[136] Some Methodist class leaders felt revulsion at being told to collect more money from people who were already suffering deep hardship – as the story of Thomas Jones, earlier in this chapter, illustrates. As a result, many of them found refuge in the IM fold where non-payment became for them a matter of principle. Finally, Watts noted that non-payment was to prove a major weakness since it impeded Independent Methodism's potential to expand at a comparable rate to other Nonconformist bodies in England.[137]

8. Movement of Population

By the middle years of the nineteenth century, most Independent Methodists were to be found in the growing industrial towns of South Lancashire, where their numbers expanded partly through the migration of people from agricultural areas, looking for employment in mines and factories. Many of the obituaries of those who joined the churches during these years show that a high percentage of them had travelled from place to place in search of employment. One such was John Holgate who abandoned handloom weaving to avoid becoming a pauper. He moved to a number of towns in turn, joining the Independent Methodists on each occasion.[138] Settling alongside others with similar experience, these migrants were among the most responsive to the Independent Methodist preachers who were from the same stratum of society as they were.

Based on an examination of a number of migrants' stories, Valenze argued that 'Many mendicant preachers made the industrial town their final destination, where they founded Independent Methodist societies in an attempt to reconstitute village communities.'[139] But this argument reads into the migration process an outcome which would be hard to substantiate and which her quoted examples do not prove. There is no single recorded example of an IM society being formed through the arrival in town of a 'mendicant preacher.' While it was true that migrant workers, some of them preachers, settled in industrial towns, they usually joined existing societies which had resulted from Methodist schisms. Most of the founders of the early societies were people of different background from these agricultural migrants, such as John Broadhurst, the Manchester draper (certainly no mendicant preacher) and Peter Phillips, the self-employed chairmaker of Warrington (a third generation townsman).[140]

The 'hungry forties' highlighted the hardship experienced by many early Independent Methodists. A trade depression, accompanied by the high price of bread engendered by the Corn Laws, brought the weavers of Westhoughton (and elsewhere) to near starvation, so that when Wingates Church received notice of the 1843 Annual Meeting, it responded by saying that it was 'too poor to send a delegate.' Its report continued:

> Many of our dear friends that compose our congregation, as well as many of the members of our Society, are extremely poor; the suffering and privation through which many have had to pass during the winter, cannot be described within the limits of our report.[141]

Depressed trade also led to increased emigration, particularly to America, as spinners and weavers who were the mainstays of the churches in towns such as Bolton and Oldham headed off for the fresh opportunities of the new world. Within just a few years of 1841, Folds Road Church, Bolton, was to lose twelve families by emigration to America alone.[142] Their letters encouraged others to join them. William Parker, long-serving preacher of Macclesfield and sometime missionary, was one of the emigrants who exchanged the penury of a silk weaver for farming in the Midwest of America. Writing to his friend Thomas Bramwell at Bolton, he pointed out the material benefits of living in a country where land was cheap (two dollars an acre) and where there were no beggars. He also found a better response to his convictions than in his home country:

> My principles which caused me to be despised in the old priest and king country obtain for me universal respect here. I bitterly repent I have spent the prime of my life in England.[143]

Independent Methodists were not alone in chafing at poverty, deprivation, social injustice and a class-ridden society, but their strong egalitarianism and anti-clericalism made them natural candidates to take up life in the land of the free.

9. Conclusion

The 1820s provided several examples of how Wesleyan Methodism lost ground in areas of material poverty and among people of radical persuasion. A structure which required substantial finance, given voluntarily, for its maintenance was sustainable in circumstances where people had the means to give, but it lacked the flexibility to make allowances for its members during times of hardship. When the failure of impoverished labourers to maintain contributions became a disciplinary matter, adverse reaction was inevitable. The Independent Methodists provided a net which caught such people, but their new allegiance, at least initially, was for practical rather than ideological reasons.

Similar inflexibility on political involvement (albeit for understandable reasons) again created a wedge between Methodist officialdom and ordinary members who saw the political route as the only way to remedy social injustices. While Independent Methodism had no stated policy on this matter, it left local members free to pursue their interests unchallenged. From their point of view, religious and political freedoms now stood together. Though Independent Methodism would never be large enough to be a force in the nation, to its adherents each local chapel was home to a people's church which took their concerns seriously.

Notes to Chapter Two

1. E.J. Evans, *The Forging of the Modern State* (London: Longman, 1983), 181.
2. D. Bythell, *The Handloom Weavers* (London: Cambridge University Press, 1969), 206.
3. J. Crowther, *Thoughts upon the Finances or Temporal Affairs of the Methodist Connexion* (Leeds, 1817), 33.
4. D. Gowland, *Methodist Secessions* (Manchester: Chetham Society, 1979), 98.

5. 'Memoir of Thomas Jones', *United Methodist Free Churches' Magazine* 1866, 634-5.
6. A.H. Williams, *Welsh Wesleyan Methodism 1800-1858* (Bangor: Cyhoeddwyd gan Lyfrfa'r Methodistiaid, 1935), 201. Williams points out that this is a one-sided account, based on a pamphlet published in Welsh by Thomas Jones under the pseudonym 'Arthur o Bowys'. There is no Wesleyan account of the event.
7. Williams, *Welsh Wesleyan Methodism,* 205.
8. Doctrines and Rules of the Independent Methodist Church established July 1818 in Liverpool, *passim.*
9   *Ibid.*
10. See Chapter 3.
11. S. Rothwell, *Memorials of Folds Road Independent Methodist Chapel, Bolton* (2 vols.; Bolton: Independent Methodist Bookroom, 1887), 1:81. There is no independent evidence of this statement, but this church continues as an Independent Methodist Church to the present day.
12. The chapel was vested in a local deed which gave the trustees complete autonomy.
13. A. Mounfield, *A Short History of Independent Methodism* (Wigan: Independent Methodist Bookroom,1905), 66f.
14. W. Sanderson, *The Life and Labours of William Sanderson* (Wigan: Independent Methodist Bookroom, 1899), 225.
15. Anon. 'Rise and Progress of Methodism in Lancaster. Part 19: 1822-25. The Secession of 1824' in *Lancaster Circuit Wesleyan Methodist Church Record,* February 1903.
16. *Ibid.*
17. *IMMag.* 1825, 641.
18. See Introduction.
19. D. Hempton, *Methodism and Politics in British Society 1750-1850* (London: Hutchinson & Co. 1984), 104.
20. *Ibid.*
21. 'Address of the Preachers to the Methodist Societies', Leeds, 27 July, 1812.
22. 'To the Societies in the Connexion Established by the late John Wesley A.M.' (Committee on Religious Privileges, 12 November, 1819).
23. *Wingates Messenger*, September 1895, 39.
24. *Ibid,* 40.
25. 'A Short Account of the Rise and Progress of the Independent Methodist Interest in Bolton', *IMMag.* 1824, 271.
26. Vickers, *History of Independent Methodism* (Wigan: Independent Methodist Bookroom, 1920), 147f; Mounfield, *Short History,* 106f.
27. Rothwell, *Folds Road,* 1:10.
28. Register of Baptisms, Folds Road Independent Methodist Church, Bolton.
29. Rothwell, *Folds Road,* 1:25.
30. Bolton Report to Annual Meeting, IMMins. 1821.
31. *Newcastle Courant,* 16 October 1819, 2.
32. W.R. Ward, *The Early Correspondence of Jabez Bunting* (London: Royal Historical Society, 1972), 21ff. For an examination of the significance of the Stephenson case to Wesleyan Methodism, see Hempton, *Methodism and Politics,* 106ff.

33. Hempton, *Methodism and Politics,* 107.
34. W.H. Stephenson, *The Loyalty of Methodist Preachers exemplified in the Persecution of their Brethren* (Newcastle: 1819), 8.
35. H. Kelly, *An Impartial History of Independent Methodism in the Counties of Durham and Northumberland* (Newcastle: Edward Walker, 1824), 9.
36. *Ibid,* 12.
37. MS History of Gateshead Independent Methodist Church, und. (IMA)
38. H. Kelly, *A Rude Sketch or Good Days in Sarre Louis, (*Newcastle, 1824). Born in 1792 in Sunderland, Kelly was apprenticed as a mariner at the age of 11 and was a prisoner-of-war during the Napoleonic Wars. While in a French prison, he came under the influence of a group of Methodists, embraced their faith and learned to read and write.
39. H. Kelly, *The Stone cut out of the Mountain* (North Shields, 1821), preface.
40. Kelly, *Impartial History,* 15f.
41. Ward, *Bunting,* 39n. The 'late Spence' was Thomas Spencer, minister of Newington Chapel. The 'Independent youth' was almost certainly Hugh Kelly, then 27 years of age.
42. IMMins. 1820.
43. Kelly, *Impartial History,* 23.
44. G.E. Milburn, *The Christian Lay Churches and their Origins* (Sunderland: Independent Methodist Circuit, 1977), 7.
45. IMMins, 1824.
46. *Rules of the Independent Methodist Churches in Durham and Northumberland,* 37.
47. Kelly, *Impartial History,* 18.
48. *Ibid,* 19.
49. *Ibid,* 22. W.H. Stephenson, *A Sermon preached in the Independent Methodist Chapel, Newcastle . . . the day of the Coronation of His Majesty George IV* (Newcastle: John Marshall, 1821), 19.
50. Kelly, *Impartial History,* 19.
51. *Ibid,* 21
52. Stephenson was received back into Wesleyan Methodist membership and resumed his role as a local preacher some time afterwards. W.H. Stephenson, *A Funeral Sermon occasioned on the Death of Mr. John Dungett* (Newcastle, 1833), 9.
53. For the reasons for their change of allegiance, see account of the Protestant Methodists in Chapter 3.
54. Sermon notes recorded in Vickers, *History,* 32f.
55. *IMMag.* 1827, 331.
56. H.L. Tyldesley, *The Duke's Other Village* (Radcliffe: Neil Richardson, n.d.) 8.
57. 'Memoir of James Ashton', *Zion's Trumpet,* 1860, 4ff. *IMMag.* 1908, 161.
58. *IMMag.* 1827, 323.
59. W.R. Ward, *Religion and Society in England 1790-1850* (London: B.T. Batsford, 1972), 135f.
60. P.B. Cliff, *The Rise and Development of the Sunday School Movement in England 1780-1980* (Redhill: National Christian Education Council, 1986), 6f.

61. J.M. Turner, 'Methodist Religion 1791-1949' in R.E. Davies et al (eds.) *History of the Methodist Church in Great Britain* (4 vols.; London, Epworth, 1978), 2:103.
62. IMMins. 1824
63. Cliff, *Sunday School Movement,* 68.
64. 'Life and Labours of Peter Phillips', *Zion'sTrumpet,* 1855, 183.
65. J.A. Dolan, *From Barn to Chapel* (Warrington, 1989), 123
66. Hymnsheet for Stockton Heath and Friars Green Chapels, 1821 (Warrington Library Archives).
67. A. Mounfield, *Brick Street Sunday School 1823-1923* (Warrington, 1923), 4.
68. George Street Independent Methodist Church, Oldham, Account Book 1825-63. This details the running expenses of the schools at each place. *Independent Methodist Magazine.* 1862, 188.
69. Ward, *Religion and Society*, 137.
70. 'Neither the Art of Writing, nor any other merely secular branch of knowledge shall be taught on the Lord's Day.' *Wesleyan Methodist Magazine* 1827, 696. Cliff, *Sunday School Movement,* 81.
71. 'On the Propriety of Teaching to write in Sabbath Schools', *IMMag.* 1828, 667ff.
72. T.W. Laqueur, *Religion and Respectability* (Yale, USA, 1976), 128.
73. Rothwell, *Folds Road,* 1:105.
74. Cliff, *Sunday School Movement,* 74.
75. Mounfield, *Brick Street*, 4.
76. The Bishop of Rochester had launched a particularly fierce attack earlier in the century. *Gentleman's Magazine,* November 1800, 1076ff.
77. Poster, Independent Methodist Church, Numbers Garth, Sunderland, 1822 (IMA).
78. Charlestown Sunday School, Ashton-under-Lyne, Minute Book 1824-1857. The outcome was a decision to stay with the Independent Methodists.
79. For the former view, see Laqueur, *Religion and Respectability,* 42, 63; for the latter view, see Patrick Joyce, *Work, Society and Politics: the Culture of the Factory in Later Victorian England* (1980), 178f.
80. E. Howell, *Whispers of Wingates* (1984), 12.
81. Dolan, *Barn to Chapel*, 49 (from a Hymnsheet in Warrington Library Archives)
82. Cliff, *Sunday School Movement,* 56.
83. Charlestown Minute Book; IM (Minority) Mins. 1858, 8.
84. *Wesleyan Methodist Magazine* 1827, 696.
85. Rothwell, *Folds Road,* 1:134.
86. Laqueur, *Religion and Respectability,* 133.
87. *Centenary History of the Independent Methodist Church and School, Greenough Street, Wigan* (1930), 12ff.
88. See obituary of Ralph Tinsley, an early scholar, in *IMMag*, 1860, 297.
89. A. Mounfield, *A Village Centenary* (Warrington, 1906), 18.
90. G.M. Trevelyan, *English Social History* (London: Longmans, Green & Co. Ltd. 3rd edition, 1946) 543.
91. Charlestown Minute Book.
92. Poster advertising the opening of the Independent Methodist Chapel, Gateshead

Fell, 1823 (IMA).

93. IMMins. 1837, 14.

94. H.L. Tyldesley, *The Duke's Other Village* (Radcliffe: Neil Richardson, n.d.),
    12. The 'Wesleyan' was the local Independent Methodist leader and
    entrepreneur Richard Clarke, who proved a moving spirit in many aspects of
    community life.

95. K.D.M. Snell and P.S. Ell, *Rival Jerusalems* (Cambridge University Press,
    2000), 303.

96. George Street, Oldham, Account Book.

97. W. Pilkington, *The Makers of Preston Methodism and the Relation of
    Methodism to the Temperance Movement* (London, 1890), 179.

98. A. Mounfield, *The Beginnings of Total Abstinence* (Warrington, 1902), 18.

99. Rothwell, *Folds Road*, 1:113; George Street, Oldham, Account Book.

100. 'Parsnip Wine', *IMMag.* April 1827, 310.

101. H. Carter, *The English Temperance Movement: A Study in Objectives*
    (London: Epworth, 1933), 25

102. S.J. Webb, *The History of Liquor Licensing in England principally from
    1700 to 1830* (London: Longmans & Co. 1903), 118f.

103. Carter, *Temperance Movement*, 32.

104. Mounfield, *Total Abstinence*, 11f.

105. *Kaleidoscope (Literary Supplement to the Liverpool Mercury)*, Vol. 10
    (1830), 162.

106. MS Roll Book of the Warrington Temperance Society, (IMA) 1830-70;
    Mounfield, *Total Abstinence*, 18f.

107. P.T. Winskill, *The Comprehensive History of the Rise and Progress of the
    Temperance Reformation from the Earliest Period to September 1881* (4
    vols.; Liverpool, 1881), 1:65.

108. Carter, *Temperance Movement*, 21.

109. Winskill, *Temperance Reformation*, 59.

110. Rothwell, *Folds Road*, 1:125.

111. *Preston Temperance Gazette*, 1834, 94; Rothwell, *Folds Road*, 1:127.

112. IMMins. 1838.

113. IMMins. 1841.

114 IMMins. 1851, 9.

115. Pamphlet, 'The Association for the Promotion of the useful Knowledge in
    Connexion with Temperance.' (IMA).

116. J. Livesey, *Reminiscences of Early Teetotalism* (Preston and London, 1872),
    33.

117. W. Brimelow, *Centenary Memorials of the Independent Methodist Church,
    Roe Green Worsley* (1908), 21. This is still the case to the present day.

118. H. McLachlan, 'The Christian Brethren,' *The Story of a Nonconformist
    Library* (Manchester University Press, 1923), 163.

119. E.P. Thompson, *The Making of the English Working Class* (London: Victor
    Gollancz Ltd., 1965), 398ff.

120. See Chapter 3 for further details on the Gospel Pilgrims. *IMMag.* 1827, 326;
    IMMins, 1834, 17; *Bradford and Leeds Gospel Pilgrims Plan*, 1834.

121. A.J. Peacock, *Bradford Chartism 1838-1840* (York: St. Anthony's Press,
    1969), 19.

122. W. Cudworth, *Rambles around Horton* (Bradford: Thomas Brear & Co. Ltd., 1886), 27.
123. E.P. Thompson, *Working Class,* 398ff.
124. D. Thompson, *The Chartists* (London: Temple Smith, 1984), 226.
125. B. Wilson, *The Struggles of an Old Chartist* (Halifax, 1887), 22.
126. Howell, *Wingates,* 34.
127. Sanderson, *Life and Labours,* 39.
128. Deborah Valenze, *Prophetic Sons and Daughters* (Princeton University Press, 1985).
129. *Ibid*, 241.
130. *Ibid*, 215.
131. See 8. Movement of Population
132. See Chapter 4.
133. Valenze, *Sons and Daughters*, 211ff. Max Weber, *The Sociology of Religion*, Ephraim Fischoff, trans. (1922; Boston: Beacon Paperback ed. 1964), 111.
134. See Chapter 5.
135. M. Watts, *The Dissenters*, (2 vols. Oxford, Clarendon Press, 1995) 2:164f.
136. *Ibid*, 238.
137. *Ibid*, 239.
138. 'Memoir of J. Holgate of Dewsbury', *IMMag.* 1877, 355.
139. D. Valenze, *Sons and Daughters*, 234.
140. See Chapter 1 for details of Broadhurst and Phillips.
141. Howell, *Wingates*, 35.
142. Rothwell, *Folds Road*, 1:155.
143. William Parker to Thomas Bramwell, 18 August 1840 (The Correspondence of Thomas Bramwell, Shoemaker and Preacher of Bolton and Liverpool, Bolton Library Archives).

Chapter 3
The Shaping of the Movement 1815-60

Up to the middle of the nineteenth century, not only did social and political influences shape Independent Methodism's character, but events in the wider field of Methodism and the emergence of significant new leaders affected its structures and corporate activity, turning it gradually into a more cohesive body.

1. Alexander Denovan (1794-1878)
and the Church at Glasgow

Scotland was not fertile territory for Methodism and Glasgow was no exception. The Wesleyan Methodists had only one society in the city prior to 1819.[1] The Methodist New Connexion's presence dated from 1814 and reached its zenith with a membership of 123 in three societies in 1827; however, numbers soon dwindled and the cause had disappeared by 1834.[2] Not until 1826 did the Primitive Methodists arrive.[3]

Despite this unpromising picture, in 1820 the Independent Methodists started a church in Glasgow, which grew rapidly and held its strength through the greater part of the nineteenth century. Its success has to be understood in the context of the life and career of its founder-leader, Alexander Denovan, who became a commanding figure in the denomination for over fifty years. His church warrants specific attention as it was the only Independent Methodist Church to take root in Scotland for any length of time and, paradoxically, the largest Church the Independent Methodists ever had.

Denovan was born at Bannockburn in 1794, the youngest of seven sons of a handloom weaver, with a Covenanter ancestry. As a child, he received an elementary education at a Parish School and was, nominally, a Church of Scotland adherent. In 1806, he left his village and went to Glasgow where he was apprenticed to a grocer. Four years later, he was appointed as a clerk to a firm of West India shipping merchants where he spent the rest of his working life.[4]

In 1812, Denovan married Ann Bell, a local young Methodist. Under her influence and that of her mother, he started attending Methodist meetings and, despite his initial scepticism, was converted a year later. Shortly afterwards, he began studies at Glasgow University, on a part time basis, financed by some private teaching which he undertook in writing and arithmetic. In his studies he excelled in Greek and Hebrew and finally matriculated in 1819.

During these years, Denovan struck up a friendship with some people who had seceded from a Presbyterian Church, three of them being office-bearers who, 'feeling themselves aggrieved by the ruling powers, ceased to have fellowship with their mother church.'[5] Part of their grievance related to what they saw as the failure of the Established Church to preach the Gospel to the poor.[6] They started to meet for worship in a shop in Candleriggs and later moved to larger premises as their numbers grew. At around this time, they heard of the advent of Independent Methodism in Newcastle and were attracted to its principles and practices.[7] A letter from Newcastle offered guidance on the formation of a church, whereupon they drew up some basic principles of church government which centred on the appointment of three groups of officers – pastors, teachers and deacons. They believed that one-man ministry put unbridled power into a single pair of hands, while their study of the New Testament convinced them that a plural pastorate was more scriptural. They also believed that local ministry should be unpaid, arguing that Scripture taught that pastors should maintain themselves. Concessions were made for those engaged in missionary service which took them away from home and those who were unable to work through 'affliction or old age,' in which case relief would be supplied according to need.[8]

However, they felt that public credibility would require their officers to be ordained by the laying on of hands by others so ordained. Providentially, two men who met their requirement joined them: John Virtue, a retired Church of Scotland minister and Robert McPherson, a Church of England clergyman who had become convinced of the Independent Methodists' views. In due course, these two officiated at a service to ordain those who had been elected as pastors, teachers (class leaders) and deacons.[9] Four pastors were appointed, including Alexander Denovan who, at twenty-six years of age, was the youngest; together with the teachers, they constituted an eldership. Ordination was not usually practised in Independent Methodist Churches, but, as the denomination had no centrally-appointed ministry at this stage, the churches seem to have been content to allow each other considerable latitude on such matters.

In 1821 a large house in Low Green Street[10] was purchased at a cost of £1,500 and adapted for use as a chapel. Taking advantage of its strategic location, Denovan obtained a movable pulpit, which he frequently took out on to nearby Glasgow Green, where he exercised a vigorous outdoor preaching ministry.[11] His son's biographer wrote: 'believing that the Gospel should be preached literally without money and without price, he began a mission of his own in the lower parts of Glasgow, which he designated, "The Free Gospel Church." '[12] Like the Independent Methodists of England, his passion was to offer good news to the poor without making any financial demands of them.

Denovan's wider efforts led to the establishment of preaching stations at Hamilton, Lanark, Bothwell and Paisley, all of which he visited frequently.[13] He also visited Ireland to follow up an enquiry which brought a short-lived affiliation by a church at Downpatrick,[14] but the contact with it soon lapsed. The church in question had no preacher of its own and geographical separation meant that it had no prospect of support from outside.[15] Nor did any of the Scottish preaching stations last for very long. The small church at Lanark, for example, lost its pastor and family through emigration to the United States.[16] The remaining members joined the Old Independents.[17]

The Scottish Independent Methodists found, along with Methodists generally, that their very name created a problem, so, a decade after their inauguration, they concluded that a new name was needed and came up with an ingenious solution to their dilemma:

> The propriety of changing our name having been discussed at several church meetings, and it having been shown that Methodists were classified with Arminians, who were alleged by many to expect to obtain heaven by their own works, which doctrine we as a church abhor, and declare to be a principle contrary to the doctrines we have espoused from the beginning, that in consequence of this, the work of the Lord was hindered, and as names were nothing of themselves, and we should become all things to all men so far as one can do with a clear conscience, it was resolved, without a dissenting voice, that from the first day of January Eighteen hundred and thirty one years, we be called, what properly and scripturally we are, and have always been, namely *Church Presbyterians*; as in our church we have a plurality of presbyters, or elders, or pastors, forming a presbytery quite independently of any sister churches' pastors associating with them.[18]

Their decision reflected the overwhelmingly Calvinistic ethos of the Scottish Churches and the limited scope for an Arminian Church to gain a foothold. Nevertheless, the change of name taken by the Independent

Alexander Denovan (1794-1878)

Methodists did not signify a deviation from their Wesleyan-Arminian beliefs. Alexander Denovan used his considerable powers to demonstrate that his church was steering a careful passage between Calvinism and Pelagianism, following Wesley who, he believed, had struck the right balance with due attention to the sovereignty of God and the free choice of humankind.[19] Denovan defined his church's mission not merely in terms of extending Independent Methodism, but 'to lend our best energies to the reconstruction and remodelling of the Christian Church 'from its present unscriptural encumbrances and [to bring it] to its primitive simplicity and original purity.'[20] He passionately believed that the Christian Church in its totality should abandon the practice of paying local church ministers and wrote extensively to outline his personal vision of a New Testament Church. If his method was sectarian, his goal was ultimately catholic.

Denovan's eldest daughter described him posthumously as 'impulsive, unrestrained in purpose, ready to take fire with his own heat, and to go to extremes in action,' tendencies fortunately tempered by his calm and practical wife. His single-mindedness was reflected in his arduous work on Sundays, when 'He would come home in the evening almost speechless from fatigue.' He walked to all his appointments, some of which took him several miles away. In his habits, he was abstemious almost to the point of asceticism. He was a strong advocate of the temperance movement and regarded tobacco as an abomination. In his early life, he had to be pressed by his employer to take a better position elsewhere, as he disliked change and refused further offers of improved employment, giving as his reason that the pursuit of wealth would be a temptation to leave the evangelistic work to which he was committed.

In addition to his preaching and pastoral work, Denovan found great personal fulfilment in his writing. From his pen came several pamphlets[21] and two books, while he edited a hymn book in 1827[22] and the denominational magazine for several years. His first major book consisted of a comprehensive account of his own and the church's views on the Calvinist-Arminian question.[23] It was a lucidly argued and vigorous defence of the Arminian position on the subject of election and a withering denunciation of the doctrine of double predestination which, in Denovan's view, was a slander on the character of God. His second book aimed to build up the picture of what a New Testament church should be and was used to vindicate IM views on church and ministry.[24]

The social composition of his church was highlighted when cholera struck Glasgow in 1832, claiming three or four members, a surprisingly small number, considering that the church, like its English counterparts, was 'composed generally of people in the humbler circumstances of life.'[25] But poverty brought no discrimination within the life of the church and Denovan showed himself ready to develop the limited talents of some of his poorer members. One such man, William Hamilton, spoke proudly of his new-found opportunities:

> After I married my late Wife, Mr. Donovan [sic] married us, he came and talked to me on the subject of coming back to the church, so accordingly I went back and I am now, unworthy though I be, raised in Divine Providence to address my Brethern [sic] from the Pulpit on the Lords Day. . . .[26]

Denovan was no 'ranter', unlike many of the Independent Methodists of northern England, but he identified with his radical brethren in Newcastle on issues of social injustice and brought his intellectual weight to bear on the case for change. Dissenters throughout Britain were pressing for the abolition of church rates in the 1830s and a pamphleteers' war on the subject arose in Scotland. Denovan entered the lists, arguing against the concept of an established church, on the basis that Christ's kingdom should be understood as being separate from the kingdoms of the world. He cited Jesus and the apostles as avoiding temporal power, but urged for the spirit of Christianity to enter into national councils. From this, he proceeded to attack the principle of mandatory payments to the established church, whether through church rates or through tithes.[27] He aired his views on the subject to the other Independent Methodist Churches, and the outcome was a petition from the Annual Meeting to the House of Commons, advocating disestablishment.[28] This was a landmark event which reflected, for the first time, the adoption of a common view on a national issue by the Independent Methodists.

From the beginning, Denovan's pursuit of his ideological objectives ensured that he would aim for significant contact with kindred minds elsewhere. Consequently, he made his first appearance at the Independent Methodist Annual Meeting, held in Oldham, only a year after his church was founded. A year later, he served as secretary to the Annual Meeting, a position which he held again in 1827 and 1834. His literary prowess and administrative ability were soon recognised by the churches and, in 1823, he became the founding editor of the denomination's magazine, *The Independent Methodist*. The product of his own initiative, it became a vehicle for his own thinking and that of others on the Independent Methodist view of church and ministry. It was issued quarterly for the following six years, after which publication lapsed for the lack of someone else to take the editor's position. After a seventeen year break, Denovan resumed his editorial role between 1847-49 and the magazine was re-named, *The Magazine of the United Free Gospel Churches*. At a time when there was little cohesion among the IM churches, the magazine was an important unifying influence.

Over the years, Denovan grew in stature among the Independent Methodists, who had few strong leaders and virtually no one to match him in scholarship. In 1833 he was appointed as President of the Annual Meeting for the first time. As in the other branches of Methodism, this position was usually taken by a different person each year, though some people had held it on several occasions. However, over the next forty-five years, Denovan was to occupy it on no less than thirty occasions, despite the fact that he came from the remotest church in the denomination. In one person, he combined the gifts of evangelist, scholar, writer, pastor and administrator, all of which were exercised with a consuming sense of purpose and direction. As an unpaid pastor, he had (at its zenith) the largest church in the denomination with over 600 members. Strongly Arminian in a Calvinistic country, he attacked Calvinism, Roman Catholicism and Unitarianism with equal force.

To use an analogy which should not be over-pressed, if Peter Phillips was the John Wesley of Independent Methodism, Alexander Denovan was its Jabez Bunting – strong, resolute and sometimes overbearing, but standing head and shoulders above everyone else of his generation in leadership ability and acumen.

2. The Missionary Society

By the early 1820s, the number of IM churches had reached about seventy, many of them added for the reasons shown in the last chapter. They valued their new-found freedom but some were dissatisfied with a form of association which merely consisted of an Annual Meeting and an exchange of preachers. For a body bearing the name 'Methodist' it inevitably contrasted with Wesleyans, New Connexion and, in particular, the current rapid growth of Primitive Methodism.

In 1824 the subject of sending out 'missionaries' to evangelise and proselytise in new areas was raised during discussion at the Annual Meeting and deferred for a year.[29] The Liverpool Church had already declared its aim to send someone into Wales and now proceeded to do so, despatching a missionary to the principality for three months.[30] The North-East Churches declared that the principle was supported by Scripture and confirmed in church history. Their assertions highlighted the tension between those who wanted to stay with a purely congregational polity and those who wanted the union of churches to become a Connexion, with mechanisms for growth and expansion:

> Local systems, confining the energies of ministers within narrow limits, produce a withering influence on the general interests of vital religion. It was the love of ease, and a want of zeal for God, that first gave them existence, and He therefore shows His disapprobation of them by cursing them with barrenness.[31]

This was neo-connexionalism asserting itself against the congregational polity adopted by the churches for the previous twenty years. It heralded the clash between opposing ideologies which was inevitably to come.

The man who proved the catalyst for action was George Turton (1791-1851), a Sheffield doctor who advocated the formation of a denominational missionary society, funded by donations from churches. The society was to send out missionaries to weaker churches or to places where there were signs of interest in the free gospel system. The missionaries were to be people who could be released from their employment temporarily. In each locality they would form classes, visit the sick and absentees and preach. No missionary was to stay for more than three Sundays at any one place.[32] This rule was almost certainly designed to deflect any possible criticism that itinerancy was being introduced by the back door.

Turton's proposals were received with acclaim and adopted unanimously. The subsequent address to the churches, published with the Minutes, defended the establishment of the mission vigorously, stating that 'it affords not the least encouragement to a hireling system', but insisting that 'missionary exertions' were essential if the great commission was to be fulfilled. However, by the following May, the project had barely got off the ground. Turton wrote to Denovan, the magazine editor, castigating the churches for their apathy:

> at present, our influence is circumscribed, our exertions confined within so narrow a sphere, and our principles unknown; hence, in many places we are branded as a selfish, narrow-hearted people, when, in fact, the opposite should be more manifest, from the privileges we enjoy. [33]

One obvious weakness of the system was soon realised: limiting a missionary's visits to a maximum of three Sundays was proving expensive and ineffective. Longer visits were needed for lasting value so greater latitude was allowed. The 1826 Annual Meeting voted to have 3000 copies of the amended *'Rules of the Independent Methodist Mission'* published and formally appointed nine members of the Sheffield Church to act as the committee for the following year. In the event, this proved the most active year in this particular phase of missionary activity, with a spate of preachers going out in different directions and sending back detailed reports.[34]

The principle of using people who could take time off work to undertake a few weeks of missionary activity inevitably restricted the number of people available from a group where giftedness was in short supply. Moreover, even after the three-week limit was removed, no missionary could stay in an area long enough to achieve anything of lasting worth. Their task was essentially hit-and-run proselytisation; not surprisingly it made little impression, as samples of the missionaries' experience show.

The isolated Driffield Church in the East Riding of Yorkshire was virtually a lost cause from the beginning, having no obvious leader in its ranks and depending on a single preacher who lived thirteen miles away at Bridlington.[35] They informed William Parker on his visit that they would continue as an independent church, provided that they could have the services of a missionary every two months until someone was raised up from among them. Parker noted, 'I gave them all the encouragement and instructions I was capable of affording; *but particularly recommended exertion among themselves as the most effectual means of promoting their prosperity.'*[36] John Eckersley, who followed him, resorted to finding employment in the area so that he could continue his work without draining the limited finances of the Missionary Committee. A year later, the congregation asked for Eckersley's return and insisted that without a missionary they could not continue.[37] By 1828 the church had disappeared from the records. Like many others, its members were really hoping for a paid minister, in all but name, at someone else's expense.

The most prolific missionary, Joseph Woolstenholme (1800-1846), was compared by his biographer to William Bramwell.[38] His later career outside Independent Methodism showed that his potential was never fully realised at this time. Woolstenholme was twenty-five years of age when the Missionary Committee first engaged his services and he concentrated on Scotland where he travelled widely. In addition to his evangelistic preaching, he promoted the IM system, but found Scotland unpromising territory. After meeting a group in Edinburgh, he commented,

> But though they have nothing to say against such a system, yet, it is extremely difficult to get them to see their privilege and duty in the gospel: especially that of having men raised up from among themselves, who shall be enabled to take the oversight of them.[39]

In effect, Woolstenholme was encountering a cultural barrier in the minds of Presbyterian Scots who had no national tradition of lay ministry and where Methodism itself had only made limited inroads. Kirk and minister were deeply embedded institutions and the idea that a congregation should produce a plurality of ministers from within its own ranks generally ran against the grain of Scottish thinking.[40] Furthermore, although Alexander Denovan and his friends were experiencing a modicum of success at this time in the Glasgow area, they had the advantage of being indigenous Scots. Eventually, Woolstenholme's health failed and, for the time being, his evangelistic labours were ended.[41] Later, he went on to fruitful ministry with the Protestant Methodists and thereafter in the Wesleyan Methodist Association.

If the missioning of Scotland resulted from the initiative of a single evangelist, the corresponding work in Wales was due largely to the vision and enterprise of an entrepreneur, Thomas Jones, leader of the Welsh Independent Methodists at Liverpool, who combined business trips with evangelistic work. Samuel Ashton (Macclesfield) accompanied him to the small church at Chirk on one occasion and commented in his report on Jones's practical commitment to the missionary cause:

> we arrived in the little village about four o'clock and sat down to dinner in company with two friends whom Brother Jones employs here in his business and who preach the gospel on the Lord's Day. He gave me to understand that his business in this country does not answer, and but for keeping the little cause alive, he

would give it up. The more I know of this truly excellent man, the more I love and admire him. His steady and persevering piety, his disinterestedness where the cause of God is concerned, and his firm attachment to the Independent Methodist cause and interest, are such traits as we find but in few.[42]

Small, cottage-based communities, promoted and encouraged by Jones and his employees, represented Independent Methodism in Wales, but none of them became strong or lasting. However, Jones saw a different outcome in the following decade.[43]

The Independent Methodist missionaries found their best reception in small communities which most resembled their own. Samuel Ashton, a silk weaver by trade, found in the eyes of the miners of Parr (St. Helens) the credibility which he was totally unable to achieve during his efforts in the city of Liverpool.[44] William Yates, carter by trade and a protégé of Hugh Bourne's early ministry at Warrington,[45] had a similar experience in east Lancashire where his characteristically revivalist style of ministry was well received in the open air, preaching rooms and cottage meetings.[46]

The missionaries' lack of success on the ground was matched by poor support from the churches, with Sheffield, Newcastle and Liverpool as the exceptions. Frustrated at beating its own drum to little effect, when Sheffield reported to the 1828 Annual Meeting it criticised 'the ill-managed zeal of those who were the first promoters of Independent Methodist principles.' A year later, the Newcastle report openly stated that its churches felt less attached to the Independent Methodists and saw no point in sending anyone to the Annual Meeting as it achieved nothing.[47]

3. Wesleyan Methodist Schisms 1829-1838

Events in the wider field of Methodism impacted upon the Independent Methodists from the late 1820s onwards. Wesleyan Methodism experienced further fragmentation, in the form of the 'Leeds Organ' dispute of 1827 (bringing into being the Wesleyan Protestant Methodists),[48] the Welsh 'Minor Wesleyan' secession of 1831[49] and the Warrenite conflict of 1834, (resulting in the formation of the Wesleyan Methodist Association).[50] The Independent Methodists briefly gained by the affiliation of the Minor Wesleyans to their ranks, but in the long run lost heavily to the other two bodies.

3.1. The Wesleyan Protestant Methodists

In 1827 a conflict arose at the Wesleyans' Brunswick Chapel, Leeds, when the trustees resolved to install an organ in the chapel at the request of a number of the seatholders. The majority of the leaders and local preachers of the society opposed this, believing that it would spoil the simplicity of

Methodist worship. Having failed to get the backing of circuit or district for their proposal, the trustees lobbied some of the more influential ministers to gain their support, presenting opposition to the organ as the work of fractious dissidents who needed to be put down.[51] As a result of their successful lobbying, the Conference granted their request.

The organ issue brought to a head a clash between Conference and the itinerant preachers, on the one hand, and local societies in the form of leaders and local preachers on the other. In fact, other issues played their part too, such as the imposed division of the circuit and the control of work done locally, such as the Sunday Schools and the prayer bands. It all amounted to a collision between the opposing forces of ministerial authority and the democratic aspirations of church members. What followed was a period of mounting conflict as aggrieved local preachers and leaders fought, unsuccessfully, to have the organ decision reversed. The Leeds Methodists included a number of people of involved in radical politics who were not prepared to be compliant and accept the over-ruling of their local decisions.

The eventual outcome of this conflict was the formation of a new division of Methodists, known initially as the Nonconformist Methodists and later as the Wesleyan Protestant Methodists.[52] Not surprisingly, they created new structures which left no scope for Conference or itinerants to overrule local people. The result was a body which was congregational in polity, Methodist in doctrine and which recognised only a lay ministry.[53] *Prima facie*, the Protestant Methodists were based on exactly the same principles as the Independent Methodists. This was sufficient to prompt Alexander Denovan to urge them to consider throwing in their lot with the Independent Methodists rather than to start yet another denomination. In an open letter, which was an eloquent *apologia* for Independent Methodism, he outlined the praxis of his church at Glasgow, which, he believed, the Leeds people could adapt to their requirements. All the main Methodist offices could be adapted, he argued, into a kind of quasi-Presbyterian system:

Methodist Office:	Independent Methodist equivalent:
class leaders	teachers
stewards	deacons
'most pious' of local preachers	pastors, bishops, presbyters or elders
itinerant preachers	evangelists

Turning to the subject of payment, Denovan argued that if it was right to pay itinerant preachers, it should be right to pay local preachers too – but in his view payment was warranted for neither. Pastors, he said, should work for the supply of their own wants and for the assistance of others. Financial support could only be justified for those who had 'no settled place of abode' such as apostles and their present equivalents, and this should be in the form of 'relief' based on need, rather than the payment of a stipend. Evangelists who were supported in this way could pay occasional visits to the churches, but the bulk of the work at home should be done by those who were currently local preachers.[54]

There is no record of any reply to Denovan's letter, but when the WPMs produced a constitution, the pattern of leadership and ministry which it laid down was remarkably similar to his suggestions. Each church was to have seven elders, who would be a mixture of preachers and leaders. There were to be no itinerants as such, but evangelists were supported on a full time basis, while church leadership was entirely in the hands of local people. Only three evangelists could sit in the Conference and then only by permission of the Ministerial Committee.[55] This, wrote a contemporary writer, put them 'lowest in the scale of influence and authority and condemns them to be treated with the utmost jealousy and suspicion.'[56] It was free gospelism, in essence if not in name, and a union of the two bodies came near to happening, but not in the way that Denovan had anticipated. There were a number of possible reasons for the non-convergence of the two groups.

Firstly, the Protestant Methodists had formulated a constitution which put all churches on the same footing, unlike the numerous local constitutions of the Independent Methodists. Secondly, the WPM Connexion effectively made each circuit an independent entity and the primary unit of the denomination. Each circuit had an annually elected Presiding Elder, the aim being to replace Wesleyan centralised government with a democratic form of government at local level. However, experience showed that the elected elders could, during their terms of office, be just as dictatorial as the Wesleyan itinerants.[57] Thirdly, while there seemed little difference in practice between the two groups in relation to ministry, the ideological basis was not the same. The WPMs took a lower view of itinerancy (in this case, in the form of evangelists) than the Methodist New Connexion or the Primitive Methodists, but they took a higher view of it than the Independent Methodists. Their main objection was to power, not to payment, of which they seemed to take a fairly pragmatic view.

A year after Denovan's letter, a group of dissident Wesleyans in Sheffield approached the Leeds WPMs to ask for their help in forming a society on the principles laid down in their rules. As a result, in October 1829 three WPM leaders visited Sheffield, where they held a public meeting in the Independent Methodists' commodious Bow Street Chapel.[58] Subsequently, a Protestant Methodist Society was formed. Bow Street allowed the occasional use of its premises to the new body, but this was more than just the generous gesture of sharing a building; the Sheffield Independent Methodists, dissatisfied with the failure of their brethren to support missionary work, liked the appearance of the Protestant Methodists. They appeared to be more structured and apparently more committed to missions than the Independent Methodists, but had also disavowed Wesleyan style itinerancy and centralised authority. In December, a public meeting of both bodies was held at Bow Street and a merger was agreed. At the 1830 Yearly Meeting of the Protestant Methodists, Sheffield was added to the list of circuits with 480 members.

George Turton, leader of the Sheffield Independent Methodists and founder of the Missionary Society, saw a possible future for all the Independent Methodist Churches in this new body. In January, 1830, he circularised them, pointing out the weaknesses in their system and encouraging them to join a body which could give them a better future.[59] This met with a very limited response. Eight churches in the Tyneside area took up his recommendation;[60] the rest of the churches reported to the 1830 Annual Meeting that they saw no point in doing do.

Turton was for one year the President of the Wesleyan Protestant Methodist Connexion, gave distinguished service to the medical profession and became a town councillor on the incorporation of the Borough of Sheffield in 1843, rising to alderman a few years later.[61] In many ways he prefigured the kind of Free Church person who would bring church, professional and civic life together so powerfully in the later years of the nineteenth century. The Independent Methodists were undoubtedly the poorer for having lost him.

3.2. The Genesis and Exodus of the Minor Wesleyans

Thomas Jones, leader of the Welsh-speaking Independent Methodists of Liverpool, saw his claims of interest in different parts of Wales validated when a body of churches came into being as the result of a split in the ranks of the Welsh Wesleyan Methodists. On 8 August 1831, twelve local preachers met in a tavern near Menai Bridge to consider the state of their denomination. They had no problems with Methodist doctrine but they believed that God had raised up many gifted local preachers who were prevented from moving from one circuit to another by edict of the superintendents.[62] This, they felt, was hindering the progress of Methodism in Wales. Further meetings were held, to which other local preachers were invited. The outcome was a series of resolutions for the reform of ministerial and local preaching arrangements. A modified version of the resolutions was sent by the circuit superintendent to the Financial District Meeting which turned them down.

The reformers' action had already antagonised the superintendents of the Beaumaris and Caernarvon Circuits who wrote to their colleagues in other parts of the province to warn them that some lay preachers had formed 'irregular committees' with the intention of launching a new non-Wesleyan organisation. They proposed to call them to account at the next Quarterly Meeting and to expel any who failed to conform to WM doctrine and discipline.[63] Further meetings and discussions took place over the following weeks and feeling intensified among the would-be reformers against Wesleyan discipline. On 6 October, the day of the Beaumaris Circuit Quarterly Meeting, the reformers met and passed a resolution to the effect that unless the Quarterly Meeting agreed to a 'change in the organisation absolutely and entirely they would no longer be members or preachers in the Wesleyan Body.'[64] It seems extraordinary that a rift should have arisen over an issue which should have been amicably resolved – the interchange of preachers between circuits. However, the presenting issue was less significant than the attitudes on both sides which lay behind it. Once again, the underlying cause of the impasse was the assertion of lay rights on the one hand against perceived clerical domination on the other.

On 13 October, the reformers, who became known as the 'Wesle Bach' or Minor Wesleyans, held their first meeting at the home of Owen Owens, the leading figure of the group, at Llaneilan. At the beginning of November a meeting was held between the reformers of Anglesey and Caernarvonshire at Cemaes, when Thomas Jones of Liverpool was present and the decision to link with the Independent Methodists was probably taken. Reference was made to their affiliation at the 1832 Annual Meeting:

> In Anglesey, the work of the Lord broke out in November last, seven local preachers tired of the yoke of bondage united themselves with us and exerted themselves to spread in conjunction with the glorious gospel of Christ, the liberal principles of Independent Methodism. Thank God He has owned their labours.[65]

Owen Owens travelled throughout Anglesey and Caernarvon, undertaking missionary tours which resulted both in conversions and in additions to the new body. Some chapels seceded in the Beaumaris, Caenarvon and Pwllheli Circuits, while new churches were also established in homes. During their brief existence, the Minor Wesleyans held their own Annual Meetings and were only once present in significant numbers at the IM Annual Meeting; they were effectively a linked sect.[66] At their high point they counted twenty-four societies with thirty-one preachers.[67] The movement spread to other parts of the principality – to the Wrexham area, south to Aberystwyth and then further south into Carmarthenshire, but its centre was always in Caernarvonshire.

For five years, until 1837, the Minor Wesleyans functioned with varying degrees of success in their different localities, with support from the

Independent Methodist Missionary Committee. Collections were taken for various chapel building projects and some of the churches were given leave to appeal to the rest of the Union's Churches for funds. Under the surface, however, dissatisfaction was brewing, inadequate support for missionary work being again a bone of contention. Much of the cost of sending missionaries to Wales was borne personally by Thomas Jones. In 1837 the Minor Wesleyans received a body blow when a group of churches in the middle of their territory returned to the Wesleyan fold.[68] Then in March 1838, Owen Owens, their inspirational figure, died at the age of forty-four.[69]

3.3. The Wesleyan Methodist Association

At the time of these setbacks, the newly formed Wesleyan Methodist Association (WMA) appeared to offer a new opening to the Minor Wesleyans. Although scarcely two years old, the Association had formed a missionary fund to aid circuits which wanted an itinerant minister but which could not afford one. Thomas Jones and the leaders of the Welsh churches saw an opportunity which offered them similar freedoms to those which they had enjoyed with the Independent Methodists, but better financial support. In 1838, the WMA Assembly, meeting at Rochdale, resolved to admit to its ranks the Liverpool Church and the remaining Minor Wesleyans.[70]

The Association's statistics two years later showed that its Welsh section consisted of 366 members, with eleven chapels and six meeting rooms. For a time, the Welsh Churches received better support than previously, but eventually the Association faced financial difficulties of its own and most of the former Minor Wesleyan Churches went into other denominations – Wesleyan, Calvinistic Methodist and Independent. Like other groups which constantly hankered for missionaries, the Minor Wesleyans' brief attachment to the Independent Methodists seems to have been based on dubious motives. They appear to have wanted the benefits of a paid ministry without having to pay for it. Those same motives drove their application to the WMA. Perhaps the ones which returned to the Wesleyan fold showed greater integrity by accepting the undisputed obligations which this entailed.

The fusion of the WMA with the WPM Connexion in 1836 brought together the former Independent Methodists of Sheffield, Newcastle, North Wales and the church at Kendal.[71] By the mid-1840s, its Connexional Committee included three former prominent Independent Methodists – George Smith of Preston, George Turton of Sheffield and Thomas Jones of Liverpool while Joseph Woolstenholme was now one of its evangelists. Conversely, however, the WMA also suffered one significant loss to the

William Sanderson (1811-1899)

Independent Methodists in the form of a small group in Liverpool who went on to form one of the largest of all the Independent Methodist churches. Its founding leader was William Sanderson (1811-1899), a tailor by occupation and a class leader in a Liverpool Wesleyan Society. Sanderson withdrew his membership during the Warrenite controversy in 1835, whereupon he became an evangelist with the WMA. After some time, he became uncomfortable with his paid status and resigned, resuming his trade as a tailor. Hearing of the Independent Methodists, he and his followers linked with them and he attended his first Annual Meeting in 1841.[72] Sanderson proved totally uncompromising on the non-payment issue, while his pulpit oratory made him hugely popular as a preacher.[73] Though he would never accept an appointment as evangelist, he operated independently in this capacity and drew several churches into the denomination.[74] He served in turn as President, Secretary and Editor on a number of occasions.

4. Primitive Methodist Schisms 1830-55

From their beginning, Primitive and Independent Methodists had much in common in terms of revivalist spirituality, the role of lay people and their appeal to the poor. Primitive Methodism had expanded rapidly, reaching a membership of 33,507 by 1824, but the years 1825-28 saw a time of crisis when issues of finance, poor practice in local leadership, discipline and the admission of unsuitable people into the ministry had to be addressed.[75] The outcome was a more centralised denomination, which made good progress in the following years. However, not all the PM people responded well to the changed situation and various schisms followed over a twenty-five year period. In most cases, the result was a localised free gospel sect – in many ways like those which resulted from Wesleyan schisms earlier in the century.[76]

4.1. Sects Resulting from PM schisms

In addition to schismatic PM groups which immediately joined the Independent Methodists, three discrete sects and their eventual relationship to the Independent Methodists should be briefly noted:

The Independent Primitive Methodists of Nottinghamshire arose out of discontent in the rural societies centred on the village of Bingham, where most of the members were agricultural labourers earning very low incomes and finding the support of an itinerant a heavy burden on their already limited means.[77] Some of their local preachers held services of their own outside of Primitive Methodist jurisdiction, sometimes in the same buildings where the Primitive Methodist societies met. In June 1832, this led to the expulsion of five of them, all members of the Bingham society, from the Nottingham Primitive Methodist Circuit.[78] Consequently, several village-based societies, mainly those in private or rented accommodation, withdrew from the circuit. They adopted the name 'Independent Primitive Methodist', denoting their adhesion to the beliefs and spirituality of Primitive Methodism, but their rejection of its developing polity. The functions of paid ministers (including pastoral work) were taken over entirely by local preachers. They maintained many of the customs and practices of Primitive Methodism, including Camp Meetings. The new churches formed themselves into a circuit which published a preachers' plan and held quarterly meetings. In 1851, the Ecclesiastical Census showed ten churches, with evening congregations totalling 865 adults and three Sunday Schools totalling 137 children. They remained as a distinct sect until they affiliated to the Independent Methodists in 1892. Only one church, Lowdham, continues to the present day.

The Primitive Methodist Revivalists and Gospel Pilgrims. Schism was often stimulated by headstrong individuals and the PMs were not always sorry to see them go, as a comment of Hugh Bourne's concerning the Bradford Circuit shows:

> This circuit had a good increase the last quarter and is doing well. Much trouble had been made by a few disturbers; but they have taken themselves away, have drawn off some of the members and have begun a connexion of their own; and we are happily delivered from their further trouble; peace is restored, the circuit has begun to move in harmony and we have every cause of thankfulness to Almighty God.[79]

The 'Connexion' to which Bourne refers was almost certainly one which subsequently split into the two groups named.[80] Few records of the Primitive Methodist Revivalists remain and their existence was brief. The Gospel Pilgrims, probably as a result of contact with existing Independent Methodists at nearby Halifax and Rastrick, joined the Independent Methodists *en bloc* in 1834.[81] Their most notable figure was John Parkinson (1793-1860), an ex-PM preacher[82] and bookseller, who went on to become a travelling evangelist with the Independent Methodists.[83] One Gospel Pilgrim society at Thornhill Edge, near Dewsbury, remained in existence until 1987.

A second group of Gospel Pilgrim churches was formed in Norfolk, apparently through dissension in the North Walsham Primitive Methodist Circuit. They were first noted in Independent Methodist records in 1839. Their leading figure was William Frost, brick and tile maker of Banningham.[84] Most of the churches were in rural locations, the one exception being a church in Norwich. In 1840, with a colleague, John Codling, Frost made the long journey to the IM Annual Meeting at Bolton, the only occasion on which the Norfolk Gospel Pilgrims were represented.[85] This group of churches had disappeared from the records by 1851, but Frost was later involved in a further group of Free Gospel churches in the south of the county; this also proved short-lived.

The Original Methodists of Derbyshire and Nottinghamshire. In 1839, the Belper Primitive Methodist Circuit, Derbyshire, resolved to increase the modest payment of the superintendent minister, William Carthy, from fourteen to sixteen shillings a week.[86] This seemed little enough, but members who were suffering from the effects of a trade depression resented it. Their resentment was compounded by the fact that Carthy had suspended three local preachers. PM members in the village of Selston accused Carthy of dictatorial conduct and ill-treatment of one preacher in particular. Writing in later years, one of their number described what happened next:

> His [Carthy's] despotic conduct and avaricious disposition, added to all that had occurred before of the same kind, had the effect of causing many to think that travelling preachers were an evil in the Christian Church and a few active local preachers in that circuit, determined to make an effort to establish a society which should not employ any paid preachers and, as a commencement in such an enterprise, they began by holding a Camp Meeting on Selston Common on Sunday, 7 July, 1839.[87]

Churches sprang up in the surrounding area and they formed themselves into a body which they termed 'The Original Methodist Connexion,' though they were often dubbed 'Selstonites' after the village where they began. Unlike the older Independent Methodist body, this group of churches could legitimately claim to be a 'Connexion'. It had a written constitution from the beginning and, although its societies were internally autonomous, they bound themselves together by common discipline. Contact with the Independent Methodists came in 1851 through William Doughty, one of the Independent Methodist leaders at Oswestry.[88] At this time, the Original Methodists numbered twenty churches with 406 members.[89] They resolved to apply to join the Independent Methodists[90] and were accepted at the 1852 Annual Meeting,[91] but they never took up the membership for which they applied. Evidently they had concluded that they could not be fully united with the Independent Methodists because the older body occasionally provided financial maintenance for travelling evangelists who were allowed 'to live off the fruits of the gospel.' The Original Methodists showed themselves, thereby, to be even more inflexible on the issue of payment than the Independent Methodists.

Strangely, when the Original Methodists went out of existence, their churches all went into branches of Methodism which had a paid ministry. Their second generation apparently saw little reason to demonise godly men whose payment represented sacrifice rather than pecuniary gain. In effect, the movement had lost its initial impetus and there was no reason for it to continue.

As the above account shows, PM schisms often had more than one cause. Certain factors occurred frequently:

4.2. Finance

The pecuniary demands placed on PM members initially were not great; in 1820 they were asked to pay a penny a week 'if they can afford it, and more if they choose', together with whatever they could afford at the quarterly ticket renewal.[92] There was a genuine concern not to over-burden the poor in the difficult post-Waterloo years, thereby falling into the same trap as the Wesleyans. The reluctance to set higher financial targets partly stemmed from some of the free gospel thinking which pervaded Primitive Methodism in its earliest days, which persisted into the 1820s, not least through two of its most successful ambassadors, John Benton and John Wedgwood.[93]

However, as time passed, inadequate funding and repeated financial embarrassments made it necessary to tighten financial regulations and the conference of 1826 ruled that each circuit thereafter must pay its own itinerant and that no circuit could accumulate a debt.[94] This was a prudent and practical move, but it reflected growing centralised direction and a larger budget as more chapels were built and new areas were missioned. The PM members were therefore now under an obligation to fund a paid itinerant, albeit on a pittance of a wage that would be accepted only by the most dedicated people. This was often resented, especially among the low-paid handloom weavers, framework knitters and agricultural labourers who formed the bulk of the Primitive Methodist membership in many places. What followed mirrored the issues within Wesleyan Methodism which brought the first free gospel societies into being thirty years earlier. As the Selston story indicates, it needed only a modest increase in a travelling preacher's stipend to precipitate the schism which led to the formation of the Original Methodists.

4.3. Preachers and leaders

Primitive Methodism distinguished between 'local', 'hired local' and 'travelling' preachers, but was careful to affirm equality of status between them.[95] Generally the balance of authority in Primitive Methodism was weighted far more to local societies and their leaders than in other branches of Methodism. However, during this period, among some PM local preachers there was a growing sense of a widening gap between themselves and the itinerants, which was sometimes exacerbated by the high-handed actions of men such as William Carthy, who unilaterally suspended local preachers, and George Herod who angered his Warrington congregation by sawing off the backrests of the free seats to make the point that some of the people concerned could really afford to pay pew rents.[96] One man's authoritarianism was other men's marginalisation; free gospelism offered restored status to local preachers in such situations. Its attractions reduced the Barnsley PM Circuit's membership fell from 913 to 680 in 1853-54:

> James Gilpin, local preacher and leader; Joseph Pollard, local preacher and leader; John Hawksworth, local preacher and leader; Thomas Hawksworth, exhorter; Henry Hewitt, exhorter and leader; and John Myers, leader, all of Barnsley, left society all

together; because they were not allowed to trample down Connexional discipline in a certain case and carry it violently their own way. They therefore withdrew from society and set up an opposition society on what is called free-gospel principles, and have used their utmost efforts to divide our society; and have succeeded to draw away about 34 of our members in and about the town and they make use of most unchristian efforts to injure our interests and damage our society in the public estimation.[97]

In the Burland Circuit, Cheshire, preaching in Free Gospel churches resulted in disciplinary procedures.[98] One of those so disciplined, Matthew Darlington, a preacher of twenty years standing, proved to be the area's most enduring supporter of the free gospel movement which he served until his death in 1885.[99] At Blackburn, William Dale received a letter from the circuit meeting, requiring him to give a written assurance that he renounced the doctrines of the Free Gospellers.[100] In the Black Country, John Wilkins preached at the opening of the Free Gospel Chapel at Wednesfield Heath, after which he was summoned to a special committee meeting and asked to undertake not to preach for them again. He refused the request, was expelled and duly joined his local Free Gospel Church.[101] Primitive Methodism was at root a lay movement and its local preachers would see their own gratuitous service as not fundamentally different from that of the Free Gospellers.

4.4. Free Gospel Proselytism

By the middle years of the nineteenth century, some Independent Methodists were no longer satisfied with the freedom to work according to their beliefs, but exchanged tolerance for polemic, leading to verbal attacks upon other denominations, often other Methodist bodies:

> So far as Methodistic bodies are opposed to Independency, they are opposed to *Scripture*. Submitting their necks to Conference, &c., they obey *man* rather than *God*. . . .
>
> What a difference is there between the hireling ministry of the present day, and the ministry of the New Testament! What a fearful departure is there around us from the simplicity of the gospel![102]

This kind of strident anti-hireling invective castigated an uncollared PM itinerant in the same way as a powerful Anglican rector. The Independent Methodists could see the unsettled state of Primitive Methodism in certain areas. Preachers such as William Sanderson saw PM troubles as heralding the collapse of the 'hired system' and readily exploited the situation for sectarian gain, making preaching tours of areas where Primitive Methodism was known to be having internal difficulties.[103]

The Primitive Methodists recognised this process for what it was and warned people against it; when Sanderson arrived in Colne, Lancashire, news of his agenda had already reached the town. He commented: 'I arrived there about noon, and was informed that the enemies of a Free Gospel had circulated that I was an infidel, and had warned the people not to go near me.'[104] However, in Colne he was meeting with a church which had left the Primitive Methodists some months previously, with no knowledge of the Independent Methodists.[105] Sanderson's visit was to prove the start of a process which would see Independent Methodism firmly established in the area. In contrast to some of the other PM schisms it would see sustained growth and stable expansion, leading to the formation of an IM circuit which, by the end of the century, would be the largest in the Connexion. The causes which led to the formation of these churches were little different from those elsewhere, but they found a niche at a critical time, as the following account shows.

Just outside Colne, a small PM chapel existed in Bradley, a hamlet on the fringe of what would later become the town of Nelson. News of the events at Colne, which was in the same circuit (Burnley), had reached Bradley where some of the members became sympathetic to free gospel ideas. Two of the chapel's local preachers gave expression to these views, as a result of which they were summoned to a Quarter Board Meeting and duly put off the plan.[106] Shortly afterwards, a minister from Burnley arrived to take the service at Bradley, allegedly tried to assert his authority and suffered a walk-out of the entire congregation which subsequently took a former handloom weaver's workshop at Bradley Lane Head.[107] They could not have known that this location would soon place them at the centre of one of the fastest-growing towns in the country. A year later, with a membership of thirty, they built their first chapel at the cost of £1,000 and named it 'Salem'. In 1855 they joined the United Free Gospel Churches (as the Independent Methodists were currently known) and had sufficient confidence to host the Annual Meeting in the following year.

The town of Nelson was entirely a product of the cotton industry. During the second half of the nineteenth century, it grew from a collection of hamlets in the parish of Great Marsden to a town of over 40,000 people, re-named after the hero of Trafalgar. Mills and mill workers' houses went up rapidly, but there were few churches or public buildings at the beginning of this period. This was a town of migrant workers, most of whom had no roots in the new community, and Salem Chapel, with its strong egalitarianism and appeal to working people was well placed to meet both the spiritual and the social needs of the new population. Its building proved

The first Salem Chapel, Nelson, built 1853

to be a focal point for the town for many years, serving as the birthplace of several local institutions and as an unofficial Town Hall.[108] It was equally successful in its evangelistic work, as its open-air meetings saw hundreds of conversions, which in turn resulted in large congregations.

Salem was strong in its advocacy of the unpaid ministry but, unlike some other churches which resulted from PM schisms, it was fortunate in the quality of its leaders, who were men of ability and enterprise. Although some were mill workers and tradesmen, others had entrepreneurial skills and made their mark in the expanding town. One such was John Landless who established an iron foundry and went on to become the principal engineer in the area. In many ways, he epitomised the kind of person (of whom the Independent Methodists of this area had many) who made a major contribution to church, town and business alike.[109] The adaptability of men such as Landless was seen in their leadership of the church as well as of industry. Salem was a church in a constant process of development and expansion, adding to its buildings and activities, looking for new doors of opportunity and eventually spawning daughter churches as well.

4.5. The Character of the PM Schisms

While some PM schisms resulted from understandable grievances, others were simply the work of fractious and unstable people. This was a phase of its history which reflected badly upon the Independent Methodists in terms of both wisdom and integrity.[110] For apparent sectarian gain, they often played into the hands of headstrong individuals, such as Joseph Duckers in the Burland PM Circuit, who resisted discipline and then presented himself as a victim of oppression.[111] In the long term, their courtship of these dissident Primitives proved largely unfruitful and they found themselves burdened with malcontents who simply caused further trouble. William Sanderson soon discovered their deficiencies and rued his earlier readiness to embrace them. Of the group of churches in the Wolverhampton area, he wrote: 'In company with Bro. Dodd, I visited several of the preaching stations and surely there is want of organisation, yea, even piety!' After visiting Stourbridge, he added, 'From what I saw and heard, I advised Bro. Dodd to commence afresh and receive none into communion, but those who were living according to the gospel.'[112]

By 1870, only seven of at least 120 churches and preaching stations which resulted from splits in Primitive Methodism during this period were still in membership with the Independent Methodists, though the Independent Primitive Methodists of Nottinghamshire were to form links at a later date. Some, like the Original Methodists, gradually dispersed into other branches of Methodism. Even some of the leaders of these groups lost their appetite for free gospelism, such as John Parkinson of Bradford, leader of the Gospel Pilgrims, who settled at Colne in his later years and re-joined the Primitive Methodists, even though a vigorous IM Church had recently started in the town.[113] Other churches simply died out when their main activists were removed from the scene.

This happened in Norfolk, when Thomas Andrews, a watchmaker, found himself the only remaining preacher. In a letter which expressed the depth of his feelings, Andrews wrote to William Sanderson, telling him that William Frost, the founder of the churches in the area, had gone to London, another key family had emigrated to Australia and he had now closed the one remaining chapel for a time, due to pressure of business and the demands of a large family. In a final comment, he expressed the same wish that had echoed from struggling churches in earlier years – that the Independent Methodists would send a missionary to the area.[114] In effect, this was a call for someone else to fund the equivalent of a full time, paid minister.

4.6. Reactions against Free Gospelism

The aggressive opportunism showed by Independent Methodists during this period brought them an unsavoury reputation. The feelings of Wesleyans were encapsulated in the words of a minister who delivered a combative lecture on the subject:

If you spend your time in abusing other churches, and insulting other Christian ministers, remember that this is a Free Gospel indeed with a vengeance! Ripe and rampant, free from all restraints of common sense, decency and religion. . . . I look upon the leaders of such an opposition as free gospelism as engaged in a deadly work, which will do much to damage the cause of God, and Christian righteousness. . . .

According to some persons, these leaders must be permitted to travel the town and the country over – to go from house to house, abusing the ministers of the sanctuary – to do all they can to get the poor away from our churches – and the very moment you speak a word against them, they cry, 'Shame! Where is your charity? We are suffering persecution!'[115]

This view was by no means unique. A Burland PM Circuit report reflected the Primitive Methodist view of Free Gospel divisiveness:

We are sorry to say we are not more prosperous through the agitation kept up by the divisionists disseminating the free gospel herisy [sic], and railing against our connexional discipline.[116]

In 1854, the PM Conference reflected on its losses over the previous three years; they represented its first setback after many years of continuous growth. Among the causes was a reference to 'laxity of discipline.' It was noted that people of 'questionable moral character' had gained prominence and that 'doubtful, self-styled revivalists ought not to be patronised.' They had caused 'internal strife and damage' to the churches.[117] Primitive Methodism's recognition of these problems seems to have coincided with a virtual end to the incidence of proselytism of its members by free gospellers, the more stable of whom now recognised how dubious their short-term gains had been. After 1853 this process effectively came to a halt, at least until the 1870s when very different issues were at stake. The decline in Primitive Methodist membership also ended and numbers began to grow again. The change may have resulted from the fact that some of the weaknesses of free gospelism were now more widely recognised and also by a greater preparedness on the part of the Primitive Methodists to repel further intrusions.

5. Joseph Barker and the Christian Brethren

The fluid state of the Independent Methodist constituency, with its constant procession of churches joining and leaving, was just one indication that it remained a disjointed collection of mini-sects even after forty years of existence. More crucially, however, it showed itself to be weak and exposed theologically for the want of a definitive doctrinal statement. This was illustrated during the period 1840-60, partly through the influence of Joseph Barker, an expelled Methodist New Connexion minister, whose heterodox views attracted a following in several parts of the country.

Barker was arraigned before the Annual Conference of the Methodist New Connexion at Halifax in 1841, on charges of doctrinal unsoundness. He had published a pamphlet denying the validity of creeds of any kind and had also instituted a periodical in which he openly rejected infant baptism. Along with a colleague, William Trotter, he was duly expelled from the ministry. In the ensuing years, Barker drew a following which caused great damage to the Methodist New Connexion, leading to the loss of twenty-nine societies and 4,348 members. Some properties were recovered only after expensive litigation.[118]

Barker was the kind of individual who quickly moved from one new idea to another. In turn, he embraced a variety of causes including teetotalism, pacifism and the rejection of oaths and lawsuits.[119] As well as opposing infant baptism, he denied that the Lord's Supper needed to be observed in perpetuity. At one stage, he rejected civil law (an antinomian trait) and wrote: 'A Christian should not be cognisant of such a thing as government or legislation in the world, and should regard all such laws and lawmakers as non-existent or curses.'[120] Later, he reversed his attitude, began to dabble in politics, embraced Chartism and advocated the abolition of the monarchy, House of Lords and Established Church.[121]

Some of Barker's thinking was influenced by Quakerism. To this he attributed his views on infant baptism, his advocacy of peace and his refusal to take oaths. It probably also influenced his objection (for a time) to a 'hired ministry' on which he wrote a paper.[122] In support of his anti-credalism, he insisted that the Bible should be the only creed or confession of faith to which ministers should be expected to subscribe. Eventually, his ideas on the Godhead led him to adopt a Unitarian position.

Barker's followers formed themselves into churches which were locally autonomous, had no paid ministers and took the name 'Christian Brethren', reflecting the idea of absolute equality of all members. At the height of their strength they numbered about 200 churches, with an average membership of thirty each. Although they adopted Barker's views on the sacraments and the non-payment of ministers, they retained many Methodist features such as Lovefeasts, Prayer Meetings, Class Meetings and even (like the Primitive Methodists) Camp Meetings. This gave them an attraction to dissatisfied Methodists, offering them what seemed to be a similar spirituality, but linked to autonomy and anti-clericalism.

During the years 1841-1851, Barker wrote and travelled extensively, finding audiences wherever he went, as people gathered to hear his novel views. Where he succeeded in convincing people, the result could be a rift in a church of any branch of Methodism. The Independent Methodists were particularly vulnerable, as some of them were attracted by his apparently similar views on ministry. At Bolton he made a number of visits to the town and, in 1848, stood as a Chartist candidate in the parliamentary election. His religious and political views were remembered many years later:

> His advocacy of certain opinions on religion . . . had a material influence on some Bolton people; and the Independent Methodists – even in the pulpit – did not remain unaffected. Between 1840 and 1850 some of the preaching, while not professedly unmethodistic, was noted for the absence of such pointed references to Christ as are customary in Methodist sermons.[123]

The Bolton IM leaders were able eventually to turn the situation around without significant loss, but the town's New Connexion Church lost some of its members who formed a Barkerite Church which ran for a number of years before joining the Unitarian body.

William Sanderson personally confronted Barker on one occasion, but noted that he had already made his mark on some of the Independent Methodist Churches, including Lancaster:

> he was a paid New Connexion minister who had ceased to believe in a paid ministry, and that fact had weight with the members of our churches. He visited Lancaster along with several other places, lecturing and preaching, and did a great deal of damage to our Churches. I heard him lecture in Liverpool on the right of private judgement and there was a regular row. . . . I asked some questions, being the means, under God, of exposing him, though not before he had entirely deluded two churches, and Lancaster was just on the eve of following him.[124]

Whether or not the two churches which had been 'entirely deluded' were Independent Methodist is not indicated. In Lancaster, the Primitive Methodists were also affected by Barker's ministry and lost their chapel in Buck Street to his followers, though it was later recovered.[125] The fact that Lancaster, a church to which Sanderson had a great personal attachment, could be so nearly won over to another cause was undoubtedly one of the factors that led him and others to consider how they could ensure that this could not so easily happen again.[126]

The Barkerite schism which proved of greatest significance to Independent Methodism occurred at Bradford. There, all but about twenty members of the MNC Circuit, where William Trotter was stationed, separated under him as their pastor.[127] One of the churches, Holme Lane,

Cleckheaton Chapel, Yorkshire, built 1874

seceded *en bloc* at the time of Barker's expulsion and immediately adopted the 'Christian Brethren' name.[128] Also in 1841, at nearby Batley, a few members from the New Connexion Church opened a Christian Brethren Church, which became known locally as 'Trotter's Chapel'.[129] This church even retained its epithet over forty years later when a new chapel was built. However, Trotter's views on primitive Christianity took him in a different direction from Barker and led him to link with the 'Plymouth' Brethren no later than 1844.[130]

The Holme Lane and Batley churches became founding members of a group entitled the Holme Lane District, which operated in a similar way to an IM Circuit, with a plan supplied by local preachers.[131] However, other churches which were added to this group came into existence by the defection of members from various branches of Methodism, attracted by the ideals of equality, local freedom and anti-clericalism.

How far they leaned towards Barker's views is hard to tell, as the autonomy of Barker's churches meant that they could be widely varied in character.

At Cleckheaton, a number of Wesleyan Methodist local preachers were enthusiastic supporters of the temperance movement and asked for permission to hold a temperance meeting in their new schoolroom. The trustees granted permission but the superintendent minister vetoed them. The preachers in question declared themselves 'heartily sick of the absolute power of the priesthood in that body', rented a room and met informally for a while.[132] Three years later, they formed themselves into a 'Christian Brethren' Church and linked with the Holme Lane District. In 1843, the new Wesleyan Methodist minister at Baildon introduced the payment of weekly class pence, a practice which had long been rejected by this society. Finding the minister inflexible on this point, Jeremiah Halliday, one of the class leaders, sent in his class book and his resignation from the society. Along with another class leader, Thomas Lister, he formed a new society on a free gospel basis and named 'Christian Brethren'. Lister had long been troubled by the fact that some of the poor people from his community declined to attend any church because of the financial expectations that would be held of them and felt that he could now 'preach the gospel free from all shackles.'[133] The new society linked with another at Birkenshaw, where a similar occurrence had happened and a circuit was formed. A few years later, this circuit was augmented by a church at Bingley which had resulted from the disciplining and ensuing resignation of a Primitive Methodist local preacher. In each case, the causes were those common enough in new churches of a free gospel character, but the new circuit soon linked with the Christian Brethren of the Holme Lane District.

By 1850, John Parkinson Jr., who had struggled to keep the Gospel Pilgrim cause alive in Bradford,[134] took up Christian Brethren membership and became a preacher on the Holme Lane plan. He was almost certainly the man who encouraged the Christian Brethren to make contact with the Independent Methodists. An invitation to visit them was duly extended to William Sanderson. On 1 April 1850, he preached at Cleckheaton and spoke at the Circuit Meeting on the following day, when he explained the advantages and conditions of a union.[135] He made further visits at later dates and, a year later, the Holme Lane District resolved to apply 'to join the Free Gospel Church Union.'[136] The district by this time consisted of fourteen preaching places, with thirty preachers.

There is insufficient extant documentation to evaluate how the Independent

Methodists and the Christian Brethren reached agreement on their basis of union, nor how aware the Independent Methodists were of the roots of their new members. Certain Barkerite aspects, such as temperance and the unpaid ministry, gave them a natural affinity, but the lack of a doctrinal test for applicants to the Independent Methodists could have left open any number of unresolved issues. It is probable that the Christian Brethren had renounced Barker's more extreme views, but, as later events showed, they still shared his rejection of creeds.[137] The Church at Birstall, clearly retained Barkerite tendencies. When William Daughtery, one of its leaders, provided an article for the Independent Methodists' magazine in support of an unpaid ministry, he cited as its source an 1843 edition of *'The Christian Brethren's Journal and Investigator'* – Barker's magazine.[138] In a subsequent letter, Daughtery stated that the Christian Brethren acknowledged 'no law book but the New Testament' (a classic Barkerite expression of anti-credalism, which occurred in other reports of this group of churches).[139] The inclusion of an article from a Barkerite source in the IM magazine underlined the theological vulnerability of the Independent Methodists at the time.

In Yorkshire, the new union suffered an immediate credibility problem which William Sanderson encountered when he went to Bradford in the following October to lecture on free gospel principles. A report of his meeting drew the comment that: 'The attendance was not so good as was anticipated, owing, partly, to the prejudice awakened by the errors of Joseph Barker. . . .'[140] Independent Methodists evidently did not baulk at the idea of augmenting their ranks with Christian Brethren Churches, but if the two uniting parties felt that the Christian Brethren name could be used without Barkerite connotations, the wider Christian public thought differently.

Separately from the Holme Lane District, a Christian Brethren Church at Lees, near Oldham, had already joined the Independent Methodists in 1849. Here, the members followed Barker out of the New Connexion in 1841[141] and built a chapel eight years later. The attraction of their new denomination seems to have been its inexpensiveness. In introducing themselves, they commented:

> We see, and have seen for some time past, that there is nothing like free gospel, free seats, free chapels, and free schools: and that 'God helps those that help themselves'. We would just mention that we are all teetotallers, and we make it subservient to religion; and our labours in that cause have been abundantly blessed. We have no creed but the Bible; no lawbook but the Bible; no ruler but Christ, whom we acknowledge to be 'Lord over all.'[142]

The Barkerite emphases were unmistakable, but most of those who read this statement would see only its similarity to Independent Methodist values. This church remained in union with the Independent Methodists until 1858, after which the association lapsed, and later became a Congregational Church. However, one of its members, Ben Dyson, removed to Oldham where he became a founder of Broadway Street Church and eventually President of the Connexion.[143]

Little is known of what happened to the 200 churches which Barker claimed as those of his followers. Herbert McLachlan, author of their sole, brief history, stated that some became Unitarian, while 'many' became associated with the Independent Methodists on the basis of their similar views of separated and salaried ministry; others joined the Bible Christians and United Methodists.[144]

6. The Structure of the Union 1830-1854

As the previous sections show, Independent Methodism's corporate development included the entrance and exit of different mini-sects in turn. Few records remain to tell the story of the years 1838-1845 when the lowest ebb was reached. In 1839, only fifteen delegates from eleven churches attended the Annual Meeting. Taken as a whole, this was an unpromising time, which could have resulted in the eventual dissolution of the Union. The main core remained in south Lancashire, centred on Manchester, Stockport, Liverpool, Warrington, Oldham, Bolton and Wigan. However, by 1855 even this area had only twenty-six chapels, with about nine other meeting places.[145]

After the loss of Sheffield in 1829, the Missionary Society was based at Bolton, but it continued to depend on the loyal donations of the few, as churches focused on chapel building projects. Nevertheless, John Parkinson of Bradford could report some successes over a period of about fifteen years, while William Parker of Macclesfield also travelled widely, serving as diplomat and trouble-shooter, as well as missioner, prior to his emigration. In 1833, the Union looked at its deficiencies in the light of recent failures. The Annual Meeting agreed a short statement of agreed principles, but it was neither a constitution nor a creed.[146] They also adopted the name *United Churches of Christ* and resolved to pursue the unification of all churches based on similar principles, regardless of local nomenclature.[147] To provide a point of reference for churches seeking union, they agreed that the President and Secretary should stay in office between Annual Meetings.[148] However, there was still no central committee, other than the Missionary Committee, until 1851.

Two years later, in a further enhancement of the presidential role, it was resolved that he should inquire of each Annual Meeting delegate in turn whether 'the purity of our doctrines be preserved in the United Societies, and whether discipline be duly maintained.'[149] Despite the treasured local autonomies of the churches, there was a growing recognition

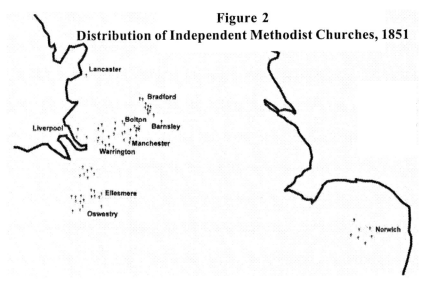

Figure 2
Distribution of Independent Methodist Churches, 1851

of the need for the whole group to have theological congruity. The turbulent experiences of the 1830s were already prompting a closer study of the movement's *raison d'être*. Now, whether intentionally or otherwise, they had given the President a role that would take them nearer to the connexionalism which they had hitherto avoided. The decisions of 1835 led to action a year later. A doctrinal problem had arisen at Wigan and the 1836 Annual Meeting called on the Wigan Church to 'remove those persons who imbibed Arian principles.'[150] This was another example of the vulnerability of independent churches, led by people of limited knowledge and literacy, to infiltration and to deviation from their foundational doctrines. However, the resolution could only advise and not enforce; the only available sanction for inaction by the church would have been its expulsion from the union of churches.

7. The Testimony and Principles of Union

Independent Methodism's looseness of association and lack of stability was a matter of deep concern to two of its leading figures and others who agreed with them. Alexander Denovan and William Sanderson were both conscious that many churches had been lost over the years because the Union had no means of holding its churches or ensuring that they did not deviate from their founding principles. When a church ran into difficulties, possibly as the result of a dominant faction taking it off course, the Union could do nothing but stand helplessly by. Consequently, some churches were taken into other denominations, some lost their properties and others simply closed down. When forceful but erratic preachers such as Joseph Barker made inroads into particular towns, the Independent Methodists were more vulnerable than most, having no overseeing body to ensure that their principles were not violated, and no centrally accepted creed to serve as a yardstick of doctrine. Memories still lingered of the Arian incident at Wigan, a church dissolved through Chartist emphases at Leigh[151] and the allure of other branches of Methodism which seemed to offer more. Independence to some of the churches meant that they opposed a unifying creed, not so much through disagreement over specific doctrines, but because it represented an infringement of local freedom. In the case of some of the Yorkshire 'Christian Brethren' churches,[152] any creed at all was unacceptable.

In December 1851, an allegation of heterodoxy arose in a church in Preston, resulting in a division and the formation of a new congregation. A correspondent from the new church made an appeal for doctrinal consistency:

> In order to [ensure] the future prosperity of the churches, we think it will be necessary that you adopt some plan, in order to protect our churches from anti-scriptural innovation, and at the same time bind the churches to the fundamental doctrines of the New Testament.[153]

Denovan's response was to draw up proposals for a *Testimony and Bond of Union* and presented it for consideration at the Annual Meeting of 1852.[154] Its objects were to help the churches to speak with one voice, to provide answers to anyone who asked about the beliefs of the union of churches and to give themselves theologically orthodox credentials. What followed was a Wesleyan-Arminian doctrinal statement containing eighteen articles of faith, and a constitution which provided a model for internal government, based on the Presbyterian pattern of elders and deacons, with (controversially) a provision for the Annual Meeting to have 'general superintendence' of the churches.

While the *Testimony* was primarily concerned with denominational cohesion, its author, Alexander Denovan, clearly wanted to see the churches operate a form of ministry which carried more weight than was currently the case. In so doing, he boldly introduced the contentious subject of authority which had been studiously avoided up to this time. In the absence of the rule of a single pastor in a church, where did the church's locus of authority lie?

In the first draft of the *Testimony*, Denovan tackled this issue by proposing the following definition:

> Regular officer-bearers, chosen by the brethren from among themselves, shall be appointed in each church, so soon as properly

qualified persons are found. These are presbyters or elders and deacons – the elders also being called overseers or bishops and may be designated pastors.

The duty of the pastors shall be to teach, rule, baptise, dispense the Lord's Supper, and, when sent for, visit the sick of their charge; at the same time they are to watch for the souls of their flock as they who shall give account, and be careful that no one lead any of them astray, and that whoever may attempt to instruct them, may do so with sound doctrine.[155]

The importance of the pastoral office was then further stressed:

Pastors, having been regularly installed into office, should have the authority given them by Christ, through the choice made of them by the brethren, upheld and respected; their instructions listened to with a seriousness and attention; and a cheerful obedience manifested to all that they require according to the Scriptures.

The terminology of 'rule', 'authority', 'instructions' and 'obedience', together with explicit responsibility for oversight, suggested a role for elders/pastors which was comparable with that of their paid counterparts in other denominations.

After a year for consideration, Denovan's proposals were brought to the Annual Meeting of 1853. Almost as a harbinger of troubles to come, the revered Peter Phillips died just a week before the Annual Meeting. From his deathbed, he denounced the *Bond*, saying: 'It sprung [*sic*] from hell, it is from the devil, it is a strife for mastery, it cannot be right.'[156] The Annual Meeting delegates, mainly people with little or no theological training, focused mainly on practical issues, seen through the eyes of a purely congregational ecclesiology. This inevitably affected their perception of doctrines such as the nature of the Church, Christian freedom and the place of corporate discipline. The word *Bond* itself was interpreted to mean a device which could bind and enforce, rather than a tie of mutual, willing obligation to one another. Several speakers argued that the Annual Meeting should retain its current status as a deliberative rather than a legislative assembly. Joseph Spencer of Cleckheaton, whose Christian Brethren Church had broken from the Wesleyan Methodists only a few years previously, echoed the Barkerite roots of the Yorkshire group of churches: 'If it had not been for men-made creeds, and men-made laws we should not have been here – we have been driven by laws similar to those proposed.'[157] He feared that instead of binding the churches it would scatter them. In response, Sanderson spoke of how churches had been damaged, not at their point of admission, but through errors creeping in later and said that the

Union could have helped to resolve such problems. The clauses on ministry were also challenged. Many of the churches were plainly not prepared to see authority placed in the hands of a pastoral oligarchy and some kind of compromise was inevitable.

In order to mitigate the fears of his opponents, Denovan agreed that the word *Bond* (to which several people had objected) should be dropped and that the title should be *The Testimony of Union*. Sanderson also further amended the resolution by adding, 'That this Annual Meeting has not power to legislate nor interfere in the internal government of the churches or with their independency.'[158] The much-feared reference to Annual Meeting having 'the general superintendence' of all the churches in the Union was deleted. The clause which specified the role of pastors was altered to make their functions less exclusive. The statement, 'The duty of pastors shall be to teach, rule, etc.' now read, '*While the brethren are not be excluded from what is required of them* . . . it shall *more especially* be the duty of the pastors to teach, rule, etc.'[159] In other words, no function was to be exclusively ministerial. This went some way towards allaying the fears of those who foresaw the rise of a new ministerial hierarchy, but left the degree of authority accorded to a minister unclear.

Despite this softening of tone, opposition to the very principle of a constitution remained. Shortly before the 1854 Annual Meeting, John Roberts, Peter Phillips' successor at Warrington, sent a circular letter to all the churches, alleging that the *Testimony* infringed the rights of each church, as it had long been understood that 'one church shall not interfere with another church respecting its faith and form.'[160] This went even further than the classic position of Congregationalism, as defined in the Savoy Declaration:

> that amongst all Christian States and Churches, there ought to be vouchsafed a forbearance and mutual indulgence unto saints of all persuasions, that keep unto and hold fast the necessary foundation of faith and holiness, in all matters extrafundamental, whether of Faith or Order.[161]

There was no qualifying phrase such as 'matters extrafundamental' in Roberts' statement. To Denovan, this was unacceptable. He replied:

> Does it not imply? Be what you will and be of any faith – believe what you please – be Roman Catholic, Unitarian, Swedenborgian, Southcottian, Mormonite, Calvinist, Arminist – what you choose – as latitudinarian as you may – only shout for 'freedom' – maintain 'liberty' and all shall be well![162]

In the *Testimony*, Denovan was attempting to do what neither Congregationalism nor John Roberts would have done: to provide a detailed, prescriptive set of doctrines to which the churches were expected to be committed.

The majority of churches upheld the *Testimony*, but a substantial minority who supported Roberts' position withdrew and met separately over the next six years. During this time, they made little reference to the *Testimony* in either their magazines or their Annual Meeting Minutes, but a report of 1857 shows that they were experiencing exactly the problems which it was designed to address:

> We as churches must not consider ourselves a refuge for the dissatisfied, we have perhaps been too anxious to increase our numbers, rather than make ourselves lovely and attractive, and for want of discrimination we have received into our churches those whose characters would not bear investigation, and whose opinions were not in accordance with the 'Methodist doctrine' which we *believe* and *teach*, hence we have discovered when too late our error in receiving those among us who are not lovers of true liberty, good order, and sound discipline but have rather, been votaries of licentiousness.[163]

In the meantime, the majority churches modified the constitution still further, but kept to the doctrinal statement in its entirety. After repeated overtures, the rift was healed in 1860 and the minority churches accepted the revised document, now entitled *Testimony and Principles of Union* without further alteration.[164]

Of the dissident churches, only two did not join the re-unified body, one of them being the Preston Church which had been accused of heterodoxy. (It was reputed to be Unitarian in teaching and 'erroneous' in its views of the atonement).[165] Its defection symbolised the new era into which the churches had moved together, in which local independence of church government had to be matched by doctrinal conformity.

8. Conclusion

Most of the leaders of the newer churches of the 1820s had come out of a connexional system which contrasted sharply with the local autonomies (and sometimes isolationism) of the Independent Methodists. They had virtually gone from one extreme to another and the weaknesses of the new system soon became obvious. What followed was the emergence of conflicting expectations between those who expected to take full responsibility for themselves and those who wanted a system that supported them. By the same token, there was a corresponding conflict between those who had no aspirations beyond local freedom with a fraternal relationship and those who wanted to develop an expansionist movement. Those churches which left for the newer Methodist bodies clearly had fewer qualms about paid ministry than those which retained their IM allegiance, but the reaction to this by the remaining churches seems to have been a reinforced determination to maintain the unpaid system as a matter of inviolable principle.

The final stage of this period, though marked by the controversy which surrounded the *Testimony and Principles of Union*, represented the most significant change in the ethos and dynamics of the Independent Methodists since they first began to hold Annual Meetings in 1806. The adoption of the *Testimony* showed that the leaders of the churches had accepted in principle that they were part of something greater than their own local congregations. This body of churches would, hereafter, place a greater premium on its collective identity and agreed *modus operandi*. It had undergone an ecclesiological sea-change and was a major step for the Independent Methodists on their journey from sect to denomination.

Notes to Chapter Three

1. W.F. Swift, *Methodism in Scotland. The First Hundred Years,* (London: Epworth, 1947), 75f.
2. A. Skevington Wood, 'Methodism in Scotland', R.E. Davies et al (eds.), *History of the Methodist Church in Great Britain* (4 vols.; London: Epworth, 1983) 3:275.
3. Swift, *Methodism in Scotland,* 65.
4. *IMMag.* 1879, 35ff.
5. *IMMag.* 1874, 279.
6. Anon. *Joshua Denovan,* (Toronto: Standard Publishing Company, 1901), 12.
7. James Vickers, *History of Independent Methodism* (Wigan: Independent Methodist Bookroom, 1920), 37f.
8. MS Minutes of the Independent Methodist Church, Glasgow, 1820-1840, together with statements of doctrine and other material, 48f, IMA.
9. Glasgow Minutes, 4. 'Rise and Establishment of the Independent Methodist Church, Glasgow', *IMMag.* April 1828, 622ff.,
10. Glasgow Minutes, 11. Low Green Street is now known as Turnbull Street, facing Glasgow Green.
11. Vickers, *History,* 38. Glasgow Green was a popular place for outdoor speakers of many religious and political persuasions.
12. *Joshua Denovan,* 13.
13. Vickers, *History,* 38.
14. *IMMag.* August 1825, 687ff.
15. A. Denovan, 'Visit to the Independent Methodist Church, Downpatrick (Ireland)', *IMMag.* 1825, 687ff., IMMins.1826, 7.
16. IMMins. 1834, 13.
17. IMMins. 1835, 13.

18. Glasgow Minutes, 19f.
19. 'Wesley Clear of what kept Arminius from the Whole Truth', *IMMag.* 1828, 635.
20. IMMins. 1833, 22.
21. Vickers, *History,* 41. As pamphleteers often wrote anonymously or pseudonymously, it is difficult to establish whether any of Denovan's other pamphlets are extant or not.
22. A. Denovan (ed.) *The Songster or A Collection of Hymns and Sacred Songs, 2nd edition, improved with Appendix* (Glasgow, 1828). This ran to a third edition in 1839. The second edition contained a supplement of hymns *'for the use of the Independent Methodist Sabbath-day School, Oldham, and other schools in connection with it.'*
23. A. Denovan, *Election According to Holy Scripture*, (Glasgow: Bell and Bain, 1832) This was revised and re-printed in 1861.
24. A. Denovan, *An Appeal to the Christian World* (Glasgow: Bell and Bain, 1866).
25. IMMins. 1833, 22.
26. Letter: William Hamilton to his father Andrew in Canada, 14 April 1842, IMA.
27. A. Denovan, *Observations in Relation to Mr. Fleming of Neilston's 'Critique in favour of Civil establishment of Christianity in two discourses.'* [*A reply to Alexander Fleming's 'A Critique on Dr.R. Wardlaw's Civil Establishments of Christianity.'*] (Glasgow: George Gallie, 1834), *passim.*
28. IMMins. 1834, 22.
29. IMMins. 1824, 321.
30. IMMins. 1825.
31. *Ibid.*
32. *Ibid.* See Appendix 2.
33. G. Turton, 'Observations on Missions', *IMMag.* 1826, 916ff.
34. See Appendix 9.
35. The preacher concerned was John Coulson, who had pioneered the area for the Primitive Methodists a few years earlier, in which case this suggests that the Driffield Church was a splinter group from the Primitives, who had become well-established in the area. H.B. Kendall, *The Origin and History of the Primitive Methodist Church* (London: Edwin Dalton, und.) ii, 98; IMMins 1824.
36. W. Parker, 'An Account of a Mission to Several Churches and Observations on the Independent Methodist System', *IMMag.* 1826, 922.
37. IMMins. 1827.
38. J. Sigston, *A Brief Memoir of Joseph Woolstenholme* (London: Wesleyan Methodist Association Bookroom, 1846), preface.
39. J. Woolstenholme, 'Letter to the President of the Missionary Committee', *IMMag.* 1827, 291.
40. There were some notable exceptions, such as the Glasites and sects which derived from them such as the Old Scots Independents and the Scotch Baptists. A.L. Drummond and J. Bulloch, *The Scottish Church 1688-1843* (Edinburgh: St. Andrew Press, 1973), 45f.
41. Sigston, *Woolstenholme*, 9; Second Report of the Independent Methodist Missionary Committee, *IMMag.* 1827, 339.

42. S. Ashton, 'Missionary Excursion into Wales', *IMMag.* 1827, 283.

43. See 3. Wesleyan Methodist Schisms 1829 - 1838

44. 'Work of God at Parr', *IMMag.* 1827, 315.

45. J. Walford, *Memoirs of the Life and Labours of the late Venerable Hugh Bourne,* (2 vols.; London: T. King and Burslem: R. Timmis, 1855) 1:373.

46. W. Yates, 'Missionary Intelligence', *IMMag.* 1827, 285ff.

47. IMMins. 1829. In fact no delegate had attended from Newcastle for several years.

48. J. Vickers (ed.) *Dictionary of the Methodist Church in Britain and Ireland* (London: Epworth, 2000), 283.

49. *Ibid,* 378.

50. *Ibid,* 385.

51. Benjamin Gregory, *Sidelights on the Conflicts of Methodism 1827-1852* (London: Cassell and Co. Ltd., 1899) 73.

52. For the most detailed accounts of the Leeds Organ Case and the story of the Wesleyan Protestant Methodists, see D. Colin Dews, 'Methodism in Leeds from 1791 to 1861' (Unpublished M.Phil thesis, University of Bradford, 1984) and Margaret Batty, *Stages in the Development and Control of Wesleyan Lay Leadership 1791-1878,* (Peterborough: Methodist Publishing House, 1988).

53. Dews, 'Methodism in Leeds', 502f.

54. A. Denovan, 'To the Nonconformist Wesleyan Methodists at Leeds, and to all who unite in sentiments with them', *IMMag.* 1828, 758.

55. J.C. Bowmer, *Pastor and People* (London: Epworth, 1975), 117.

56. Careful Observer, *Sound Thoughts for Sound People*, 14. (MCA)

57. Dews, 'Methodism in Leeds', 586.

58. *The Wesleyan Protestant Methodist Magazine* 1829, 382.

59. Minutes of the Wesleyan Protestant Methodist Society of Sheffield 1829-1839. No copy of the circular survives, but the Independent Methodists' reply shows that it alleged, predictably, that they had failed to support missionary work, that the Annual Meeting was an obstacle to progress and that they were a disjointed body. IMMins. 1830, 32f.

60. *WPM Magazine*, 1830, 127f. See Chapter 2 for the story of the Tyneside Independent Methodists.

61. *A Short History of the Rise and Progress of the United Methodist Free Church, Surrey Street, Sheffield*, 1855.

62. A.H. Williams, *Welsh Wesleyan Methodism 1800-1858* ((Bangor: Cyhoeddwyd gan Lyfrfa'r Methodistiaid, 1935), 221ff.

63. *Ibid*, 330f.

64. *Ibid.*

65. IMMins. 1832, 24.

66. IMMins. 1834, 14ff.

67. IMMins. 1833, 19.

68. Tregarth, Bethesda and Rhiwlas.

69. Obituary recorded in *Caernarvon and Denbigh Herald*, 24 March 1838.

70. Minutes of Wesleyan Methodist Association Assembly, 1838.

71. The members of this church (which seems to have had no premises of its own) were solicited by the WMA Church, recently formed in the town, to join them.

At first, they declined, as they wished to retain their unpaid ministry. However, the effect of a trade depression made them think again and they opted for WMA affiliation. IMMins. 1837, 12ff.

72. W. Sanderson, *The Life and Labours of William Sanderson* (Wigan: Independent Methodist Bookroom, 1899), 38.

73. Vickers, *History,* 44f.

74. *Ibid,* 165. Sanderson, *Life and Labours,* 71.

75. J.T. Wilkinson, 'The Rise of other Methodist Traditions', *HMCGB*, 2:311.

76. See Appendix 10 for a summary of the places concerned, with their dates and causes of origin. They totalled about 120 chapels and meeting places.

77. Vickers, *History,* 205.

78. Much of this information is based on unpublished notes by Douglas Harrison, Ph.D., of Radcliffe-on-Trent who has made an extensive study of the Independent Primitive Methodists.

79. *PMMag.* 1833, 111.

80. Circuit plans for the Birstall Primitive Methodist Revivalists and the Bradford and Leeds Gospel Pilgrims are preserved in the Cryer Collection, Wakefield Library.

81. *IMMins.* 1834

82. *PMMag.* 1861, 261.

83. Rothwell, i, 153ff.

84. William White, *History, Gazetteer and Directory of Norfolk* (1845), 457.

85. Rothwell, ii, 95.

86. H.B. Kendall, *The Origin and History of the Primitive Methodist Church.* (2 vols.; London: Edwin Dalton n.d.), i 248f. This story is extensively covered in a series of articles entitled 'The Original Methodists' by Donald Grundy in *Proceedings of the Wesley Historical Society,* (1966) 35:5, 116ff; 35:6, 149ff; 35:7, 170ff; 35:8, 189ff. (1967) 36:1, 22ff; 36:2, 49ff; 36:3, 80ff; 36:4, 115ff; 36:5, 143ff; 36:6, 181ff.

87. *PWHS.* 35:6, 150.

88. *IMMag.* 1851, 237ff.

89. *IMMag.* 1851, 258

90. *PWHS.* 35:8, 192.

91. *IMMins.* 1852, 42.

92. *Primitive Methodist Magazine 1* (1820), 208-13, 215.

93. J.S. Werner, *The Primitive Methodist Connexion, Its Background and Early History* (London: University of Wisconsin Press, 1984), 138. Both men had an independent streak which was accommodated with some degree of compromise on the part of the Primitive Methodist hierarchy.

94. J.T. Wilkinson, *Hugh Bourne 1772-1852* (London:Epworth, 1952), 130.

95. K. Lysons, *A Little Primitive* (Buxton: Church in the Marketplace Publications, 2001), 68.

96. *Zion Methodist Church, Legh Street (Warrington), Souvenir* (1954), 14. Two churches in the Warrington PM Circuit defected during Herod's ministry and continue as IM Churches to the present day. Appendix 10.

97. Barnsley Primitive Methodist Circuit Report, 21 March, 1853. The 'opposition society' later merged with the town's existing Free Gospel Church and, by 1869, after steady decline, it had folded up.

98. Burland Primitive Methodist Circuit Quarter Day Meeting Minutes 1845-56, 145, 186.

99. *Burland PM Minutes* 145, 186. Vickers, 185f. Under Darlington's leadership, the Shavington IM Circuit (later Hook Gate Circuit) became established and went on to have a long history.

100. *IMMag.* 1854, 19

101. *IMMag.* 1853, 31.

102. 'Reasons for being an Independent Methodist', *IMMag.* 1850, 333.

103. See *IMMag,* 1851, 275 and 1852, 261 for details of his proselytising work in South Cheshire.

104. Sanderson, *Life and Labours,* 71.

105. A. Dalby, *The History of Waterside Chapel 1821-1951*, (Colne, 1951), 10.

106. *IMMag.* 1852, 262.

107. J. Robinson, *Salem Independent Methodist Church, Nelson, Centenary Booklet* (Nelson 1952), 6.

108. *Nelson Chronicle,* March 26, 1891, 8; Robinson, *Salem,* 12; *Independent Methodist Year Book* 1899, 6.

109. G. Whittaker, *The Family of Landless* (Colne, 1970), 39.

110. The Independent Methodists were not alone in engaging in this type of practice at this time. The Churches of Christ, who also rejected a professional ministry, made systematic attempts to capitalise on internal problems in Methodism during the 1850s. D.M. Thompson, *Let Sects and Parties Fall: a Short History of the Churches of Christ in Great Britain and Ireland* (Birmingham: Berean Press, 1980), 62.

111. Burland PM Minutes, 1850, 167. 'Memoir of Joseph Doughty', *IMMag.* 1852, 54ff.

112. *IMMag.* 1854, 32f.

113. 'Memoir of John Parkinson', *Primitive Methodist Magazine* 1861, 261.

114. IMMins. 1857, 24. See 2. above for the example of Driffield, Yorkshire, where a similar appeal was made.

115. Lecture delivered by the Rev. J.F. Moody on Free Gospelism at the Wesleyan Chapel, Prescot, on Tuesday Evening, 23 May 1852, 37 (IMA)

116. Burland Primitive Methodist Circuit Report 1852, 7.

117. Primitive Methodist Minutes 1854, 24ff.

118. Wilkinson, *HMGB*, 2:293.

119. J.T. Barker (ed.), *The Life of Joseph Barker, written by himself* (London: Hodder & Stoughton, 1880), 254.

120. H. McLachlan, 'The Christian Brethren' in *The Story of a Nonconformist Library* (Manchester: University Press, 1923), 157.

121. Barker, *Life of Barker,* 286.

122. *Ibid,* 265, 278.

123. S. Rothwell, *Memorials of Folds Road Independent Methodist Chapel, Bolton* (2 vols.; Bolton: Independent Methodist Bookroom, 1887) 1:159.

124. Sanderson, *Life and Labours,* 227f.

125. Kendall, *Origin and History,* 2:125.

126. Barker's teachings were one of the reasons why Denovan and Sanderson proposed *The Bond and Testimony of Union.*

127. W. Trotter, *The Justice and Forbearance of the Methodist New Connexion,*

as they were illustrated in the case of W. Trotter (London, 1841), 91.

128. C. Higham, *Holme United Reformed Church, 1835-1985, A Short History* (Bradford, 1985), 14.

129. J. Willans, *Batley Past and Present*, (Batley: J. Fearnsides, n.d.), 22. R. Coad, *A History of the Brethren Movement* (Exeter: The Paternoster Press, 1968), 78.

130. H.H. Rowdon, *The Origins of the Brethren, 1825-1850* (London: Pickering and Inglis, 1967), 175.

131. There is no record of a founding date for the Holme Lane District, but the records of the Batley Church show that it was functioning at least by 1845. Minutes of Batley Providence Street Christian Brethren Chapel, 1845-1932.

132. G.Terry, *The Joint Celebration of the 150th. Anniversary of the founding of Nook Independent Methodist Church, Cleckheaton and 250 Years of Methodist Preaching in Cleckheaton.* (1995), 5.

133. *Memoirs of Thomas Lister, written by himself.* (Bingley, und.). 14f. IMMins. 1850, 26.

134. The Gospel Pilgrims were a slightly earlier Free Gospel group, also centred mainly on Bradford. Information about them is largely confined to a single Preachers' Plan for 1834 and some reports in IM Minutes during 1834-37 and 1847-49.

135. *IMMag*. 1850, 213.

136. Batley Minutes, 1851.

137. When the Christian Brethren eventually published their doctrines in 1858, they were an abridged form of the 1833 'Sentiments' of the Independent Methodists, but omitted the references to the work of Christ in redemption and sanctification. IMMins. 1833; MS Rules and Doctrines of the Christian Brethren Churches of the Holme Lane District, 1858 (IMA).

138. 'The Ministry', *IMMag*. 1852, 37f.

139. *IMMag*. 1851, 88.

140. 'Brother Sanderson's Missionary Tour in Yorkshire', *IMMag*. 1851, 255.

141. McLachlan, 'Christian Brethren', 178. William Walker, *Builders of Zion* (London: Henry Hook, und.), 73.

142. IMMins. 1849, 26.

143. Vickers, *History,* 224f.

144. McLachlan, 'Christian Brethren', 182. McLachlan's estimate was generous to the Independent Methodists; there were fourteen churches in the Holme Lane District when they affiliated in 1851, plus the church at Lees. IMMins. 1851, 26. The churches at Cleckheaton, Dewsbury and Bingley (the last of which retains the 'Christian Brethren' name in its stonework) continue to the present day.

145. See Figure 2, p. 105 for the overall distribution of churches at this time. Many of the churches shown, especially in Norfolk, Shropshire and south Cheshire were no more than cottage meetings.

146. 'Sentiments', IMMins. 1833. The doctrinal statement of 1822 (Appendix 2) seems to have been abandoned.

147. IMMins. 1833, 30ff.

148. *Ibid,* 33f.

149. IMMins. 1835, 19.

150. IMMins.1836 in Journal of the Independent Methodist Annual Meetings 1828-1882, 37.
151. Sanderson, *Life and Labours*, 39.
152. *Ibid.*
153. IMMins. 1852, 38.
154. A. Denovan, 'Proposed Testimony and Bond of Union' (Glasgow, 1852), 1.
155. Denovan, 'Proposed Testimony and Bond of Union'.
156. 'The Life and Labours of Peter Phillips' in *ZT,* December 1855, 75.
157. Notes of the proceedings of the Delegates of the United Free Gospel Churches, at the Annual Meeting assembled at Manchester, Whitsuntide, 1853, in *ZT,* August 1853, 9.
158. *Ibid,* 17.
159. New words italicised.
160. IMMins. 1854, 21.
161. Bettenson, *Documents,* 250.
162. IMMins. 1854, 21.
163. IM (Minority) Mins. 1857, 18
164. See Appendix 3 for the full text of the finalised document.
165. A. Hewitson, *Our Churches and Chapels by Atticus* (Preston, 1869), 103; Sanderson, *Life and Labours*, 81.

Chapter 4
From Sect to Denomination
1860-1927

After the churches were reunited in 1860, following the rift over the *Testimony and Principles of Union*, their future began to be shaped partly by the emergence of a new generation of leaders with a different outlook and partly by wider events, two of which should be noted at this point.

1. External Influences in the early 1860s

1.1. Revival 1859-62

The reunification of the churches in 1860 coincided with the impact of a Christian revival which began in America in 1858. This was reported by the Independent Methodist editor, Samuel Fitzgerald,[1] who followed the course of the revival as it came to Ulster a year later, whereupon he published reports of remarkable phenomena which accompanied it.[2] From Ulster, the revival spread to Scotland and then, during 1859, into Wales and England. Though its impact in England was limited, it aroused great interest among the Independent Methodists for whom it provided a welcome new focus after years of wrangling over internal politics. The 'majority' group of churches set aside the first Sunday in October 1859 for united prayer for revival.[3] It is possible that the revival, including the process of praying for it, softened attitudes between the two IM factions and aided the moves towards reconciliation.

The pattern of revival seems to have contained a mixture of planning and spontaneity and was not unique to any denomination. The idea of 'planning' a revival had been sown in the minds of British church leaders through the ministry of the American evangelist Charles Finney, who first preached in Britain in 1850-1. This placed less emphasis on passion and excitement than the style of Lorenzo Dow, but encouraged the ministry of lay people, which sat well with Independent Methodists.[4] Finney returned to Britain in 1859 at the time of the revival and one of his centres of ministry was Bolton, where Folds Road IM Church responded enthusiastically to his meetings. Finney had argued, contrary to Calvinistic thought, that revival was not necessarily a sovereign work of God, but that it could be achieved by use of the right means, one of which was prevailing prayer. Therefore Folds Road Church began to pray for revival and started to hold evangelistic events, with considerable success as large numbers of converts were added week upon week.[5] Other IM churches observed and followed suit; the Bolton pattern, in Finney's style, was adopted elsewhere. Moreover, there was evidently receptiveness to the message which was markedly different from before, as William Sanderson noted:

> In this revival men have been astonished at the success with which they can 'preach the gospel'. They have been astonished at the efficacy of free labour and individual effort. Impenitent men have been found ready to hear and ready to obey the gospel call. . . . Men have been surprised at the success of a little labour, and this has encouraged more labour. . . . It has pleased God to clothe that message with amazing power – the power of the Holy Spirit.[6]

Over the next two years, the *Independent Methodist Magazine* published numerous reports from churches which had experienced revival. Elizabeth Street, Liverpool, recorded fifty converts in seven weeks,[7] while a six week stay at Barnoldswick by one of the evangelists resulted in 100 conversions.[8] At Batley, it was reported that 140 people had given in their names for church membership.[9] It was said that Christians had been prompted to share their faith more readily with unbelievers[10] and that many had experienced sanctification.[11] The lasting results, at least numerically, are difficult to evaluate as the Connexion published no detailed statistics before 1865. However, other periods of revival occurred at intervals over the coming decades.

1.2. Cotton Famine 1862-65

Hard on the heels of the revival, a transatlantic event of a very different kind also began to affect the churches. The outbreak of the American Civil War brought with it disruption to the English cotton trade during the years 1862-65. This was felt acutely in single-industry Lancashire and Cheshire towns such as Oldham, Bolton and Nelson, where many IM churches were composed almost entirely of mill workers and their families, now living in tightly-packed terraced streets and devoid of the land which would have supported them in earlier generations. The 'Cotton Famine', brought severe hardship and reduced people to starvation level. In common with Methodism generally, the visible plight of the British poor drew greater apparent concern than that for the anonymous slaves on the American cotton plantations.[12]

The scale of the problem was such that it stretched the finances of the Poor Law Unions to breaking point.[13] Individuals and churches therefore recognised the need for action to alleviate the poverty of those worst affected by the collapse of the cotton trade. In Stockport, pauperism rose from 1.5% to 6% of the population[14] and the IM church was located in one of the poorest parts of the town. Its secretary reported: 'The gaunt visitor, poverty, has held us with his skeletal hand and iron grasp for more than two years amid suffering on every side.'[15] Here, help came from William Sanderson and some Manchester members whose gifts helped the church to give relief to those who were out of work. Although Sanderson's church at Liverpool was not in a cotton manufacturing area, its members collected forty pounds in money (no mean sum) and clothes for the people of the worst-affected churches.[16] Manchester (Hanover Street) and Bolton (Folds Road) both organised collections for their distressed members,[17] as did churches of various denominations. However, the materially poor Independent Methodists were at a distinct disadvantage when comparisons were inevitably made between the relative beneficence of individual churches. Pendleton, near Manchester, deplored the fact that thirty scholars had gone to other schools where they could receive greater pecuniary assistance[18] and Barnoldswick, Yorkshire, reported that adults too had changed allegiance for the same reason.[19] The reduced state of the cotton trade lasted beyond the Civil War years and inevitably led to removals as people migrated in search of other employment. For the Independent Methodists, with a disproportionate number of churches and members in cotton towns, this represented a significant loss of ground.[20]

2. The Leadership of the late Nineteenth Century

The 1860s saw the emergence of a man who would initiate and steer through most of the developmental changes up to the end of the century. William Brimelow (1837-1913), more than anyone, oversaw Independent Methodism's transition from a loosely connected group of churches to a denomination with structure and order.

Brimelow, a third generation Warrington Independent Methodist, started work as an apprentice basket weaver, but outside working hours he studied shorthand, which enabled him to find employment as a newspaper reporter in Bolton, where he and his wife settled and raised a large family. His rise in the newspaper world was rapid and he went on to become the first full time editor of the *Bolton Evening News*, eventually taking on a partnership with the paper's owner and in due course establishing a chain of local newspapers.[21] He became active in public life as a borough and county magistrate, member of the Bolton School Board and member of the Committee of Management for the Infirmary, among numerous other public interests. Politically, he was an ardent Liberal, serving as secretary for the Westhoughton Division Liberal Association; at one time he was invited by the Prime Minister, Sir Henry Campbell-Bannerman, to stand for Parliament, but he declined.[22] In his professional life, he was active in the wider field of journalism and in 1903 was Chairman of the Press Association.

Brimelow's skills were soon recognised in the denomination and, in 1868, two years after his first appearance at an Annual Meeting, he was appointed editor of the magazine at the age of thirty-one. During his twenty-eight year tenure of office the magazine changed from a quarterly to a monthly magazine which gradually acquired greater significance and popular readership as literacy levels rose during the last quarter of the nineteenth century. In a group of churches as small as this, drawn mainly from the poorer section of the population, it was inevitable that commanding figures would be few. Independent Methodism had grown accustomed to look to two men for its leadership, namely Denovan and Sanderson. Now, in Denovan's declining years, Brimelow became seen as the heir apparent, showing the way forward and drawing ever-increasing respect. His well-prepared initiatives included the production of a denominational hymn book, establishment of the Bookroom, creation of a permanent evangelistic agency, preparation of a new Model Deed, establishment of a Ministers' Assistance Fund and the formation of a unified approach to ministerial education. He also drove the process which led to the acceptance of a single name by the churches. While no single individual of his generation ever matched the stature of Brimelow, who served four Presidential terms, the denomination increasingly benefited from having men of business acumen and, from 1876, full time evangelists who contributed significantly to the Connexion's expansion.[23] Together, they changed its structures and character.

The President gradually became more significant as a focal, unifying figure. In the early years, it was simply his role to preside at Annual Meetings and, later, to deal with any matters which arose during the year, in consultation with the secretary. From 1862, it became presidential practice to visit as many churches as possible once each year, with the Missionary Committee supplying a visitor when the President was unavailable.[24] Some believed that the presidency should change annually, while others felt that it should be in the hands of the most capable person at the time. The latter view seems to have predominated in the mid-nineteenth century, reflected in the constant re-election of Alexander Denovan, whose employment apparently allowed him considerable freedom to travel from time to time, fitting in as many visits to churches as possible during a stay of perhaps two weeks in a given area. Of the five other Presidents of this period, William Sanderson retired early on his earnings as a tailor, Edward Twiss was a self-employed builder and Thomas Oxley

William Brimelow (1837-1913)

owned an ironfounding business. Only two came from humbler backgrounds: John Nield, an operative hatter, and John Knowles, an agricultural labourer; both held office once only. Their appointments reflected the view of at least some that even the highest office in the Connexion should be open to people who were respected for their service rather than any social or academic attributes. In 1880, two years after Denovan's death, the Annual Meeting agreed that steps should be taken to curtail automatic re-election as President; thereafter no President ever served for more than four terms.

3. Connexional Development

Up to 1869, the only two committees in the Connexion were the Connexional Committee (which met only as required and sometimes did not meet for a whole year) and the Missionary Committee (whose members were always formed from a single church). Organisation therefore remained at a minimal level. Not until 1876 did Connexional organisation take on the elaborate form of a larger General Committee with sub-committees.[25] In 1882, this was further enlarged by the appointment of representatives from each of the circuits.[26] By this time, its remit had been greatly increased, to the point at which it was handling disputes between churches[27] and was borrowing money to help churches in need.[28]

By the middle of the nineteenth century, the era of the denominational hymn book had arrived. William Sanderson, believing that the Independent Methodists should have such a book, attempted on his own initiative to produce and distribute one, for which purpose he purchased a printing press. The outcome was disastrous.[29] As he had no experience of printing, the ensuing document was full of mistakes, had an incorrect and incomplete index and was generally a poor product which the churches embraced eagerly at first but then criticised bitterly.

The embarrassment felt by others proved the spur to improvement. In 1867, William Brimelow and Robert Entwistle put forward proposals to the Annual Meeting for a new hymn book. This was initially opposed by Sanderson and his close circle, on the grounds that it would leave large quantities of the existing book unsold, but a year later the position was reversed and a committee of five was appointed to compile a new book. Of these, Brimelow, Entwistle and William Oxley were to be the editors. Because all three were businessmen, progress was slow and the book was not completed until 1870. Entwistle claimed that the final product had achieved a better balance between the hymns of Wesley and Watts than the hymn books of the Methodists, Baptists or Independents (which he felt leaned too much to one or the other). He also argued that the delay had made possible the inclusion of newer hymns of a different genre which had recently been brought from America by Philip Phillips. Dissent was minimal; the hymn book was received with acclaim by the churches and met with approving reviews in the Christian press. The *Literary World* was quoted as observing that at one time each important Nonconformist congregation had its own hymn book, but that this 'sectarian practice' had given way to denominational hymn books, of which this one was an 'ample and admirable collection'.[30] For Independent Methodists, this was to be one of the steps, albeit a small one, along the road from sect to denomination.

The printing of a hymn book in large quantities raised the question of storage, as no facility existed for the purpose. This led to a decision, again urged by Brimelow and Entwistle, to establish a Bookroom to produce and issue connexional publications, just as other denominations had operated for many years.[31] The members of the Bookroom Committee were drawn from the Bolton churches, and the stock was housed at the home of the secretary, Robert Entwistle, where the committee also met each month.

His initial task was to distribute hymn books and magazines, but as further suggestions for literature were made, the task grew in size. Alexander Denovan presented 400 copies of his *Election According to Holy Scripture* for sale, while his recently published *Appeal to the Christian World* was strongly promoted by the Committee as the most comprehensive set of arguments yet produced in favour of the IM system of church and ministry. [32] The Society of Friends also offered copies of Robert Barclay's *Apology for the True Christian Divinity* which were accepted on the basis that they endorsed IM ideas of unpaid ministry. [33]

Despite increased activity, the Connexion remained in many ways a collection of sub-groups, each with its own identity. Local names persisted, often to the point that members who knew their own church as 'Independent Methodist' were unaware that a nearby 'Free Gospel' Church was attached to the same denomination. Eventually, William Brimelow wrote a lengthy paper, arguing for the matter to be addressed in the interests of cohesion. He listed the number of churches known by the various names: [34]

Independent Methodist	62
Free Gospel	20
Christian Brethren	12
Christian Lay Churches	10 (this increased to 33 within two years)
Independent Primitive Methodist	8
Names unrecorded	8

Brimelow clearly had his own views on a preferred name, but prepared his ground by saying that it should be a name which described what the denomination was. He was particularly concerned that it should include the word 'Methodist' and stated, 'We think Methodist thoughts and enjoy Methodist experience, and our ways are the ways of Methodists.' The 1895 Annual Meeting voted overwhelmingly in favour of the name 'Independent Methodist', but as the thirty-three strong group of Christian Lay Churches affiliated at the same meeting, the matter was deferred for three years to allow them to contribute to the debate. [35]

Finally, in 1898, Brimelow formally moved the adoption of the name 'Independent Methodist' for the denomination and encouraged individual churches to start to use it. A further survey had shown a majority in favour, but the northern churches wished to retain the word 'lay' in the title. Brimelow felt that 'lay' implied 'of an inferior order' which was exactly what they were against, to which William Branfoot, leader of the Christian Lay Churches, replied that 'lay' implied 'of the people' (*laos*) which indicated that they were non-clerical. He wondered if the term 'Independent' would soon date, given the fact that the once-named 'Independents' had now become 'Congregationalists'. [36] A compromise was reached, whereby the denomination would take the name 'Independent Methodist', but the Christian Lay Churches would use the term 'Independent Methodist Lay Church'.[37] In the event, within a few years, they dropped the term 'Lay' and fell in line with the rest.

The adoption of a single name had a profound significance in giving a sense of unified identity which was previously unknown and gave Independent Methodism a better claim to be regarded as a denomination. The choice of name, significantly, took the churches back to their origins and initial ethos as a hybrid of two streams of ecclesiology, but gave them a firm sense of Methodist identity at a time when the various branches of Methodism were coming closer together.

4. Evangelism and Expansion

4.1. The Demographic Aspect

This period proved to be Independent Methodism's greatest phase of growth. In 1871, there were 3,496 members in eighty-seven chapels and meeting places; by 1911 this had increased to 8,316 members in 159 places of worship, the greatest growth occurring in large, urban centres.[38] However, Alfred Roscoe, in his 1885 presidential address, noted that not all growth was the result of evangelistic effort;[39] there were gains through the affiliation of existing churches, some from other denominations and others from none. Also, while urban churches of all denominations grew rapidly during these years, as the towns themselves grew, they were actually declining in proportion to population growth.[40] Nevertheless, the Independent Methodists had learned through experience and were now better organised and more competently led. Whatever the position relative to the population, their absolute growth gave rise to an enormous sense of confidence and well-being.

In Independent Methodism's early days, the dominant occupation of members was handloom weaving, later to be subsumed into power weaving in cotton and woollen mills. However, from the middle of the nineteenth century, the balance tilted towards coal mining, as the result of the industry's growth and the denomination's expansion in two mining areas.[41] From the 1860s churches mushroomed in and around the central Lancashire mining towns of St. Helens, Wigan and Leigh, while the accession in 1877 of the Christian Lay Churches of North-East England brought into the denomination a considerable number of churches, most of which were based in pit villages.[42]

As Robert Moore has pointed out, miners tended to be found in relatively isolated and homogeneous working class communities with their own distinctive culture.[43] Here, community solidarity gave a sense of identity. Congregations developed, often in miners' homes, where self-reliance in ministry underpinned their independence from any external authority. Churches led by miners acquired a character of their own and identified with the tribulations which often touched their communities. In such situations, Independent Methodism had a ready appeal, with its lay leadership, local autonomies and working class sympathies.

Churches formed in mining areas were usually the result of personal or group initiative. James Garner, who began his journey of faith at a cottage meeting at Billinge organised by the Wigan IM preachers, conducted open air meetings in mining communities, followed by cottage meetings and eventually the establishment of churches, first at Lamberhead Green and later at Haydock.[44] Miners from New Springs, Wigan, followed the same pattern in the newly developed mining area of Westwood, where another church was formed.[45] Of twenty-one churches started in the mining villages of the North-East between 1877 and 1890, fourteen began in a miner's home, a miners' hall or a colliery school, the remainder using modest rented premises.[46]

Low Green, near Wigan, (later known as Platt Bridge) began in 1866 with the conversion of two miners, formerly PM members, who started cottage meetings, hiring a room for 1s. 6d., because they felt that 'they had to do something for the Lord who had done so much for them.' As some of their workmates scarcely knew the alphabet, they resolved to provide weeknight teaching for them, in the hope that it would keep them from the public house. However, the curriculum evidently included more than just the alphabet and after three weeks they had three converts. Hearing of the Independent Methodists, whose beliefs and practices seemed best to accord with their own, they contacted them and asked for assistance.[47]

Towards the end of the nineteenth century, for all their earlier shortcomings, the Independent Methodists were in a better position to offer such locally formed groups the help they needed. One group at Thatto Heath, St. Helens, consisted mainly of miners and workers in other local industries who met in a disused colliery engine winding house. Contact with the Independent Methodists of Liverpool brought them not only evangelistic help, but the expertise of those who could guide them in financial matters and the necessary procedures for building a chapel.[48] But help in this case (and others) depended on the beneficence of individuals. Thomas Backhouse, a Liverpool preacher and cowkeeper, mortgaged his cows to help to save the Thatto Heath Chapel at a time of crisis, and came near to losing them. The contrast between Thatto Heath and its Wesleyan Methodist neighbour church reflected a pattern which was common wherever IM churches were found: the Wesleyan Nutgrove Chapel was attended by managers and foremen, while Thatto Heath was the spiritual home of the miners.[49]

Growth in mining areas could be prodigious, but it was also precarious. A year after it began, Low Green lost a number of members by removal following a dispute with the owners of the local mine. Strike action, a further hazard, hit the Wigan area in 1868, affected all the churches and caused a notable reduction in membership at New Springs, due to members' removal.[50] The greatest threat to colliery churches, however, was the sheer physical danger of members' occupations. An explosion at Seaham Colliery in 1880 took the lives of 164 men and boys; one of the side-effects of this tragedy was that a three year old nearby IM church which still met in miners' homes was brought close to extinction.[51] Low Green suffered the loss of its leader Richard Hilton and another member who were killed in a pit explosion;[52] here again, the church's future became suddenly uncertain. Mine closures could result in the removal of an entire workforce to a new area in a very short space of time. The church at Easington Lane, County Durham, touched its lowest membership in 1893 when the local colliery closed and members left the district.[53] Sometimes, however, a church could close and resurface somewhere else. A Free Gospel Church was established in 1881 by miners at Neston, Cheshire. Their colliery closed in 1884 and the workers were scattered, but two families removed to the mining community at Sutton, St. Helens, where they opened a cottage for services and thus resumed their activities in a different location.[54]

4.2. The Addition of Churches

Some of the larger churches extended their borders by planting new congregations, usually at short distances away. This would be a major factor of denominational growth, accounting for at least twenty-eight churches formed during the years 1850-1900, particularly in towns which grew rapidly in the latter part of the century, such as Nelson (leading to four additional churches), Bolton (four), Wigan (three) and Liverpool (four). Earlier experience of unsuccessful church plants led some churches to adopt a more rigorous policy of control. This was advocated by William Sanderson, whose Liverpool Church had established new societies in Kirkdale (North Zion) and Maghull, but retained direction of them for many years until it was clear that they could maintain themselves. Others, like Bolton, ensured that there was a large enough work force from the beginning and released the churches at Noble Street and Chalfont Street to move quickly to complete independence.

However, IM expansion rarely resulted through migration of members further afield. By the late nineteenth century, migrant members would find other branches of reformed Methodism well established and little appetite locally for the free gospel ideology. One exception resulted when James Slack, a Manchester member, moved to Crewe in 1869 for reasons of employment and started a meeting in a small rented room.[55] The Connexion's Missionary Committee was sufficiently keen to ensure the success of his venture by fortnightly provision of preachers, all of whom had to travel some distance. In due course a chapel was built and the church became a lasting one. By contrast, when William Wilson moved from Loughborough to Great Yarmouth in 1904, the church he started failed to provide the bridgehead into East Anglia for which the Connexion hoped.[56]

Divisions in churches sometimes led to the formation of new churches, which often had no wish to become part of a different denomination, while local circuits and the Connexion were willing to admit them into membership alongside the churches they had left. Geographical absurdities sometimes resulted. In Oldham two churches existed only a street apart for over 100 years, while in both Warrington and Glasgow, two churches stood in the same street. Other 'breakaways' retreated to more sensible distances. Barkerhouse Road (Nelson), formed through a rupture at Salem in 1869, and High Street (Bolton) whose founders left Noble Street in 1893, subsequently improved their relationships with their former brethren and carved out niches in separate communities.

Mid-nineteenth century revivalism brought added momentum to lay evangelistic initiatives which were not necessarily linked to any denomination.[57] Westmorland shepherd, Thomas Buck, had an early Quaker experience, which led him to believe in an unpaid ministry,[58] but he owed his conversion to the Primitive Methodists whom he served as a local preacher for a time. However, his independent spirit led him to branch out on his own, establishing small congregations in his own county and into County Durham. For six years until 1865, they were connected with no denomination until they heard of the Independent Methodists.[59] Westmorland's Quaker heritage, mixed with the revivalist preaching of the Primitive Methodists, could have made the county ripe for free gospelism, but in the event its emergence provoked the same reactions in other denominations that it did elsewhere and this group of churches encountered much opposition before it passed out of existence about 1881.[60]

Although IM preachers abandoned their disreputable practice of proselytising among other denominations from the mid-1850s, they still added to their numbers through localised schisms, usually among the Primitive Methodists. The most significant of these happened as the result of a PM Conference decision to divide the Sunderland Circuit, creating a second circuit based on the newly built central chapel in Tatham Street. The proposal to do so had been discussed for the previous two years or so in the circuit, where it was vigorously opposed, particularly by local preachers and circuit officials. Summing up the reasons for the opposition, Milburn commented that many Primitive Methodists saw the proposed step as symbolic of a move away from their roots towards a greater focus on imposing chapels, formal worship and general respectability.[61]

The opposite side of the argument was, of course, that Primitive Methodism needed to broaden its appeal and cater for former working class members who now had greater educational and social expectations. As Milburn concluded, it was basically 'a division of opinion between modernisers and traditionalists.' After a protracted dispute, the Conference referred the matter to a special committee, made up of fourteen members, twelve of whom were ministers. They came to Sunderland in February 1877, heard the case from both sides and enforced the formation of the new circuit. The immediate outcome was a series of resignations that would take several local preachers and their families out of the circuit. In total, about 300 members left, some 200 of whom formed themselves into a new body. To their credit, the people concerned were conscious that the circuit they were leaving was in debt, so they promptly resolved to pay it.[62] Initially, they called themselves 'Primitive Methodist Secessionists' and began to meet in rented premises, but later they adopted the title 'Christian Lay Churches.' Within a month, they had opened six places of worship.

The inclusion of such a high percentage of ministers on the special committee had led the local preachers to feel that, as lay people, they were becoming disenfranchised and to allege that the Conference's move had been made to 'bolster up priestly power'.[63] This would point them in the direction of establishing a church structure that would be operated entirely by laymen. On their first plan, in a lengthy apologetic for their action, they announced: 'We have resolved to return to the primitive usages laid down in the New Testament, believing that a hired ministry is by no means essential. . . .' They lamented what they saw as the tendency of ministers to 'lord it over God's heritage' and resolved to hold to the principle that 'One is your master, even Christ, and all ye are brethren.'[64] Without knowing it, they were echoing the same sentiments as the early Independent Methodists.

Most of the first Christian Lay Churches were located in the poorest parts of the town. Within a few years they were augmented by others in the colliery villages surrounding Sunderland who had heard of the events in the town and who were apparently inspired to follow suit. The early members were mainly shipwrights and miners, possibly attracted by the democratic polity of the new churches. However, among their ranks were men of some stature who provided strong and able leadership, such as William Branfoot (colliery and ship owner), Robert W. Collin (engineer and ironfounder) and John W. Johnson (accountant and town councillor). The first chapel was built in 1878, a year after the secession and others quickly followed. All were simple, modest buildings. Milburn noted that in 1904 the combined value of the eighteen chapels in the circuit was little more than the cost of the Tatham Street PM Chapel of 1875.[65]

The former PM local preachers rose to the occasion of their new role and undertook functions normally done by the ministers, such as weddings and funerals. At first, in true sectarian style, the use of non-Lay Church people as preachers was discouraged, but by 1889 the increase in the number of preachers had not matched the increase in the number of churches, which had now reached twenty, and the shortfall began to be felt. It was therefore agreed to accept non-accredited preachers on the plan, together with some preachers from other denomi-

William Branfoot (1825-1903)

nations.[66] The movement continued to expand in the North-East. By 1882, there were five circuits: Sunderland, Newcastle, Kip Hill, Stockton and Darlington. Spennymoor was added a few years later.[67] These circuits combined to form the Northern Counties Christian Lay Churches' Confederation, which held an annual weekend assembly and developed a concerted policy of further expansion.

Not long after the initial secession, the Sunderland pioneers became aware that a body based on similar principles to their own already existed and this led to contact between the two bodies in the form of correspondence and deputations. A 'courtship' of some years would precede the eventual union, but from an early stage the Christian Lay Churches adopted the hymn book and magazine of the Independent Methodists. Initially, there was some reluctance to affiliate, possibly from a fear of loss of independence and possibly from a sense that a link with churches far away in Lancashire would be meaningless. This was similar to the attitude of the Independent Primitive Methodists of Nottinghamshire who existed for over sixty years before joining the Independent Methodists. The very smallness of each of these free gospel groups led to a mindset which tended not to see beyond the group's own horizons, finding pleasure in small accessions, but steering clear of anything which threatened to absorb them.

Eventually, the churches affiliated individually from 1881 onwards, having joint membership of the two bodies. In 1883, the Sunderland Circuit hosted the Independent Methodist Annual Meeting, even though most of its churches had not yet applied for membership. This greatly helped to strengthen the links, but the Confederation as a whole did not affiliate until 1895, largely because of arguments over the mode of representation to the Annual Meeting.[68] The addition of this substantial group of churches inevitably impacted on the make-up of the Connexion, bringing to its ranks people of stature and a whole new geographical area. This was an accession of far more profound significance than those of earlier years, such as the Gospel Pilgrims and Minor Wesleyans, which lasted only briefly, and then in an age when the Independent Methodists did little more than hold an Annual Meeting.

In certain respects, there were differences between the Northern Counties Confederation and the rest of the Connexion, which sometimes led to tensions. The Confederation had a strong sense of corporate identity and would tend to speak with a single voice, while the other churches were more disparate. The Northern churches continued to be more overtly working class, while those in Lancashire in particular were experiencing 'redemption and lift', making some of them at least more sedate and respectable. By the same token, the plain and simple chapels of the North East looked rather different from the increasingly elaborate buildings which were being built in Lancashire as the nineteenth century drew to a close. However, the stability and order for which William Brimelow and others had worked so hard helped the process of bringing the two groups together and the union proved a lasting one.

Reference must also be made to Independent Methodism's only success in establishing itself in southern England. This began in 1885 when a group of Primitive Methodists in the Bedminster area of Bristol came into conflict with their minister and left to establish a new church which was made up mainly of miners, quarrymen and their families.[69] After meeting for some time in a rented hall, the secretary of the new church heard of the Independent Methodists while in London. He contacted the Bookroom and visits were exchanged.[70] The church affiliated to the Connexion and later formed a circuit with other unattached churches operating on a similar basis. In the 1890s they were further augmented by three small missions in South Wales and became the 'Bristol and South Wales District', though the Welsh missions proved short-lived.[71]

4.3. Connexional Evangelists

During the years 1825-1875, evangelistic work amounted to no more than different preachers taking time off from their employment to serve churches for a few weeks. This system was inevitably 'hit and miss', not always achieving a match between an evangelist's availability and a church's need. Perhaps it was the dearth of readily available evangelists within the Connexion that caused some churches to use the services of freelancers such as Richard Weaver and Henry Moorhouse,[72] the latter being associated with the IM Church at Stretford, near Manchester. This became a point of criticism, especially when churches resorted to the use of so-called 'Hallelujah Bands' which rose out of the Black Country revivals of 1863-4. According to William Booth, they 'were not troubled with any scruples about vulgarity'[73]; the Independent Methodist Annual Meeting evidently took a similar view and discouraged their use, warning people not to use anyone who was not attached to a recognised denomination.[74] However, the same objections were not raised towards the missions of D.L. Moody to Britain during the years 1873-75; these were welcomed by the churches generally, reported with approval in the Connexional magazine and endorsed in the official address to the 1875 Annual Meeting.[75]

By the 1870s, the Independent Methodists began to compare their own slow progress with the successes of other denominations. The Wesleyan Methodists had inaugurated their Home Missions Department, the Congregationalists had engaged in rural evangelism and the Baptists had undertaken special missions and services for working men.[76] Once again, the Independent Methodists sought to keep in step with what was happening among others. Some wished to see permanent evangelists appointed; others feared that this would compromise their non-payment principle. During 1869, the extensive service given by James Greenhalgh of Manchester was recognised and the Missionary Committee concluded that it would be justified in employing him for several weeks at a remuneration of twenty shillings per week.[77] This, however, was only a short term measure; the prospect of a permanent evangelist had to be deferred as funds were so low that the Treasurer found it necessary to advance a large amount of his own money to keep the Mission Fund afloat. The quandary facing the Connexion was that there were few people of the necessary ability to give themselves to the work, funds were inadequate and the low demand from the churches did not appear to warrant such a major undertaking. Once again, it fell to William Brimelow to take the initiative and draw up detailed proposals, which he submitted to the Annual Meeting of 1875. Brimelow rightly recognised that the long-established practice of accepting volunteers who could take a week or two off work each year to undertake evangelistic work elsewhere would never achieve anything of substance. Moreover, it inhibited the use of the most gifted people who were tied by the most demanding employment and who were unable to have leave of absence.[78]

Brimelow's approach was to propose the establishment of a 'Guarantee Fund for the Employment of Evangelists.' By tackling the financial issue first, he aimed to create a situation in which able people could be employed with some degree of job security and, by the same token, he argued that the appointment of suitably gifted evangelists would provide an incentive for the churches to engage their services. He proposed a contribution of two shillings per member per annum to maintain the fund. William Sanderson and other Liverpool delegates greeted the proposal with suspicion, arguing that it potentially brought in a paid ministry by the back door. They moved an amendment to refer the proposal back to the churches, but the tide was against them and the proposal was carried with only seven votes against.[79]

During the following year, Brimelow used his editorial position to advantage, preparing the ground for the following Annual Meeting when the method of implementing the scheme was to be launched. In a major change from historic practice, this heralded the end of the old Missionary Committee, located at different churches in turn, and its replacement with an Evangelistic Committee more representative of the Connexion as a whole. At the 1876 Annual Meeting, the existing Missionary Committee, based at Primet Bridge Church, Colne, expressed a sense of failure and declined to continue. Brimelow therefore submitted his proposed scheme which outlined in detail how permanent evangelists would operate. Realising that he faced opposition from Sanderson and his Liverpool colleagues, he outmanoeuvred them by couching his resolution in terms which merely required the Connexional Committee to 'attend to the evangelistic objectives of the *Testimony and Principles of Union*'. The Annual Meeting duly voted in favour of the resolution and a week later the Connexional Committee quickly acted upon it. John Knowles, a Cheshire agricultural labourer and long-serving preacher with a homely, domestic manner, was appointed as an evangelist, while Thomas Worthington of Lamberhead Green, an auctioneer and estate agent, was appointed as the first Evangelistic Committee Secretary.[80]

William Sanderson, who was present at the meeting, wrote afterwards:

> This result caused deep distress to me and my friends. I could not see how we could, with our views of the question, submit to the majority without violating conscience, and sin against what we considered a fundamental truth we held. The only way that we could get out of the difficulty was to resign, and carry on with the Lord's work as we had done. . . . Our churches in Liverpool unanimously decided to have nothing to do with paying for any preaching, and they requested me to draw up a circular and send copies to every church in the Union.[81]

When the Connexional Committee met in August, the circular was considered and arrangements were made to send deputations to all the Liverpool District Churches, which included such outposts as Crewe, Chester and Lancaster, to attempt a reconciliation.[82]

Notwithstanding the Liverpool revolt, the Connexional Committee was determined to press ahead with its evangelistic scheme and made further plans. One of the issues which needed to be resolved was the fact that the Warrington and Wigan Circuits were already employing their own evangelists. They were now asked to come under the Connexional umbrella by putting their financial and human resources into the wider body. The Warrington response was unequivocal – they would hand over 'their work, their man and their funds.' The Wigan response was rather more reserved and included a request to have an evangelist for at least a year to take care of its newest missions. The Committee took this request into account, appointed a second evangelist, Robert Berry, and located him in Wigan.[83]

To rebut charges of giving payment where this was unnecessary, the Committee later defined appointments on a three-fold basis.[84] There were to be voluntary evangelists, who gave time periodically and who received expenses only, occasional evangelists, who served for slightly longer and who were recompensed for lack of earnings and permanent evangelists who were full time employees of the Connexion and remunerated accordingly.

In order to select locations for possible church plants, the Evangelistic Committee wrote to circuit secretaries, asking four questions:[85]

Were there any suitable neighbourhoods in the circuit's vicinity?
What assistance could the circuit give?
Were there any districts further afield to which three or four members had removed?
Were there any local undenominational missions run on IM lines?

Evangelists spent at least some of their time attending to the needs of churches which were running evangelistic campaigns. This was usually short-term but intensive work, whereby they would spend two or three weeks at a church, conducting nightly evangelistic meetings and engaging in visitation work during the day. Each evangelist would keep a detailed record of work done, noting how many people had made professions of faith and how many families had been visited.[86]

After a period of travelling around the churches, visiting homes and conducting mission services, John Knowles, the first of the evangelists, was directed by his committee to consider the possibility of starting a church in Leigh, Lancashire, now a burgeoning town and home to several Independent Methodists from other places (most notably nearby Lowton) who had moved there for reasons of employment. In December 1876, Knowles and the Warrington Circuit evangelist, Joseph Birchall (who now transferred to the Connexion's employment), hired the Good Templars' Hall in King Street and started to hold services there.[87] Attendances were encouraging and it was obvious that there was great potential for a thriving church. Realising that this would need a substantial investment of time, Knowles found himself accommodation in the town and for the next two years made it his home.

During the following year, work began on building Leigh Chapel in The Avenue. While this was still under construction, Knowles and others saw a new opening at nearby Atherton, where a few 'earnest, but poor men' were holding cottage meetings. Together, they took possession of a building which had formerly been used as a smithy and, with the help of a grant from the Connexion, turned it into a school and preaching room.[88] Within two years, the churches at Leigh and Atherton were sufficiently established for Knowles to relinquish his post and return to his home at Lymm.

In the meantime, Robert Berry had spent time successfully building up the new church at Ince, but his greater work lay in establishing another mission a short distance away at Spring View, a growing mining community. On his advice the Wigan Circuit took a cottage in the centre of the village, adapted it for use and continued services in it until a chapel was built until 1880. Once this mission was on its feet, Berry turned his attention to the established but near-defunct church at Stubshaw Cross where, despite initially slow progress, his efforts again proved fruitful.[89] The pattern set by Knowles and Berry was exactly what the Evangelistic Committee had in mind and other evangelists were appointed in due course to undertake similar work, which went on until the First World War. Under the direction of R.B. Woods, the longest serving and most prolific of all the evangelists, new churches at Hindley, Leigh (Bright Street and Mill Lane), Ashton-on-Mersey, Blackley, Blackpool and New Easington were opened in the early years of the twentieth century. In addition to the use of permanent evangelists, the Committee also kept a supply of material resources. Tents, tin chapels, forms, harmoniums and hymn books were used for the launch of new places of worship, then moved on when the churches thus formed became independent and provided for their own needs.

The process of contacting undenominational missions, which proliferated from the 1890s, was pursued with great vigour. In some places, there were few gaps to be filled by the formation of new churches and the best hope for expansion was to persuade existing unattached churches of the merit of IM principles and practice. Such churches invariably found no problem with the IM concept of independence; their response really hinged on whether or not they identified with the principle of unpaid ministry. One of the successes of this policy was the accession of the long-established Independent Primitive Methodists of Nottinghamshire who, after years of intermittent contact, finally joined in 1893. However, this group had long been committed to free gospelism[90] and had no ideological barriers to union. Moreover, it was now reduced to eight churches, where once there had been sixteen. It is difficult to avoid the conclusion that decline may have driven the decision to affiliate at this particular time, though an additional factor was the formation of a new church in Nottingham, started on the initiative of one Thomas Walker who was keen to link his church to the Connexion.[91] By 1897, the Committee reported that sixty missions had been visited in the previous five years and that thirteen of these had joined the Connexion, representing 560 members and 1003 Sunday School scholars.[92] These included Runcorn Gospel Mission (Cheshire), Rotherham, Loughborough, Haslingden (Lancashire), Dumfries, Hull, Pensnett (Dudley), Talywain and Trealaw (South Wales), though some of them proved unstable and short-lived.

Matthew Kennedy (1839-1922)

At a later stage came Morecambe, Salford (Weaste), and three churches in the Oldham area: St. Mary's Street Medical Mission, Grasscroft and Failsworth.[93]

As the evangelistic policy showed its worth, confidence grew in both its methods and its people. Churches more readily accepted advice and called on connexional expertise to help with their problems. This also brought successes, a notable example occurring in the new church at Nottingham, which hit problems at an early stage. Matthew Kennedy (1839-1922), then one of the evangelists, was asked in 1894 to visit the church which appeared to be on the verge of collapse. What he found was a mixture of financial mismanagement, resulting in a crippling debt (for which the church's leader, Thomas Walker, bore much of the responsibility), factionalism and general incompetence. Out of concern for the Connexion's reputation in its new Midlands location, Kennedy secured the Evangelistic Committee's permission to stay at the church for three months. Moving rapidly, he rescheduled debts with short-term help from the Connexion, dissolved the church and reconstituted it. By the time he left it was on a secure footing and went on to become a thriving community.[94]

The Nottingham situation was not unique. Many IM Churches, like the unattached missions which they courted, were set up on the local initiative of people who often abounded in enthusiasm but lacked financial awareness or basic management skills. Some, like Nottingham, had built chapels without the necessary financial security and found themselves mortgaged beyond their means. In earlier years, few were fortunate enough to secure the necessary remedial help.

Connexional intervention, albeit with the consent of the churches concerned, marked a new phase in denominational development as churches realised the benefit of external support. There was a general realisation that the Connexion now had more people than ever with the necessary expertise to give churches the guidance they needed.

4.4. The Healing of a Schism

During the years 1876-78, the Connexional Committee turned its attention to the Liverpool defectors. Initial deputations proved unsuccessful so, in September 1877, legal advice on the Liverpool Chapel Deed was sought. This resulted in counsel's opinion that none of the churches on this or any other version of the Model Deed had any power to withdraw from the Union.[95] The Liverpool Churches were advised accordingly. A further deputation met with them and the matter was evidently settled, according to Sanderson, to the satisfaction of both parties.[96] The settlement evidently included a concession which acknowledged the right of churches to contribute or not to the Evangelistic Fund.

When the matter came up for discussion again some years later, it was clear that the Liverpool Churches remained opposed to the scheme and neither contributed to it, nor received the evangelists in their circuit. Nevertheless, Sanderson was elected back on to Connexional Committee at the 1878 Annual Meeting and also (remarkably) on to the Evangelistic Committee. Whether legal coercion or a genuine change of heart brought about the reconciliation is difficult to tell. The recourse to legal advice on this matter was a defining moment for the Connexion. For the first time, the binding effect of the Model Deed was put to the test and it achieved its desired object. From this point on, the notion of complete independence would never be as unchallengeable again. The churches became aware that, for good or ill, their futures lay in membership with a central body to which they were committed. It was a further move away from unbridled sectarianism and separatism.

4.5. Chapel building

As the nation became more materially prosperous in the late nineteenth century, church leaders built bigger and more impressive edifices than the small, plain chapels of their poorer forebears. In 1865 (the first year for which there are comprehensive statistics) only fifty-three out of eighty-eight churches (60%) could claim their own properties, but this was about

The second Salem Chapel, Nelson, interior (built 1892)

to change rapidly. During the 1860s, twenty-five churches built new chapels, varying in cost from a modest £200 to the £4,200 it took to build the 1,000 seater Charlotte Street Chapel in Glasgow. A further fourteen built extensions. The rate of building accelerated in the following four decades, with the result that by the early twentieth century, few churches were meeting in cottages or rented premises or even early nineteenth century chapels.

1914 provides a useful snapshot of the progress of chapel building up to that point, since it coincided with the end of Independent Methodism's height of prosperity and, in any case, building effectively ground to a halt during the war years and never resumed at the same pace afterwards. By this time, eighty-one of the chapels (51%) were less than thirty years old, while only fifteen (9.7%) were over fifty years old. Building peaked during the years 1874-1894 and gradually tailed off afterwards, though the buildings of the 1890s included the largest and most opulent of all at

Nelson and Barnoldswick. Both these buildings, and others, compared well for architecture and furnishing, with the structures of the larger Methodist bodies. Independent Methodism was plainly working towards an improved image and moving further from its earlier simplicity.

Some of the older generation observed, with regret, that pre-occupation with buildings often led to neglect of a church's spiritual life. Fund raising activities now took on a different aspect, as Christmas fairs, bazaars and sales of work became a normal part of chapel life. Stonelaying ceremonies were almost as important as actual opening services and the honour of laying a foundation stone could be a means of eliciting a donation. William Oxley, speaking at the 1868 Annual Meeting, deplored this practice:

> If there was a foundation stone to be laid, instead of looking for the man of the deepest piety, and the man who did most service in the service of Christ, and putting him in the post of honour, it was too often the practice to look for some titled gentleman – an M.P., a Mayor, or something of that sort – and, although he might be a Unitarian or Swedenborgian, exalt him that they might succeed in getting a trifle out of him.[97]

By the end of the century, Independent Methodism's own more prosperous men were in considerable demand for foundation stone laying, with the same pecuniary expectations as 'titled gentlemen'. William Boote, once Connexional President and large-scale furniture remover, laid foundation stones for at least twelve chapels, at considerable self-sacrifice.[98]

The late nineteenth century saw the Independent Methodists give long overdue attention to the matter of chapel deeds. Most of the earlier churches had individual deeds which secured the properties to the original owners and their heirs and successors. Thus, chapels could be taken out of the denomination at will or the congregation could lose its home without redress. For this reason, a Model Deed was introduced in 1860 to secure church properties for Free Gospel purposes[99] and the churches were encouraged to adopt it.

In 1894, possibly with Methodist union in mind, William Brimelow introduced a new Model Deed which stipulated that churches based on it must remain linked to the United Free Gospel Churches (as they were then known) and adhere to evangelical doctrine, but allowed for the fact that the Connexion might change its rules and practices.[100] It was an astute balancing act, but one which won the favour of the churches. Thereafter, most new trusts adopted it and some older ones were able to transfer to it, though some were still based on the 1860 Deed.

Stonelaying, King Street, Oldham, 1905

4.6. Overseas Activity

Unlike other branches of Methodism which established themselves overseas, the Independent Methodists were simply too small to follow suit. However, during these years, emigration led to a few isolated attempts to start churches on a free gospel basis in other parts of the world, but mainly in Australia. The earliest known instance occurred in 1863 when John W. Cullen, an IM preacher, began a society at Jamberoo in the Kiama District of New South Wales. Delighted at the prospect of an overseas branch, the Independent Methodists in England sent liberal supplies of literature for him to distribute, but correspondence was inevitably slow and some materials never arrived.[101] Cullen persevered and saw growth in the ensuing years. However, free gospelism was not welcomed by other churches and Cullen wrote home to complain of persecution.[102] Hoping to be accepted as a minister, he encountered problems in the eyes of the Australian authorities, to whom he could offer no credentials. This dilemma was resolved when the Connexion in England supplied him with a certificate of accreditation, which enabled him to enrol with the Registrar General as an Independent Methodist minister.[103] In so doing the Connexion found itself faced with a new situation. The accreditation of ministers was normally a function of local circuits; there was no such thing as a 'Connexional' minister. On this occasion, for the first time, the Connexion had to act as an accrediting body in the absence of a denominational network in Australia. Unwittingly, this event would serve as a pointer to a time fifty years ahead, when the matter of central accreditation would arise on a much wider scale. However, the opposition experienced by Cullen continued and gradually his members returned to their previous churches. This followed a similar pattern to the experience of Free Gospel Churches in England which drew opprobrium upon themselves for their public attacks on paid ministry during the middle years of the nineteenth century. Cullen died in 1879 and his church died with him.[104]

A more indigenous attempt to form a church on a free gospel pattern occurred in 1885 at Adamstown, New South Wales, where a group of members of the Free Methodist Church left and formed themselves into a Lay Church. Hearing of the Christian Lay Churches recently formed in Sunderland, England, they contacted them and were duly put into contact with the IM Connexion. In justifying their actions, they alleged that the Free Methodist ministry had become a matter of business rather than a love for souls and money given for mission had been used for buildings and the furnishing of parsonages, while the poor were neglected and Christian duty was being done by proxy.

The Adamstown officers sent a detailed report of their current situation and appealed for help with provision of materials, especially for Sunday school work.[105] Information was intermittent over the following years, but by 1904 there was a circuit of seven churches. The same number was cited again in 1911, but membership totalled only 100, with 400 scholars.[106] Evidently, the membership was made up mainly of mining families, as they reported in 1913 that they had sustained losses due to people moving to a new coalfield.[107] In 1914, they reported shortage of workers and lamented the fact that 'in this land of sunshine the people are given up to pleasure.'[108] Contact finally lapsed in the 1920s.

The Independent Methodists took their first steps into formal overseas missions work in an age when it would have been neither practical nor appropriate to start a denominational missionary society. In 1898, Joseph Robinson of the Stretford Church, a member of the Student Volunteer Movement at Owen's College, Manchester, felt a calling to serve overseas and challenged the Connexion to send him out as a missionary.[109] On the encouragement of missionary speakers at the college, he undertook medical training and the Connexion accepted him as a missionary candidate shortly before the completion of his course. A Foreign Missions Committee was formed in 1903 and work began on raising funds. The Committee investigated possible avenues of service and entered into an arrangement with the Friends' Foreign Mission Committee who accepted Dr & Mrs Robinson as members of staff at one of their hospitals at Itarsi in Central India, beginning in November 1904.[110] The choice of the Friends as a partner body reflected a trend in Independent Methodist thought at the time, influenced greatly by Arthur Mounfield, the first chairman of the Foreign Mission Committee, who had strong Quaker sympathies. The whole project caught the imagination of the

Connexion and the churches enthusiastically undertook responsibility for the couple's maintenance. A precedent was thus made for later missionaries, whereby each would serve through an existing missionary society, with the Connexion giving full or partial financial support.

The Robinsons served in India until 1913 when they resigned on grounds of ill-health. A gap followed until Nurse Edith Bevan went out in 1927, again to Itarsi with the Friends Foreign Mission Committee. In the years between, the Connexion continued its links with the Friends and gave support to their work in India, but other areas beckoned too. The Committee gave support to two 'native' evangelists working with the China Inland Mission and made arrangements for individual churches to adopt such workers also. As churches responded, there were seven native evangelists in China, two in India and one in Korea. By 1917, six churches were raising sufficient money for each to support a worker fully.[111]

5. Ministry Issues

Using data from the census returns of 1881,[112] together with Independent Methodist Year Books and church returns, it is possible to build up a picture of the occupations of those who served as ministers/preachers at these times. In 1881, the churches returned 261 ministers; occupations have been traced for 180 of them and these indicate that a total of 70% of the people concerned were either white collar workers of modest status or skilled manual workers.[113] Figures for people at the upper and lower end of the occupational scale were much smaller; the unskilled labourer and the large employer were both atypical of Independent Methodism's corpus of preachers. Aside from their actual occupations, their spheres of work reflected the predominant industries of areas where Independent Methodists were to be found. Eighteen were involved in the coal industry and thirty in textiles. Few were agricultural workers, which illustrated the largely urban nature of the denomination. Twenty-three were retailers.

Twenty seven of the respondents to the census indicated not only their occupations, but their preaching ministries too. This is perhaps most significant for the fact that twenty three of these styled themselves as 'local preachers' rather than 'ministers' – perhaps the clearest single piece of evidence from the late nineteenth century of their self-perceptions. Descriptions varied from 'Free Gospel Minister' to 'wheelwright and Methodist local preacher', 'bricklayer and lay preacher', 'independent preacher' and even one who declared himself as 'provision dealer and vagrant Methodist local preacher.' Of only four who used the word 'minister', two were currently working as evangelists for the Connexion and had no other occupation. Whatever the later claims made for the Independent Methodist ministry, its nineteenth century practitioners saw themselves primarily as preachers, with no pretensions to be anything else.

Occupation was an important factor in a person's capacity to fulfil the functions of ministry. Most pastoral visitation (where it was done) would be covered in evenings. Baptisms took place on Sundays and weddings on Saturdays, so employment demands, in most cases, allowed room for these. The difficulty came with funerals which, invariably, took place on week days. For the shopkeeper who could leave his shop to an assistant or the self-employed tradesman who managed his own working hours, this presented no difficulty, but for a schoolteacher to leave a class was a different matter. Moreover, for a miner or mill worker to take time off to conduct a funeral meant loss of income for someone who was already on a low wage. Despite its no-payment policy, recompense for loss of earnings was permitted within Independent Methodism, but, since this was dependent on arrangements by local churches, it is impossible to establish how many ministers received recompense and how many simply forfeited their income.

During these years, Independent Methodism's unpaid ministers experienced new problems, as the main free churches moved towards a college-educated ministry. The miners, mill workers and small tradesmen who made up the bulk of the IM ministry's workface began to look decidedly inferior and less competent in educational terms to their paid counterparts. In due course, this impacted on inter-church relations and public life, partly arising from the gradual removal of religious disabilities which had benefited the larger Free Churches. In 1872 the Free Churches of Bolton had an arrangement with the Burial Board whereby a number of ministers took charge of cemetery services on a rota basis, but Independent Methodists were not included. When the Bolton Circuit meeting challenged this, the local Free Church ministers replied that 'the duties pertaining to cemetery interments are distinctly trusted by the Burial Board to those who are *bonâ fide* ministers and pastors of congregations' and that exceptions could only be made 'wherein it is intimated by the friends of the deceased that they prefer the service of someone not ordinarily recognised as a minister.' In a rather condescending sideswipe at the Independent Methodists, the writer added,

> If the public and the Burial Board will admit that about 50 tradesmen be put upon the cemetery list, I shall be very thankful that thus it may be. . . . But there can be no doubt that if the congregations now enumerated with your own, and others becoming destitute of an officiating minister, are to be generally represented by tradesmen who shall take religious duty at the cemetery, other societies not professedly Christian, will ask for a similar privilege of appointing a nominee to take a turn with the rest.[114]

In other words, the 'ministers' of the Independent Methodists were no ministers, but merely tradesmen appointed by their churches to officiate at services which should normally be conducted only by *bonâ fide* ministers, though this expression would prove notoriously difficult to define. The unwritten perception of a *bonâ fide* minister in the minds of church and public alike was that of one who was appropriately educated, ordained, given pastoral oversight of a congregation and who served in a full time capacity. In fairness to the Independent Methodists, it has to be said that this perception was as much the result of an evolutionary process as their own ideas, but as the odd ones out of a much larger picture, they were inevitably at a disadvantage. The Bolton situation reflected the widening gulf between IM and other Free Church ministries. The disregard of its ministry by other Free Churches continued into the twentieth century and proved even more galling than its familiar rejection at the hands of the Anglicans who accorded no recognition to any form of Free Church ministry.

One further fact about the IM pattern of ministry should be noted at this point. From earliest times, the Independent Methodists were ready and willing to use women as preachers, though the percentage of them in relation to men remained small until well into the twentieth century. Sometimes they had to face public opposition for doing so. John Landless recorded what happened in Nelson when Salem Church, only three years into its existence, received the talented Sarah Fitzgerald of Lancaster to preach in 1855:

> After our placards were put out, numbers of the Brethren were attacked by the opposers of female preaching, who stated that we were wrong in permitting our females to preach. Our sister in her first discourse was, without any previous knowledge of such opposition, led to dwell on female preaching, and very ably proved to the delight of the Brethren, and the entire satisfaction of all that heard her, that she had a right to labour in this important work.[115]

The Independent Methodists resisted all such pressures to discontinue female preaching and gradually more women preachers emerged in different parts of the Connexion. Nanny Butler of Dicconson Lane, Westhoughton (Lancashire) was a particularly respected and effective preacher who, in 1864, took under her wing the young Richard Lee (a future evangelist and President of the Connexion) and guided his first steps in preaching.[116] Later, in 1894, the Evangelistic Committee engaged the services of its first female evangelist, Clara Green of Oldham. There was no formal policy to recognise women as preachers at any given point; it was simply understood that if a woman had a calling and a gift, then like a man she would be given the opportunity to use it.

6. The Changing Character of the Churches

Cottage meetings, street preaching and tract distribution featured in the activities of many of the churches. Street singing was used to invite people to attend services. Mass evangelism maintained the patterns set by Finney, Moody and others. Churches continued to experience times of revival and held mission campaigns which often gave them a significant boost. However, as the nineteenth century drew to a close, church reports were often in similar vein to one from Batley, Yorkshire, which lamented, 'The Lord's Supper is only moderately attended, the Class meetings much neglected, the Band Meeting almost forgotten and the Prayer Meeting dead.'[117] Others deplored lack of commitment from members and lack of conversions. More positively, an new outlet for the young came with the arrival from America of the Christian Endeavour movement, which aimed to train young people for service. This became widely popular in Britain from the late 1880s onwards. It had a strong appeal to Independent Methodists, as it implicitly reflected their ethos of grassroots ministry. In 1894 it was officially adopted by the denomination and a Christian Endeavour department was established.[118]

Limited opportunities for travel meant that artisan members of IM churches spent most of their lives in the towns and villages of their birth and therefore lived in a culture shaped by the chapel and its leaders. Whereas other churches experienced change as one minister succeeded another, Independent Methodists were generally slower to pick up on changes in the wider nation. Consequently, they became followers of trends rather than instigators of them. Edward Ralphs, by occupation a contractor's chief clerk and cashier and longstanding leader of his church, depicted chapel life at Wingates, Westhoughton (Lancashire), during the last quarter of the nineteenth century.[119] A Dramatic Society, Social League, Home Reading Circle, Elocution Class and Debating Class now featured in the church's programme, all of them responding to perceived needs in the community. A Pleasant Sunday Afternoon Society (a move away from a Bible Class) discussed public issues. Money was raised and sent to support victims of disaster and persecution. Ralphs had a strong political bent and, as one of the church's leaders, his views on the democratic process would inevitably be followed by others. The chapel itself, once the home of Radical Reformers and Chartists, entered a new phase of influence, in which members of the community found a place where their opinions would be formed, expressed and channelled into other areas of activity, such as local government and philanthropic organisations. Wingates was by no means unique in this respect; other chapels had similar personalities and produced similar results.[120]

Churches in urban areas provided for the whole person in an age when the factory system created a hemmed-in, unvaried pattern of life. At Smith Street, Oldham, the church invested in a recreation ground which would be used as 'a safe retreat from more questionable places.' The Adult Class was regarded as a college for the working man, giving an opportunity for a step up in the world. Having an eye for the unchurched poor who lived in the teeming streets of their town, the Sunday School leaders sent helpers to take part in the 'Free Breakfast Mission' which operated in the town every Saturday morning.[121] Other churches provided free breakfasts for the poor children of their area on Christmas morning, when hundreds would crowd in for their only treat of the day.[122]

Mutual Improvement Societies, Libraries, Literary Societies and Sewing Circles abounded. The Charity Sermon was re-named the Sunday School Anniversary (or Sermons) – still with a focus on raising school funds for the coming year, but with ever more sophisticated contributions from the scholars. As the musical talents available to churches became greater, singing classes were formed, eventually leading to able and accomplished choirs.[123] The pipe organ – a source of controversy earlier in the century – was now almost an icon, reflecting the desire of Independent Methodists of this era to enjoy parity with other denominations. Organ openings mirrored the openings of chapels; often, a magazine report of an organ installation would be accompanied by a picture and full specifications of the organ which had become its church's pride and joy.[124] The choir and organ era had arrived in Independent Methodism as in other denominations. But this had a social as well as a spiritual dimension. It was not merely a matter of producing better music for the greater glory of God. The choirmaster at Smith Street, Lunn Inman, perceptively affirmed the value of his choir to its *members*, believing that music was a corrective to the monotony of industrial life.[125]

Recreational provision for Sunday Schools was enhanced. Herculean efforts were made for Sunday School outings which were just beginning in the middle years of the century. In 1866, Stubshaw Cross, Wigan, along with other local schools, went on a train outing to Llandudno (a major undertaking and adventure for the time), departing at 5.30.a.m. and arriving home at 10.00.p.m.[126] Three Sunday Schools in Oldham followed their 1887 Friday Whitsun procession with a field day for children to play. The next day each took its scholars on an outing: Smith Street to Llanberis, King Street to Coniston (with a Singers' trip to Matlock) and Bethesda by wagonette to the Ashworth Valley.[127] Such events, which took town children and adults to countryside and coast for the first time in their lives, provided lifetime memories for those concerned.

The changes in church life among the Independent Methodists at the end of the nineteenth century mirrored those in other free church denominations as all were similarly affected by the social and theological changes of the times.[128] Poverty gave way to prosperity (at least for some) and preachers urged their hearers to imbibe the Spirit of Christ rather 'flee from the wrath to come'.[129] While spirituality continued to run deep, it began to find different expressions, some Quaker rather than Methodist, exemplified at Stockton Heath, Warrington, where the church's leader, Arthur Mounfield, introduced the practice of Quaker silences into the church's Sunday services. As a further expression of his Quakerism, the Lord's Supper was not observed in the church during his years of leadership.[130]

7. Temperance Activity

IM commitment to the temperance movement deepened during the middle years of the nineteenth century to the point where it became positively totemic.[131] To be an Independent Methodist was to be a teetotaller, and the temperance pledge almost equalled the 'decision card' as a symbol of Christian commitment. It even added to motivation for chapel building. When William Crumblehulme set out to establish a church at Horwich, he was 'determined that the Gospel should be freely preached in the village and that a place could be built where total abstinence could be advocated.'[132] Churches were encouraged to establish Bands of Hope, while printed addresses were sent, from time to time, to church officers and Sunday School teachers, commending the practice of total abstinence. The fact that many IM churches were located in areas of poverty where alcohol abuse was rife made the issue emotive and poignant. A Band of Hope report from the church at Accrington stated that the economic effects alone made a severe impact on trade, five times as much being spent on alcohol as on cotton. Female drunkenness in the streets was common in the area, while Sunday School scholars (presumably adolescents) were seduced by the ready availability of alcohol, with the result that many ended up in prison.[133] As the temperance movement was concerned to promote healthy pursuits to young minds, the curriculum of its various groups became educational and cultural as well as religious. This could lead to secondary activities which became significant in their own right. At Wingates, temperance spin-off activity led to the formation of a drum and fife band, later augmented by brass, which went on to become the world-famous Wingates Temperance Band.[134]

By the later part of the nineteenth century the temperance movement was a powerful coalition of organisations which sought to promote its cause nationally as well as locally. Almost every organisation – the Band of Hope, United Kingdom Alliance, Good Templars, Sons of Temperance and Blue Ribbon Army, among others – had IM supporters.[135] In 1900, the Connexion established a Temperance Committee, effectively making total abstinence the formal policy of the denomination, and drew up a comprehensive agenda for action.[136] Seventeen years later, a new membership rule book made total abstinence a condition of church membership and prohibited members from working in the drink trade. The temperance issue, more than any other, came near to putting Independent Methodism back on a sectarian track by making a secondary issue an article of faith and a defining point of required conduct.

8. The Ecumenical Movement

From the last two decades of the nineteenth century, the Independent Methodists found themselves increasingly faced with the challenges and opportunities of the ecumenical movement. This affected most notably their relationship with other Methodist Churches and the Free Churches generally.

8.1. Methodist Union

The first Methodist Ecumenical Conference, held in London in 1881, saw William Sanderson and William Brimelow attend as the Connexion's representatives. Their subsequent report focused almost entirely on how the Conference had affirmed lay people; it was a report of men anxious to find support for their sectarian peculiarities.[137] However, when he looked back on the occasion in later years, Sanderson, who 30 years earlier had poured vitriol on all other Methodist systems, wrote:

> All the meetings were attended with marvellous unction and divine power. . . . Though holding different views of church polity,
>> All were of one heart and soul
>> And only love inspired the whole.
> It was indeed a grand sight, one never to be forgotten.[138]

Others found through this Conference hope for a unified future rather than vindication of a sectarian past. At the second Conference, held ten years later, the mood had changed dramatically and Methodist union was openly advocated.[139] At the third Conference, held at Wesley's Chapel, London, in September 1901, minds were clearly focused on taking positive steps forward. Such was the euphoria of the occasion that Thomas Worthington, one of the IM representatives, made bold to say that the Independent Methodists would welcome the reunion of all Methodists. The Wesleyan Reform Union expressed a similar view.[140] The Conference agreed to inaugurate 'Methodist Concerted Action' which would embrace all Methodist bodies. Its purpose was to promote co-operation in areas such as mutual defence, social action and the better distribution of Methodist Chapels across the country.[141] The Independent Methodists joined this body and identified enthusiastically with its aims, which gave them access to a strong, corporate voice in ways previously unknown to them.

During the 1901 Conference, a spontaneous move was made by three Methodist bodies – the United Methodist Free Churches, the Methodist New Connexion and the Bible Christians – to pursue organic union.[142] This came before the annual gatherings of all the Methodist denominations in 1902 and four of them (the above three and the Wesleyan Reform Union) agreed to their executives pursuing the matter.[143] A Joint Committee representing the initial three denominations then drew up a series of tentative resolutions which were designed to outline a basis for union. In March 1903, representatives of the Wesleyan Reform Union also attended the Joint Committee's meeting and it was resolved to send a communication narrating progress to date to the secretaries of the Wesleyan Methodists, Primitive Methodists and Independent Methodists, asking each body to consider the matter at its next Conference.[144]

At the IM Annual Meeting in June 1903,[145] three representatives were appointed to attend a joint conference in London on 13 November. The President, Arthur Watson, expressed the mixture of hope and apprehension which this step represented:

> That our own denomination presents special difficulties is patent to anyone; but . . . I feel it is imperative that we place no obstacle in the way. If they prove insuperable our case will be all the stronger for our willingness to discuss them with our brethren, and they respect us nonetheless if we are afterwards compelled to withdraw from the conference. We value our liberty in the control of our own churches. But other churches are not so chained and bound as we have imagined and may be in the framing of a basis of union the aspiration for freedom and elasticity may make itself felt to a degree most welcome to us who love it so dearly. Undoubtedly the most serious, most delicate subject will be the ministry. We have stood out like our friends, the Quakers – with whom we have so much in common – for a voluntary ministry. I confess I do not see my way round this difficulty, but it may be God will have in readiness, when the time comes to consider it, a man who will have conceived such a statesmanlike scheme in his heart that when it is elaborated we shall find the barriers of difficulty melting away one by one. If it should be proved that the time is not ripe, we must quietly abide God's time.[146]

Watson's Micawberite optimism was to be disappointed. The three main players already had a clear idea of the eventual shape of the new denomination, the basis of which created great unease in the minds of the

IM delegation to the November meeting. Their subsequent report to Connexional Committee, which met later the same month, indicated that they were on the horns of a dilemma:

> It is a very grave matter indeed to withdraw from the movement for Methodist Union; and to go forward now means for our Connexion the giving up of a great deal we have hitherto considered vital and fundamental.[147]

Most particularly, the proposals would have required the Independent Methodists, along with others, to provide funds for a maintained ministry and all the associated commitments – Ministers' Annuity, Ministers' Children's Funds and the funding of colleges. This ran counter to all their long-held convictions and left them with the problem of deciding whether those convictions were more or less important than the goal of Methodist Union. To hold on to them carried the price of future isolation; to surrender them was tantamount to either an admission of previous error or the betrayal of a vital principle. It is difficult to overstate how much hung on their decision. In the event, the Connexional Committee bought time, pulled back from the brink of withdrawal and resolved 'that it is not at present desirable to withdraw from the Conference on Methodist Union, but that a definite statement of our position should be prepared by our representatives and laid before the conference appointed to discuss this question.'[148]

Some of the reservations felt by the Independent Methodists were apparently also shared by the Wesleyan Reform Union. At the February 1904 Connexional Committee, Arthur Mounfield reported that, as a result of representations made by both groups, the negotiating body wished to meet the IM and WR committees in Manchester later that month to hear and address their concerns. The IM Connexional Committee appointed seven representatives to the meeting, but recorded in its minutes that it was opposed to the intended basis of union.[149] When the meeting came, the three larger denominations stood their ground and were not prepared to make any significant changes. William Brimelow wrote to the following Connexional Committee meeting to explain the tension he felt:

> In regard to Methodist Union, I do not see how the present proposals can be accepted by us. But a simple refusal on our part does not seem to meet the case, because at Annual Meetings and by other action, we have expressed a desire for Methodist Union, and in some way we should justify our professions in this matter.[150]

However, the only tangible suggestion he could offer was that the IM and WRU committees should hold a conference to define their position in relation to the proposals and to consider how they could give effect to their declarations in favour of Methodist Union.

The next Connexional Committee meeting considered their representatives' report and, in Brimelow's absence, his letter. They concluded that the proposed basis of union was not acceptable and that the reasons should be given to the next meeting of the Joint Committee.[151] Ellis Barker later wrote to the Joint Committee to confirm the IM views on the proposals. The Committee, having considered his letter and expressed regret at the IM decision, gave a reply with a sting in its tail:

> Remembering that your churches are independent, and that final decisions on so vital a matter must be reached by them individually, the Joint Committee ventures to suggest that the opportunity of consideration be given to them.[152]

In effect, they wished to see individual IM churches have the opportunity to secede from the Connexion and join the proposed United Methodist Church. There is no record of the reaction to this suggestion, but as the Connexion had taken numerous measures during the previous fifty years, such as the introduction of the *Testimony and Principles of Union* and the Model Deed, to secure churches to the Connexion, it was unlikely to be welcomed. However, to show that no information was being withheld, the 'Tentative Proposals' were published to the churches prior to the 1904 Annual Meeting and the Connexional Committee reported that it was 'unable to recommend for acceptance by the Annual Meeting of the Independent Methodist Churches the Bases of Union on which these three bodies have tentatively agreed in their present form and the present advanced stage of the negotiations.'[153] The IM Annual Meeting evidently took no vote on the subject, but simply accepted the Committee's recommendation. There seems to have been little appetite on the ground for a scheme of union which would have made increased financial demands upon them (to which they were unaccustomed) and which would have introduced a maintained ministry which their forebears had consistently denounced as unscriptural.

The logical conclusions of the ecumenical movement caught the Independent Methodists unprepared. They had expressed a buoyant enthusiasm for unity, without properly thinking through its potential impact on their cherished principles. As Brimelow's comment implied, by their affirmations of the desirability of Methodist Union, they had put themselves into a position from which any alteration necessarily denoted a retreat. But their case for church autonomy and voluntary ministry had been forcefully propounded for so long that participation in this particular act of union would have seemed inconceivable. It was to take generations, not decades, for Independent Methodists to draw different conclusions from their forebears on the subject of maintained ministry and thereby to look afresh at schemes of union in an age when denominational loyalties would carry far less weight than in former times.

8.2. The Free Church Council Movement

Moves towards greater Christian unity were also advancing on another front during the last decade of the nineteenth century. In 1892 the first Free Church Congress was held and two years later the Independent Methodists, by invitation, sent representatives. Thereafter they became fully and enthusiastically part of the Free Church movement, encouraging churches to support the formation of local councils in their towns and districts.[154] The Connexion strongly affirmed the 1901 Simultaneous Mission of the National Free Church Council (NFCC), under the leadership of Gypsy Smith. Many Independent Methodists, including the Connexion's evangelists, had charge of centres during the mission.[155]

In 1912, the NFCC began to pursue the concept of a United Free Church of England, at the instigation of J.H. Shakespeare, Secretary of the Baptist Union.[156] This led to a Free Church Inquiry which investigated the matter; notwithstanding their retreat from Methodist Union, the Independent Methodists participated in the process.[157] Further stimulus came in a landmark address by Shakespeare to the 1916 Free Church Council Assembly in Bradford. There he spelt out forcefully his view that Free Church divisions were wasteful and caused the Free Churches to be weak and ineffective in the life of the nation. He proposed, as a first step, a Federation of all Free Church denominations. This was received with acclaim by all the denominations and various committees were appointed to produce comprehensive proposals:

> designed not for absorption or amalgamation, but for concerted action and economy of resources. No attempt was made to interfere with the distinctive witness and practice of each body, and the statement of Faith, drafted by Dr. Carnegie Simpson, was never designed to be an exhaustive creed but simply a public and corporate testimony.[158]

From the Independent Methodists' point of view, the only problem was that the draft form of the constitution contained a list of denominations whose ministries were recognised. This did not include the Independent Methodists, as they had 'no regular ministry in the ordinary acceptation of the term'.[159] They duly registered an objection to this part of the proposals, as a result of which the following representatives' meeting agreed to omit the list of denominations, thereby granting ministers of all member denominations the right of recognition.[160] The 1918 Annual Meeting thereupon resolved to join the new Council.[161] With the exception of the Wesleyan Methodists, who deferred their decision for a year, all the Free Churches came together for the first assembly of the Federal Council of Evangelical Free Churches in 1919. Thereafter, this body and the earlier NFCC operated on parallel lines until they were merged in 1940. The Independent Methodists maintained a strong commitment to both bodies throughout this time. However, all the denominations remained attached to their distinctive characteristics and Shakespeare's dream of a United Free Church was never realised.

8.3. A Possible Amalgamation: the Wesleyan Reform Union

For many years, the IM Connexion had maintained links of varying kinds with the Wesleyan Reform Union, a denomination which had its roots in the Wesleyan schism of 1849. Most of the Wesleyan Reformers who separated at the time joined the United Methodist Free Churches in or after 1857. The WRU consisted of those societies and members which chose not to do so.[162] It was of similar size and polity to the Independent Methodists, but had a different geographical base. The main difference between the IM Connexion and the WRU was that the latter allowed for a paid ministry in those of its churches which opted to have it. Contact was first made in 1869,[163] leading eventually to an exchange of visitors at Annual Meetings. In the 1890s an agreement on federal union was made, but in practice little happened.[164]

Fraternal contacts continued during subsequent years, including the time of the Methodist Union discussions, and in 1913 a formal decision was taken to pursue the federal plans of twenty years earlier. A year later, the two denominations met in Bradford, when the WRU put forward a proposal for organic union, whereby each church in the new body would choose its own form of ministry. This was declined by the Independent Methodists, who argued that any church which appointed a single minister would effectively exclude all others from the pulpit. The presenting issue, therefore, was not so much an objection to payment as to the principle of maintaining an open pulpit.[165]

In the 1920s, the matter came under fresh consideration and a scheme of full union was proposed, but again it foundered on the question of paid ministry. This time, the Independent Methodists urged the Wesleyan Reform Union to phase out its paid ministry gradually, but the latter refused, basing its objection on what it saw as a matter of democratic principle:

> If the principle of democratic government is the accepted basis of any institution, religious or civil, then should be accepted also [*sic*] the natural and logical outcome of such democracy, which

must necessarily admit the liberty of the institution to legislate completely for its own affairs, and in so doing it cannot fairly be charged with impinging on the rights of its neighbour, for the rights of the neighbour are precisely the same as its own.

Hence they could not accept the IM proposals:

They are based on the ultimate relinquishing of the rights of our churches to avail themselves individually or in co-operation with other churches of the services of a minister if so determined.[166]

In fact only a minority of WRU churches had paid ministers. The majority operated no differently from the Independent Methodists, who no doubt hoped that their support would provide the necessary leverage for change. However, the WRU argument basically gave independence the moral high ground over other considerations, such as whether a local church chose to pay its minister or not – which in their view was mainly a matter of local preference. The IM President, T.R. Openshaw, was near to the mark when he stated that the reason for the failure of the talks was that the Independent Methodists were coming primarily from a Quaker perspective, while the Wesleyan Reform Union saw the issues through Congregational eyes.[167] Discussions continued for some time, but the possibility of union finally foundered on this issue. No other denomination resembled the IM Connexion remotely as much as the WRU, so this final, failed attempt at union made negotiations with other bodies virtually pointless. While the WRU involved itself with the initial talks leading to the 1932 Methodist Union, the IM Connexion did not. The only course open to it ecumenically was continued co-operation with other free churches locally and nationally.

9. The Schism of 1907-23

The Independent Methodists suffered a major fracture in their ranks, ironically, at a time when ecumenism was on the rise. However, this was not related to theology or even to internal matters of church government; it was entirely a dispute over the nature of Connexional trusteeship. The legal position of those who held funds or property on behalf of the denomination had been raised as long ago as 1875, but remained unresolved at the time.[168] As the nineteenth century gave way to the twentieth, some of the younger men of the Connexion felt that this matter should now be addressed, since the funds were held in the names of three men under a Declaration of Trust to abide by the decisions of the Annual Meeting. Counsel's opinion was sought, resulting in a recommendation to form a company limited by guarantee (to be known as the Independent Methodist Association Incorporated), as other denominations had done, to act as permanent trustee of Connexional funds, thus removing liability on individuals and the recurring need to make new deeds of appointment. The members of Connexional Committee as constituted at each Annual Meeting would be the directors of the Association, which could also act as trustee for individual churches if they so wished.

In 1876, William Brimelow had submitted a proposal to incorporate, but it proved impractical, so the matter was dropped. However, when it was raised in 1903, he was implacably opposed to it, giving as one of his reasons: 'Because Jesus Christ is the head of the Church and that all things therein should be done through the guidance of the Holy Spirit and not through Acts of Parliament.'[169] His considerable weight of influence undoubtedly had the effect of slowing the process down. Not until 1905 was it fully debated at the Annual Meeting and Brimelow further stated his case. He argued that it was wrong that the proposals should be advertised in the secular press, allowing members of the public to object, and that the Connexion should subject itself to having a state document to authorise its object of 'promoting evangelical religion'.[170] He saw it as creating two ranks in the Connexion – one enjoying the privileges of association (the Connexional Committee) and one not. Brimelow was one of the three Connexional trustees at the time, another being Thomas Worthington who was also opposed to the proposals.

The younger leaders (or progressives) took a different view, seeing greater risks in private trusteeship and stressing that the proposed Association could act only with the authority of the Annual Meeting. It was pointed out that churches already had to abide by the law of the land and that the proposals gave the state no say in the doctrines which they preached. At the 1906 Annual Meeting, their proposals were passed by a large majority. However, the strength of feeling on the part of those opposed was such that they pursued all legal means possible to prevent the process of incorporation from materialising. In a formal notice of objection to the Board of Trade, they alleged that the matter had not been properly discussed and that it contravened the fundamental principles of the denomination.[171] In due course, both parties were invited to send delegations to the Board, so that each could state its case. The Board's President (and future Prime Minister), David Lloyd George, chaired the meeting personally and expressed the wish that the two parties would resolve their differences satisfactorily. In a subsequent letter from his secretary, he concluded that there was no reason to refuse the application to incorporate.[172]

Not satisfied with Lloyd George's verdict, the opposing group now took the drastic step of withdrawing their churches from the Connexion and forming a small union of their own which had its own Annual Meeting and published its own magazine. There was undoubtedly great bitterness over the whole matter and the wound took many years to heal. That a legal and domestic issue should have proved a source of division was a tragedy for all concerned. During the earlier part of the division, preachers from one camp were not invited to churches in the other. However, with the passage of the years, attitudes changed. William Burrows wrote from the perspective of the person in the pew at the time:

> Whilst the division emanated from the top, I recall that unity returned from the bottom. Slowly, the division disappeared and the churches began to come together again at circuit level for different purposes. It was with delight that I saw our pulpit filled one Sunday by a preacher from the 'opposite camp' who for years had not been invited to preach because he supported incorporation which our church opposed. What started as a trickle soon became a flood.[173]

The leaders of the majority group made overtures to the minority in 1911 and both groups (paradoxically) were represented at the Methodist Ecumenical Conference in Toronto that year.[174] However, the matter was pursued with greater alacrity from 1916, bearing out Burrows' comment that there was a thaw at grass roots level in some churches. The deaths of some of the leading opponents of incorporation and the geographical moves of others took some of the heat out of the situation. However, not until 1923 did formal reconciliation took place, when an amendment to the Articles of Association satisfied all of the dissident churches. Once again, the desire to stand by an identity and a set of beliefs had overcome conflicts over power and control.

10. The First World War and Its Effects

The Independent Methodists had long raised their voices against armaments and warfare, though their views on the subject were by no means uniform and the outbreak of the war would expose tensions among them. As early as 1901, the Annual Meeting passed resolutions deploring the growing militarism in the country and criticising the government for its continuation of the Boer War.[175] Two years later, it protested against the use of military drills in public elementary schools. The same year saw Salem Church, Nelson, submit a Notice of Motion expressing the desirability of churches observing Peace Sunday in their public services and Sunday Schools.

Before the war even broke out, the Annual Meeting passed a resolution opposing the introduction of compulsory military service and sympathising with conscientious objectors in Australia and New Zealand.[176] However, many young men from the churches volunteered for service from the beginning of the war. Their loss was reflected in a dramatic fall in the number enrolling for the Ministers' Education Scheme.[177] On the home front, churches supported relief funds and assisted the war effort in other ways. Beverley Road Church, Bolton, held a weekly meeting for soldiers' wives, while Wingates members received Belgian refugees into their homes.[178]

The whole issue of war proved contentious. For the first time since the outbreak of hostilities, it was debated openly at the 1915 Annual Meeting. Here, the Independent Methodist attitude showed itself to be less supportive of the war than that of the other Free Churches.[179] Feelings ran high as one speaker asserted, 'The soldier is a murderer. He must murder to save himself.'[180] A resolution tabled by James Vickers urged the immediate seeking of terms of peace and calling on the government to enter into no secret treaties or undertakings without the sanction of Parliament. This was insufficient for the pacifist element who argued that it gave tacit endorsement to the kind of treaty obligations which could take the country into future wars. The proportion of pacifists in the meeting was probably reflected in the voting figures, which saw the resolution passed by fifty-eight votes to twenty-four, suggesting that nearly a third of the delegates opposed British involvement in the war.

As the war took its toll, the Conscription Act was introduced in 1916 to increase the number of soldiers available for service and to replace those lost in battle. However, the Act allowed Ministers of Religion to be exempted from military service. This caused a dilemma for the Independent Methodists, most of whose ministers were engaged in secular employment. Sixty-eight out of 402 were eligible for military service and thereby liable to be conscripted.[181] Should the denomination retain its emphasis on the equality between ministers and members and thereby lose over one-sixth of their ministers (the whole younger generation) to the armed forces – or should they set out to prove that their ministers were a defined body of people, differentiated from other members by the work they did, and thereby risk creating the very kind of spiritual caste which they had always rejected? In the event they opted for the latter course and effectively moved from a semi-Quaker view of ministry to one which bordered on a clerical order.[182]

The Connexion therefore appointed a Sub-Committee to take steps if necessary to make clear the status of IM ministers. A letter was eventually received from the War Office confirming that they were exempt, but this did not prevent the summoning of ministers to local tribunals. It was, in any case, contradicted by a subsequent War Office circular which, on the advice of the Interdenominational Advisory Board of Chaplains, said that all ministers who did not give their whole time to the ministry should prove their status before a court of magistrates.[183] The matter was finally resolved by a Test Case, using a Swinton (Manchester) minister, Arthur Howell, which acknowledged that IM ministers were 'regular ministers of a regular denomination'.[184] From then onwards, a minister only needed a letter from the Connexional Secretary to prove his exemption. This was very significant; for the first time the IM ministry was officially recognised by the civil authorities in the same way as that of other denominations.

Despite the outcome of the Test Case, some ministers chose to undertake military service, while others refused exemption and made their stand as conscientious objectors. One man became a *cause célèbre* both in his town and the IM Connexion. Wilfred Wellock, a minister at Salem, Nelson, wrote:

Mrs Margaret Embleton of Sunderland, first President of the Women's Auxiliary (1916) and the first woman to become Connexional President (1934)

I did not apply for this letter, but the [Connexional] secretary, who knew my stand against war sent me a letter which I had in my pocket when I was before the Tribunal. I refused to produce it because I had opposed the right of ministers to be exempted from military service as a special privilege, since most ministers supported the war, many indeed calling it a holy war.[185]

He was duly imprisoned. Views on conscientious objection varied in the churches as in the country, but, as many Independent Methodists were opposed to the war, there was a tendency to be sympathetic to the objectors and to deplore their repeated prison sentences.[186] The Connexion also protested at the transference of people from service corps to combatant units.[187] As the war continued, the churches counted their losses. A large number of churches reported that nearly all their young men had gone to the war, numbers varying between thirty and 130 in each case.[188] The pages of the magazine each month contained tributes to young men killed in action. Of eighty who had gone from George Street, Oldham, thirteen had lost their lives; other churches had similar experiences. Few families were untouched.

11. Wartime and Post War Innovations

By the end of 1915, about 1,300 men from the IM churches were serving in the armed forces, albeit some of them in ambulance corps and other non-combatant roles. This created a huge gap in the churches, which coincided with a time when female suffrage was a national issue. The Independent Methodists had never formally refused to accord women equal rights with men, but the war put some of them into the forefront of church life in a new way. This led to the idea of having a denominational women's movement which would give women the experience of organising themselves and thereby of learning the skills of leadership. The inspiration came from the Wesleyan Reform Union which already had an organisation which it called the 'Women's Auxiliary' (WA). This had been launched in 1911 with the aim of providing a midweek meeting for women in poorer areas who felt unable to attend Sunday services for want of suitable clothing.[189] Having been made aware of the existence of this organisation, in 1916 Edward Ralphs, Will Price and R.B. Woods took the initiative to encourage the establishment of a similar body in the IM Connexion.[190] Its first meeting took place during the Annual Meeting at Leigh, when over 300 women assembled for the purpose. Among the speakers was Mrs. E. Jacques of Rushden, Northants, who represented the WRU and was able to share its experience over the previous five years.

Within a year, fifty-four branches had been established and 1,610 members had been enrolled. Eventually, nearly every church had its own WA branch, while at Connexional level the women met regularly for devotional purposes and to plan activities, which included the training of women as speakers, magazine articles directed to women's interests, the provision of a Benevolent Fund to assist women dependants of deceased ministers, financial support of overseas missionaries and the issuing of statements, sometimes to the government, on matters of concern. The Women's Auxiliary, albeit much reduced since the vigorous days of its beginnings, continues to the present time.

The aftermath of the First World War prompted the Social Service Committee of the Connexion to launch a new organisation to meet the needs of another group: the young men of the churches, particularly those who had recently been demobbed.[191] Unlike the Women's Auxiliary, which had a devotional emphasis, the Young Men's Fellowship (YMF) concentrated on a social programme and adopted a minimalist theological position, reflecting the extent to which theological liberalism had become the norm among the younger generation of men.[192]

In 1920, no doubt influenced by the success of the recently established Holiday Homes started by other denominations and, notably, the Christian Endeavour movement, the Independent Methodists took steps to establish a Holiday Home of their own. This was largely on the initiative of T.R. Openshaw, an emerging leader in the Connexion and a cotton mill owner. Openshaw became aware that 'Burnside', a large country house near Skipton, Yorkshire, was available for rent, with an option to purchase. In order to secure it, he laid out the initial capital himself and then launched a limited company with individual members of churches as shareholders.[193] This proved an extremely popular move. The house was not only used for holidays, but became a venue for ministers' conferences, teacher training weekends and young people's events.[194] For the first time in its history, the Connexion had premises which provided a focal point for its activities.

Conclusion

Independent Methodism's times of change were met with that conflict between conservative and progressive elements which invariably characterises such times. Ironically, two of the main players during this period would be identified as progressive at one point, but conservative at the next. William Sanderson pressed the adoption of a doctrinal statement and constitution but baulked at the appointment of paid evangelists which the same constitution allowed.[195] William Brimelow advocated the appointment of paid evangelists, but opposed the incorporation of the Connexional Committee, a concept which he had favoured at an earlier date. Yet despite these conflicts, the Independent Methodists were able in time to heal their divisions and move forward together with an ever-increasing programme of corporate activity as they aimed to take their place as an accepted and recognised denomination.

Notes to Chapter Four

1. Quoted from the *New York Tribune* in *IMMag.* 1858, 179.
2. *IMMag.* 1859, 7, 27, 108ff, 332. The papers cited were the *Ballymena Observer, Coleraine Chronicle* and *Banner of Ulster.*
3. *IMMag.* 1860, 30.
4. R. Carwardine, *Transatlantic Revivalism: Popular Evangelicalism in Britain and America 1790-1865* (London: Greenwood Press, 1978), 169.
5. 'Revival at Bolton', *IMMag.* 1859, 57ff; S. Rothwell, *Memorials of Folds Road Independent Methodist Chapel, Bolton* (2 vols.; Bolton: Independent Methodist Bookroom), 1:191.
6. 'All can do Something', *IMMag.* 1860, 253ff.
7. 'Revival in Liverpool', *IMMag.* 1859, 75f.
8. *IMMag.* 1859, 138.
9. *IMMag.* 1861, 439.

10. *IMMag.* 1860, 252.

11. *IMMag.* 1862, 156.

12. M. Edwards, *Methodism and England* (London: Epworth, 1943), 166.

13. W.O. Henderson, *The Lancashire Cotton Famine 1861-1865* (Manchester University Press, 1934), 52f.

14. *Ibid,* 56.

15. IMMins. 1864, 13.

16. IMMins. 1863, 15

17. IMMins. 1863, 6, 11.

18. IMMins. 1863, 33.

19. IMMins. 1864, 39.

20. IMMins. 1864, 38; 1869, 36. This contrasts with the growth in Wesleyan Methodism in the Lancashire cotton towns during these years. R.B. Walker, 'The Growth of Wesleyan Methodism in Victorian England and Wales', *Journal of Ecclesiastical History* vol. 24, no 3 (1973), 270. Perhaps this bears out the IM lament that, as the poorest of the poor, they had less to offer in material terms than other, more prosperous churches.

21. J. Vickers, *History of Independent Methodism* (Wigan: Independent Methodist Bookroom, 1920), 55ff.

22. *Bolton Journal,* 13 June, 1913, 6.

23. See 4.3. Connexional Evangelists for detailed account of the evangelists and their work.

24. IMMins. 1862, 41.

25. *IMMag.* 1876, 202f.

26. CCMins. 1883, 64ff.

27. IMMins. 1881, 15

28. IMMins. 1882, 10.

29. W. Sanderson, *The Life and Labours of William Sanderson* (Wigan: Independent Methodist Bookroom, 1899), 67.

30. *IMMag.* 1870, 85.

31. IMMins.1869, 9

32. The enduring interest of this work, at least for the specialist reader, is reflected in a twentieth century reprint (Orange, California: Ralph E. Welch Foundation, 1961.)

33. IMMins. 1870, 56.

34. W. Brimelow, 'Our Denominational Name,' *IMMag.*1894, 185ff.

35. *IMMag.* 1895, 230.

36. *IMMag.* 1898, 226.

37. *Ibid,* 229

38. See Appendix 12.

39. IMMins. 1885, 107f.

40. J. Munson, *The Nonconformists: In search of a lost culture* (London: SPCK, 1991), 11, 90.

41. During the years 1841-1881, the number of miners in the Lancashire and North-Eastern coalfields trebled. R. Church, *The History of the British Coal Industry,* (3 vols.; Oxford: Clarendon Press, 1986), 1:189.

42. See 4.2. for an account of the Christian Lay Churches.

43. R. Moore, *Pitmen, Preachers and Politics* (Cambridge University Press,

1974), 15.

44. 'Memoir of James Garner, late of Haydock in the Liverpool Circuit', *IMMag.* 1870, 86f.

45. Details collated from IMMins. 1870 and A. Mounfield, *A Short History of Independent Methodism* (Independent Methodist Bookroom, 1905), 132.

46. Mounfield, *Short History,* 189ff.

47. *Independent Methodist Church, Platt Bridge, Jubilee Celebrations,* 1916, 3.

48. W.G. Burrows, *Independent Methodist Church, West Street, St. Helens, Centenary 1892-1992,* 5.

49. Information supplied by W.G. Burrows.

50. IMMins. 1868, 38.

51. *Souvenir, Independent Methodist Church, New Seaham, Jubilee Celebrations 1877-1927,* 6.

52. *IMMag.* 1870, 105.

53. *Independent Methodist Church, Easington Lane, Jubilee 1881-1931,* 14.

54. Mounfield, *Short History,* 148.

55. *Ibid,* 181. IMMins. 1869, 45.

56. Mounfield, *Short History,* 203.

57. N.T.R. Dickson, 'The Church itself is God's Clergy' in D.W. Lovegrove (ed.) *The Rise of the Laity in Evangelical Protestantism* (London: Routledge, 2002), 221.

58. 'The Late Thomas Buck of Ravenstonedale', *IMMag.* 1869, 31ff.

59. IMMins. 1865, 50.

60. IMMins. 1881, 8.

61. G.E. Milburn, *The Christian Lay Churches and their Origins* (Sunderland, 1977), 9.

62. *Ibid,* 13.

63. *Sunderland Daily Echo,* 3 March 1877, 3.

64. Christian Lay Churches, Preachers' Plan, February-May 1877.

65. Milburn, *Lay Churches,* 29.

66. *Ibid,* 23.

67. *Ibid,* 31.

68. *Ibid,* 38.

69. *Jubilee History, Mount Zion Independent Methodist Church, Bristol, 1885-1935,* 2.

70. Vickers, *History,* 198f.

71. Mounfield, *Short History,* 199.

72. J. Macpherson, *Henry Moorhouse, the English Evangelist* (London: Morgan and Scott Ltd, und.) Moorhouse was credited with influencing D.L. Moody and also brought Ira D. Sankey to sing at the Stretford Church. 'The Moody Centenary', *IMMag. 1937, 42.*

73. J. Holmes, *Religious Revivals in Britain and Ireland 1859-1905* (Dublin: Irish Academic Press, 2000), 148.

74. IMMins. 1867, 54.

75. 'Times of Refreshing', *IMMag.* 1874, 75; W. Boon, 'Christian Unity', *IMMag.* 1876,102. IMMins 1875, 60. Two of the three reports make the point that Moody's mission was an example of Christians working together regardless of

denominational differences. This appears to have been one of the factors that caused Independent Methodists eventually to re-think their sectarianism in favour of a more ecumenical spirit.

76. I. Sellers, *Nineteenth-Century Noncomformity* (London: Edward Arnold, 1977), 9.
77. IMMins. 1868, 39.
78. *IMMag.* 1875, 244.
79. *IMMag.* 1875, 247
80. CCMins. June 1876.
81. Sanderson, *Life and Labours,* 129.
82. CCMins. August 1876.
83. *Ibid.*
84. Evangelistic Committee Minutes 1889-1924, 16.
85. ECMins. 70.
86. ECMins. *passim.*
87. Minutes of the Warrington Independent Methodist Circuit, 1877.
88. IMMins. 1878, 17.
89. IMMins. 1878, 18.
90. See Chapter 3 and Appendix 10.
91. Vickers, *History,* 202.
92. ECMins. 179.
93. For the spread of the Connexion when the major era of evangelistic expansion was at its height, see Figure 3, page 193, which shows the distribution of churches in 1901. With the exception of the agricultural areas of Nottinghamshire and North Staffordshire, it remained predominantly an urban denomination.
94. Letter: Matthew Kennedy to William Brimelow, 25 September 1894; Letter: Matthew Kennedy to Evangelistic Committee, 19 June 19 1895.
95. CCMins. 1877.
96. Sanderson, *Life and Labours,* 130.
97. IMMins. 1868, 48.
98. *IMMag.* 1900, 215.
99. Printed as an Appendix to IMMins. 1866.
100. Independent Methodist Churches Model Deed and Deed of Reference (Wigan: Independent Methodist Bookroom, 1898).
101. Letter: J. Cullen to W. Sanderson, *IMMag.* 1866, 944.
102. *Ibid.*
103. Letter: J. Cullen to J. Vickers, *IMMag.* 1869, 274.
104. *IMMag.* 1880, 130ff.
105. *IMMag.* 1889, 200
106. *IMMag.* 1911, 104.
107. *IMYB* 1913, 46
108. *IMYB* 1914, 53
109. Vickers, *History,* 308.
110. *Ibid.*
111. i.e. Bolton (Noble Street), Barnoldswick, Horwich, Moorside, Roe Green, Nelson (Salem).
112. Figures drawn from the website: Family Search, www.familysearch.org, © 1992-2002 Intellectual Reserve Inc.

113. For comparable figures of local preachers in other branches of Methodism, see C.D. Field, 'The Methodist Local Preacher: An Occupational Analysis' in G.E. Milburn and M. Batty (eds.), *Workaday Preachers* (Peterborough: Methodist Publishing House, 1995), 223f. See also Brown, *Nonconformist Ministry*, 20ff. for analyses of entrants into nonconformist ministries in the nineteenth century.

114. 'Claiming Equality with other Ministers', *IMMag.* 1874, 270f.

115. *IMMag.* 1855, 19. Sarah Fitzgerald, originally from the IM Church at Oswestry, was a successful author of Methodist fiction

116. R. Lee, *Sixty Years a Preacher* (Wigan: J. Starr and Sons, 1923), 38f.

117. IMMins. 1889, 69.

118. *IMMag.* 1894, 229f.

119. E. Ralphs, 'Church Life Fifty Years Ago' in *Independent Quarterly* 1936, 145.

120. If anything, the Connexion encouraged political involvement. See Chapter 5.

121. A. Walker, *A Souvenir Centenary History, Smith Street, Oldham 1837-1937*, 70.

122. *IMMag.* 1898, 45, 54.

123. A. Dalby, *The History of Waterside Chapel 1821-1951* (1951), 26. E. Howell, *Whispers of Wingates* (1984), 96.

124. E.g. the organ opening at Sindsley (Lancashire), *IMMag.* 1879, 178f.

125. *Ibid,* 39f.

126. 'A Sunday School Excursion to Llandudno in North Wales', *IMMag.* 1866, 749ff.

127. *Local Notes and Gleanings: Oldham and Neighbourhood in Bygone Times* (Oldham: Express Office, 1887), n.p.

128. See Chapter 5.

129. R.M. Jones, 'Has Christianity been tried?' *IMMag.* 1903, 220.

130. Information supplied by W.P. Lockley and confirmed by church members who remembered this practice.

131. See Chapter 2 for an account of Independent Methodism's early involvement with the temperance movement and the impact of temperance on the denomination during the ensuing decades.

132. Rothwell, *Folds Road,* 1:198.

133. *IMMag.* 1869, 310f.

134. Howell, *Wingates*, 74.

135. See Chapter 5 for the Connexion's responses to various licensing bills.

136. See Appendix 4.

137. 'The Ecumenical Methodist Conference', *IMMag.* 1881, 361ff.

138. Sanderson, *Life and Labours,* 160f.

139. W. Redfern, 'Unions and Reunions Effected' in W.J. Townsend et al, *A New History of Methodism.* (2 vols.; London: Hodder and Stoughton, 1909), 2:447f.

140. 'The Ecumenical Council', *IMMag.* 1891, 375.

141. Paper: 'United Methodist Committee on Concerted Action amongst the Methodist Churches of Great Britain', 1903.

142. R. Currie, *Methodism Divided* (London: Faber and Faber, 1968), 240ff.

143. O.A. Beckerlegge, *The United Methodist Free Churches* (London: Epworth,

1957), 100. The IM Annual Meeting reported the development with approval but took no action. *IMYB* 1902, 98.

144. Letter: G. Packer to E. Barker, 9 May 1903. The involvement of the IM Connexion in the pre-1907 discussions, albeit briefly, has been largely unmentioned by historians of Methodist union.

145. *Independent Methodist Year Book,* 1903, 101.

146. *Ibid,* 105f.

147. W. Brimelow and A. Watson , 'Notes on Methodist Union', November 25th, 1903. See Appendix 5 for the full text of this circular.

148. CCMins. November 30th, 1903, 284.

149. CCMins. 11 February 1904, 285.

150. Letter: W. Brimelow to E. Barker, 7 March 1904.

151. CCMins. 8 March 1904, 290.

152. Letter: G. Packer to E. Barker, 16 May 1904.

153. *IMYB* 1904, 49.

154. CCMins. 1892, 606; *IMYB* 1894, 31.

155. *IMYB* 1901, 47

156. E.K.H. Jordan, *Free Church Unity* (London: Lutterworth, 1956), 127ff.

157. *IMYB* 1913, 51.

158. Jordan, 133. His comment on the Statement of Faith is significant to IM history, since the Independent Methodists in 1927 adopted it in a modified form as a replacement for its far more credal predecessor, the 'Testimony and Principles of Union'.

159. *IMYB* 1917, 42f., CCMins. 1917, 220f.

160. *IMYB* 1918, 48. The Independent Methodists received support in the meeting from the Wesleyan leaders J. Scott Lidgett, Luke Wiseman and Maldwyn Hughes.

161. *IMYB,* 1918, 15.

162. J.A. Vickers (ed.) *A Dictionary of Methodism in Britain and Ireland* (London: Epworth, 2000), 386.

163. *IMMag.* 1869, 172f.

164. *IMMag.* 1893, 233f.

165. CCMins. 1915, 141.

166. *IMMag.* 1922, 97ff.

167. *IMYB* 1926, 26.

168. Incorporation Proposals Explained (Wigan, 1904), 1f.

169. Letter: William Brimelow to George Hunter (President), 5 October 1903.

170. *IMMag.* 1905, 150ff.

171. Proposed Independent Methodist Association (Incorporated), Notice of Objection, 17 November 1906.

172. Letter: G.S. Barnes, Board of Trade, to Messrs. Taylor and Sons, Solicitors, 7 February 1907. An account of the meeting was recorded in an undated MS by Will Price (IMA).

173. W. Burrows, 'Independent Methodist History Part IV, Period 1907-1923', *IMMag.* August 1982, 6.

174. J. Murray, *Independent Methodist History 1905-1955* (Wigan: Independent Methodist Bookroom, 1955), 4.

175. *IMYB* 1901, 19.

176. *IMYB* 1913, 26f.
177. This became more marked as the war progressed. *IMYB* 1917, 21.
178. *IMYB* 1915, 44.
179. David Lloyd George addressed a large Free Church gathering at the City Temple in November 1914. In response to his address, the meeting passed a resolution 'pledging nonconformity to the fight.' Jordan, *Free Church Unity*, 140f.
180. *Oldham Daily Standard*, 23 June 1915, 2. *IMMag.* 1915, 123ff..
181. MS List of ministers eligible for military service, compiled by the Connexional Secretary, James Vickers.
182. The denomination would never admit that this was the implication of its decision and continued to deny any distinction between ministers and others.
183. *IMYB* 1917, 36f. The IM Connexion failed to secure the appointment of any its ministers to chaplaincy work. Few requested to be appointed and the war was almost over when they applied. The Chaplaincy Board would therefore have been unfamiliar with IM practice and would simply have been concerned to prevent spurious applications.
184. Murray, *History*, 20f..
185. W. Wellock, *Off the Beaten Track* (India: Sarva Seva Sangh Prakashan Varanashi, 3rd Edition, 1980), 33. See also Chapter 5 for details of his influence on IM theology and his career as a politician.
186. *IMYB* 1918, 40.
187. CCMins. 1917, 218.
188. *IMYB* 1918, 41f.
189. W.H. Jones, *One is Your Master* (Sheffield: Wesleyan Reform Church House, und.) 56f.
190. F.E. Woods and G. Rodgers, *History of Women's Auxiliary 1916-1966*, 2.
191. CCMins. 1919, 274.
192. See Chapter 5.
193. CCMins. 1920, 292.
194. Murray, *History,* 28.
195. See Appendix 3, Constitution Clause 10.

Chapter 5
The Wider Interface:
Independent Methodism in its
Contemporary Context, 1860-1927

As Chapter 4 has shown, Independent Methodism changed almost beyond recognition during the period 1860-1927. However, no account of its metamorphosis would be complete without an examination of the various external factors which served to re-shape it. Most notable among them were the increasing involvement of its members in politics, the education controversies which touched all churches, the impact of theological change and IM attitudes on social issues such as temperance. Out of these came changed perspectives and values, while growth in the denomination and increased material prosperity in their own lives made the IM people more vocal and self-assured than in previous generations.

1. Theological Change

It is difficult to establish exactly when new trends in theology began to impact upon Independent Methodism. Other denominations present the same problem, but with one major difference. While new learning had a natural seed-bed in nonconformist theological colleges, Independent Methodism had no equivalent establishments. It would have been entirely understandable if this small denomination had remained aloof and isolated from theological change, but the opposite was the case. Though late starters, they were just as affected by this process as other denominations and had to learn their way through it.

Just as the nation's chapels fostered elementary education through their Sunday Schools in the early nineteenth century, so they promoted the wider pursuit of knowledge in the latter part of the century and so opened young minds to a world of intellectual enquiry. In 1859, William Sanderson acknowledged the churches' need to increase their 'intellectual level',[1] which was a *volte-face* from his attitude less than a decade earlier when he locked horns with an Independent minister on the subject of ministerial education. On that occasion, he argued that ministers could derive all the wisdom they needed from the Bible and everyday life, and that there was no need for 'metaphysical reasonings.'[2] Within a few short years, the growing sense of the importance of advanced learning had begun to focus even the minds of those, such as Sanderson, who had been resistant to change.

Two sources of mental stimulation, common to other nonconformists, facilitated the Independent Methodists' learning and opinion-forming. Firstly, the ubiquitous chapel library opened a window into the world of learning for a generation which was gradually becoming literate but remained too poor to afford books. The leaders of Folds Road Church, Bolton, proudly declared that they had a library of 1,100 volumes 'containing standard works upon religion, moral philosophy, art and science, adapted to elevate the mind, and shield young people from the light & mischievous literature of the present day.'[3] Some libraries contained material mainly of a religious nature, but others carried a wide range of subjects; far from 'shielding' young people, they served to open their minds to fresh arenas of thought.

Secondly, from the middle of the century, many churches established Mutual Improvement Classes or Societies, often started by the young men of the churches, where essays were read or lectures given by the members. Like the libraries, some societies were purely theological, while others gave themselves a much wider brief. In either case, they helped young people to learn to express themselves or to expound and defend arguments. However, in the characteristically poor areas where Independent Methodists were often found, the prospect of presenting papers to an audience was simply too daunting for some manual workers. Salem, Pendleton, Salford, situated among mills and factories, claimed some success in overcoming this problem by the use of a manuscript magazine in which the older Sunday School scholars could write pseudonymously on any subject of interest, sacred or secular.[4] Pendleton was hardly the easiest of areas for the seed of advanced learning to take root, but efforts such as its manuscript magazine provided important stepping stones to cultural and material advancement as well as spiritual challenge for its younger generation. At a slightly later date, the Pleasant Sunday Afternoon Societies found in several IM churches provided further opportunities for members to consider topics of interest, religious or otherwise. Such groups sometimes attracted people with no church allegiance and therefore served as part of the church's interface with the local community. Through them, the rising generation inevitably re-evaluated its faith in the light of its learning.

In an address to the 1867 Annual Meeting, James Vickers, Sr. (1822-1879) spoke of 'The Importance of the Acquisition of General Knowledge.'[5] Referring to a teachers' preparation class of earlier years, he described how their discussions on creation had led to an interest in geology and astronomy. He contrasted the experience of the older generation who had few resources for learning in their younger days, with the younger people who, he said, should now be equipped to use their learning in defence of their faith. Vickers' church at Bolton also had a thriving Young Men's Association, begun in 1863, which went into these subjects in some depth. Darwinism was currently challenging long-held beliefs about creation, while geological researchers argued for a much older Earth than the biblical timescale seemed to suggest. In a lengthy paper to the Association, later printed in the denominational magazine, an anonymous writer aimed to reconcile geology with the Bible.[6] Having described current thought on the Earth's structure and rock formation, he turned to the six days of creation, citing various early Christian writers in support of his view that the 'days' actually represented much longer periods.

This group of young men faced the same issues as others across the country as they wrestled with the impact of scientific theory and discovery upon certain aspects of Christian belief. While awareness of biblical criticism would come only at a later date, the Independent Methodists of the 1860s were just as conscious of scientific issues as their contemporaries in the larger denominations. The publication of an article questioning the literality of the creation account in the denomination's magazine (without any published counter-argument) indicated how quickly the rising generation was absorbing new thinking. By the end of the century, Independent Methodism, in company with the Free Churches generally, had largely embraced evolutionism. Edward Ralphs described how, at the 1896 Free Church Congress, 'speakers vied with each other to commend Darwinism.'[7] Initially, many were concerned to use their new-found knowledge (as Vickers senior had hoped) to defend traditional views of faith, but as other factors entered the debate in the ensuing years, the entire corpus of Christian belief would gradually acquire very different interpretations.

Towards the end of the nineteenth century, biblical criticism began to impact on the Independent Methodists as on other denominations and traditional views of biblical authority came to be questioned. The choice of books for the Ministers' Education Scheme reflected the critical approach, prompting some controversy at the 1908 Annual Meeting, as not everyone had embraced the new thinking. John Wright Johnson (1861-1915), businessman and Sunderland town councillor, argued that some of the chosen textbooks contradicted the Connexion's official beliefs, particularly in relation to the authority of Scripture, as expressed in the *Testimony and Principles of Union*. Arthur Mounfield, one of the examiners and editor of the connexional magazine, refuted Johnson's allegations and reported the discussion in a way which affronted Johnson even further:

> What did they[8] understand by 'Word of God?' In the New Testament it was Christ and not the Bible who was spoken of as the Word. When Paul said, 'Preach the Word,' he did not mean Preach the Bible but Preach Christ. 'In the beginning was the Word,' and 'Word' was a general and common title for the Messiah. Then again to say, as had been said, that the Bible is the only rule of faith was misleading. Christ committed His Church not to the guidance of a book, but to the guidance of the Spirit. The Bible is precious as bearing witness to Christ, and Christ is infinitely greater than the Bible. The Bible, like the Church, was one of the fruits of the Spirit; it has been mightily used of the Spirit, but to put the Bible in the place of the Spirit was to reverse the true order and to make confusion.[9]

Johnson's response came in a lengthy letter to Mounfield, intended for publication in the magazine, with a point-by-point rebuttal of his remarks, focusing on what he regarded as Mounfield's disingenuous use of language and questioning his Word-Spirit antithesis.[10] He also accused the editor of not reporting his own statements correctly. Johnson then circulated copies of his letter to all members of the Connexional Committee and demanded an embargo on using the magazine to propagate doctrines other than those held by the Connexion. He also continued, without success, to press Mounfield to publish his letter.

The Connexional Committee's tardy response mirrored the doubts which many members felt. Ellis Barker, the Connexional Secretary, regarded the matter as an unwelcome theological controversy and attempted to placate Johnson by suggesting that he and Mounfield resolve the matter privately and amicably.[11] However, Johnson was not prepared to settle for anything less than an open vindication of his position and a public repudiation of Mounfield's published statement. He wrote:

> I have done my best I could [*sic*] to get the Editor to face the position he has placed himself and the Connexion in, but he persists in his attempts to evade the issue. . . . The matter is of so great importance, in my opinion, that I cannot agree to its being shelved. I am determined that my reply shall reach our people. If the Editor be permitted to print such matter and then to close the pages against correction and prevent my access to those who have read his words, I must adopt another way to reach them, and reach them I certainly will.[12]

A week later, a letter from the Northern Counties Confederation gave full support to Johnson's position.[13] Connexional Committee – still unwilling to grasp the nettle – appointed a sub-committee to consider the matter.[14] The outcome of its deliberations was to ask Mounfield to write a paragraph in the magazine indicating that 'it was not his intention in his remarks in the Annual Meeting . . . to express any want of adherence to the Constitution of the Connexion in its reference to the Bible as the "Word of God" '.[15] Mounfield finally complied and wrote:

> The passage 'To say that the Bible is the only rule of faith is misleading' was used in conjunction with the passage 'The Spirit of Truth shall lead you into all the truth.' We cannot imagine the guidance of the Spirit being at variance with the guidance of the Bible, since the Bible is the gift of the Spirit for guidance and instruction.[16]

Johnson's tenacity had finally won him a reply, even if it fell short of what he wanted. Thereafter the matter was dropped.

At the following Annual Meeting, the new President, Ward Riding, referred positively to biblical criticism and added, 'We can never return to a theology which demands us to accept the Bible as a book of astronomy or geology or natural history.'[17] He then quoted Marcus Dods: 'I never understood what the infallibility of scripture was, and wherein it consisted until criticism demanded that I should cease to identify infallibility with literal accuracy.' At a later stage, even the Canon of Scripture was challenged. Arthur Mounfield, commenting on the Apocrypha, observed, 'Some of the writings are crude and are better left out, but on the other hand there are some we would gladly put back within the covers of the Bible.'[18] By this time, his nemesis, Johnson, was dead and no one challenged him. When, eventually, the Connexion rescinded the *Testimony and Principles of Union*, the new *Statement of Faith and Practice* (1927) would capture the more muted ideas of biblical authority held by the current generation of leaders:

> The Scriptures, delivered through men as moved by the Holy Spirit . . . record and interpret the revelation of redemption, and contain the sure Word of God concerning our salvation and all things necessary thereto.[19]

Of course, by implication, if the Scriptures merely 'contain' the Word of God, they can also contain that which is *not* the Word of God. Such subtleties of wording would satisfy those who could no longer affirm the plenary inspiration of Scripture, without necessarily disturbing those who adopted a more conservative view. On the basis of this form of theological accommodation, the Connexion operated for the next 57 years.

The Johnson-Mounfield conflict revealed an important factor in IM theological development during the earlier part of the twentieth century: the renascent Quakerism which Mounfield and others embraced. As Editor of the magazine for forty years, Mounfield made it a vehicle of Quaker thought, using the distinguished Friend Dr Rufus Jones as a monthly columnist and adding numerous articles of his own on Quaker history. Quakerism featured in other aspects of denominational life, including overseas missionary work.[20] When the Young Men's Fellowship was launched in 1919, the syllabus used for its meetings was the one published by the Quaker Adult School Union.

The theological dimension of new thought surfaced in 1889, when William Brimelow gave the Annual Meeting a foretaste of ideas which were later propagated through the writings of Adolf von Harnack.[21]

> Christ taught the great truth of the common Fatherhood of God and the common brotherhood of man; and when mankind arrives at a proper conception and realization of the fact that we are all brothers and sisters, members of the vast family of whom God is the Father, then injustice and wrongdoing, and anger and strife will disappear, and love and peace and righteousness and concord will take their place.[22]

Brimelow's son, James, spoke in similar terms two years later:

> The life and purpose of Jesus Christ was to establish a Gospel of brotherhood on this earth. . . . To this end, Christ gave the world a new conception of God and a new conception of man; he taught the Fatherhood of God and the divinity of human nature.[23]

To the average Independent Methodist hearer, these messages sounded noble, high-minded and credible. Few would be sufficiently discerning to see that their implications would sound the death-knell of their ideas of the corruption of human nature, the need for personal salvation and the call to repentance. This switch of focus, which was widespread by the early years of the twentieth century, effectively took the heart out of orthodox, evangelical Christian belief and would later prompt the often-quoted dictum of H. Richard Niebuhr, that, 'A God without wrath brought men without sin into a kingdom without judgment through the ministrations of a Christ without a cross.'[24]

The biblical picture of the Kingdom of God was gently being replaced by a form of universalism – the brotherhood of man. Some have expressed the view that this new doctrine had the effect of feeding nationalism in Germany, leading up to the First World War.[25] However, its effect among

British Christians was not a strident nationalism, but an internationalist outlook which eventually became expressed in enthusiasm for the League of Nations. The Independent Methodists warmly welcomed its formation:

> The effectiveness of the League being entirely dependent upon the weight of an informed and Christianized public opinion behind it, we earnestly urge the members of our churches and congregations to take a live interest in this supremely important matter. . . .[26]

The general emphasis of most preachers was on the 'spirit and example' of Jesus, rather than the historic doctrines of justification by faith, atonement and redemption. Richard Knight wrote, 'I was once told that I was a disciple of a certain saintly teacher because I looked up to him as an ideal and loved and esteemed him. I think that is a true conception of discipleship.'[27] The picture of Jesus Christ as incarnate Son of God, Saviour and Lord, was giving way to the image of a heroic, admirable figure, the embodiment of humanity at its best, representing the immanent God and imbued with divinity much as all living things were. As Kenneth Brown has observed, by 1900 liberal theology had become the accepted norm and 'many ministers were left preaching little more than an amorphous gospel of good works and ethics.'[28]

Matthew Kennedy, currently one of the Connexion's evangelists, took up the theme of the social implications of the gospel and linked it to the anti-credalism which was becoming increasingly a characteristic of the age:

> Something more than dogma is required to convince a reading, thoughtful, observant community that Christianity is a reality. Creeds without deeds will never win the world for Christ. It is not enough to preach the doctrines of faith, repentance and conversion. In addition to these doctrines which are necessary to save souls, there must be other doctrines promulgated that will save bodies. The church of the past has been too much a manufactory of creeds, but the church of tomorrow will be a manufactory of character. . . . The church of the past has preached the doctrine of contentment to the toiling masses who were working twelve hours a day for starvation wages. . . . But the church of the future will preach a more acceptable doctrine than that.[29]

The seeds of Kennedy's ideas came not only from increased Christian concern for humanity, but also from a re-interpretation of certain doctrines. When R. W. Dale expounded the significance of the atonement, he expressed the work of Christ in orthodox terms, but made the redemption of the human race its goal, thus taking it beyond a purely individual application.[30] This interpretation sat well with the emerging 'social gospel' which, as S.E. Keeble put it, was 'bent on saving not only the individual but society; of setting up in the earth the Kingdom of Heaven.'[31] It had a ready enough appeal to Unitarians, but in effect attacked sacramentalism and pietism alike as being inadequate expressions of the gospel.[32] Henry Brimelow, leader of the Mission Band at Folds Road, Bolton, felt that its work ought to include material relief to the poor in the church's vicinity:

> The whole neighbourhood is wretched – filthy – vile – and it seems to me that if there is anything in the gospel of the Lord Jesus Christ, here is a splendid opportunity for putting it on its trial . . . so far as I am concerned, my faith in that gospel is so bound up with this work that, just according to whether it succeeds or fails, that faith stands or falls.[33]

The views of Kennedy and Brimelow reflected the 'social gospel' which was emerging at the time. It should not be confused with theological liberalism, though the two sets of ideas often came together. The 'social gospel' tied in with socialist convictions and attracted men such as Wilfred Wellock (1879-1972), a preacher from an early age at Salem Church, Nelson, and Independent Labour Party activist.[34] His autobiographical account of his theological views reflected what was happening in the denomination. To Wellock, it was a mistake to accept a theology which focused only on man's battle against sin. Issues such as social justice and peace were at the fore of his thinking, just as they were with others of his generation.[35]

Nevertheless, throughout this period, evangelistic work continued, appeals were made, converts were counted and new churches were formed. Spiritual fervour persisted and, in some places, echoes of earlier revivalism remained. At Sutton, St. Helens, 'Curly' James Johnson, miner and church trustee, initiated a prayer meeting early on Sunday mornings, to pray for revival. In January 1905, he saw its outcome as six weeks of open air meetings and nightly evangelistic meetings resulted in 130 conversions amid scenes of Pentecostal-style fervour.[36] Similar stories came from other churches. Many churches and preachers showed little interest in theological debate, while some of those who promoted a social gospel saw it as complementary to the call to personal commitment rather than an alternative to it. George Hunter (1858-1932) shared many of the ideas of his contemporaries but retained an evangelistic edge. During the years of theological change, despite his numerous civic and business interests, Hunter was constantly looking out for new mission opportunities. By the 1920s, he had been instrumental in the establishment of the churches at Tyldesley, Westleigh, Mill Lane (Leigh) and Astley, using the classic methods of open air preaching, visitation and consolidation.[37]

At Connexional level, only John Wright Johnson remained a significant counter-voice to overt liberalism. His views were largely influenced by his association with the Pentecostal League of Prayer, having met its leader, Reader Harris, while on one of his business trips to London in 1893. The League encouraged its members to pray for revival and the spread of scriptural holiness as taught by John Wesley. Johnson began its first branch outside London and his church (Robert Street) became the venue for its meetings.[38] Later, he became the League's North of England Secretary.[39] In 1913 he began a two year term of office as IM President and used his inaugural address to warn against what he saw as the danger of a liberal treatment of Scripture.[40] A year later, he spoke of the decline which seemed to him inevitable where 'modernist' teaching was accepted and called for strong personal prayer life, family prayers and tithing.[41] Tragically, he and his son were killed in a train crash in 1915, though his church and others in the area maintained their strong holiness position long afterwards, despite the Connexion's drift in the opposite direction. The involvement of prominent Keswick Convention speaker W. Graham Scroggie as speaker at his funeral indicated something of Johnson's stature among the evangelicals of his time.[42]

The tensions between conservative and liberal evangelicals reached breaking point in a series of controversies between 1913 and 1928.[43] It is relevant to note which way the Independent Methodists jumped in relation to the divide which followed. One of the most widely publicised points of conflict came in Dayton, Tennessee, in 1925, when a young teacher was brought to trial for teaching evolution, despite state laws forbidding him to do so.[44] Commenting on this incident, the Independent Methodist President, T.R. Openshaw, defended the young man and expressed support for Darwin's principle of the survival of the fittest. He then contended (in a strange piece of anthropology) that Pentecost supported the evolutionary principle, causing the human race to become a higher species than in pre-Christian times.[45] According to his logic, it had effected an ontological change not merely on Christians but the entire human race. This had massive implications, not only for pneumatology, but also for missiology. The school of thought which Openshaw and his contemporaries had embraced would plainly take them further towards a humanitarian rather than a conversionist gospel.

2. Political Involvement

2.1. The Conflation of Religion and Politics

It remains a matter of debate whether nonconformists' spirituality shaped their political thought or whether their politics ultimately hampered their spirituality. In examining this subject, Timothy Larsen concluded that perhaps the relationship between faith and politics could be symbiotic rather than competitive.[46] However, most denominations experienced this symbiosis at least partly through the balance between a theologically trained ministry and the influence of powerful lay people who were making their mark in public life. Late nineteenth century Independent Methodists were under the leadership of lay people who were untrained theologically and whose statements showed all the signs that the religion-politics symbiosis, in this instance, was unequal in proportion. Political thought was increasingly informing faith rather than *vice versa*. Church democracy became the corollary of democracy in public life as the words of Matthew Kennedy indicated:

> What is Independent Methodism? Or what is an Independent Methodist Church? It is composed of a number of persons who accept the doctrines and assent to the polity of the Union. One distinctive feature of the polity is the principle of democracy. Each church manages its affairs, and we have not only household suffrage, but also manhood suffrage – yea, even womanhood suffrage. The lodger franchise has also been secured. This comes in for poor bachelors. So that we may safely conclude that an Independent Methodist Church is a Democratic society. If that be so then we are democrats. Democracy means government by the people and for the people.[47]

To Kennedy and others of his generation, the concept of democracy had become as sacred as any biblical doctrine. This had its roots in the denomination's history of connections to the Radical Reform movement and Chartism and now flowered in the new age of extended suffrage.

2.2. The Second Parliamentary Reform Act, 1867

After the demise of the Chartists, the Independent Methodists had shown little evidence of involvement in reformist politics, but this simply reflected the wider picture in the nation.[48] However, the passing of the second Parliamentary Reform Act of 1867 effectively doubled the electorate, which now included the more prosperous elements of the working class.[49] This brought an unprecedented opportunity for newly-enfranchised free church people to become an influence in both municipality and nation. Those Independent Methodists who were now eligible to vote took part enthusiastically in the following year's General Election.

IM political interest was further boosted at the end of 1868, when Alexander Denovan finally retired as editor of the *Independent Methodist Magazine*, to be succeeded by William Brimelow, then a young journalist with an eye to the wider world and an active member of the Liberal Party. From this point on, matters of public concern, particularly points of legislation affecting nonconformists, were regularly brought to readers' attention and became the subjects of published correspondence. The transition of editorship at this point was remarkably timely, bringing the Connexion into a wider sphere just at the time when nonconformity was beginning to be a significant force in the political realm.

2.3. The Liberation Society

The IM Annual Meeting in 1867 allowed representatives of the Liberation Society to commend to the churches their agenda of church/state separation and the ending of all discrimination on grounds of creed.[50] This almost certainly indicated that some of the IM leaders of the time were linked with the Liberation Society, particularly at local branch level. The Liberationists' message was received with acclaim and the representatives duly distributed papers and tracts for the delegates to take back to their churches. Disestablishment had a ready appeal to Independent Methodists, who, like other nonconformists, resented the privileged position of the Church of England.

2.4. The Liberal Party

Independent Methodists in general wanted to see a just society where self-determination belonged to the many rather than the privileged few. This would inevitably draw their allegiance to parties or pressure groups which were concerned with democratic reform, not least in the removal of the religious disabilities which dissenters had long suffered. Despite some reservations, mainly from the Wesleyan Methodists, nonconformists generally were more inclined to be politically Liberal since the Liberal party had a more overtly reforming agenda (though it was Disraeli's Conservatives who carried the Second Reform Act). Independent Methodists, like other nonconformists, had enormous personal respect for the Liberal leader, William Gladstone, whose views on moral values at personal and corporate levels were similar to their own.[51]

In 1868, with an eye to the first General Election under the new franchise, when many of their people would be voting for the first time, they tabled a potentially controversial resolution to the Annual Meeting:

> That this meeting rejoices in the effort now being made to place all sections of the Christian church on an equal footing, and would earnestly urge all our friends to aid by their votes and influence at the next General Election, those candidates only who pledge themselves to support the measures of the Right Hon. William Ewart Gladstone with reference thereto.[52]

In the debate which followed the resolution, some speakers disapproved of the principle of introducing political matters while others objected to endorsing particular candidates or parties. However, one voice provided the response which would encapsulate the IM political stance for the next forty years:

> Mr. Brimelow remarked that there was a point at which religion and politics closely touched each other, and we should be careful in discountenancing politics lest we were refusing our aid to the cause of religious progress. The question before the country was not a mere matter of Toryism or Reform, but of religious freedom and equality.

John Holland (Manchester) thought all Independent Methodists should go with the Liberals, while William Sanderson argued that Toryism was inconsistent with Independent Methodist principles. Those who disagreed were heavily outnumbered and, in the years that followed, political debates and resolutions featured regularly in Annual Meetings, invariably supporting Gladstone and the Liberals. The fact that Gladstone was the sitting member for South-West Lancashire, where many IM churches were located, as well as Liberal leader, gave weight to their support for him. The Liberalism of Gladstone made a natural home for people whose roots were in the political radicalism of the earlier part of the century. It matched the aspirations of the mainly working class Independent Methodists who wanted a more equitable social structure in an age before British socialism had taken root. More significantly, however, the widened franchise meant that they now operated not from the margins of society but with direct access to people whose hands were on the levers of power and who wanted their votes.

2.5. Compulsory Church Rates

1868 finally saw the end of an injustice long resented by nonconformists, namely the compulsory payment of church rates.[53] Independent Methodism's corporate political awakening came too late for it to make its voice heard on this subject, but individual members had already made their stand in a personal capacity. At Horwich, Lancashire, the church's leader, William Crumblehulme, made himself unpopular with the local Vicar by holding public meetings of protest against Church Rates, 'and got up petitions, signed in the dark night by men who hardly dared openly call their souls their own'. According to his chronicler, he then 'got John Bright to present them to Parliament.'[54] Like many others, he suffered distraint on his goods as a result of refusing to pay the church rate.

However, Independent Methodism's most celebrated skirmish over church rates occurred in Scotland. A Glasgow IM preacher, Archibald

Pollock, chose to take a stand on this issue when property owners in his home parish of Calton were called upon to pay for an increase in stipend for the parish minister, John Murray. In Pollock's case, this amounted to fifteen shillings a year. Many people objected, but Pollock alone continued to resist the demand for payment. Eventually, this led to a warrant being obtained for recovery of costs and word was sent to Pollock that this would be enforced promptly. Still refusing to pay, he published a pamphlet in which he gave his reasons for refusal. His central argument was that 'as the Established Church has now the right to appoint their pastors, they ought, like honest people, to pay for what they get and not be paupers on other people's bounty or be obliged to harass at the point of the bayonet the widow, the orphan, and the fatherless to pay for the grand sermons that they are privileged to hear.'[55] The outcome was that Pollock suffered the distraint of household goods, the first person to do so in Glasgow. However, public sympathy was aroused and the incident served to highlight the injustice felt by free church people at having to maintain a church which they did not attend.[56]

2.6. Licensing Legislation

Like the majority of nonconformists, Independent Methodists were strongly committed to the temperance movement and added their support to any measure that would curb the drink trade. From 1862 onwards, Sir Wilfrid Lawson, MP, put before Parliament a 'Permissive Bill', the effect of which would be to allow individual localities to prohibit the sale of alcohol. Each year, the IM Annual Meeting passed a resolution supporting Lawson's Bill, but each year it was predictably defeated. Further resolutions were passed in favour of other licensing measures: the abolition of grocers' licences;[57] the proposed compensation of publicans when licences were abolished;[58] and most strongly of all, Sunday closing, which was never achieved.[59] Temperance and sabbatarianism stood closely together in the Independent Methodist mind.

2.7. Ireland

While Ireland was of indirect concern to the Independent Methodists, who had no churches on the island, they immediately interested themselves in the Bill of 1868 for the Disendowment and Disestablishment of the Irish Church, no doubt hoping that similar measures would follow in England. The Independent Methodist magazine kept readers informed of legislative progress, and expressed support for the Bill.[60] This was duly endorsed by the following Annual Meeting.[61]

Ireland became an issue again in the 1880s when Gladstone's Home Rule Bill came before Parliament. Some Methodists feared that this would result in a Roman Catholic majority regime which would create difficulties for Irish Methodists.[62] For the Independent Methodists, this was not directly relevant and they remained silent when Home Rule became the defining electoral issue of 1886, resulting in the fall of the Gladstone administration and the return of the Conservatives under Lord Salisbury. However, the ensuing punitive legislation aroused their ire and resulted in their open support for Home Rule thereafter. The 1887 Coercion Act was designed to give protection to Irish landlords, including those who were absentees, by banning workers' combinations. Its effect was, as the Independent Methodists saw it, 'to crush the liberties of our fellow subjects in Ireland'.[63] Absentee landlords had used powerful influence to have such acts passed[64] – including the Marquis of Londonderry whose mines were places of employment for many Independent Methodists living on the Durham coalfield. Notwithstanding his powerful position, the Annual Meeting of 1887 passed a further resolution:

> That this assembly hereby records an emphatic protest against the unchristian character of the Coercive Measures carried out in Ireland under the Crimes Act of 1887, whereby the just liberties of the people of that country have been invaded, and feelings of bitterness engendered towards the Government of England; and hereby calls upon Parliament to adopt a policy of conciliation towards the people of long misgoverned Ireland.[65]

Robert Entwistle, moving the resolution, reminded the Annual Meeting members that they were advocates of religious liberty and of the right of people to join in lawful combinations. Similar resolutions were passed in 1888 and 1889. The Independent Methodists were plainly prepared to allow the religious question to take second place to the need to secure basic human rights for all Irish people, regardless of creed.[66]

2.8. Churchyard Burials

The last of the major religious disabilities to be addressed was that of the right of nonconformists to bury their dead according to their own rites and traditions in Anglican parish churchyards. While public cemeteries allowed for nonconformist rites, only Anglican clergy could conduct funerals in churchyards. This created a particular dilemma for any nonconformist who lived a long distance from a public cemetery; those who lived in the countryside usually had no viable option other than to bury their dead in the local churchyard. As a result, a clergyman who would possibly have little knowledge of the deceased would conduct the burial service. In 1877, the Independent Methodists discussed the matter at their Annual Meeting and called for a recognition of 'the rights of all parishioners to be buried in their churchyards with such religious ceremonies as may be deemed fit by their surviving relations.'[67]

In 1880, a Burials Act finally removed this last grievance and, on October 10, the first Independent Methodist funeral in an Anglican churchyard took place in Murton, Co. Durham.[68] However, not all Anglican clergy readily co-operated with new the Act and an incident occurred at Lowton Common, Lancashire, which received extensive coverage in the national press. The young son of Simon Boydell, superintendent of the local IM Sunday School, had died and his father wished to bury him in the nearby St. Mary's churchyard, where he owned a family grave. Boydell followed the required procedure and gave the vicar due notice of the time for interment and of his wish to have the service conducted by a preacher of his family's choosing. The vicar raised various objections, mainly based on the fact that the family lived just outside the parish boundary. Boydell, however, was determined to assert his rights and made the situation known in the locality. On the day of the funeral, the cortege arrived at the church gates to find them locked and the grave not dug. This led, later in the day, to a confrontation at the gates between the vicar and a group of nonconformists of various denominations who had assembled to make their protest. Finally, under sufferance, the vicar allowed the service to proceed later that afternoon.

The saga reached the attention of the Manchester and District Committee of the Liberation Society, who took legal advice on the matter and passed a resolution approving Boydell's persistence and congratulating him and his friends on having vindicated their claim. The *Manchester Guardian*, reporting the story, expressed sympathy with the clergy whose powers were being steadily eroded, but observed that the vicar in this instance had acted unwisely. It concluded, 'Every occurrence like this at Lowton pushes a new and effective weapon in the hands of the Liberation Society.'[69] Boydell's action reflected the determination of nonconformists generally to assert their hard-won rights; its outcome illustrated the changing balance of power in the religious life of the country.

2.9. Personal Involvement in Public Life

Independent Methodists generally came into municipal life at a later stage than people of the larger nonconformist denominations, probably because of the impoverished circumstances of even many of their leaders. However, by the later years of the century, many of them had become successful businessmen and were able to move into the new sphere of local politics, taking their places among the large number of Nonconformists who played such a major part in the social and economic life of mid-Victorian Britain, though none were of the stature of great Christian industrialists such as William Lever who could exercise powerful patronage over churches built with their own money.[70] Furthermore, unlike Lever, they did not appoint ministers to churches; in fact many of them *were* the preacher-ministers who led the churches.[71]

While it is difficult to establish the full scale of the part which IM leaders took in civic life, an analysis of those who served as Presidents over a period of approximately fifty years gives some idea. Of the twenty-eight people who held this position between 1879 and 1927, nineteen held at least one public office and some held several:

Independent Methodist Presidents holding public office
1879-1927

Office held	Number of holders
Councillor/Alderman	11
Mayor	3
Magistrate	5
Member of School Board	5
Member of Board of Guardians	3
School Governor	3
Secretary to School Governors	2

Added to these were memberships of various public committees, academic boards and business forums. Twelve of the twenty-eight were Managing Directors or owners of companies, ten were professional people or owned small businesses and only six were employees, just one of whom (Thomas Lomax) was a manual worker who came to the Presidency after retirement. In 1919, Thomas Robinson of Stretford Church, standing as a Liberal candidate, became the first Independent Methodist to be elected as a Member of Parliament; a year later he became the first Independent Methodist knight.[72] Civic-minded, philanthropic entrepreneurs were leading the denomination, bringing their combined skills to the organisational aspects of the Connexion and raising the standing of their churches in their respective communities. Some of them also proved significant benefactors to their own churches, other churches and the Connexion. Despite their little-understood ministry, the Independent Methodists had moved a long way from their 'poor and despised' forbears of the early nineteenth century. This was truly 'redemption and lift' at work; they had become respectable and socially significant.

2.10. Independent Methodists and the Labour Party

The Labour Party made little impact upon IM political attitudes in its earliest days, largely because the denomination was single-mindedly Liberal and church leaders treated the advent of socialism with some caution. However, as Leonard Smith has pointed out in a meticulous case study of the rise of the Independent Labour Party, Independent Methodism, with its radical heritage, lent itself more than most other denominations to becoming a channel for new forms of radical thought.[73]

In 1890s Nelson, Lancashire, the Young Men's Mutual Improvement Society at Salem IM Chapel proved to be the breeding ground for ideas which led to the formation of the town's branch of the ILP, largely through the use of speakers with socialist ideas at the society's meetings.[74] Wilfrid Wellock, was a leading figure in both the Mutual Improvement Society and the ILP. He came into some degree of conflict with the politically Liberal leadership at Salem as his preaching and Sunday School teaching increasingly dealt with the socialist consequences of capitalism.[75] Wellock represented the new political trend which would acquire greater significance in the denomination as the Liberals were eventually replaced by Labour as one of the two parties of government. He went on to contest the Stourbridge Constituency for the Labour Party at the 1923 and 1924 General Elections, eventually serving as its Member of Parliament for 1927-31, during which time he chaired the House of Commons India Committee. Meanwhile, in 1925, another Nelson IM preacher, Rennie Smith, was elected to serve as Labour Member for the Penistone Constituency. Despite their removal from IM 'territory', both men retained their denominational links. As writers in the cause of peace, as well as the promotion of their political views, they were greatly admired and respected by their peers in the denomination.

Commenting on the tendency of Independent Methodist young men (in at least one church) to go into Labour politics, Smith pointed out that leadership was less autocratic or oligarchical than in mainstream Methodism, the churches were not led by professional ministers and there was a longstanding tradition of supporting radical and progressive causes. Moreover, at Nelson specifically, the large membership necessitated the sub-division of the church into several auxiliary societies, each controlling its own affairs. The Young Men's Mutual Improvement Society, which nurtured ILP ideas, was a case in point.[76] While Smith's analysis was based on a single church, the basic principles held true of most IM churches, particularly in respect of the underlying radicalism in their origins and the absence of a professional ministry. In the North-East coalfield, where there was a strong antipathy for capitalism, these features were even more pronounced than in Lancashire, with scarcely a middle-class individual to be found in many of the mining chapels. The ethos of the chapel was strongly linked to the welfare of the miners, their places of work and the institutions that held them together, including trade unions and village politics.

Trade Unions provided the route into Labour politics for a number of Independent Methodists. During his apprenticeship as a wheelwright and wagon builder, William Burrows (1887-1993) became interested in the welfare of his fellow craftsmen and started to take part in union work in his home town of St. Helens. Realising his need for further education, he attended night school and later joined the Workers' Educational Association, where he studied local and central government, industrial history and economics. As branch secretary of his union and a member of the St. Helens Trades and Labour Council, he was encouraged to stand as a candidate for the Town Council. After two failed attempts, he was elected in 1925 and went on serve for over forty-eight years, holding numerous positions, including those of Mayor, Alderman and Leader of the Labour Group.

County Borough of St. Helens

Municipal Elections, Monday, Nov 2nd. 1925.

WEST SUTTON WARD

WORK and VOTE
FOR
William Burrows
The Labour Candidate.

(Please Turn Over)

Election poster for William Burrows, 1925

Burrows' experience in union activity gave him a unique perspective when he was later appointed as the Independent Methodist representative to the British Council of Churches. As the only member of the Council with an industrial background, he was called to assist in drawing up a document entitled, *'The Ethics of Strikes'*. Looking at this from the angle of a shopfloor worker, he pointed out that, in disputes, the church was often perceived to be more sympathetic to employers than to their workers. To show that the fault was not always on one side he successfully persuaded his colleagues to change the title of the document to *'The Ethics of Strikes and Lockouts'*.[77]

3. Education

In 1843, Sir James Graham's Factory Bill proposed to regulate the working hours of young children and provide schools for their compulsory elementary education. The incumbent and churchwardens of the local Anglican Church, together with four others nominated by the local magistrates, would manage each school so created.[78] To the nonconformists, who were already alarmed by the rise of Tractarianism, this amounted to a state subsidy to the Anglican Church. Their protests led the government to abandon the education clauses of the bill. Thus began a battle over the provision and management of elementary education which would last into the twentieth century. More than any other issue, it served to politicise nonconformity and draw it closer together, with the Church of England rather than the state as the perceived enemy.[79] Education, in effect, became nonconformity's chosen battlefield for religious equality.

For a small denomination such as the Independent Methodists, the education controversy was one of the main factors which propelled them away from an isolationist sectarianism and into the broad stream of free church life during the last third of the nineteenth century. Realising that they had a common interest with other nonconformists, they stood firmly alongside them in opposing successive acts of seemingly pro-Anglican legislation, readily taking the lead from men such as Edward Miall, Edward Baines, R. W. Dale, and, later, John Clifford.

3.1. The 1870 Education Act

When the Liberal government of 1870 drew up an Education Bill which was designed to make elementary education available to all, it received strong protests from the nonconformists who welcomed the concept of universality but objected to concessions which allowed Anglican teaching in the proposed new schools. Baines argued that state support for the Church of England would help it to indoctrinate children with its distinctive denominational teaching.[80] Two Independent Methodist Churches – Warrington (Friars Green) and Liverpool (Elizabeth Street) – lost no time in presenting petitions to the House of Commons, without waiting for the Connexion to formulate a collective response. Fearing Anglican domination of school boards, they protested against the powers to be given to the boards to determine the form of religious education to be given.[81] The subsequent IM Annual Meeting made a similar point, as did nonconformists across the country. After a sustained campaign against the bill in its existing form, it was amended to exclude the teaching of anything distinctly denominational in board schools.

3.2. Nonconformist Day Schools

By the 1870s, the nonconformists had opened many more day schools. The Congregational Union had established a Committee of General Education in 1843, in the wake of the Factory Act; the Wesleyan Methodists had done so six years earlier, but in 1843 began to set targets on the number of schools to be established. The Primitive Methodists were active on a smaller scale, but they regarded the provision of schools as a church rather than connexional responsibility.[82]

Data on IM day schools is limited, but a pattern similar to that in Primitive Methodism emerged. As connexional structures and resources were minimal, no central body oversaw or even co-ordinated them. The schools reflected local independence as much as their churches did. Most appear to have entered the field at a very late stage. Apart from a school which operated at Lowton Common, Lancashire, from 1793 until 1863,[83] the earliest known examples were at King Street, Oldham (c.1858),[84] Stockport (1864)[85] and Pendleton, Salford (1868),[86] but only passing references to them remain. Lowton Common resumed in 1880 and six others entered the field in the years following the 1870 Education Act.[87] All ten known schools were in or near Lancashire, the Connexion's main stronghold. Allowing for the fact that the Independent Methodists had sixty-seven churches in this area in 1880, this meant that 15% of them operated day schools at some point between 1860-1900.

In each case, the initiative to start a school was based on a perceived need in a chapel's locality. Lack of provision or Anglican hegemony provided the impetus. Rapid population growth through industrial development sometimes prompted the kind of action which occurred at Horwich, near Bolton, where the establishment of the railway works suddenly quadrupled the village's population. The Independent Methodists seized the opportunity and in 1887 opened a school to provide for the children of the railway workers.[88]

A village school near Burnley came about under rather less usual circumstances when Thomas Butcher, head of the Mereclough Wesleyan Day School (and also the Sunday School Superintendent), was sacked and asked to leave his lodgings.[89] This led to a schism at the Wesleyan Chapel, with the result that a breakaway society established itself in a weaving shed at nearby Walkmill and became affiliated to the Colne and Nelson IM Circuit which began to supply it with preachers.[90] Two months later, the new society opened a Sunday School in the same weaving shed and on the following day opened a day school, with Butcher as its head.[91] A subsequent report in the local press indicated that Butcher attracted much public sympathy and his new school soon numbered 170 children.[92] The action of the dissident Wesleyans indicated that local issues took precedence over denominational allegiance and that the church-school link was important to them. Independent Methodism offered them the support they wanted without the external control of a body such as the Wesleyan Education Committee. Public support was sustained in the following years and the community moved quickly to raise funds for the building of a school-chapel.[93]

Voluntary schools could obtain Department of Education grants, which gave nonconformist churches the financial means to operate them, but grants entailed inspections which were designed to ensure that only competent establishments received them. And the inspectors had teeth – with the result that problems were addressed with haste. Noble Street, Bolton, had 550 scholars in 1881, but, as a result of an inspection, the Department of Education had threatened a withdrawal of aid because there were too many scholars for the space available. The church promptly built a £900 extension and secured public endorsement by inviting the chairman of the Bolton School Board to give the address at the opening service.[94] Horwich, where the initial influx of children exceeded all expectations, was placed under similar inspectorial pressure and built an entirely new school at the cost of £1,200 to avoid the threat of closure.[95] When Lowton Common re-opened its school in 1880 after a seventeen-year gap, the independent-minded villagers found that their action now required government approval.[96] Despite having 170 pupils, the school managers, all chapel members, were informed that they would not qualify for a grant until they had been operational for three years.[97] This placed a considerable strain on the church finances, but the school continued until the necessary grant was finally secured.

The story of the school at Wingates, Westhoughton, illustrates how nonconformists sometimes established schools reluctantly, through the dilemma of wanting a state system of elementary education and the reality of having only an Anglican school available in the locality. During the 1885 General Election, a local Anglican clergyman allegedly made provocative speeches describing nonconformists as 'cuckoos' whose children were educated in nests provided by Church people. Reacting bitterly, local nonconformists banded together to establish an undenominational day school using the IM premises.[98] The Westhoughton School Board raised no objection to the school, but the change of government from Liberal to Conservative in 1886 led to a less sympathetic treatment from the Department of Education, which insisted that a new school be built within the next twelve months. The school was successfully established, but recognition was still refused, so no grant was made. The support of sympathetic Members of Parliament was enlisted and the matter ultimately came to the Minister of Education, who sanctioned the school without any conditions. Nonconformist doggedness and determination paid off.

The whole issue of nonconformist children attending Anglican schools was heightened when, in 1876, the Conservative government introduced legislation to make elementary education compulsory in many parts of the country.[99] This meant that, in rural areas particularly, the only school available was the church school. The government's bill went unchallenged nationally, but feelings of injustice remained among nonconformists. These were compounded in 1897, when a bill was passed which allowed £0.5s. per child to voluntary schools, but not to board schools.[100] By this time the Independent Methodists had only three day schools, and education was compulsory in all parts of the country. The following IM Annual Meeting expressed displeasure that denominational schools which were outside public control should be so financed. As a result, their children often had to attend schools 'where creeds were taught of which their parents disapproved.'[101] While a conscience clause allowed exemption from (Anglican) religious education, few took this option, since it effectively stigmatised the children who were separated from their peers, often in uncomfortable conditions.

Part of the nonconformists' battle for a system of public, non-sectarian education was to show that their schools offered an even-handed approach to people of all denominations. The opening of the school extension at Noble Street IM Church, Bolton, illustrated this:

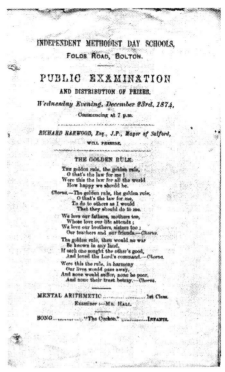

Public Examination and Prizegiving Programme, Folds Road, Bolton, Day School, 1874

> Mr. W. Brimelow, after expressing his pleasure at seeing the Chairman of the School Board presiding over that meeting, said that if the school was not at present a Board School, it was the next best thing, it was an undenominational school. While he heartily rejoiced in the establishment and extension of schools by whomsoever established or extended, he still more rejoiced in the establishment of undenominational schools, because he thought as they increased in number it brought nearer the time when there would be one general system of education in the country.[102]

The chairman of the School Board underlined the same point:

> Their object . . . was not the training of children in the doctrines and practices of the United Free Gospel churches, or any other, but to give a good education to children of any denomination, in which an important part was the giving of religious and moral instruction from the Scriptures.

The fortunes of Independent Methodist schools under the inspection regime varied. The school at Folds Road, Bolton, began in 1873 and by 1877 was able to report that it had received both a favourable inspection and a commendation following a public examination by the Recorder of the town. This school, among others, benefited from local exhibitions and scholarships which were largely instigated by William Brimelow, one of the church's leaders and a prominent townsman. These enabled a number of pupils to enter university.[103] Among the Folds Road alumni was a distinguished local educational pioneer, Frederick Wilkinson, whose career illustrated the possibilities which nonconformist voluntary schools opened up to their pupils. After a time as a pupil teacher, he underwent college training and eventually become headmaster at Noble Street, which was by now a Board School. Later, when the town's Mechanics' Institute was changed into a Technical School, he became its first Principal and went on to become President of the Lancashire and Cheshire Institutes. Such was his success as Principal that, when the 1902 Education Act was passed, he was invited to become Director of Education for the Borough of Bolton, a position which he occupied for many years.[104] Wilkinson retained his IM links and served for a time as Connexional Secretary.

Of all the IM day schools, the largest and most successful was at Salem, Nelson, begun in 1881. Almost from the beginning, its examination grades were high and by 1886 the standards passed reached 98%. Starting from a base of 430 children, by 1889 its numbers reached 1,190, making it the largest school in the town. Not all places were so successful, however, and the school at Walkmill, Burnley, was closed after a chequered fifteen-year existence which culminated in a series of bad reports.[105]

The voluntary system was a heroic response to a national problem, but it was totally inadequate. The scale of the task facing the denominations was far beyond even their collective resources. To a denomination as small as the Independent Methodists, any contribution to the voluntary sector would be of local significance only. Leading nonconformists such as R. W. Dale came to the view that a national system of education, publicly funded, was the only way to provide for the needs of all the nation's children.[106] The Independent Methodists concurred with this view and gradually gave over their schools to the school boards, though the schools often continued to meet in church premises long afterwards. The Bolton Schools, Folds Road and Noble Street, made the change as early as 1882. Salem, Nelson, gave over its huge school to the newly formed Nelson School Board in 1897.[107] Horwich, which had no local School Board until long after the school was established, remained in church hands until 1905, when it was handed over to Lancashire County Council.[108] Wingates followed suit in 1915.

3.3. Independent Methodists and School Boards

Since people of all denominations and none were eligible to sit on school boards, numerous nonconformists successfully stood at the three yearly elections to the boards, including many Independent Methodists. Others served as managers, governors and clerks. At Colne, Ellis Barker became chairman of the School Board and thus gained a position of some influence in his town.[109] In the adjacent borough of Nelson, Arthur Watson topped the poll in the first election to the town's Board and served as its Vice-Chairman on three occasions. At Salford, Eliza McDougall, a member at Salem Church, Pendleton, stood for

PLUMP 15 FOR
Mrs. J. P. McDOUGALL,

THE CHILDREN'S CHAMPION.

Printed and Published by Geo. Wheeler & Co., 46 King St. West Manchest

School Board Election notice, Eliza McDougall, 1900

election in 1900 under controversial circumstances. There was evidently feeling among the members of her church and others that the local 'Progressive Party' (Liberals) which advocated non-sectarian education, was monopolised by 'the ministerial element and the well-to-do chapel-going people.'[110] As a result, a large number of members took matters into their own hands and nominated McDougall, who was active in local philanthropic work, using the name of the Progressive Party, of which they felt some ownership. This prompted a backlash from a party member who wrote to the *Manchester Guardian*, alleging that her nomination was unofficial, denominationally motivated and that it would split the Progressive Party vote.[111] McDougall's action, clearly supported by her church, perhaps reflected the fact that Salem still retained some of early Independent Methodism's slightly anarchic readiness to break ranks with other denominations when it felt the need to do so. In the event, she finished near to the top of the list of candidates.[112] This may have been due to a wide level of support in the local community, but equally it could be attributable to the fact that voters in School Board elections had as many votes as there were seats on the Board. A voter could legally use all his votes for one candidate, a device known as 'plumping', which often ensured the representation of minority interests.[113] By this means, a partisan candidate such as McDougall could secure election by the number of votes cast rather than the number of supporters who endorsed her.

3.4. The 1902 Education Act

The Free Churches' hope for a national, non-sectarian system of education was dashed with the passing of the 1902 Education Act, which strengthened the position of denominational schools. The Church of England which had held firmly on to its schools, would benefit enormously by this Act, but the free churches, including the Independent Methodists, were to lose, having largely relinquished their much smaller stake in educational provision. This generated enormous anger among the Free Churches, the outcome of which must be noted as far as it affected the Independent Methodists.

The Education Bill of 1902 proposed to sweep away the school boards and to establish Local Education Authorities in their place. It also imposed on LEAs the responsibility of aiding voluntary schools from the rates. As these were now mainly Anglican and (especially in Lancashire) Roman Catholic, the Free Churches saw this measure as tantamount to a re-introduction of church rates by the back door. They were being required to subsidise the Church of England and Roman Catholic Church by funding their schools. The Bill also made no provision for the protection of teachers from ecclesiastical tests, a serious matter for Free Church people aiming to enter the teaching profession. In the eyes of Independent Methodists and others, the new legislation would mean that they would be paying to hand over their children to denominational teaching that would destroy nonconformity, while some of their young people could be driven reluctantly into Anglican allegiance in order to secure employment as teachers.[114]

Opposition to the Bill grew as the constituent denominations of the Free Churches motivated their members to take a stand on the issue. The Independent Methodist magazine kept its readers up to date on the latest stage of developments each month, reflecting the denomination's support for the overall position adopted by the Free Churches, that one authority should supervise all grades of public education.[115] Schools supported by public funds, they argued, should be managed by representatives of the people, directly elected for the purpose. The leading figure in the fight against the Bill was Dr. John Clifford, minister of Westbourne Park Baptist Church, London, whose theme of 'Rome on the rates' became a popular outcry which was received with acclaim and resulted in large-scale support throughout the country.[116] Nonconformity was more united and passionate on this issue than any other before or after.[117] Even before the Bill's first reading, voices had been raised to urge passive resistance to the proposed measures, in the form of a refusal to pay the education portion of domestic rates bills.

The responses of Free Churches varied. The Free Church Council itself stopped short of calling for outright support for passive resistance.[118] The Wesleyan Conference expressed sympathy but took no stand on the issue, partly because its own voluntary schools stood to benefit from the new measure. The Primitive Methodists, on the other hand, were firm resisters, since many of their churches were in rural areas where the Anglican day school was the only one. When the IM Annual Meeting was held in June, a motion was passed expressing the denomination's view on the subject:

> That this Meeting of Representation of Independent Methodist Churches protests against the Education Bill of the Government as being an entire reversal of the principles of the Act of 1870, as making no provision for the compulsory establishment of a secondary system of education or for the protection of teachers from ecclesiastical tests, and as being designed to promote the interests of sectarian schools by checking the future development of unsectarian education and by giving still larger grants of public money to denominational schools without any adequate public control; it condemns the superseding of board schools except by local authorities popularly elected for educational purposes in suitable areas.[119]

The main points of this resolution were unexceptional and reflected the common ground of the free churches. What is striking is the lack of any reference to the passive resistance movement. While this was viewed sympathetically in the columns of the magazine, there seems to have been little determination to pursue it at Connexional level. A year later, when passive resistance was at its height, the matter came before the Annual Meeting again. This time, there was no discussion and the meeting simply voted to leave the matter to individuals, while expressing broad sympathy with those whose consciences called them to be passive resisters.[120]

Some Independent Methodists responded to the call to passive resistance. Like other Free Church people they were taken to court and suffered distraint of goods, though none appears to have suffered imprisonment.[121] Later in 1903, a correspondent to the magazine wrote to advocate passive resistance and expressed surprise that there had been so little correspondence on the subject. Thereafter, little reference to the Education Act appears in IM records, though the issue was far from over and Free Church opposition continued for several years afterwards. However, it would be wrong to assume that Independent Methodists simply lost interest; too many were involved in Liberal politics to let the matter drop. It is probably fair to say that the Connexion was preoccupied with other matters, particularly its dilemma on Methodist Union[122] and the looming crisis over Incorporation.[123] Thus, the Education issue was left to individuals, with the result that those concerned now operated through channels other than their denomination. When, eventually, opposition to the 1902 Act waned, Independent Methodists, along with other Free Church people, came to accept that the dual system had come to stay. The age of a nonconformity politicised by education effectively ended with the First World War.

4. Conclusion

Throughout this period, the thinking of the IM people, like that of their contemporaries in other denominations, was profoundly influenced by developments in the world of scientific discovery, Biblical criticism and theology. But why did the less educated Independent Methodists absorb new ideas with such apparent eagerness? There were probably three reasons. Firstly, critical work can only be properly evaluated when critical skills are brought to bear upon it. Without these, readers too easily stand in awe of the scholarship which faces them and the result is uncritical acceptance. The Independent Methodists had no theological colleges to provide the intellectual rigour which develops such critical skills. An examination of the writings of Brimelow and Vickers, able men though they were, reveals extensive awareness of the scholarship of their time but no inclination to challenge it.[124] Secondly, it is impossible to follow Independent Methodism's development from 1881 (the year of the first Methodist Ecumenical Conference)[125] without discerning a picture of people anxious to find acceptance in the wider Church and in community life generally. This inevitably entailed keeping abreast of the thinking which now permeated other denominations. Rather naïvely, perhaps, they proved more willing to embrace changes to their theology than to their distinctive polity, which they continued to defend as vigorously as ever. Thirdly, the Quaker aspect of Independent Methodism, virtually forgotten in the middle years of the nineteenth century but now renascent, featured significantly in its process of its theological change. Quakerism eschewed creeds, which were falling from favour almost universally at the end of the nineteenth century; its stress on the Spirit rather than the Word also sat well with current thought. For some Independent Methodists, the departure from their conservative evangelical roots became too much and some left to find new homes in Brethren or Free Evangelical Churches.

Linked to all three of the above factors was the influence of denominational literature: in particular, the magazine which was probably the only religious journal read by most Independent Methodists. As literacy increased, its readership grew and a new generation readily absorbed the

Figure3
Distribution of Independent Methodist Churches, 1901

thinking which it projected. Only two editorial partnerships covered the seventy-three years from 1868 and 1941. The Brimelow family, William and his sons Richard and James, between them served until 1901, after which Arthur Mounfield took up the position, with the support of Edward Ralphs for fifteen out of forty years. Aside from the magazine, James Vickers wrote several small booklets on denominational polity which sold widely. Between them, these men were hugely influential in shaping readers' ideas on church polity, politics, education and theology.

In 1927 the Connexion's doctrinal position was defined by the *Statement of Faith and Practice*.[126] Thereafter came a long period of theological ossification. There is little evidence that later denominational leaders re-evaluated (for instance) the ideas of Harnack in the light of his pupil and critic, Karl Barth, who steered twentieth century theology in a very different direction from his teacher.[127] Nor was any critical consideration given to the writings of Brimelow, Vickers, Mounfield and Ralphs which acquired almost canonical status and remained unchallenged until the late twentieth century.

The period from 1867 to 1914 represented a window through which Independent Methodism saw the outside world virtually with a single eye. These years saw an interweaving of many aspects of their activity. As successive acts of Parliament widened the franchise, political aspirations grew. Facing political issues together served to strengthen internal unity and also prepared the ground for the embryonic ecumenical movement of the 1880s and 90s. In turn, ecumenical contact opened channels of communication which facilitated the spread of new theological ideas. Such ideas, especially those which endorsed the 'social gospel', stimulated further interest in issues such as politics and education. It would be impossible to disentangle this complex web of processes.

On the basis that success breeds success, churches and people motivated each other. One church saw another's successful enterprise in launching a day school and followed suit; one man was successfully elected to a Council or School Board and others followed. This was a time of enormous confidence, but it is impossible to isolate Independent Methodists from other denominations in this context, since they shared a common mindset and set of aspirations, even though some of their largest goals were to go unrealised. Like other nonconformist denominations, they produced people who had the courage of their convictions to face perceived injustice and, if necessary, to suffer for it, whether in battles over burial rights, church rates, the 1902 Education Act or wartime conscription.

Involvement in public life, whether as councillors, magistrates or school board members, inevitably entailed a readiness to be identified with the institutions in question and to build positive relationships with others of different convictions who worked in the same spheres. As with Christians of all eras who have had to come to terms with the society of their day, late nineteenth century Independent Methodists had to balance loyalty to their principles with commitment to public office and all that it involved. Such community involvement would take the edge off their sectarian separatism. By its nature, sectarianism has a more natural proclivity for the prophetic mode of relationship with civil authority, critiquing it from the margins rather than engaging with civic processes. Once a religious body (or at least its leadership) enters the corridors of power it moves to a Constantinian form of relationship and, thereby, away from sectarianism. The successful political involvement of many of its people played a significant part in translating Independent Methodism from derided sect into accepted denomination.

Notes to Chapter 5

1. *IMMag.* 1859, 114
2. W. Sanderson and T. Sturges, Is a Located Hired Ministry in direct opposition to the letter and spirit of the Scriptures, particularly of the New Testament? A discussion between William Sanderson and the Rev. Thomas Sturges (Liverpool, 1852), 17, 26, 54.
3. IMMins. 1866, 21.
4. 'Manuscript Magazines' *IMMag.* 1866, 611.
5. IMMins. 1867, 75ff.
6. R.E. 'Geology and the Bible', *IMMag.* 1869, 299ff.
7. E. Ralphs, 'The Christian and the Scientific Attitudes towards Truth', *Independent Quarterly* October 1927, 16.
8. i.e. Johnson and his supporters.
9. *IMMag.* 1908, 130. Mounfield's response reflected his Quaker view that the 'Word' was the Logos or Divine Spirit rather than the Bible. E. Grubb, *What is Quakerism?* (London: George Allen and Unwin, 3rd edition, 41). The Statement of Faith of the Federal Council of the Evangelical Free Churches (1917) also gave supremacy to the Spirit rather than the Scriptures, but this was altered by the Independent Methodists when they adapted it for their own purposes in 1927. It suggests that this issue was an ongoing point of debate among Independent Methodists, though there is no record of the discussions which led to the final form of the IM Statement. See Appendix 6.
10. Letter: J. W. Johnson to Arthur Mounfield, 9 July 1908.
11. CCMins. 1908, 421.
12. Letter: J. W. Johnson to Ellis Barker, 22 September 1908.
13. Letter: G. W. Collin to Ellis Barker, 30 September 1908.
14. CCMins.1908, 431.
15. CCMins.1909, 442.
16. *IMMag.*1909, 44.
17. *IMYB* 1909, 48
18. A. Mounfield, 'The Book of Ecclesiasticus', *IMMag.* 1920, 68
19. See Appendix 6.
20. See Chapters 4 and 6.
21. A. von Harnack, *What is Christianity?* 5th edition (London: Ernest Benn Ltd, 1958), 54ff.
22. W. Brimelow, 'Does Christianity embody the Truest Ideal for Man's Aspirations', *IMMag.* 1889, 262.
23. J. Brimelow, 'The Gospel of Brotherhood', *IMMag.* 1891, 242.
24. H.R. Niebuhr, *The Kingdom of God in America* (New York, Harper & Row,

1959) [orig. 1937], 193.

25. G. Wainwright, 'Types of Spirituality', C. Jones et al, *The Study of Spirituality* (London: SPCK, 1986), 597.

26. *IMMag.* 1920, 104.

27. R. Knight, 'The Field of Service for Young People in Disciple Making', *IMMag.* 1921, 157.

28. K. Brown, *A Social History of the Nonconformist Ministry in England and Wales 1800-1930* (Oxford: Clarendon, 1988), 50.

29. M. Kennedy, 'The Church of Tomorrow', *IMMag.* 1892, 251.

30. R. W. Dale, *The Atonement* (London, 1897), 410-40.

31. S.E. Keeble, *Industrial Day Dreams* (London, 1896), 62f.

32. D.M. Thompson, 'The Nonconformist Social Gospel', *Studies in Church History 7*, 256.

33. Letter: H. Brimelow to D. Whitehead, Church President, 1 July 1891.

34. See 2.8. for details of his political activities.

35. W. Wellock, *Off the Beaten Track,* (India: Sarva Seva Sangh Prakashan Varanashi, 3rd Edition, 1980) 15ff.

36. E. Simpson, *Miners and Saints in Sutton* (St. Helens, 1999), 8.

37. E. Ralphs, 'Experiments in Evangelism. Interview with G. Hunter', *IQ* January 1927, 41ff.

38. This remains so to the present day.

39. *IMMag.* 1916, 27.

40. *IMYB* 1913, 108ff.

41. *IMYB* 1914, 58ff.

42. Scroggie was the minister at Bethesda Evangelical Church, Sunderland, at the time.

43. D. W. Bebbington, *Evangelicalism in Modern Britain* (London: Unwin Hyman, 1989), 217.

44. D. Tidball, *Who are the Evangelicals?* (London: Marshall Pickering, 1994), 68.

45. *IMYB* 1925, 61.

46. T. Larsen, *The Friends of Religious Equality: Nonconformist Politics in Mid-Victorian Britain* (Woodbridge, Suffolk: Boydell Press, 1999), 10. Larsen contrasts Michael Watts' dualism between theology and political philosophy with J.P. Ellens' view that nonconformists' politics hindered their spirituality. M. Watts, *The* Dissenters, vol. 2. (Oxford: Clarendon Press, 1995), 510f; J.P. Ellens, *Religious Routes to Gladstonian Liberalism: The Church Rate Conflict in England and Wales 1832-68.* (University Park, Pennsylvania: Pennsylania State University Press, 1994), 85f.

47. M. Kennedy, 'Independent Methodism. What it is. What it has done. What it ought to do.' *IMMag.* 1886, 297.

48. E. Royle, *Chartism* (London: Longman Group, 1980), 49, 83.

49. A. Wood, *Nineteenth Century Britain 1815-1914* (Singapore: Longman Group, 1982, 2nd edition), 266.

50. IMMins. 1867, 8; 72f.

51. J.M. Turner, *Conflict and Reconciliation* (London, Epworth, 1985), 141.

52. IMMins. 1868, 55.

53. O. Anderson, 'Gladstone's Abolition of Compulsory Church Rates: A Minor

Political Myth and its Historiographical Career' in *Journal of Ecclesiastical History 25* (1974) 195.

54. *Wingates Messenger*, July 1910. John Bright, Quaker and Member of Parliament for Rochdale, campaigned vigorously against compulsory payment of church rates from 1840. W.G. Addison, *Religious Equality in Modern England* (London: SPCK, 1944), 65.

55. A. Pollock, *Priestcraft, Priestcraft, Priestcraft* (Glasgow, 1876). The right of a parish to appoint its own minister had been granted by an Act of Parliament in 1874, abolishing patronage. J.H.S. Burleigh, *A Church History of Scotland,* (London: Oxford University Press, 1960), 375.

56. *North Bristol Daily Mail,* Monday 16 October, 1876.

57. IMMins. 1880, 9.

58. IMMins. 1890, 34.

59. 'Sunday Closing – Urgent', *IMMag.* 1883, 121; IMMins. 1880, 9f.

60. 'Irish Church Measure', *IMMag.* 1869, 86; J. Cherry, 'The Disestablished and Disendowed Church' *IMMag.* 1869, 214; 'The Irish Church Bill Passed', (from *The Liberator*) *IMMag.* 1869, 223.

61. *IMMag.* 1869, 175f.

62. M. Edwards, *Methodism and England,* (London: Epworth, 1943), 167.

63. IMMins. 1887, 13.

64. Edwards, *Methodism and England,* 182.

65. *IMMag.* 1888, 227.

66. This was consistent with the support for religious equality which lay at the heart of dissenting belief. Larsen, *Religious Equality,* (Woodbridge, Suffolk: Boydell Press, 1999), preface.

67. *IMMag.* 1877, 242.

68. 'The New Burials Act', *IMMag.* 1880, 419.

69. Quoted in *IMMag.* 1880, 449ff.

70. D.J. Jeremy, *Capitalists and Christians: Business Leaders and the Church in Britain, 1900-1960* (Oxford: Oxford University Press, 1990), 2; Sellers, *Nineteenth Century Nonconformity,* 76.

71. One such example was William Oxley of Manchester, described in the 1881 census as 'Candlewick Spinner and Free Gospel Minister, employing 78 men, 6 boys and 28 females.'

72. CCMins. 1919, 255; 1920, 227.

73. L. Smith, *Religion and the Rise of Labour* (Keele: Ryburn Publishing, 1993), 137.

74. *Ibid,* 133.

75. *Ibid,* 134. Wellock, *Beaten Track*, 19. See also Chapter 4 for Wellock's stand as a conscientious objector.

76. Smith, *Labour*, 138. Salem Church had over 500 members at the time.

77. W. Burrows, *Recollections* (St. Helens, 1975), 15ff.

78. H. Townsend, *The Claims of the Free Churches* (London: Hodder & Stoughton, 1959), 178f; Addison, 87.

79. D.W. Bebbington, *Nonconformist Conscience* (London: George Allen and Unwin, 1982), 127; Larsen, *Religious Equality,* 2.

80. Bebbington, *Nonconformist Conscience,* 128.

81. *IMMag.* 1870, 99.

82. K. Lysons, *A Little Primitive* (Buxton: Church in the Marketplace Publications), 245ff.
83. This was operated by the Wesleyan Methodists until 1819.
84. *A Centenary History of King Street, Independent Methodist Church, Oldham, 1854-1954*, 7.
85. IMMins. 1864, 14.
86. E. Cooper, *Salem Independent Methodist Church, Pendleton, History of the Church and School*, 1955, 10.
87. See Appendix 11 for a full list of the schools concerned.
88. S. Rothwell, *Memorials of Folds Road Independent Methodist Chapel, Bolton* (2 vols.; Bolton: Independent Methodist Bookroom, 1897), 2:305f.
89. *Burnley Advertiser*, 15 May 1878.
90. *Burnley Express*, 13 July 1878.
91. C. Scholes, *History of Mount Zion Independent Methodist Church, Walkmill, Cliviger 1880-1980*, 4.
92. *Burnley Advertiser,* 27 July 1878.
93. Scholes, *Cliviger,* 8.
94. IMMag. 1881, 17ff.
95. Rothwell, *Folds Road,* 2:306.
96. Independent Methodist Church and Schools, Lowton, Empire Bazaar Handbook, 1912, 57.
97. IMMins. 1882, 34.
98. E. Howell, *Whispers of Wingates* (Bolton, 1984), 51.
99. Bebbington, *Nonconformist Conscience,* 133.
100. *Ibid,* 138.
101. IMMins. 1898, 239ff.
102. *IMMag.* 1881, 19
103. *Bolton Journal*, 13 June 1913, 6.
104. J. Vickers, *History of Independent Methodism* (Wigan: Independent Methodist Bookroom, 1920), 260.
105. Headteacher's Log Book, Walkmill School, Cliviger, 1895, 125.
106. Bebbington, *Nonconformist Conscience,* 128.
107. J. Robinson, *Salem Independent Methodist Church, Nelson, Centenary Booklet*, 1952, 37.
108. J. Vickers, *Horwich Independent Methodist Church and School, A Jubilee History 1862-1912,* 10ff.
109. Vickers, *History,* 237.
110. Undated Cutting from Evening Chronicle, Salem Church Scrapbook.
111. Undated Cutting from Manchester Guardian, Salem Church Scrapbook.
112. Cooper, *Salem, Pendleton,* 28. To put the place in context, the area where Salem Chapel stood was used by Walter Greenwood for his fictionalised account of poverty in Salford, *Love on the Dole*. Greenwood's novel and the events of 1900 suggest the same picture of an alienated and almost abandoned community. This was often the kind of environment where Independent Methodism flourished and where people readily accepted the kind of artisan ministry and leadership which struggled to find acceptance in more prosperous communities.
113. J.S. Hurt, *Elementary Schooling and the Working Classes 1860-1918*

(London: Routledge and Kegan Paul, 1979), 75.

114. Bebbington, *Nonconformist Conscience,* 142.

115. *IMMag.* 1901, 204.

116. Lysons, *A Little Primitive,* 252f.

117. Bebbington, *Nonconformist Conscience,* 143.

118. Lysons, *A Little Primitive,* 253f.

119. *IMYB* 1902, 93.

120. *IMMag.* 1903, 146.

121. Murray, 9. J. Munson, *The Nonconformists* (SPCK 1991), 272. Prominent Independent Methodists who were passive resisters included Arthur Watson (Vickers, *History,* 229) and William Hindley (*IMMag.* 1937, 25). Given the fact that only 0.5% of Free Church members were active resisters, this would translate into no more than 50 Independent Methodists.

122. See Chapter 4.

123. *Ibid.*

124. Note in particular Vickers, *History,* chapters 9-13, and W. Brimelow, *A Free Church and a Free Ministry,* (London: Elliott Stock, 1883), *passim.*

125. See Chapter 4.

126. See Appendix 6.

127. This reflected the extent to which IM theology was shadowing Quaker thought at the time. The Quakers, similarly, were little affected by the neo-orthodox theologians. E. Isichei, *Victorian Quakers,* (London: Oxford University Press, 1970), 41.

Chapter 6
An Established Denomination 1927-1959

The period from 1927 to the outbreak of the Second World War proved to be Independent Methodism's high watermark of corporate activity. Several factors made this possible. The reunion of the churches in 1923 after a sixteen year division led to renewed confidence and greater collective resources. More than ever, Independent Methodism was now a denomination in the true sense of the term and its members took great pride in their identity. The instruction of their young people in IM principles was regarded as an essential part of their education. Anything which promoted 'the cause of Independent Methodism' or which brought Independent Methodists together was to be welcomed. Moreover, while the denomination remained predominantly working class, a small percentage of members had gained experience of leadership in business and civic life and those concerned were able to apply their skills to the leadership of the denomination. Combined with all these factors was the increased availability of public transport which made distant places more accessible than ever. Thus, a new era of denominational life began. The years following the First World War no longer saw single, dominant individuals such as Alexander Denovan or William Brimelow standing head and shoulders over the rest in the Connexion's leadership. There were able leaders in the current generation, but not necessarily with the charisma of the earlier 'giants'. But this was an era when Christian confidence had taken a severe knock, both on the theological front and as the result of a catastrophic world war. If, therefore, the leaders of the time appear to have been less charismatic than before, they need to be understood in the context of their cultural milieu.

1. Denominational Activity between the Wars

The inter-war years saw a major emphasis on learning and the development of interest in the wider world and its needs. From 1922 onwards, a weeknight lecture scheme, initiated by Edward Ralphs, offered lectures to the churches on a range of subjects, such as 'Christian Statesmen', 'The Christianisation of Society', 'The Reasonableness of the Christian Faith', 'Democratic Ideals' and 'Religious Experience: Its Nature and Value'.[1] Over 130 lectures were available in total, all delivered by the Independent Methodists' own people. However, the response to this scheme was less favourable than the organisers anticipated and much of the material prepared was never used.[2]

The recently-established Holiday Home at Burnside, Skipton, provided a ready-made venue for education and training.[3] From 1926 until the outbreak of war in 1939, a conference for ministers was held annually, drawing an attendance of about seventy on each occasion. From 1935, two lecture weekends each year were introduced to supplement the Ministers' Education Scheme and so bring together those studying the course in different areas. This had a profound effect in building relationships between those engaged in study, who previously would not have met, but who now found new friendships which opened up the wider denomination to them.[4] From this sprang a Students' Association which met periodically and which, on one occasion, organised a mission at Newtown Church, Wigan.

In the same way that students found common identity, there was a programme of training for Sunday School teachers which introduced much larger numbers to each other. Weekend conferences were held at Burnside and, on one occasion, a training week was provided, with lecturers from Westhill College.

Non-residential events also played their part in meeting the training needs of the churches. From 1932 onwards, a yearly conference was held at Lowton Church in Lancashire, when speakers from the denomination addressed large gatherings of Sunday School workers. The 'Lowton Conference' promoted ideas which emanated from the National Sunday School Union and effectively guided the teaching methods of a generation. It also provided a market place for the exchange of ideas and for reflection on current problems, such as the abandonment of morning Sunday School sessions.[5] The conference was initially well attended, but waned towards the end of the decade and was curtailed by the Second World War.

One of the major innovations of this period was a new magazine, *The Independent Quarterly*, which was launched in 1927 and ran for ten years. Its moving spirit was Edward Ralphs who was appointed as its editorial secretary. In a modest way it emulated similar publications from other branches of Methodism, such as *The London Review* and *The Holborn Review*. In launching it, the editorial board claimed:

> It will be seen that the *Quarterly* appeals to the thoughtful among us. It is also definitely constructive and aims at helping those who feel that we should not just look at the religious and social problems of our time and just pass by on the other side.'[6]

The contents reflected this view, with features on social, political, philosophical and topical subjects. Articles on science, archaeology, history and poetry also appeared, written by the most able people in the denomination and some from outside it, including several Quaker writers. At a theological level, it was generally liberal and anti-credal.

The *Quarterly* never achieved the measure of support for which its editorial board hoped. In a denomination which was still predominantly working class, it failed to win the hearts and minds of people whose daily lives found little space for the lofty themes addressed by its writers. Some alleged that its articles were too advanced for many people.[7] More than sixty churches took no copies at all.[8] By 1937, circulation was down to 800 and the decision was taken to discontinue it.[9]

Autumnal conventions were held in the various regions of the Connexion, while the Northern Counties Confederation met annually in conference at Easter, as it had done from its beginning. The Women's Auxiliary by the 1930s numbered over 4,000 members and its rallies drew large attendances. The Young Men's Fellowship found strong support for its conferences at first, with 200 attending the 1928 Conference at Pendleton (Salford). However, by 1934 its influence was waning and it ceased to exist for a time, later to be resurrected as the Men's Fellowship.[10] Through the denominational magazine, a 'Children's Circle' was formed and rallies were held from time to time.[11] In total, this was a time of abounding activity which strengthened the sense of common identity of the Independent Methodist people.

At local level, circuit activity thrived. Bolton Circuit held an annual gathering at the town's Albert Hall Methodist Mission, drawing over 1,000 people on each occasion over several years.[12] Manchester Circuit held an annual Music Festival which proved very popular among its Sunday Schools. Hook Gate Circuit (Staffordshire), despite its rural location, held an annual rally when a marquee supplemented the accommodation of one of the tiny chapels and large crowds gathered to listen to visiting speakers.[13] It also continued to hold Camp Meetings (reflecting its Primitive Methodist origins).

2. The Social Outlook of the Time

2.1. The Political Dimension

The pacifism which had proved so strong an ideal for some in the years prior to the First World War found able exponents and advocates in the twenties. Those who had witnessed the horrors of the war or had suffered bereavement were determined to do everything in their power to ensure that it never happened again. Throughout the British churches there was a tension between those who stood for total disarmament and those who wanted peace but saw the dangers of making the nation defenceless.[14] But however great the tension under the surface in Independent Methodism, its public face was resolutely pacifist. The Annual Meeting of 1929 expressed support for the Peace Pact of Paris which had been signed a year earlier and for the covenant of the League of Nations, which many of the Connexion's leaders came to regard as the answer to the world's problems.[15] It was a subject frequently aired in sermons at the time.[16] Rennie Smith (1887-1962), a Nelson IM minister who had served for a single term as a Member of Parliament, became a leading thinker, writer and campaigner in the cause of peace.[17] For a time he served as secretary to the National Council for the Prevention of War and as editor of *Central European Observer*.[18] He proved an inspirational figure to his generation and was warmly welcomed at least in some of the churches where his peace theme was received with acclaim. Arthur Mounfield, who edited the denomination magazine from 1901 to 1941, was also a staunch pacifist and ensured that the subject of peace was well covered in the magazine's columns. Pacifism was just one political issue among many in a denomination which had become a quasi-political body with a strong Labour party influence, where subjects such as poverty, unemployment, industrial relations and housing conditions were regularly debated at Annual Meetings, often resulting in resolutions to the government.[19]

2.2. Temperance and Social Concern

The temperance movement was at the height of its strength during the inter-war years and its supporters confidently stated that Britain, at the time, was the most sober nation in the world.[20] Alcohol consumption had been falling steadily since the beginning of the twentieth century and the churches had good reason to believe that prohibition could be extended from the USA to Britain.[21] The IM Connexion's Temperance Committee secured over a thousand total abstinence pledges and 284 re-affirmations in a single year.[22] However, when an attempt was made to introduce smoking into the Committee's remit, this was defeated by a vote of the Annual Meeting;[23] little was known at the time about the effects of tobacco on health and, in a largely working class denomination, the level of smoking among male church members in particular was high. On the other hand, the Temperance Committee had no hesitation in addressing the rise of gambling, in the forms of greyhound racing, football pools and sweepstakes.[24] It also attacked the opening of cinemas and theatres on Sundays.[25]

In 1933, the Director of the Brewers' Society, Sir Edgar Sanders, drew the attention of the Midland Counties Wholesale Brewers' Association to the fact that most drinkers in public houses were elderly men and that, unless younger men could be encouraged to take up drinking, the industry faced the prospect of continued decline. The outcome was an advertising campaign designed to attract young men to beer drinking and it proved highly successful. The temperance tide retreated from this point onwards.[26] At their 1935 Annual Meeting, the Independent Methodists expressed concern over the brewers' campaign and feared its consequences for those who were drawn into the drinking habit.[27]

After the Second World War, it soon became evident that enthusiasm for the temperance movement even within the churches was diminishing. When the Civic Restaurants Bill clause permitting drink to be consumed in restaurants came before Parliament in 1947, there was little opposition to it.[28] When, in 1952, the IM churches were asked to include total abstinence teaching in their young people's meetings, only a third agreed to do so.[29] By 1956, there was a shortage of speakers willing to speak at temperance services and many churches abandoned them altogether.[30] The Temperance report of 1959 expressed a sense that the battle was being lost.[31] In truth, many church members had quietly dropped their total abstinence practice, though few would say so in IM Annual Meetings where most delegates were still staunchly teetotal. The denomination's Model Rule Book, which had not been revised since 1927, still contained a requirement for church members to be total abstainers, but each church was, of course, independent and could frame its own rules. From this period onwards, a steadily increasing number of churches took their own decision to drop the abstinence rule, leaving the Connexion to follow suit many years later.

2.3. Social Provision and Recreational Life

Hints of a more liberal approach to some social, recreational and personal practices were evident from the years immediately following the First World War. This was particularly so among the younger generation of churchgoers who chafed at the perceived strictness of their elders. Early in 1919, a group of ten young men left the Foundry Street Primitive Methodist Church at Dukinfield, Manchester, having returned home from the war with changed attitudes and expectations. A church member recalled what happened: 'There was frustration and annoyance at the old fashioned ways and regulations of the church. The church's intolerance of things like smoking was one of many things which forced the young men to turn their backs on established religion and go their own way.'[32] Those concerned established the 'Excelsior Young Men's Mission' which not only took a tolerant attitude to smoking, but placed a high premium on its recreational activities from the beginning; its first list of church officers included Football Captain and Vice-Captain. The Mission steadily grew, built its own premises and joined the Manchester IM Circuit in 1924.

Football played a major part in the formation of another church, two years later. In 1921, the Wesleyan Methodist Church at Horden (Co.

Durham) suffered a schism when a group of young men arrived at a meeting one evening in dirty football boots, with the result that the caretaker refused them entry by locking them out. Some church members supported the caretaker's action, but others left the church along with the footballers and established a thriving, evangelical mission which duly linked itself to the Sunderland IM Circuit.[33]

Throughout this period, churches saw an expansion of recreational activity; cricket and football teams, billiard clubs and concert parties abounded. Undoubtedly they met real needs in their communities and provided light relief after the horrors of the First World War. Some urban churches continued to fulfil a social welfare role, much as they had done in the previous century. During a period of heavy unemployment in the 1920s, Buckley Street Church (Warrington) ran a soup kitchen for a month, when people from the neighbourhood came with jugs and bowls to receive the soup.[34] Several churches continued to hold poor children's breakfasts on Christmas Day or Boxing Day. In 1933, Brighouse Street Church, Salford, provided for 350 children in this way.[35] In the same town, Fitzwarren Street Church in 1935 entertained a similar number of children on Christmas Day and on a later day gave tea to 270 old people.[36]

However, on both social and recreational fronts, from 1918 onwards churches were diminishing in significance as major providers, as secular entertainment eclipsed anything which churches could offer and the state eventually became the great provider of welfare services. Churches which had been the hubs of their local communities began to look out-of-date and irrelevant as many of them struggled to maintain the activities which had held memberships together. As cinema, radio and later television became part of everyday life, churches which had majored on social activity rather than spiritual life were faced with a virtual loss of significance. In some ways, this paved the way for the restored evangelical emphasis which was to follow.

3. The Process of Decline

3.1. The Causes of Decline

From the 1920s onwards, it became increasingly obvious that organised religion, especially nonconformity, was experiencing steady decline and making little headway among the non-churchgoing element of the population. From time to time, conference speakers attempted to analyse the causes. Tom Grey, Durham miner and IM preacher, dwelt on this theme at the 1929 Annual Meeting. Referring to empty churches, especially on Sunday mornings, he cited 'the lure of the world', dependence on social activity and the churches' loss of faith in their core doctrines as causes of decline.[37] In fact a major cultural shift was under way, as the population embraced new leisure pursuits. Nonconformity was seen by many as the bastion of temperance and Sabbath observance and thereby in opposition to everything in life that was enjoyable.[38] By 1936, the Connexion was looking back on a decade which had seen the loss of 5,000 Sunday School scholars.[39] Arthur Ince (1903-1977) speaking at the 1937 Lowton Conference, analysed the causes of Sunday School decline and listed declining birthrate, population removal, Sunday distractions, the increasing antagonism to organised religion and lack of conviction in the churches themselves.[40] His point about population removal had a specific relevance to the Independent Methodists, whose churches were situated in areas where the predominant industries were cotton and coal, both of which were, by this time, in decline.[41]

T.R. Openshaw placed the process of decline in a wider context, linking it to social and political trends:

> The history of the past twenty years has revealed two ominous tendencies: the growth of irreligion and the deterioration of political morale – there appears to be something more than a casual connection between them. Steadily, year by year, the statistics of organised Christian bodies have shown a reduction in the numbers attached to and attending the Churches and Sunday Schools in this country. Similar trustworthy evidences – the reports from political organisations, the increasing proportion of non-voters and parliamentary representatives, the betrayal of the League of Nations – all indicate a definite declension in the sense of citizenship and social responsibility.[42]

Openshaw's connection between the decline in the churches and increasing disinterest in political matters was profoundly significant. It demonstrated that some of the problems experienced by the churches were due to an indifference which was more than merely irreligious, but it also showed that the spiritual and moral vacuum which accompanied church decline was now impacting on matters of social and political concern. However, what Openshaw and others failed to highlight was the loss of any sense of sacrificial service which was becoming increasingly evident in Independent Methodism as its political leanings took precedence over its spiritual values.

3.2. A Case Study: North-East Lancashire

The connection between IM losses and industrial decline can be illustrated from events in North-East Lancashire. Nelson in the 1920s was a town with 15,000 cotton operatives, of whom a quarter were unemployed by 1932, while 3,000 had become permanently redundant in the previous five years.[43] The result was a drift of population away from Nelson and similar towns, which would continue for the next fifty years. This inevitably affected churches of all denominations, not least the Independent Methodists who lost some of their most valued workers through removal. By the late 1930s, the impact of population movement, together with the general spiritual malaise of the time, brought inevitable and unwelcome results. The Colne and Nelson Circuit, which only forty years earlier had been the most thriving in the Connexion, was now in serious decline. In 1936, a survey showed that the circuit's Sunday Schools had lost 1,177 scholars in fifteen years.[44] This was only the prelude to the church closures which followed: Every Street, Nelson, (1938), Brierfield (1939) and Haggate (1942). The large chapel at Barkerhouse Road, Nelson, kept open by a handful of people, survived only as a result of help from Salem Church, but finally succumbed to closure in 1957. Several others struggled on and it was a common complaint that even the largest chapels had only small congregations. High unemployment also affected the small town of Westhoughton, Lancashire, and the leaders of Wingates IM Church lamented that their Sunday School was now only half the size it once was.[45] A general sense of defeatism was widespread.[46]

3.3. The Scale of Losses

While Colne and Nelson was the worst affected circuit, others suffered losses too, with the effect that the Independent Methodists disappeared from some areas altogether. In 1928 the solitary church at Darlington was the first of several to close.[47] Glasgow followed in 1932, ending the IM presence in Scotland.[48] The two churches at Lancaster merged in the same year[49] and, despite the best efforts of evangelist Clara Green who was sent in at an impossibly late hour, the church in nearby Morecambe closed in 1933.[50] Stockport, one of the Connexion's founding churches, closed in 1937. Two of the six rural Nottinghamshire churches were lost during the Second World War, while the Northumberland churches were reduced from five to two in a few short years. In 1939, the isolated church at Hull came to an end, as did St. John's Lane, Bristol.[51] On the other hand, Spennymoor Circuit in County Durham enjoyed a time of growth and prosperity which continued into the Second World War years. Its chapel at Brandon, given originally by the local colliery proprietors, was replaced with a new building in 1931.[52] Metal Bridge, an existing mission, affiliated itself to the circuit in 1939 and, a year later, the Circuit's energetic Home Missions Committee established a new church in the village of Kelloe.[53]

4. Developments in Overseas Missions

On the Overseas Missions front, 1928 saw two important developments. After several years of having no missionary on the field, a new candidate emerged in the person of Edith Bevan (1903-1989), a young nurse from Moorside Church, Swinton (Manchester). She was posted to the same location as Joseph and Jessie Robinson, at Itarsi in Central India, through a

*Horace Banner giving a reading lesson to Paiakan, a Brazilian boy
who later became international ambassador for the Kayapo Indians*

similar arrangement between the Connexion and the Friends Missionary
Society. This provided a new impetus for missionary interest, once again
in the form of a medical missionary. In 1947, Edith Bevan's outstanding
contribution to Christian medical work in the area was recognised by the
British Government, which still ruled India at the time, and she was awarded
the Kaiser-I-Hind medal by King George VI.[54] Her service in India continued
until 1967.

Far less publicised at the time was the departure of Horace Banner
(1906-1974), a young IM minister from Grappenhall Church (Warrington)
who answered the call to missionary service, not via the IM Connexion but
with the Unevangelised Fields Mission. He set sail for Brazil in 1928, with
his fare paid by Mrs. C.T. Studd, whose husband had founded the Worldwide
Evangelisation Crusade (WEC) and who greatly admired the eager new
recruit. His service began in the coastal areas of the country but in 1936
he responded to a new challenge. Three young American missionaries had
set out to contact tribal Indians in the Xingu River region, but nothing had
been heard from them. It fell to Horace Banner and another missionary,
Jock Johnstone, to investigate. They eventually found the wreckage of their
predecessors' boat and later discovered that they had been killed by the
Indians.[55] Thus began a mission to the remote tribal Indians of Brazil, which
not only saw Christian churches established among the tribes, but which
eventually brought national honours to Horace Banner from the Brazilian

government. The IM Connexion belatedly recognised his work twenty years after his arrival in Brazil and started to give him support, following strong representations by some of the churches where his 'furlough' visits had made a great impression. This created a precedent in the whole IM approach to Overseas Missionary work which gradually changed to a pattern whereby a candidate would apply directly to a missionary society; the Connexion, if it was satisfied with the arrangements, would agree to provide some support.

5. Theological Trends between the Wars

5.1. Biblical Authority

Theologically, the liberalism of earlier years continued unabated throughout the 1920s and 1930s.[56] The nature of belief in biblical authority had been under question for some time and, by the 1920s, most IM leaders held very different views from their forebears.[57] Responding to the fundamentalist controversy in the United States, Arthur Ince refuted ideas of infallibility and inerrancy, on the basis that the Scriptures did not claim them.[58] At the Sunderland Ministers' Conference, William Foreman spoke against literalism and argued that modern scholarship had improved the understanding of the Bible.[59] Charles Thornton (Ashton-under-Lyne, Manchester) agreed with the New Testament scholar, T.R. Glover, 'The old doctrine of verbal inspiration has wrought havoc with the faith of the younger generation. It is useless trying to bolster up the illogical formulas of bygone ages.'[60] His observation reflected the genuine dilemma of an age when informed evangelical scholarship had yet to provide an adequate response to the onslaughts of scientific knowledge and biblical criticism. Many years were to pass before a confident, biblically rooted evangelicalism was to assert itself.

5.2. Christology and the Kingdom of God

However, and more importantly, the most foundational doctrines to come under re-interpretation at this time were those concerning the person of Christ and the Kingdom of God. Christology had been changed not by science or textual criticism but by an emphasis on the immanence of God, rather than His transcendence, which made only the vaguest distinction between the human and divine. This inevitably impacted on doctrines such as the incarnation and led to a view of Jesus which concentrated on the 'Son of Man' rather than the 'Son of God.'[61] Although such thought was past its high watermark by the 1920s, to many Independent Methodists it was still new and revolutionary. At the Ministers' Conference of 1928, T.R. Openshaw stated that 'Jesus' and 'Christ' were not synonymous terms to him: 'Christianity was the final faith because

Jesus won his Christship. In the forty days of the Temptation he became, *he became* the Christ, the Saviour of the world.'[62] Charles Thornton observed that the humanity of Christ was being stressed at the expense of his divinity, and concluded 'but that has been a gain rather than a loss. It has brought him nearer, showing to us that he is our true elder brother. Let the human element be admitted at once in the Bible and the divine element will shine out more clearly.'[63] The Men's Fellowship presented Christ as 'the ultimate ideal'[64] and 'the sound guide to life'.[65] Ernest Lawrenson described him simply as 'the exemplar of service.'[66] Rarely was there any explicit reference to His deity. The picture of Christ given by James Murray in a 1933 address, reflected the general failure of many of the IM leaders of the time to appreciate His true identity:

> Christ was no narrowminded sectional thinker; his philosophy
> was comprehensive and all embracing. He had a reverent attitude
> to God and to God's universe and that gave Him His religion.

Having relegated Christ from God the Son to mere philosopher, Murray turned to the related theme of the Kingdom of God, which he equated with universal brotherhood and linked with the freethinking ideas of the Hindu poet, Tagore. He continued:

> The Kingdom of God embraces 'every kindred, clime and land';
> men of all colours and all creeds; it is bigger than the systems of
> religion; it is to be a Universal community of the loyal.[67]

Murray's conflation of the Kingdom of God with universal brotherhood was a widely held view among Independent Methodists at the time, having roots in the ideas of the German theologian Albrecht Ritschl (1822-89), who saw the Kingdom as a static realm of ethical values in which religion and culture were virtually identical.[68] Its secularised eschatology failed to acknowledge the flaws in human nature and argued that humankind was progressing upwardly. Even in 1933, this view was beginning to look rather dated and came under heavy criticism from theologians such as Karl Barth and the brothers Reinhold and H. Richard Niebuhr who could see the weaknesses of liberal Protestantism's excessive optimism.[69]

Changes in interpretation of both Christ and the Kingdom of God impacted on the whole nature of religious experience and evangelistic work. In true Methodist style, Independent Methodists had traditionally stressed new birth and the inward witness of the Holy Spirit, but immanentism scaled them down to experiences which were common to all men.[70] The divine distinctive was lost and universalism became the order of the day. In the process, the doctrines of the creeds were sidelined or even denied. The outcome (not only among the Independent Methodists) was a vagueness of belief which was often behaviour-centred rather than theological.[71] Decency, good living and neighbourliness provided the ethos of nonconformist life generally, while doctrine was a matter of disinterest to the average church member and mission focused on the improvement of society rather than on repentance and conversion.

5.3. The Sacraments

The renascent Quakerism of the early twentieth century still carried some weight, not least through its two greatest exponents, Edward Ralphs and Arthur Mounfield. This inevitably impacted on sacramental thought and practice. Writing in a booklet for young people, Mounfield wrote of the Lord's Supper:

> When Jesus gave them [the disciples] the broken bread it was a symbolical and Jewish way of saying that He had formed a new kind of family, and when He asked them to eat and drink in his memory He was asking them to live always in fellowship with Him and with each other. The Jewish supper was the mark of the family, and we shall best understand what we call the Lord's Supper if we look at it in this way.[72]

Of baptism, he wrote:

> It is a pity that Christians have differed so much about baptism, for it is a custom that belongs to the old world and has no real meaning for us. We can make confession without water.[73]

The fact that the IM Bookroom published this booklet indicated that this was a widely held view of the sacraments, which were regarded as having little or no spiritual efficacy. However, in the years following World War 2, they received closer attention, partly through ecumenical involvement and partly due to changed views on baptism in some of the churches.[74]

Generally speaking, addresses which were reported to the magazine focused on Christian ideals of love, loyalty, altruism and heroism, as exemplified by Jesus. The Old Testament and the writings of Paul were rarely mentioned, the devil was consigned to mythology and 'hell' was merely a profanity. It was an eloquent silence.

6. Evangelistic Activity

The years between the wars still saw extensive evangelistic activity, though it fell short of its pre-war successes. During his presidency of 1927-28, Henry Barrett (1876-1930) of Nelson made every visit to the churches and circuits an evangelistic meeting and recorded large numbers of converts during the year. In his descriptions of the churches and some of the people he met, he noted with approval Christians of long standing who still bore the glow of their new-found faith. Commenting on his visit to Sutton Church (St. Helens, Lancashire), he wrote: 'There are about a dozen men who would furnish Harold Begbie with ample material for another *Broken Earthenware*. Men who in the past have been associated with all that is wicked in the world and have been literally lifted out of the mire and clay.'[75]

Mission and denominational expansion were inseparable in the minds of the leaders of the day and an evangelistic drive, known as 'The Forward Movement', was launched in 1929 with the aim of raising £1,000 each year in the hope that this would assist local efforts to build new churches.[76] However, in giving the launch address, Henry Barrett put his finger on the pulse of the denomination: 'there is not the same keenness, intensity, the great yearning and longing for the salvation of the people as in our fathers thirty or forty years ago.'[77] His assessment was borne out as the financial target fell far short of expectations and only one new church was established in the 1930s, through the enterprise of the Bolton Circuit which opened a mission on the newly built Top'oth Brow estate.[78] The overall failure of the Forward Movement project indicated the extent to which evangelistic motivation had waned.

Diminished evangelistic motivation inevitably affected the work of the Connexion's evangelists, the main one of this period being Alfred Foreman of Sunderland (1888-1964) who served from 1916 to 1942. His main bases of operation were Blackley (Manchester), Astley (Leigh) and Top'oth Brow (Bolton).[79] The work at Astley proved particularly hard and, in 1938, Foreman enlisted the assistance of W. Drummond Brown who walked several miles each week from Swinton to help him.[80] Brown's voluntary commitment to this work was typical of the unstinting devotion of many of those who maintained the IM churches without remuneration.

By contrast to his localised postings, demand for Foreman's services for weekend missions had waned even by the late 1920s, so the Connexional Committee looked at other ways of using his abilities. In 1928, four objectives were agreed:

1. The use of Burnside as a teaching centre
2. The provision of peripatetic tuition for the Ministers' Education Course
3. The formation of teacher training classes
4. The launch of a junior membership scheme among the churches.

The decision to channel Foreman's energies in this direction was opposed by his home circuit at Sunderland, which took the view that evangelists should be engaged only in evangelistic work, but the Annual Meeting was plainly determined to see the scheme launched and it was approved overwhelmingly. T.R. Openshaw made the point that the lack of demand for Foreman's services as an evangelist had made him available for tutorial work,[81] while the report of the Evangelistic Committee indicated that there was not as much enthusiasm for organising missions as there had been a generation earlier.[82]

Foreman pursued all four objectives with vigour. In later years he was remembered in particular for his work in establishing

WE WANT YOU TO KNOW

THESE MEETINGS ARE FOR YOU
COME AND BRING YOUR NEIGHBOURS

tuition centres for the Ministers' Education Course. At the 1930 Annual Meeting it was reported that he had conducted ninety-six classes in six centres.[83] He continued with this work throughout the 1930s, during which time he also wrote a basic church history textbook which became part of the syllabus for the course.[84]

Prima facie, Openshaw's comments on the lack of demand for Foreman as an evangelist were justified. But the reality was that Foreman was a self-taught scholar and social idealist rather than an evangelist in the traditional mould. Like others of his generation, his theology had been shaped in an age when old certainties about the Bible were questioned and important doctrines were being re-interpreted.[85] Those who saw evangelism in the more traditional style therefore regarded him with some caution. However, many of his contemporaries approved of his style of evangelism:

> His was an evangelism so different from the accepted kind – an appeal not to emotionalism but to a rational consideration of the claims of Jesus Christ as Saviour to a man's whole life and service. There was for him no high pressure appeal – no wearing down of the personality of a man, but the presentation of Jesus Christ as Saviour, friend and guide.[86]

By 1936, the demand for an evangelist's services was significantly greater than in 1928, but the churches by this time were prepared to go outside the Connexion in order to find suitable personnel. Several churches availed themselves of the services of W.H. Harvey and A. Blythe of Sunderland, two Cliff College students, who were known as the 'Sunshine Corner' evangelists. Their direct appeals to the unconverted were well received in churches where the liberalism of the denomination's leaders found little sympathy. At Tetlow Street (Liverpool), a mission in 1936 resulted in about fifty adults giving their lives to Christ. Similar experiences were reported at Bethany (Sunderland), Waterside (Colne, Lancashire) and Crewe.[87] A year later saw them hold a further mission at Liverpool and one at Golborne (Lancashire). In 1938 Blythe conducted a mission alone at Nottingham, resulting in twenty-two conversions. If some were uncomfortable with their methods, these churches, at least, were well satisfied with the results.

Certain pockets of firm resistance to the liberalism of the time remained in various parts of the Connexion. Robert Street Church, Sunderland, maintained the strong Wesleyan holiness tradition begun earlier in the century by John W. Johnson.[88] In the 1930s 'trekkers' from Cliff College and later from the International Holiness Mission, led by Kenneth Bedwell, came in turn to the church. November 1939 brought a mission led by Maynard James, an evangelist with the Calvary Holiness Church. Each event saw conversions take place.[89] New Year's meetings took place, when each meeting invariably ended with an appeal for those who wished to receive the second blessing of entire sanctification.[90]

Among the Connexional evangelists who served in the inter-war years were A.J. Good of Trimdon Grange, Co. Durham, who worked briefly on a full time basis, Robert Rimmer (1859-1939) of Bolton, who conducted weekend missions during the winter months, and Clara Green (1873-1958) who worked mainly among women. There was also a 'panel' of evangelists who gave occasional service.[91] After 1942, the only evangelists to serve for the next five years, albeit on a part time basis, were William Eccleston (1875-1955) of Golborne, Lancashire, and the veteran Clara Green. This war-time lull in activity was followed by a call from delegates at the Annual Meetings to appoint another permanent evangelist. In 1947, the Home Missions Committee responded to the call and John W. Davenport (1898-1987) of Tyldesley, Lancashire, was appointed on a five year contract. Initially his services were well used, but latterly demand tailed off, with only twelve churches using him during the year 1951-52.[92] The decision was therefore taken to terminate his services. Paradoxically, a new era of evangelism was on the horizon, but it stemmed from sources completely outside of the denomination.

7. Ministry

The need to use Alfred Foreman as peripatetic tutor indicated that ministerial education was almost as great a problem as it had been when first attempted sixty years earlier. The denomination simply lacked people with the necessary grounding to deliver the course and standards of tuition varied widely. Few, like the Liverpool Circuit, were fortunate enough to have the services of a man like William Logan, a minister at Tetlow Street Church and an erudite scholar in his own right.[93] Some circuits put conscience about paid ministry to one side and engaged the services of members of the local clergy; others had no tutors and the students studied alone.[94]

Since 1917, the ministry had become more centrally driven, but there was still no formal accreditation beyond local circuits. Some operated their own education schemes which amounted to little more than an oral examination on basic doctrines. People were added to the Connexion's list of ministers simply on the basis that their local circuits had approved them. There was a widely held view that some consistency was needed. In 1941, the Annual Meeting approved a document which laid down central rules for admission to the ministry of the Connexion.[95] This included a requirement to complete either the Connexion's own education scheme or one which the Ministers' Committee regarded as equivalent to it. A minister's name had to be added to the Connexional list by a nomination from his local circuit and a formal resolution at a Connexional Committee meeting. The rules covered the obligations of studentship and procedures for recognition or deposition of ministers.[96] The process of centralisation was, in effect, completed and the rules remained unchanged until 2000.

The Independent Methodists held tenaciously to their views on unpaid ministry throughout this time. At times, their inflexibility closed the doors to opportunities for wider service. In 1952, the local Free Church Council at Haslingden (Lancashire) wished to recommend an IM minister as chaplain to the Rossendale General Hospital. As this was a paid appointment, the matter came before the Connexional Committee to establish whether or not the minister in question should accept it. After some discussion, the Committee passed a resolution:

> That we appreciate the recognition of the right of an IM minister
> to be appointed as a hospital chaplain, but cannot, having regard
> to our constitution, approve of any such appointment to which a
> payment is attached.[97]

The very basis of this refusal reflected the massive change in thinking of the previous seventy years. Writers such as Denovan and Brimelow had sought sanction for their views in biblical teaching, but the current generation of leaders no longer had their forebears' confidence in the Bible, so any appeal to its injunctions would have lacked both conviction and credibility. The only way they could justify their decision was by citing the constitution which, of course, was merely the mechanism by which the denomination operated. The constitution precluded payment so, whether right or wrong, it was not permissible, regardless of the possibilities which it might open up. A once living issue of ideology had become fossilised in legality. The non-payment principle had, in effect, become more important than the principle of freedom to fulfil a God-given ministry, which was, in essence, the real aspiration of the denomination's founding fathers.

Ministry remained a controversial subject and provoked a series of letters to the denominational magazine in 1951. One correspondent, J. White, wrote to say that he saw the appointment of ministers as a contradiction of the Connexion's professed principle of the priesthood of all believers. He was supported by Joseph Robinson of Nelson who regarded the 1917 Military Test Case as a backward step which had created an artificial distinction between one servant of God and another.[98] Against them stood William Durant of Warrington who upheld the designation 'minister' as a way of setting people apart for a role and recognising their ability and training.[99] Ai Shires of Dewsbury supported Durant and, in a telling comment, deplored the fact that the ministry was singled out from time to time for attack. After so long a history of voluntary ministry, it would not have been unreasonable to expect that the denomination would by now be of one mind on how it should be understood and defined, but this brief exchange plainly showed that the position was as indeterminate as ever.

9. Ecumenical Developments

9.1. The British Council of Churches

Continuing as they had done in the years preceding the First World War, the Independent Methodists maintained their interest in ecumenical activity and continued to be represented on national bodies. One of their new spheres of involvement was the Christian Social Council, which aimed to apply Christian faith to social, industrial and economic questions. T.R. Openshaw of Gargrave, Yorkshire, (1881-1956), represented the Connexion on the Council from its inception and played an active part in its work. He was recognised for his stature as an industrialist, being a director of various cotton mills, and his involvement with the Council led to an invitation to speak for the Industrial Christian Fellowship at a Conference of Anglican clergy on the Christian faith and the economic depression.[100] In due course, he went on to represent the Connexion on other ecumenical bodies and finally became its first representative on the British Council of Churches when it was established in 1941. After the Second World War, he became involved in the work of Christian Reconstruction in Europe and the rehabilitation of refugees, to which he gave the remaining years of his life.[101] Perhaps more than anyone else, he gave Independent Methodists a broader perspective on the universal church and the wider world. When he was called to the presidential chair for the second time in 1942, he reflected on the developments that had taken place already in the field of Christian unity:

Edward Ralphs (1863-1946)   *T.R. Openshaw (1881-1956)*

The day of religious proselytising is waning. Selfish isolationism (a self-centred regard for one's creed or system) is giving way to a tolerant sympathy for all the followers of the Lord and an overwhelming concern for the triumph of His Kingdom. The speed of the growth of the sense of unity among Christians of every denomination is marvellous in my eyes; it is the Lord's doing verily![102]

9.2. Movements towards Organic Union

Certainly Openshaw spoke for Independent Methodists in expressing approval towards improved relationships and better co-operation, but organic forms of union were still far from their thinking. However, other churchmen plainly had a different view. One of the main ecumenical thrusts of the inter-war years began with the Lambeth Conference of Anglican bishops in 1920, which pointed to the vision of a reunited Christian Church. This was received sympathetically by the Free Churches and led to conversations (in which the Independent Methodists participated) which took place intermittently over the next two decades.

In 1938 a report entitled *An Outline of a Re-Union Scheme for the Church of England and the Evangelical Free Churches of England* was published, with the intention that it should be discussed by all the churches concerned. The Independent Methodists opened it up for discussion at their Annual Meeting in June of that year and delegated to the Connexional Committee the task of making a formal submission to the Federal Council of Evangelical Free Churches.[103] This was drafted by the Connexional Secretary, James Murray (1884-1964), who produced a 12,000 word response which acknowledged the spiritual unity of the church, but expressed the view that unity should exist within variety. Murray identified three problems for Independent Methodists with the proposed scheme. Firstly, his comments on the sacraments reflected the modified Quakerism which still prevailed in parts of the Connexion:

> As in the belief of the Free Churches, the individual conscience gives relative degrees of importance to the Lord's Supper and to Baptism. But since our emphasis is upon individual conversion and an open acknowledgement of the same, we feel that we should be frustrating the work of the Spirit if we should insist upon any sacrament of the Lord's Supper (Eucharist and Holy Communion are terms not used by us), or upon a ceremony of Baptism before the Lord Jesus Christ will receive men into His heart and impart His life.[104]

Secondly, the matter of ministry was inevitably a point of dispute for Independent Methodists, since the proposed scheme called for the reunited Church to be an Episcopal Church:

> when the ministry becomes exclusive, privileged, and founded upon an Episcopal order, we must frankly declare that we feel it to be inconsistent with the teaching of the New Testament concerning the Church and its ministries.[105]

Murray then turned to the associated issue of ordination, which was anathema to the Independent Methodists; in their view, it accentuated the difference between ministers and others. With this in mind, he offered an alternative proposal, couched in functional terms, which would never have been accepted by the Church of England:

> The call of the Holy Spirit is primary, and this should be recognised by the Church and confirmed by appointment to the work of the ministry in the name of the Church.[106]

By the same token, Murray's paper objected to the report's proposal to limit sacramental presidency to 'those who have received authority thereto.' As the 'authority' so accorded was to come from the proposed unified Church, this contravened the Independent Methodists' belief that the *local* church should be the primary ecclesial unit.

It was obvious from both the report's proposals and the IM response to it that the gulf between the two was too great for any serious chance of IM participation in such a reunion scheme. They were not alone among the Free Churches in believing that outward uniformity was not necessary for spiritual unity.[107] In the event, conversations between the Church of England and Free Churches were brought to a standstill by the outbreak of the Second World War a year later. The Free Churches were also preoccupied with negotiations which resulted in the amalgamation of the Federal Council of Evangelical Free Churches with the National Free Church Council in 1940.

Probably the most significant ecumenical achievement of this period was the union of the Wesleyan Methodists, Primitive Methodists and United Methodists in 1932, to form the Methodist Church of Great Britain. The Independent Methodists were not invited to join in the talks which led to this union, but were represented at the unifying meeting at the Royal Albert Hall, where Ellis Barker gave the Connexion's greetings.[108] The emergence of this new body, with over a million members, made the Independent Methodists look smaller and more anachronistic than ever, but their determination to continue for the sake of their distinctive principles remained undiminished.

10. Civic and Parliamentary Involvement

At a personal level, the political involvement of IM people continued unabated between the wars and beyond, despite the fact that nonconformity was no longer the political force it had once been. Sir Thomas Robinson, after his parliamentary career was over,[109] became the first mayor of the newly created borough of Stretford.[110] William Grundy, later to be Connexional President, became the first Labour mayor of Leigh.[111] 1938 saw a triplet of IM mayors – George Ford (Sunderland), Joseph Robinson (Nelson) and Edward Burrows (St. Helens).[112] Perhaps the most elevated civic office went to Joseph Baldwin (Nottingham) who became his city's Lord Mayor in 1939. A railway servant by occupation, Baldwin was a classic example of the type of person raised to prominence through democratic processes which pushed back the barriers of social class. He also exemplified the kind of firm nonconformist who took his principles into public life; during his tenure of office, no alcohol was served at civic functions.[113]

Trade union activity provided the route into political life for a number of people.[114] Two further Independent Methodists entered Parliament during the 1940s, both of them from North-East England, Labour Party candidates and nominees of the National Union of Mineworkers. James Dixon Murray (1887-1965), already an alderman and county councillor, was returned unopposed in 1942 as Member for Spennymoor[115] and was re-elected in the post-war election of 1945, serving until 1955, latterly in the newly formed constituency of Durham North-West. As an active trade unionist, he was a member of the Executive Committee of the British Miners' Federation.[116] The same election brought in Charles Frederick Grey (1903-1984) as Member for the adjacent constituency of the City of Durham.[117] Grey remained in Parliament for twenty-five years, during which time he served as a party whip, became Treasurer of the Queen's Household in the Labour government of 1966-70 and was awarded the CBE. After his retirement, he was accorded the freedom of the City of Durham and, later, an honorary doctorate in Civil Law from Durham University. Murray and Grey reflected the interest of many Independent Methodists of this period in both church and trade union activity which led in turn to wider political influence. No other Independent Methodist has sat in Parliament since Grey's retirement in 1970.

11. The Second World War

The IM Connexion's pacifist stand continued almost up to the outbreak of the Second World War. In 1938 the Connexional Committee issued a statement to the churches favouring disarmament and opposing conscription.[118] Prime Minister Neville Chamberlain's visit to Munich in the same year and his appeasement of Hitler were greeted with approval.[119] However, once war had broken out, the pacifist voice fell silent and the Independent Methodists, with the rest of the country, faced up to the reality of the Nazi threat and threw themselves into all aspects of the war effort. Individual churches operated 'comforts' schemes, whereby gifts were sent to members in the armed forces and some premises were requisitioned as soup canteens or evacuee centres. Bulwell Church, Nottingham, opened its own soldiers' canteen and also rented two lock up shops which it opened on weeknights as a service to the soldiers. The women of this church gave additional support to servicemen by taking in washing and helping with uniform repairs.[120] The Connexion played its part, in conjunction with the Methodist Church, by sending wallets containing two booklets *My Faith* and *A Booklet of Hymns and Prayers* to servicemen and women connected with the churches. By the end of the second year of the war, 1,749 had been issued and these continued to be sent until the war was over.[121]

Air raids took their toll on both buildings and people. Evacuation emptied several urban Sunday Schools as children were dispatched to the relative safety of the countryside. In some instances, church members lost their homes through enemy action. In Liverpool, Goodison Road Church reported the loss of Sunday School children who had been killed in bombing attacks on the city.[122] Bethany Church (Sunderland), Varley Street (Manchester) and Greenough Street (Wigan) were all completely destroyed, while Bedminster (Bristol) and Fitzwarren Street (Salford) suffered partial destruction.[123] Boldon Church (Sunderland) was extensively damaged, as was Tetlow Street (Liverpool), where the premises remained closed for two years.[124] Blackouts led to evening services being curtailed or brought forward to afternoons. The traditional IM practice whereby ministers travelled from town to town to preach in different churches was suspended and journeys were kept to a minimum. In numerous

*Members of the Connexional Committee at the 1946 Annual Meeting,
Roe Green Church, Worsley, Manchester. Left to Right.*
Back: *Charles Merrill, T.R. Openshaw, Noel lockley, Philip Lockley,
Wilfrid Sanderson, George Proudfoot, Silas Osborne, Ernest Barker, R.J.
Husband, Arthur Lambley.* **Middle:** *William Webb, Norman Allen, Albert
Davenport, Harry Bressington, Tom Backhouse, John Hassall, W.H.
Williams, William Eccleston, E.S. Mogg, John Priddle, Cyril Brown.*
Front: *Edward Embleton, George Case, Wilfrid Imeson, Ai Shires, William
Burrows, Alfred Walker, Albert Winnard, R.H. Settle, William Shaw, J.T.
Greenwood, Thomas Darlington, Ernest Woolard, H. Blacker*

ways, the churches had to adapt to a very different world.[125]

When the war ended, the churches prepared themselves to receive returning soldiers, though many never resumed their former allegiance.[126] Friars Green, Warrington, typified the experience of many churches; out of twenty men who had served in the armed forces, only three returned to the church.[127] Arthur Barrett of Nelson told the 1946 Annual Meeting that his war experience had caused him to doubt some of what he had previously believed.[128] The Connexional Committee was plainly aware of similar reactions and expressed a cautionary note in its annual report of 1945: 'It is our earnest hope that the churches may, while preserving the essentials of our Faith, do their best to eliminate the irritations of dogmatism, and will welcome back their friends without ostentation but with unmistakable thankfulness and friendliness.'[129]

12. Post-War Change
12.1. The Return to Theological Orthodoxy

It is difficult to gauge the extent to which the post-war generation of IM leaders was influenced by those whose writings they read, but certainly this was an age when orthodoxy reasserted itself in popular writers such as G.K. Chesterton, Dorothy L. Sayers and, most importantly, C.S. Lewis. The term 'thinking reader' was no longer the monopoly of the modernist; there was now a new interest in the great themes of incarnation, sin, judgement and redemption, stimulated by writers of formidable intellect whose academic credentials were impeccable.[130]

Some Independent Methodists began to question the 'social gospel', believing that it had eclipsed the spiritual message of the church. In the aftermath of the Second World War, the Connexional Secretary, W. Philip Lockley, commented on the lack of spiritual hunger in the churches and put his finger accurately on the denomination's spiritual poverty:

> We appear to have become in recent years a people of pretensions, thinking that we are called upon to solve all life's problems. We have lost much of our evangelistic fervour and are tending to subordinate faith to culture. While it may be possible to solve many of the world's difficulties and errors by culture . . . it is only as men are moved by the Gospel that they have not only the power but also the desire to do it.[131]

In a further address, a year later, he spoke of the dangers of diluting the Christian message:

> For years we have softened down the Gospel to make it attractive and 'to keep the young people'. The hours I have spent watching young folk play table tennis and billiards in the hope that it would help to hold them. It didn't – and it didn't deserve to . . . I believe that will only be attained by giving them a gospel with a Cross in it.'[132]

A development on the overseas missions front showed that this view was not an isolated one. In 1945, John and Elsie Finney from Prescot, Lancashire, went to India to serve in the same location as Edith Bevan at Itarsi, again under the aegis of the Friends, whose missionary society had now changed its title to 'Friends Service Council'. The Finneys' departure coincided with increasing interest in the work of Horace and Eva Banner in Brazil and prompted the observation of the Overseas Missions Secretary, W. Cyril Brown (1910-1995), that the Connexion's overseas involvement now had a new emphasis in terms of evangelical concern.[133] His own vision for missionary work had a decidedly conversionist agenda and illustrated his unease at the growing gap between this view and that of the Friends, who saw their priorities in terms of humanitarian work:

> One cannot help but feel that service to the community which, while presumably Christian, is suspicious of conversion and feels itself hampered by forthright evangelism, is not likely to achieve any lasting results in the regeneration of men and women which is fundamental to our service. No preaching, no form of worship, no pastoral work, will achieve their true purpose, if they fail either separately or together to bring the individual face to face with God in such a way as to demand a definite decision.[134]

The differences of views on mission policy between the Friends and their IM partners eventually came to a head, leading to the Finneys' resignation. It was the greatest crisis ever experienced in IM overseas work and culminated in the Connexional Committee's decision to terminate the Connexion's long association with the Friends Service Council.[135] The local church at Itarsi was incensed by what had happened and wrote a letter to express its support for the Finneys, expressing its 'profound disagreement with the policy of the Friends Service Council (London office)' and stating that 'the religious outlook and attitude of modern Friends is completely different from the basic teaching of the Indian Church at Itarsi.'[136] The Finneys moved to the Methodist-run Ingraham Institute at Delhi and Edith Bevan joined the staff of the United Church of Canada's mission hospital at Indore. This was an occurrence of profound significance which pointed the way to changes that would happen on the home front in the years ahead.

The comments of Philip Lockley and Cyril Brown reflected the early stages of Independent Methodism's return to its evangelical roots. They (and others) could see that the previous generation's preoccupation with the social gospel and political issues had failed to produce disciples. There was a need to re-focus on the Christ of the cross and the need for personal salvation.

As the years passed, the rise of conservative evangelicalism nationally played its part in further re-shaping IM attitudes, as individuals attended events such as the Keswick Convention and the Filey Crusade year by year. The writings of authors such as Martyn Lloyd-Jones, John Stott, J.I. Packer and F.F. Bruce also gave new stimulus to their thinking about cardinal Christian doctrines, including the inspiration and authority of the Bible.[137]

12.2. The 'Fundamentalist' Debate

In 1954, a long-running debate in the denominational magazine began as the result of an address by Henry Sharples (1896-1978), a Bolton minister and later Connexional President, to a 1953 conference for ministerial students, when he argued for the verbal inspiration of the Bible:

The theory which we adopt is that of plenary or verbal inspiration. We maintain that not only did God make a revelation of truth – of supernatural truth – to the sacred penmen, but He so influenced their minds that they used the very words in which He wished that revelation to be communicated to men. [138]

In 1953, this was such an exceptional position that some readers could hardly believe that it was being advocated in the denominational magazine. Three letters immediately followed, all expressing the opposite view. The main spokesman was Walter Hill of Wigan (1886-1983), another future Connexional President, who said that he had abandoned verbal inspiration forty years earlier because intellectual honesty required him to do so. Joseph Robinson of Nelson regarded such fundamentalism as extremist, was shocked that it should be taught to ministerial students and objected to magazine space being given to it. Geoffrey Lee of Cleckheaton argued for progressive revelation on the basis of a dichotomy between the pictures of God found in the two testaments. [139]

The matter did not rest there. Support for Sharples came from John Edwards (Sunderland) who argued that he had only expanded on the statements on the authority of Scripture recorded in the Connexion's Statement of Faith and Practice. [140] Jack Cantrell (Manchester) asserted that, as a scientist, he did not commit intellectual dishonesty by his commitment to biblical truth and deplored the superior attitude which seemed to him to be coming from Sharples' opponents. Over the following months, argument and counter-argument continued, with neither side willing to let the other have the last word, until the editor, Dr. Tom Backhouse of Liverpool (1915-1998), finally declared the matter closed. The whole debate exposed the chasm between the two viewpoints, but it also showed that the denomination was less uniformly liberal than formerly. In subsequent years, the balance gradually tilted towards those who took a more firmly biblicist view, though few would term themselves 'fundamentalist' and verbal inspiration was never formally adopted as the denomination's official viewpoint.

12.3. The Retreat from Politics

Notwithstanding the work of J.D. Murray, Charles Grey and others on the political front, the Independent Methodists were becoming gradually less disposed to tackle political issues than they had been a generation earlier. Leaders such as Dr. W.W. Kay favoured an interest in current affairs, but believed that church and politics should be kept separate. [141] Resolutions to the government became fewer as their impact seemed increasingly negligible and internal support for them was no longer a foregone conclusion. In 1957 the Connexional Committee suffered the uncomfortable experience of finding that its members' views on certain issues no longer reflected the wider outlook of their constituency. At the beginning of the year, Alfred Foreman, veteran pacifist and by now the editor of the denominational magazine, published an article in which he advocated the establishment of an International Police Force under the aegis of the United Nations.[142] Such a body would patrol the frontiers of every country in the world. Once established, the production of arms would be forbidden and all national military forces disbanded. This lofty objective was set against the backcloth of international tension following the 1956 Suez crisis, the Soviet invasion of Hungary and the acceleration of the nuclear arms race. Foreman then brought a proposal to the Annual Meeting, with the Connexional Committee's support, calling on the Independent Methodists to give a lead in campaigning for his suggested antidote to the threat of a third world war. He concluded, 'It was the Baptist Church [sic] which first stood for liberty of conscience; it was the Society of Friends who first stood for the abolition of slavery; now I should like to claim the honour for our Church [sic] to give a lead in the preservation of peace.'[143] In the event, the delegates felt that this was a political matter which could potentially cause division in the Connexion and a more general resolution was passed, urging church members to 'support every activity that will further the establishment of lasting peace.'[144] Just as the Liberal political hegemony in the denomination had fragmented after the First World War, the domination of inter-war pacifist thought had now lost ground in a more pragmatic age. Independent Methodists were more politically heterogeneous than ever and consensus was more difficult. Moreover, as the IM people gradually rediscovered their evangelical roots in the 1950s, they were less disposed to spend time on pursuing political objectives and more realistic about what a small denomination could achieve at national level.

12.4. The Recovery of the Sunday Schools

In common with the churches nationally, IM Sunday Schools experienced a renaissance, with numbers steadily rising year on year. They totalled 14,000 children by 1954, but thereafter decline continued unabated throughout the ensuing decades. The benefit of this post-war boom was reflected in increased young people's activity at Circuit and Connexional level from about 1950 onwards. Weekend Young People's Conferences took place, firstly at a retreat centre at Burley-in-Wharfedale (Yorkshire) and later in local churches. Individual Circuits, notably Liverpool, Manchester, Bristol and the Northern Counties Confederation also held their own residential weekend conferences. An annual Scripture Examination proved highly popular, with over 1,000 entrants per year at the height of its strength. Christian Endeavour continued to be a major influence well beyond 1960, with the majority of IM churches operating junior and young people's groups. As in other denominations, youth clubs and uniformed organisations also featured in the programmes of many churches. In all, the 1950s, numerically at least, brought an Indian summer of prosperity to young people's work, before the years of heavy decline set in.

12.5. New Forms of Evangelistic Work

In 1946, England experienced a new evangelistic phenomenon with the arrival of the American evangelist, Billy Graham. In some ways reminiscent of the missions of D.L. Moody eighty years earlier, Billy Graham's method was to preach simple gospel messages to large crowds of people and call on them to make a response of personal commitment. Graham's first major campaign, in 1954, took place in London, where the Independent Methodists had no churches, but as the following account shows, its effects were felt further afield.

In 1950, Jack Cantrell, a young IM minister and a powerful evangelistic preacher, joined the church at Ashton-on-Mersey (Manchester). Though never a Connexional officer, he was in great demand for his preaching ministry and especially for young people's events. He and his wife, Lee, worked through the Christian Endeavour movement in their new church, where they saw several conversions among the young people, who were nurtured through Bible study, trained in Christian service and encouraged to share their newfound faith with others.

Young people who had prayed aloud, led the meeting or presented papers for the first time in the Christian Endeavour meeting formed 'preaching teams' and took services in many churches in the Manchester and South Lancashire area. Some went on to become IM ministers or preachers. This impacted on youth work and Sunday Schools in the Manchester Circuit. One identified need was for visual aids and a filmstrip projector was purchased, which led to an arrangement with Elite Projectors whereby such machines were made available to at least eleven Connexional churches at discounted prices. Ashton-on-Mersey purchased a variety of filmstrips to provide a library from which other churches could borrow for a small charge, thus enabling more filmstrips to be purchased.[145]

A year after Billy Graham's 1954 Harringay Crusade, a film based on the Crusade, entitled 'Souls in Conflict', was shown in the Manchester area, resulting in some conversions. The young people at Ashton-on-Mersey immediately saw film as a potential medium of evangelism. Through sacrificial giving (most of them were still at school), they raised enough money to purchase a secondhand 16mm projector and a 'Film Unit' was established. Films were hired from several sources, but mainly the Billy Graham Association and the Moody Bible Institute. Under Jack Cantrell's inspirational leadership, it went on to become an important means of evangelistic work locally and further afield. In 1957, the Connexional Home Missions Secretary, Bill Maiden, encouraged the Connexion to adopt this outreach work, which then became 'The Independent Methodist Film Unit'. In the years that followed, it became one of the Connexion's main tools of mission work, travelling to all parts of the denomination for both single evenings and full scale missions. As a result of one of its journeys to the North-East, Ron Stout, a minister at Hetton-le-Hole Church (Co. Durham), caught the same vision and started a Film Unit for the churches of the Northern Counties Confederation.[146]

A resourceful and energetic Young People's Committee was formed in the Manchester Circuit during the late 1950s, with some talented youth leaders from the various churches. Most were in their late teens, newly converted and with strong evangelistic motivation. They organised numerous activities, including missionary meetings, Arts and Crafts Festivals, sports days and dinners. Social events were invariably concluded with a 'gospel' message. An annual Young People's Conference saw many commitments to Christ over the years. In a telling comment, one of the young leaders of the time, David Hill, referred to one of the least noted characteristics of the Independent Methodists: in a denomination which lacked a professional ministry, anyone who attempted to do anything new was allowed to make mistakes.[147] Experts who could have corrected them were in short supply and, in any event, ageing leaders were grateful to see the emergence of new life after years of decline and were prepared to give opportunities for the young people to serve.

From Ashton-on-Mersey, Peter Wilkes, a young university lecturer, went to the nearby IM church at Stretford and began a successful youth work which extended into the local student population for a number of years. At the 1958 Annual Meeting, he sought out Dennis Downing, currently the Connexion's representative on the Free Church Council Youth Department, to share his conviction that the various youth clubs in the Connexion needed something to bring them together. Dennis Downing described his involvement with the Methodist Association of Youth Clubs (MAYC) in his home town of Loughborough. His own IM church then had no youth club so, using MAYC ideas, he had started a youth club which had grown to a membership of fifty. From his experience with MAYC, he was able to suggest ideas for an Independent Methodist youth club network. The outcome was a meeting at Stretford in November 1958, attended by various youth leaders, who agreed to form a new organisation, to be known as IMTAKS (Independent Methodist Teen Age KlubS), the name already used at Loughborough. Peter Wilkes was its first President and Dennis Downing its first Secretary. The following Connexional Committee meeting approved its formation and details were sent to all the churches. There was an immediate take-up from a small number of churches, but the number grew steadily during the following years.[148]

After the Connexion ceased to have an evangelist of its own, those churches which were mission-minded called upon the services of establishments such Cliff College (Derbyshire), the Evangelisation Society or the Children's Special Service Mission to run missions in their churches and localities. Others simply used their own resources. The rising interest in evangelistic work among the younger generation was not confined to one area; new life was emerging in several places. A Youth Weekend at Horden (Co. Durham) in 1955 saw the church's young people engaging in open air work, testimony meetings and indoor evangelistic preaching, resulting in fourteen decisions for Christ over the weekend.[149] A campaign at Cochrane Street (Liverpool) in the same year brought twenty-eight decisions and the beginning of a new chapter in the church's life.[150] Through missions such as these, faith grew and even people who had worshipped in their churches for years experienced a new awakening.

The fruit of the new evangelicalism included a renewed interest in Overseas Missions work as the rising generation took seriously the 'great commission' of Christ. Over the coming decades, the number of missionaries going out from the IM churches grew exponentially, but the 1950s marked only the early stage of this process and saw just two candidates begin their missionary careers. Joan Caven (1929-1976) of Robert Street Church, Sunderland, went to Brazil in 1958 with Unevangelised Fields Mission as a teacher of missionaries' children. Her career was tragically cut short when she was diagnosed with multiple sclerosis and she returned to Britain in 1968.[151] From the same church, Hilda Rolfe went as a medical missionary to Vendahland in South Africa where she went on to become matron of the Donald Frazer Mission Hospital. Her work entailed teaching and evangelistic work as well as nursing and she served until 1974 when the care of her aged parents made a return home necessary.[152]

13. Conclusions

The IM leaders during the inter-war years faced a very different world from that of their predecessors. The impact of theological change had already been felt before the Great War and, along with Christians in general, they faced the challenge of the post-war world with the tools of a theology which made little of dogma, but which looked for a universalist Kingdom of God built on earth through peace and brotherhood. This matched their predominantly socialist political outlook. Quaker ideals were also held in high regard and were reflected in the denomination's strongly pacifist strain and low view of the sacraments. Education received greater stress than evangelism, perhaps not surprisingly since the evangelistic message was sounding an uncertain note; there was not the same confidence in a gospel which had once stressed that salvation was found through Christ alone. While it would be too simplistic to say that changed theology was the main reason for the numerical decline which continued throughout these years, a gospel which tacitly implied that many roads led to God inevitably took away one of the most compelling reasons for a distinctively Christian commitment and thereby for church attendance.

The aftermath of the Second World War saw a gradual decline in the theological liberalism which had dominated Independent Methodism for nearly fifty years, but denominational principles continued to be regarded as inviolable, as the Rossendale chaplaincy situation showed. The new young evangelicals of the 1950s were only a small minority in the denomination, with little influence. At this stage, they found themselves facing cultural barriers in many churches, some of which were recreationally orientated and had little spiritual life beyond Sunday worship. Their day was still to come.

Notes to Chapter Six

1. 'The Lecture Courses', *IMMag.* 1922, 138.
2. James Murray, *Independent Methodist History 1905-1955* (Wigan: Independent Methodist Bookroom, 1955), 58.
3. See Chapter 4.
4. *IMYB* 1935, 34.
5. 'The Lowton Conference', *IMMag.* 1934, 163.
6. 'The Independent Quarterly', *IMMag.* 1928, 5.
7. *IMMag.* 1937, 114.
8. 'A Letter from the Connexional Editors', *IMMag.* 1933, 40.
9. *IMMag.* 1937, 114.
10. 'Young Men's Fellowship Spring Conference', *IMMag.* 1934, 44.
11. Murray, *IM History*, 33.
12. *IMMag.* 1931, 16.
13. 'Hook Gate Circuit August Bank Holiday Rally', *IMMag.* 1939, 143.
14. J.M. Turner, *Modern Methodism in England, 1932-1998* (Peterborough: Epworth, 1998), 7.
15. E. Ralphs, 'The Peace Pact and Afterwards', *IMMag.* 1929, 136.
16. Information supplied by W.P. Lockley, Connexional Secretary 1941-47.
17. Rennie Smith wrote *General Disarmament or War?* (London: Allen and Unwin, 1927) and *Peace Verboten* (London: Hutchinson, 1943). He also wrote a foreword to Trevor and Phyllis Blewitt's translation of Hans Siemsen, *Hitler*

Youth (Lindsay Drummond, 1940) and a preface to Hans Aktuhn, *Aggression: the Origin of Germany's War Machine* (London, 1942). At one time he was reputed to be on Hitler's 'hit list'.

18. R. Smith, 'The Churches and World Peace', *IMMag.* 1929, 223.
19. Murray, *IM History*, 61.
20. *IMYB* 1932, 134. This comment evidently took no account of Muslim countries, some of which were entirely alcohol-free.
21. G.T. Brake, *Policy and Politics in British Methodism 1932-1982* (London: B. Edsall & Co. Ltd, 1984), 434.
22. *IMYB* 1931, 30
23. *IMYB* 1936, 30.
24. 'The President on Greyhound Racing', *IMMag.* 1928, 22; *IMYB* 1932, 28; *IMYB* 1939, 39
25. *IMYB* 1943, 12.
26. Brake, *Policy and Politics*, 434.
27. *IMYB* 1935, 73.
28. *IMYB* 1947, 41.
29. *IMMag.* 1952, 53.
30. *IMYB* 1956, 22.
31. *IMYB* 1959, 52.
32. Anon. Typescript History of Dukinfield Excelsior Mission, n.d.
33. R. Barnes, Typescript History of Horden Independent Methodist Church, 1999.
34. *Methodist Free Church, Buckley Street, Warrington, Centenary Booklet,* 1951, 29.
35. *IMMag.* 1933, 35.
36. *IMMag.* 1935, 38. See Chapter 5.
37. T. Grey, 'The Work of God', *IMMag.* 1929, 128
38. A. Hastings, *A History of English Christianity 1920-1990*, (London: SCM Press, 1991), 268.
39. *IMYB* 1936, 54f.
40. A. Ince, 'Stopping the Leakage', *IMMag.* 1937, 150.
41. T.H. Adams, 'Unemployment', *IMMag.* 1931, 122.
42. T.R. Openshaw, 'The President's Message', *IMMag.* 1942, 66.
43. *Ibid.*
44. *IMMag.* 1936, 111.
45. 'A Notable Achievement at Wingates', *IMMag.* 1938, 5.
46. *IMYB* 1937, 31.
47. CCMins. October 1928.
48. *IMMag.* 1932, 127.
49. *Ibid.*
50. *IMYB* 1933, 28, 39.
51. *IMMag.* 1938, 97
52. *IMMag.* 1932, 15.
53. 'Opening of the New Church at Kelloe', *IMMag.* 1940, 57.
54. *Thirty Years in India. An Appreciation of the work of Edith Astley Bevan 1928-1958* (Wigan: Independent Methodist Bookroom, 1958), 14.
55. H.H. Banner, *The Three Freds and After* (London: Unevangelised Fields Mission, n.d.) 25ff.

56. See Chapter 5.
57. *Ibid.*
58. 'Where Authority lies in Religion', *IMMag.* 1929, 206. See also Chapter 5.
59. 'Ministers' Conference in Sunderland', *IMMag.* 1930, 70.
60. C. Thornton, 'The Decline in Church Attendance: Is there a Remedy?' *IMMag.* 1928, 124.
61. Horton Davies, *Worship and Theology in England*, (Grand Rapids: Wm.B. Eerdmans Publishing Co. , Combined Edition 1996), *IV, From Newman to Martineau 1850-1900*, 192.
62. 'Ministers' Conference at Burnside', *IMMag.* 1928, 191.
63. *IMMag.* 1928, 124.
64. 'Young Men's Fellowship Conference at Pendleton', *IMMag.* 1928, 36.
65. Murray, *IM History*, 78.
66. E. Lawrenson, 'The Exemplar of Service', *IMMag.* 1933, 153.
67. J. Murray, 'Christ's Conception of the Kingdom of God', *IMMag.* 1933, 185.
68. A. McGrath, *Christian Theology* (Oxford: Blackwell, 1994), 94.
69. C. Jones et al, *The Study of Spirituality* (London, 1986, 396ff).
70. B.G. Worrall, *The Making of the Modern Church. Christianity in England since 1800* (London: SPCK, 1988), 156.
71. K. Hylson-Smith, *The Churches in England from Elizabeth I to Elizabeth II, Vol. III, 1833-1998* (London: SCM Press, 1998), 202.
72. A. Mounfield, *Pictures of the Early Church* (Nelson: Independent Methodist Bookroom, n.d.) 14.
73. Ibid.
74. See Chapter 7.
75. H. Barrett, 'The President's Campaign', *IMMag.* 1928, 60. H. Begbie, *Broken Earthenware* (London: Hodder and Stoughton, 1910), *passim.*
76. Murray, *IM History*, 36.
77. 'Our Forward Movement', *IMMag.* 1929, 138.
78. Several new chapels were built, but they were all replacements of existing buildings.
79. 'Obituary: Alfred Foreman', *IMMag.* 1965, 14f.
80. See Chapter 7 for details of W. Drummond Brown's later work as Connexional Secretary.
81. *IMMag.* 1930, 120.
82. *IMMag.* 1930, 124.
83. See Murray, *IM History*, 53ff. for fuller details of Foreman's work.
84. A. Foreman, *Christian History: A Free Church View* (Wigan: Independent Methodist Bookroom, 1932).
85. For a general view of Foreman's ideas, see A. Foreman, *The Faith of a Christian* (Nelson: Independent Methodist Bookroom, 1925).
86. *IMMag.* 1965, 15.
87. *IMMag.* 1936, 27, 80, 95, 224.
88. See Chapter 5.
89. Information supplied by Helen Gooud, formerly of Robert Street Church.
90. Information supplied by Bill Weddell, formerly of Robert Street Church.
91. Murray, *IM History*, 62f.
92. *IMMag.* 1952, 51.

93. *IMMag.* 1936, 152.
94. 'Report on Ministry', CCMins. 17 March, 1928.
95. *IMYB* 1941, 12.
96. 'Regulations for the Introduction and Acceptance of Candidates for the Ministry and Recognition of Ministers' (Independent Methodist Churches, Ministers' Committee, 1941).
97. Murray, *IM History*, 130; *IMMag.* 1952, 91.
98. *IMMag.* 1951, 75, 91. See Chapter 4.
99. *IMMag.* 1951, 83.
100. *IMYB* 1933, 47.
101. 'Obituary: Thomas Robert Openshaw', *IMMag.* 1956, 42.
102. *IMMag.* 1942, 66.
103. Murray, *IM History,* 86.
104. Murray, *IM History,* 90. See also Mounfield's comments below on the sacraments, under 'Theological Trends'.
105. Murray, *IM History,* 92.
106. *Ibid.*
107. E.K.H. Jordan, *Free Church Unity* (London: Lutterworth, 1956), 178.
108. *IMYB* 1933, 38.
109. See Chapter 5.
110. 'Mayoral Service at Stretford', *IMMag.* 1933, 218
111. 'The President – William Grundy', *IMMag.* 1934, 2
112. *IMMag.* 1938, 29.
113. 'Joseph Baldwin of Bulwell', *IMMag.* 1939, 184.
114. See Chapter 5 for the career of William Burrows and his contribution to union, civic and denominational life.
115. *IMMag.* 1942, 67.
116. 'Obituary: James Dixon Murray', *IMMag.* 51f. Fuller details of his earlier life and trade union activities are given in *Durham County Advertiser and Chronicle,* 22 September, 1933.
117. 'Labour's Man for Durham', *The Sunderland Echo and Shipping Gazette,* 15 January, 1945, 4.
118. *IMMag.* 1938, 122.
119. *IMMag.* 1938, 180.
120. 'In the Service of the Soldiers', *IMMag.* 1943, 19.
121. Murray, *IM History,* 101.
122. *IMMag.* 1941, 44.
123. Murray, *IM History,* 102.
124. *IMMag.* 1944, 47.
125. Fuller details of how the IM Connexion and its churches responded to the challenge of the Second World War can be found in an excellent chapter, based on personal memories, in Murray, *IM History,* 97ff.
126. *IMYB* 1947, 28
127. Information supplied by one of the three men in question.
128. *IMYB* 1946, 24.
129. *IMYB* 1945, 46.
130. Hastings, *English Christianity,* 493.
131. W.P. Lockley, 'Independent Methodism – Whither?' *IMMag.* 1946, 11.

132. W.P. Lockley, 'A Gospel with a Cross in it', *IMMag.* 1948, 4.

133. W.C. Brown, 'Reflections', *IMMag.* 1945, 68.

134. W.C. Brown, 'Motive and Method in Missionary Service', *IMMag.* 1947, 35.

135. A full report of the sequence of events and the issues involved is recorded in *IMYB* 1948, 35ff.

136. *Ibid.*

137. O. Barclay, *Evangelicalism in Britain 1935-1995* (Leicester: Inter-Varsity Press, 1997), 72f.

138. H. Sharples, 'The Divine Inspiration of the Scriptures', *IMMag.* 1954, 10f.

139. *IMMag.* 1954, 26ff.

140. *IMMag.* 1954, 49. See Appendix 6.

141. *IMMag.* 1962, 102.

142. A. Foreman, 'A Policy for World Security: Can Christendom lead the way?' *IMMag.* 1957, 6f.

143. A. Foreman, 'The International Situation', *IMMag.* 1957, 92. The use of the term 'Church' for the corporate bodies of the Baptists and Independent Methodists was inaccurate in both instances.

144. *Ibid.* See also votes on similar issues at the Annual Meetings of 1936 and 1937. Murray, *IM History*, 75f.

145. 'The Filmstrip Method of Presentation', *IMMag.* 1952, 68.

146. E. Headon and H.M. Ashurst, 'The Independent Methodist Film Unit', *IMMag.* 1969, 39f. Additional information supplied by Tony and Enid Headon, members of the Film Unit Team of the 1950s.

147. Information supplied by J. David Hill, formerly of Roe Green Church, Worsley, Manchester.

148. The activities of IMTAKS, its significance to the denomination and the important contribution of Dennis Downing will be examined in the next chapter.

149. *IMMag.* 1955, 35.

150. *IMMag.* 1955, 37.

151. *IMMag.* 1976, 28, 47.

152. *IMMag.* 1974, 151.

Chapter 7
Adapting to a Post-Christian Culture
1960-2005

The final phase of the story of Independent Methodism's 200 years of history faces the inevitable problem of proximity to the people and events concerned. Moreover, some of the processes of change outlined in this chapter still continue and their full significance will only be appreciated long after they have been superseded by whatever follows them.

1. Facing a Changing World

While churches of all denominations faced the changes which heralded a post-Christian culture from the 1960s onwards, there were some factors which were specific to the character and geography of Independent Methodism which influenced the course of events. Although it was a period of overall decline, this was not uniform; for some churches it was an era of innovation and growth. The overall picture now needs to be examined.

1.1. Social Change

The period from 1960 onwards saw huge changes in British society and the growth of patterns of activity which widened the gulf between church and community. It was a time marked by the post-war boom of prosperity, the growth of teenage cult movements and the beginning of a hedonistic approach to life. Television, sport, car travel, caravan ownership and a generally relaxed approach to the use of Sunday inevitably removed one of the main bulwarks of chapel culture: the strict observance of the Lord's Day. The confidence of chapel leaders was steadily eroded as they realised that their hold on adherents was becoming weaker.

On the wider front, the social trends which impacted, however subtly, on the nation's chapels and their culture were too many and too complex to permit elaboration here. As different faith groups became established in the country, multi-culturalism was not only accepted but celebrated. Moral relativism steadily gained ground, impacting on ethical issues which struck at the heart of Christian belief. As society became increasingly materialistic on the one hand and diverse in its spirituality on the other, traditional Christianity was perceived as narrow, outdated or irrelevant. The years in question also saw the gradual development of a 'low commitment' culture which impacted on personal relationships, employment and, in turn, on the internal functioning of churches. Factors such as these served to drive a wedge between chapels and their surrounding communities.[1]

1.2. Environmental Change

From the early 1960s, urban redevelopment began to affect churches in the various towns and cities of the north of England, especially in areas of industrial decline and dereliction. While this was a common experience for churches generally, for the Lancashire Independent Methodists, it was a major problem since most of their churches were situated in areas such as these. Few were to be found in the countryside or in smart new suburbs. Compensation was available and impressive modern buildings replaced old, decaying ones, but the redevelopment of the areas in question saw long-established communities broken up and the influx of new populations with no roots in the areas in question. A new IM chapel would stand in splendour amidst unrecognisable surroundings, maintained by members who travelled in from the suburbs and with no relationship to the new local population. A classic example occurred in Salford, where the chapels at Pendleton (Salem) and Brighouse Street were swept away in a massive clearance scheme, which saw thousands of terraced houses replaced by tower blocks. In the middle of the new development a new IM chapel was built to replace the two which had been demolished. Its chosen name 'Salem House' reflected a desire to retain past identities, which did not augur well. After a hopeful start, it soon became obvious that the church was making no impression on an area where social problems were escalating. The city's other two IM churches, Weaste and Fitzwarren Street, were also unable to cope with their changing environment and closed down in 1978 and 1984 respectively. In 1987, after only twenty years in its new building, Salem House followed suit, ending 130 years of IM presence in Salford.

In North-East England, the end of the coal mining industry brought new challenges to churches in former pit villages, which now experienced more diverse patterns of employment and some movement of population. However, communities generally remained more intact than in parts of urban Lancashire, a fact that worked to the advantage of the churches in the villages concerned. Only a few churches relocated, while others redeveloped, expanded or replaced their existing premises and continued to maintain good relationships with the surrounding population. By contrast with the massive losses in Yorkshire and South-East Lancashire (see below), the

Sunderland Circuit had a net loss of only church out of twenty by the end of the period in question, though membership and attendances were greatly reduced as elsewhere.

1.3. A Changing Connexion

The numerical decline which churches had experienced since the First World War accelerated from the 1960s onwards. This was compounded by diminishing confidence, a haunting sense of failure and, particularly, the loss of the younger generation. Congregations grew old together. The number of IM churches and missions dropped from 152 in 1960 to 89 in 2004 and the number of members from 7,517 in 1960 to 2,061 in 2004. Some areas were affected more severely than others – most notably the circuits on either side of the Pennines. The Yorkshire, Oldham, Bolton and Manchester Circuits collectively fell from 40 churches with 2,236 members in 1960 to 12 churches with 216 members in 2004. Town centre churches were particularly vulnerable and these years saw the demise of some of the Connexion's oldest and most historic churches – Bolton (Folds Road), Batley (Cambridge Street), Oldham (George Street), Leigh (The Avenue) and Wigan (Greenough). In some of the areas in question, churches found themselves reduced to ghettos in areas where the houses were now populated almost entirely by ethnic groups of other faiths. Equally vulnerable were the 'outpost' churches which were remote from the main blocks of churches and therefore removed from the means of support. Crewe, Wrexham, Lancaster, Market Drayton, Newbury and Nottingham were all lost. The overall effect of this trend was to make the Connexion's already small geographical base even smaller.

Church closures brought home one of the major weaknesses of Independent Methodist autonomy. Under the Model Trust Deed, each church kept its own deeds, appointed its own trustees and replaced them when necessary. However, many churches which came to the point of closure were found to have too few trustees, none at all or did not know who the trustees were. Some had even lost their deeds. Trust problems often ran on for years before properties were finally sold.

2. Innovations of the Period

Despite the overall decline which persisted from 1960 onwards, this particular phase of the denomination's history saw definite attempts made both to stem the decline and to advance Christian work on several fronts. Some of them brought lasting benefit, but not on a scale sufficient to counteract the long-term downward trend.

2.1. Youth Evangelism

The 1960s saw the rapid growth of the IMTAKS movement which had begun at the end of the previous decade.[2] By 1962, membership numbered 730.[3] Not only did Youth clubs in many parts of the Connexion affiliate to it, but also its Leaders' Council organised an extensive programme of activity. The main gathering was a weekend Congress, held in spring at a

Dennis Downing

different church each year. Young people assembled for sports tournaments on the Saturday afternoon and a 'display' in the evening. Those who travelled from a distance were accommodated overnight by members of the host church and stayed for the final event of the weekend, a Sunday morning service, which was always evangelistic and often included an appeal for commitment by the speaker. By 1963, when the Congress was held at Easington Lane, Co. Durham, attendance was up to 350.[4]

Other events included an annual residential Leaders' Training Weekend, twice yearly leaders' councils, inter-church sports tournaments and events among groups of clubs in different areas. IMTAKS also published its own magazine, *IMPACT*, for several years. Those trained for leadership through IMTAKS went on to apply the skills which they learned to roles which they would later fulfil in their churches and the wider Connexion. It was an important seed-bed for the evangelical renewal which was taking place across the denomination.

Much of the success of IMTAKS was due to its indefatigable and visionary secretary, Dennis Downing, by occupation an associate legal executive, who spent most of his weekends travelling between his Loughborough home and the churches in Lancashire and the North-East, and most of his weeknights in the administration of the movement. During this time he built relationships with youth club leaders and served as adviser and mentor to many of them. His obvious abilities were soon recognised in the Connexion. In 1963 he was appointed as Young People's Secretary, where he joined the equally visionary Assistant Secretary, J. David Hill, who had been appointed two years earlier. Their partnership laid the foundation for a vigorous and high quality programme of work which ran beyond their own time. An example of their strategic thinking

W.W. Kay (1896-1980)

was seen in an annual one-day conference for Chairmen and Secretaries of Circuit Young People's Committees, to stimulate activity at local level. Also, for the first time in many years, residential weekends for young people were held, usually in Christian Endeavour Holiday Homes; these led to major steps of faith for many of those who attended. During the 1980s and 1990s, follow-up weekends designed to provide newly-committed young people with biblical teaching were held annually at Knock, Cumbria, and later at the Quinta Centre in Shropshire.

A separate development in 1960 saw a group of teenagers from the nine churches of the Spennymoor Circuit (Co. Durham) form a Mission Band, which met together weekly for fellowship, prayer and study, but with evangelism as its central theme. Members of the Band engaged in door-to-door work in the areas around each of the circuit churches over a period of several years.[5] The Mission Band, which grew to a membership of twenty-nine, was invited to take meetings throughout the County of Durham and beyond, visiting churches of various denominations. At these meetings, the young people sang as a group, gave testimonies and preached gospel messages. Sometimes they held open-air meetings and, on one occasion, visited the Durham Miners' 'Big Meeting', where they conducted a meeting on the field throughout the day. Over the years, the Mission Band saw many conversions and in 1962, as a specific project, undertook a 'rescue' operation for the church at Metal Bridge which was near to closure.[6]

2.2. Christian Education

From the 1960s onwards the IM Youth Department made valiant efforts to improve the work of the Connexion's Sunday Schools. It organised twice-yearly teacher training weekends to stimulate teachers and offer new ideas and, in 1970, introduced a Teacher Training Course, conducted in local groups, using material from the National Christian Education Council. This ran successfully for several years; at one point over a hundred people were studying in local groups.[7] The Young People's Department aimed to reverse the decline in the Sunday Schools, but this was never achieved and was probably not achievable by denominational activity alone. Adverse social trends and the sheer lack of capable personnel to run establishments suitable to the times meant that this task was always an uphill one.

Traditionally, most IM churches had used lesson materials produced by the British Lessons Council (BLC) and published by the National Sunday School Union (NSSU). However, during this period, the BLC produced a new syllabus with a new approach, based on the research of Ronald Goldman of Reading University.[8] Goldman had advocated an experiential process of learning, with less emphasis on story-telling. At the same time, the NSSU changed its name to National Christian Education Council (NCEC), to reflect the fact that many churches were now dropping the term 'Sunday School' in favour of names such as 'Junior Church'. The IM Youth Department, which was represented on the NCEC kept abreast of developments and urged churches to prepare to adopt the new materials, which first appeared in 1968 under the title of 'Partners in Learning'. In the event, however, most IM churches quickly abandoned the new materials, largely because of their reduced biblical content and the fact that the lesson outlines demanded greater resourcefulness on the part of teachers than before. While the new BLC syllabus was used by eighty percent of churches nationally, the figure for IM churches was less than twenty percent.[9]

Another national trend was the gradual change from afternoon Sunday Schools to Sunday Morning Family Worship. This had begun earlier in the century but accelerated in post-war years. Independent Methodists were generally slower than most to make the change, which suited church-going families, but led to a gradual loss of contact with the local community.[10] Children of non-churchgoing families gradually ceased to attend and Sunday Schools (or Junior Churches) soon consisted of attendees' children only. Where congregations consisted mainly of older people, this often meant that the Sunday School was discontinued. From about the 1980s, statistics began to show that midweek work rather than Sunday School was becoming the churches' main point of contact with the growing generation.

In the later years of the twentieth century, the more resourceful churches began to develop other means of contact with children, through annual Holiday Bible Clubs and school links. Churches which engaged the services of youth workers took the opportunity to establish relationships with local primary and secondary schools, taking lessons and assemblies, inviting school classes to planned events and providing Religious Education materials for use in schools. If this made little difference in terms of church attendance, it had the very positive effect of engaging churches in their local communities and giving them a more outward focus.

2.3. The Forward Movement

At the 1960 Annual Meeting, the Connexional Secretary, W. Drummond Brown, issued a document in which he described the state of the Connexion with some concern.[11] The outcome was a project known as 'The Forward Movement,' which ran over the next two years. It was partly a fact-finding exercise and partly a stimulus to action. Each circuit was asked to form an 'Action Committee' which would visit all of its churches to discuss a series of questions about their life and work. Needy churches were to be identified and, where possible, help given. For example, the Warrington Circuit addressed the problems at Stockton Heath, currently its weakest church. A visitation project in 1962 culminated in a weekend's mission by the IM Film Unit. This brought some new growth in the Sunday School. At the end of the project, the Connexional Committee produced a summary report which highlighted its perceptions of common weaknesses. These included: lack of vision, a casual approach to worship, excessively long tenures of office and poorly prepared Sunday School work. The report's authors lamented the level of ignorance of connexional affairs and noted that forty per cent of the churches never sent a delegate to the Annual Meeting. They therefore urged that church members be instructed in denominational principles. But they made little reference to prayer (except in the context of formal worship), evangelism or even purposeful social action. The overall focus was denomination-centred, inward-looking and made little reference to the realities of the world of the 1960s.[12]

2.4. The Crusade in Evangelism

In 1964, Dennis Downing was appointed as Joint Connexional Secretary, in tandem with W. Drummond Brown. Thus, he held three major responsibilities in the denomination in addition to full time employment. Perhaps more than anyone else of his era, he illustrated the dependence of the Independent Methodists on people who were prepared to undertake heavy workloads in a voluntary capacity. His unique position in the denomination meant that during the years from 1964 to 1976, when he relinquished his last position, that of Connexional Secretary, he formed a bridge between the older, more cautious people and the eager young enthusiasts of the rising generation.

Under the leadership of Drummond Brown and Dennis Downing, a 'Crusade in Evangelism' was launched in 1967, with the remit of promoting spiritual life and outreach both within individual churches and among the churches of a given area. This resulted in a number of local initiatives, including the introduction of an annual weekend retreat by the Bolton Circuit[13] and a ten week teacher training course in Warrington and Wigan.[14] In the Colne and Nelson Circuit, assistance to Blacko Church from Bethel (Colne) resulted in the Sunday School being re-opened.[15]

2.5. Missioners and Voluntary Helpers

The evangelical resurgence of the 1960s led to pressure for the Connexion to appoint a full time evangelist once again, but views on the subject were mixed. The 1966 Annual Meeting passed a Notice of Motion agreeing to the appointment of an evangelist, but this was never implemented.[16] However, in a less formal way, individuals, some of them retired, offered their services voluntarily to assist needy churches. Granville Mason, a past President, took up the role of 'connexional helper' in 1969[17] and continued in this position for three years. During this time he visited several churches in different parts of the Connexion, undertook visitation, drew in the services of the Film Unit and enlisted the help of other people for specific projects. A year after Mason's retirement, George Williams of St. Helens succeeded him and did similar work in Lancashire,[18] while Martin Bolt and his associates in the 'Gospel Outreach Team' worked among some of the churches in the North-East.[19] In each case, short-term encouragement was often followed by longer-term disappointment, largely due to the lack of committed support from the churches which were being helped.

The 1980s saw the Connexion return to the pattern of appointing full time personnel for mission work, but termed now as 'missioners', rather than 'evangelists'. From 1980 to 1984, Douglas Ward undertook church-based work, first in Southport and later in Manchester. After a two year gap, David Hill (Missioner 1986-90) and Judith Diggins (Missioner 1987-99) were appointed with the remit of working across the Connexion, mainly with the aim of motivating and equipping people to undertake mission work in their own communities. It was clear from the outset that they were stepping into a situation of ongoing decline and that the future looked bleak.[20] Together they ran numerous projects and gave support to churches which were developing their own mission strategies. Under the heading 'Primetime', David Hill ran courses on 'Understanding the Bible' and 'Preaching and Leading Worship'. These operated in several parts of the Connexion and were well attended. 'The Macedonian Project' drew on volunteer teams to help churches on a short term basis with aspect of their mission, but the response to this scheme was small.[21] Through 'There is Hope', churches were encouraged to develop mission activities their own and share their experiences with others. This was a period of intensive activity when both missioners worked assiduously to stimulate mission-mindedness among the churches, with varying degrees of success. Fundamentally, they faced the challenge of working with churches where human resources were limited and where local talent was sometimes in short supply.

2.6. Campaign Evangelism

In 1961, the evangelist Billy Graham came right into the heart of IM 'territory' to conduct a campaign at Maine Road Football Ground, Manchester. Older IM leaders had reservations about his style of ministry, regarding it as slick, fundamentalist, emotional and excessively individualistic,[22] and the denominational magazine noticeably made no reference to it. However, a few churches acted on their own initiative and took groups to the meetings, while those closest to Manchester became involved in practical aspects of the campaign.

The following decades saw an enormous change in IM attitudes towards Billy Graham's approach to evangelism. When he undertook another major campaign, 'Mission England', in 1984, this received unreserved support from the denomination's leaders. Churches were involved on a large scale, often taking leading roles in local organisation, particularly when the campaign meetings took place at Liverpool and Sunderland football grounds. When the campaign was over, several churches held nurture groups to follow up those who had made commitments of faith. The church at New Silksworth, Sunderland, ran eight such groups for a total of sixty people.[23]

Independent Methodists in North-East England ran a series of high-profile events in their own region during the 1960s and 1970s, largely through the initiative of Charles F. Grey, CBE, MP and Betty Stout, joint secretaries of the Northern Counties Confederation (NCC) of IM churches. The first such event took place in 1965, when the 'Joystrings', then a nationally known Salvation Army music group under the leadership of Joy Webb, the Salvation Army's Young People's director, performed in the New Silksworth Church. The success of this event led to a campaign which featured visits to schools and prisons as well as church-based events.[24] In 1969, Charles Grey was able to secure the services of Cliff Richard for a concert in the Newcastle City Hall. One of the singer's requirements was a choir of 120 young people to sing with him at the concert; the NCC duly recruited the young people and a choir was formed. The concert, attended by 2,200 people and screened by Tyne-Tees Television, was regarded as huge success and spurred on further action.[25] Its most outstanding legacy was the choir, which went on to develop a ministry of its own, taking services in Durham Prison,[26] presenting regional television epilogues and serving wider gatherings such as the British Christian Endeavour Convention and a regional campaign by the evangelist Dick Saunders.

2.8. Church Planting

During the 1960s the Connexion added four churches to its ranks: Kent Street, Warrington (an existing unattached mission) and three North-East churches – Greatham, Hebburn and Willington – all of which

*Missionaries at 1985 Annual Meeting. Left to right: Edith Bevan,
Maureen Wyatt, Ken Wyatt, Iris Harrison, Miles Harrison, Jenny
Robinson, David Robinson, Anne Stanworth, Eva Banner*

resulted at least partly from local Methodist church closures. There
were no further additions for nearly twenty years until the concept of
'church planting' received a high profile among British churches in
the 1980s, following extensive research by the Bible Society.[27] The
first IM plant of this era was launched in the growing residential area
of Appleton, a suburb of Warrington, under the leadership of Gordon
Gleave, an IM minister who had recently moved into the area, with
initial assistance from missioners David Hill and Judith Diggins.[28] In
the same year, Ashton-on-Mersey began a church plant at Heald Green
in South Manchester.[29] In Sunderland, Bethel Christian Fellowship,
under the leadership of Martin Bolt joined the Connexion in 1992 and
bought a disused chapel on the Thorney Close Housing Estate as its
place of worship and outreach.[30] 2001 saw a further addition in
Warrington when members of Stockton Heath Church established a new
work on the Westy Estate. At about the same time, a group of members
from Culcheth, near Leigh, started a church in the adjacent village of
Croft.[31] The church at Stretford closed in 2002, but opened again with
a new congregation, under the name of Trafford Christian Life Centre.
Each of the newer churches was not tied to custom and tradition, with
the result that new patterns of church life began to emerge.

2.9. Missionary Expansion

From the 1960s onwards, the IM missionary 'family' grew rapidly.[32] Evangelical conviction was leading many people to respond to the call to overseas work. Barrie and Maureen Heyworth (Stretford) served in Rwanda, Uganda and Gambia as medical missionaries for several years. Ken and Maureen Wyatt (Bristol) worked in India, where Ken's radio skills were put to work in Christian broadcasting. Miles and Iris Harrison (Horwich) became church planters in Austria. David and Jenny Robinson (Manchester) spent many years in church planting in Thailand, where David eventual became field superintendent for Overseas Missionary Fellowship (OMF). After Jenny's death, he transferred to Cambodia where he re-opened OMF's missionary work after the fall of the Pol Pot regime. He and his second wife, Mary, became the nucleus of a growing body of missionaries in a country where people were openly receptive to the Christian message. Anne Stanworth (Warrington), again with OMF, served for over thirty years in the Philippines, based in turn in various church planting locations. Mark and Alison Weir (Hartlepool, Cleveland) also worked in the Philippines with Youth with a Mission, on a project to rescue young girls working in clubs and bars from a life of prostitution. Gail Jefferson (Spennymoor, Co. Durham) went first to Costa Rica and then to Colombia, where she met and married Daniel Castro. Together they worked among street children and also through the outreach ministries of their local church. Others who worked for shorter periods were based in a variety of countries, including Jordan, Cyprus, France, Italy, Ivory Coast and Pakistan. Some worked in North Africa through secular projects, with no formal missionary status. On a more mobile basis, some worked through the ships' ministry of Operation Mobilisation, while others engaged in the UK-based activities of their missionary societies. In total, the number of missionaries going out from this small denomination was out of all proportion to its size and reflected keen IM interest in overseas missions.

3. Changes in Administration and Resources

3.1. Annual Meetings

At connexional level, a new departure saw the character of the Connexion's Annual Meetings gradually change from 1975 onwards, when, for the first time, the event moved from church-based accommodation to a residential setting, usually on a university campus. This gave scope for a much wider and more imaginative programme, which could include seminars, Bible studies, drama and social

Opening ceremony of the Resource Centre, 1990, performed by Derek Yates, Connexional President (left) and William G Burrows, past President and architect

activities. From the delegates' perspective, it also facilitated informal gatherings and helped relationships to be built. Annual Meetings were invariably held at weekends, reflecting the fact that most delegates, including ministers, would be people engaged in secular employment on weekdays. This practice was interrupted only in 2000 for a special holiday convention style of Annual Meeting to mark the Millennium.

3.2. From Bookroom to Resource Centre

From its earliest days, the Connexion's Bookroom had always operated from rented premises, either at the secretary's home or in one of the churches. Its last rented home was in rooms adjacent to Greenough Street Church, Wigan. However, when this church came under a compulsory purchase order in the late 1960s, the Connexion decided to use some of its capital to purchase a property of its own – a semi-detached house at Orrell, Wigan.[33] This was opened in 1969 and served the traditional function of a distribution base for denominational literature.

During the 1980s, the amount of work covered by the Bookroom increased, as it took over from individual officers the task of sending out information. Ecumenical activity also produced more paperwork. To cope with these demands, the Bookroom obtained an offset litho printer, which generated yet further work in the form of a printing service for the churches. Hitherto, its staffing was voluntary, but this was now proving impracticable, so, in 1985, the Connexion appointed its first full time Bookroom Manager in the person of Andrew Rigby. By this time, the Orrell premises were proving inadequate as the main location of the Connexion's work. Providentially, the nearby IM Church at Lamberhead Green had decided to dispose of its large school building, so, in 1990, the Connexion purchased it for a nominal sum and converted it into a purpose-designed set of offices, together with meeting rooms. The new premises were named 'The Resource Centre', rather than 'Bookroom', to reflect their wider function. The Resource Centre thereafter became not only a distribution centre, but also the Registered Office and headquarters of denomination, a place for small group meetings and a home for the archives of the Connexion and its churches. Modern and well-equipped, it gave the Connexion greatly improved facilities which amply met its administrative needs.

3.3. The Hymn Book

Towards the end of the 1960s, the Connexional Committee was obliged to make a decision concerning the Independent Methodist Hymn Book, published in 1902, as stocks were exhausted and it was long overdue for revision. A committee was appointed to compile a new hymn book, much shorter than the old one, and this was published in 1974.[34] It was received well for a time and was reprinted twice, but the explosion of new worship songs which began only a few years later was virtually unforeseeable. When the last of the stock expired in the mid-1990s there was no suggestion of a reprint or further new book. The churches by this time had adopted their own alternatives, usually in the form of 'Mission Praise' or similar publications.

3.4. The High Legh Centre

In 1997, a project of a different nature resulted from the closure of the church at High Legh, near Knutsford. This country chapel, with an adjoining cottage and half an acre of land, was located in prime Cheshire countryside and had long been used by other churches for outings and social events. Instead of following usual practice and selling it, the Connexion took the decision to spend some of its capital on restoration of the premises and to open them as a Retreat Centre. The High Legh Centre, as it became known, went on to become a popular venue for personal and group retreats, weekend camps, church away days and many other events.

3.5. The Theatre Royal

One of the successful activities of the Connexional Young People's Department during the 1990s was an annual Christmas event, entitled, 'Let's Celebrate'. This drew large numbers of people, reaching an attendance of

850 in 1996, when it was held at the Theatre Royal, St. Helens.[35] At the time, the lease of the Theatre Royal was due to expire and another lessee was being sought. Some leaders in the Connexion felt that this offered a great mission opportunity and steps were taken which resulted in the IM Connexion holding the lease of a theatre.[36] It became the venue for many good quality Christian events, but the financial loss incurred proved prohibitive and the 1998 Annual Meeting took the decision to terminate the lease.[37]

4. Changes in the Character of the Denomination

During the years 1960-2005, Independent Methodism not only saw changes to its programme of activity, but also to its fundamental character. These may be analysed as follows:

4.1. Demographic Change

Membership migration played a significant part in the Connexion's losses in the post-war years as some of its more successful people took up new employment opportunities away from their home areas, often in the south of England. Many of its voluntary ministers were lost in this way. In an age when people of all denominations, upon re-location, would look for a church of the same denomination, the Independent Methodists could only ever be the losers through their narrow geographical base. Their migrating members, by necessity, had to find churches of other denominations, since the nearest IM Church was often over 100 miles away. For the same reason, IM churches rarely received any corresponding additions through other Independent Methodists moving into their areas.

However, the issue of transference gradually changed, as the Christian population of the country in general from the 1970s onwards gave less priority to denominational attachment. Christians moving into new areas were more likely to look for a local church which matched their personal aspirations rather than one of the same denomination. Thus, IM churches, like others, gradually became more heterogeneous. The stronger churches, at least, found themselves composed of people from a variety of denominational backgrounds, but, consequently, congregations were less interested in denominational matters than was once the case. This would be a major consideration towards the end of the twentieth century as the Independent Methodists began to ask themselves whether their continuation as a separate denomination was relevant or meaningful. Philip Lockley threw down the gauntlet on this issue as early as 1965, when he stated that Independent Methodism was no longer fulfilling the reasons for which it came into being and he saw no point in fighting the battles of 1800.[38]

4.2. Leadership Changes

Although change had been developing at Independent Methodism's grass roots during the 1950s,[39] it had yet to penetrate the senior ranks of the Connexion. A first time delegate to the 1960 Annual Meeting summed up her first impressions: 'Kindly, elderly men dominated the proceedings. These men embody of Independent Methodism – immovable, verbose, sincere and kind, always exhaling comforting spiritual qualities.'[40] Her words eloquently highlighted the fact that a whole generation, some of whom had been in

John Day

connexional leadership for over forty years, was nearing the end of its stewardship. Over the coming years, this picture changed dramatically with the arrival of several young men and women who made their mark as the innovators of their generation. They included two men who became the longest secretarial partnership in the Connexion's history: John Day, a drawing office manager from Croxton, Staffordshire, General Secretary 1976-2000 and Trevor Prescott of St. Helens, a college lecturer, Administrative Secretary 1965-2000. Both were highly effective in their positions and ensured the efficient running of the Connexion.

4.3. Changes in Doctrine and Spirituality

As a result of the evangelical resurgence of the 1950s and 1960s, Independent Methodism gradually developed different theological emphases and forms of spiritual expression. Much of this was influenced from external sources, such as Christian writers and convention speakers. Prayer Meetings and Bible Studies represented a return to earlier, lapsed values and became the new orthodoxy of the churches. The rising generation criticised the churches' preoccupation with fundraising and low levels of giving. With no paid ministry to sustain, IM churches should have been less costly to operate but, in reality, their congregations often financed them poorly. In time, this issue was taken seriously and the image of churches maintained by jumble sales began to wane.

Infant baptism came under attack from the 1970s and several churches abandoned it entirely in favour of the baptism of believers. This led to much debate within the denomination[41] and a weekend conference was organised in April 1975 to examine the subject theologically.[42] Eventually a statement was issued, acknowledging that both forms of baptism were used among the churches and urging charity and tolerance on the subject.[43]

Towards the end of the 1960s, the impact of the charismatic movement began to be felt, though initially it represented part of the spiritual journey of individuals rather than a massive change of direction for the denomination as a whole. In some churches this led to a new set of tensions in which evangelicals resisted charismatic spirituality, but others embraced it and their churches changed accordingly. If ecumenism had lowered

Trevor Prescott

denominational barriers, the charismatic movement lowered them even further. From the 1970s onwards, it was increasingly clear that many churches and individuals who had experienced spiritual renewal had little interest in maintaining denominational values. This was a marked change from the fifties and sixties when there were young evangelicals with a strong sense of attachment to the Connexion and a determination to restore its evangelical heritage.

Newer arrivals from the seventies onwards, often from other denominational backgrounds, found it irritating and frustrating to be told that they should adhere strictly to unpaid ministry and total abstinence. One of the most vigorous of all the churches at the time was Radcliffe, Bury, which was filled to capacity with a young generation of worshippers. On one occasion, the church put forward seven candidates for the ministry, but they all baulked at the Bolton Circuit's insistence that they should sign a total abstinence pledge as a condition of acceptance. Eventually, the bulk of the members left the church and went on to found a new church known as Bury Christian Fellowship, free, at least as they saw it, from the restraints of a denomination locked in its past. Shortly afterwards, a strong group of young adults in the church at Horwich, Bolton, came under the influence of a line of 'restoration' teaching which urged them to break from their denominational attachments and branch out on their own.[44] Thereupon, they left the Independent Methodists and started Bolton Community Church (Claremont Chapel). The events at Radcliffe and Horwich left those churches irreparably damaged, with small memberships and years of struggle ahead. Other churches which saw substantial losses for similar reasons during this period included Tyldesley, Bradshaw Street (Nelson) and New Silksworth (Sunderland) where some young members established Calvary Fellowship in the same village.

Charismatic renewal was perhaps most strongly experienced at Ashton-on-Mersey, Manchester, where most of the indigenous congregation, which was conservative evangelical in character, withdrew from the church in the early 1980s after a lengthy period of internal tension. The new leadership re-named the church 'King's Way Fellowship', appointed a full time worker and set about developing the life and of the church in a different way, with less structured worship and an emphasis on 'signs and wonders'. A period of rapid growth followed, during which time three new congregations were planted, though two of them only lasted briefly. The church also ran its own day school for a few years.[45] Over a period of time, King's Way's involvement with the Connexion gradually diminished and it finally ended its association in 2001.[46]

Losses sustained through defection were not, of course, losses to the Christian Church as a whole. Most of the churches which arose out of this process continue and prosper. They represent an aspect of continuity beyond Independent Methodism and illustrate the fact that the statistics of a denomination alone fail to give the full story of any process of growth or decline.

During the 1970s, the Connexion undertook an exercise to examine its *Statement of Faith and Practice* which had last been revised in 1927. This led to a lengthy process, finalised in 1984 as two new documents, the *Statement of Faith*, which was entirely doctrinal, and the *Statement of Practice*, which was a descriptive statement of how the denomination worked.[47] The *Statement of Faith* was much briefer than its predecessor and was conservative evangelical in tone, highlighting doctrines such as the authority of the Bible, the atonement, new birth, final judgement, the second coming of Christ and (with an eye to the charismatic constituency) spiritual gifts.[48]

4.4. The Ministry

During the late 1960s a committee was appointed to draw up a new Ministers' Education Scheme. The existing three-year course was the source of frequent complaints, not least because it was based on set textbooks, many of which were very dated, giving no scope for students to explore subjects using a variety of books. The most vociferous criticisms came from the new young evangelicals who objected to the fact that almost all of the textbooks were written by liberal scholars.[49] Moreover, the course simply required the students to read the textbooks and take an examination at the end of each year; there was no essay work and no practical work. In a few circuits, such as Sunderland, students were assigned to specified ministers to accompany them and take part in services, but others had no formal system of monitoring at all.

The new scheme, which came into operation in 1970, brought in a four year course which was subject-orientated, requiring students to complete written assignments throughout the year, based on broad reading, but with a particular emphasis on direct study of the Bible. The syllabus included a mixture of macro and micro studies of both Testaments, Church History, Christian theology and a forty hour assignment of social work through attachment to a professional person, such as a probation officer, child care officer or agency working with the elderly. In total, it was far more rigorous than the previous course, but still far short of the level which would have been offered through a theological college.

The question of what it really meant to be an IM minister was forever under discussion. Officially, the position was described in the Statement of Faith and Practice as 'an office within the church',[50] but with the passing of time many ministers, having been accorded connexional recognition, spent most of their Sundays preaching at other churches and were rarely seen at home. Some did little or no pastoral work. Moreover, when a minister moved to an area where there was no Independent Methodist Church and began to worship at a church of another denomination, provided he kept his membership at his home church, he would retain the office of minister. Thus, there were people who held the title of 'minister' but who did little to fulfil more than an itinerant preaching ministry. These included several of the denomination's most prominent figures.

In a few cases, the retention of IM membership enabled people living at a distance from their churches to serve the denomination in a wider capacity. One who made a distinguished contribution, particularly during the 1960s, was Dr. W. W. Kay (1896-1980), a consultant pathologist, who removed from Horwich, Lancashire to Epsom, Surrey, in 1938. His proximity to London enabled him to represent the denomination on national bodies, the most notable one being the Free Church Federal Council. In 1960 he was appointed as Moderator of the Council, the only Independent Methodist ever to occupy this office. A year later he became President of the National Sunday School Union and for a time he was Chairman of the Executive of the British Lessons Council. He served twice as President of the IM Connexion and, with his wife, was joint editor of the magazine for eight years.[51]

From its earliest days, Independent Methodism faced a recurring problem through its inability to provide a channel of service for individuals who had a calling to full time service. Consequently, several people went into the ministries of other denominations from about the 1950s onwards. From Mill Lane Church, Liverpool, three young men went into the Congregational ministry (later United Reformed). One of them (Graham Cook) served a term as Moderator of the United Reformed Church.[52] From Tetlow Street, Liverpool, John Smith went into the Baptist ministry, becoming President of the Baptist Union of Scotland and later UK Director of the Evangelical Alliance. Norman Smith of Colne became a Methodist minister and went on to serve as a Cliff College evangelist. Robert Hope of Sunderland joined the Church of England, was ordained and spent part of his career as a travelling secretary for the IVF Theological Students Fellowship. Numerous others went into maintained ministry, mainly with the Methodists or the Baptists, while others undertook missionary work overseas. For a small denomination, such losses took away some of its finest talent and inevitably impacted on its ability to find capable leaders by the end of the twentieth century. This was undoubtedly a weakening factor which would have featured far less in a denomination which had a facility for settled ministry. A few IM churches compensated for this loss from about 1980 onwards by breaking with historic practice and appointing pastors, youth workers or other leaders on a full time or part time basis. However, these were purely local arrangements which gave the people concerned no denominational support.

Leadership patterns, sometimes influenced by 'restoration' thought and sometimes simply by biblical re-examination, began to change from about the late 1960s. One of the churches which led the way was Tyldesley, Leigh, which changed from the traditional IM pattern of leadership by presidency (which often changed annually) and a church committee. It now became presbyterian, with elders and deacons holding office. The strict application of this concept left no place for the office of 'minister', which meant that the IM connexional ministry became irrelevant. In some ways, the Tyldesley approach took its people back to the concepts expounded by Alexander Denovan in the *Testimony and Principles of Union* and his *Appeal to the Christian World* a hundred years earlier.[53] Other churches followed this pattern (or variations on it) in due course. By the beginning of the twenty-first century, many had abandoned traditional structures and operated some form of corporate leadership.

The Tyldesley view of ministry was highlighted in the Connexion when the *Statement of Faith* and *Statement of Practice* were under discussion in the early 1980s. The incongruities of the IM ministry came into sharp focus and some churches openly advocated its abolition on the basis that 'ministry' in the New Testament did not refer to a specified office but that every member had a 'ministry'. Others argued for the ministry's retention and the need for some parity with other denominations. The outcome was

Group of Past Presidents at 1984 Annual Meeting. Left to right:
Arthur Smith, Eileen Tyson, Charles Grey, Tom Savage, John Edwards,
Doris Barber, Tom Backhouse, Edith Bevan, Jim Johnson, Bill Stokes,
George Turner, Gordon Gleave

the inclusion of two clauses which attempted to satisfy both views, but which inevitably contained an inner contradiction:

> a: Every believer is called to service in the Kingdom of God, there being no distinction between one service and another beyond that of function. It is recognised that differing gifts and ministries are bestowed on believers for the benefit of the Church as a whole. Each church, therefore, should recognise and cultivate the gifts and ministries of its members.
> b: To assist pastoral responsibility and the wider ministry of the Word of God, the Connexion appoints as ministers of the denomination those, called by God and duly nominated by their Churches and Circuits, who have satisfied Connexional requirements of calling and training. Such ministers serve their Church, Circuit and the Connexion without remuneration.[54]

The last sentence was inserted at a late stage of the process to satisfy those who felt that the denomination's stand for unpaid ministry was not sufficiently emphasised. At this stage, those who took a different view were outnumbered and so the traditional position was upheld. In 1991, Roe Green Church attempted to have the reference 'without remuneration' deleted, but was defeated by fifty-three votes to thirty-four with two abstentions.[55]

Three years later, Nelson Church moved that the clause be amended to read 'normally without remuneration' and this was passed by forty-five votes to thirty-eight.[56] A year later, when this was confirmed (as required by constitution), the voting had moved still further, from fifty-seven votes to twenty-six.[57] Opinion was gradually shifting, with fewer people and churches demanding strict adherence to non-payment with each passing year. One of the first practical indications of the changing situation was that several IM ministers took up chaplaincy work, mainly in hospitals and prisons, even while the payment issue was still under debate.

The last major development in the evolution of the IM ministry came in 2000, following a thorough review of both the underlying principles of ministry and the way in which it was working in practice. The final report was adopted as the *Statement on Ministry* at the Annual Meeting in 2000, with a remarkable level of agreement. The *Statement's* most fundamental principle, never previously expressed in any IM document, was that a minister's responsibility was firstly to his or her own church rather than to the wider Connexion; this went directly against the idea of the IM minister as primarily a local preacher. The *Statement* also acknowledged that some churches wished to pay ministers and proposed that suitable guidance be made available to them. Similarly, the matter of distinctive dress, long rejected by Independent Methodists, had to be addressed, since a number of ministers, particularly those involved in chaplaincy work, were finding it necessary to use clerical collars for purposes of identification. The *Statement* carefully balanced this against continuing objections and allowed for a minister to use certain dress codes subject to the agreement of his/ her church and the Connexion. Retirement of ministers was a further issue. As the IM ministry had always been unpaid, there was never any formal process of retirement; ministers either remained in their positions until death, even though this often meant years of total inactivity, or they resigned. A new term, 'minister emeritus', now left them with a form of recognition but without responsibilities. Finally, for the first time, it was acknowledged that some people might have a call to be preachers but not ministers. These too could now be accredited. In total, these were the most radical changes, at least in conception, ever undertaken in relation to the IM ministry, but they moved it much nearer to congruency with other denominations.[58]

4.5. A Renewed Social Conscience

As in previous generations, IM leaders attempted to interpret the times in which they were living and challenged their constituency to face up to new situations. In 1971, Norman Prescott of Wigan highlighted five particular trends in British life that were affecting the churches: marvellous technological development; the gradual break-up of traditional family life;

the questioning of authority; the decline in the churches' influence; and the weakening of moral values.[59] Each of these trends was to increase in significance during the coming decades as the churches found themselves increasingly isolated in a society which was steadily becoming more secularised. At the 1976 Annual Meeting, the newly appointed Connexional Secretary, John Day of Croxton, Staffordshire, gave an address in which he expressed concern on the exploding sexual revolution and matters of legislation such as relaxed licensing laws for the sale of alcohol and the use of lotteries to finance local authorities.[60] The views of both men reflected those of the whole denomination, which regarded social trends of the time with alarm. Others in the nation held similar views and grouped themselves together to protest against specific aspects of moral decline.[61] Not surprisingly, the Independent Methodists became increasingly identified with such protests. In 1995, the Connexion finally decided to join the Evangelical Alliance,[62] but by this time several churches had already joined it individually. IM churches generally had given their support to different groups which were emerging in response to social and cultural change, including the Nationwide Petition for Decency,[63] the National Viewers' and Listeners' Association on the issue of child pornography,[64] and the Keep Sunday Special Campaign.[65] They also reacted adversely to some developments in the wider ecumenical movement, such as the role of the World Council of Churches in giving funds to freedom fighters in South Africa[66] and the action of the British Council of Churches in making a grant to the so-called 'Liverpool 8 Defence Committee' in the wake of the 1981 Toxteth riots.[67]

However, the response of the IM people to the challenge of their changing world was not merely one of negative reactionaryism. From the 1970s onwards, in common with evangelical Christians across the country, there was a growing sense of social concern and responsibility. At the 1973 Annual Meeting, Eddie Maiden of Oldham urged delegates to have a more realistic view of the secular world and to develop 'hands-on' support for people in difficult social environments.[68] During the ensuing years, churches and individuals tentatively turned their eyes towards the needs of the wider community. After much debate, the 1977 Annual Meeting took the decision to change the name of the 'Temperance and Social Service Committee' to 'Christian Responsibility Committee.'[69] It was to be a change that was more than merely symbolic. For several years, the new committee undertook fundraising projects for needy causes, such as a residential centre for the mentally handicapped and a children's hospice. The churches responded enthusiastically to the projects on each occasion. However, it was the inspired efforts of individuals and small groups which proved the most impressive contributions of all, as the following accounts show.

The plight of suffering people in Eastern Europe from the early 1980s onwards roused several people to action. One of the pioneering spirits who achieved a huge amount in a short time was Nona Starosta of Loughborough who organised a major relief effort to Poland which was in a state of economic collapse at the end of 1981. Against enormous difficulties, she and her team took a lorry containing two tons of food and other supplies to a village in acute need.[70] This was just the prelude to a long-term project which became steadily more sophisticated, with ever larger shipments of goods. Other IM churches took inspiration from this project and added their own contributions.

On a different front, one young man had a particular concern for those who were suffering persecution for their faith in communist Eastern Europe. Bill Hampson of Lowton, Lancashire, became involved in a campaign for the release of a group of Christians known as 'The Siberian Seven'.[71] This was ultimately successful; later the organisation was re-formed and campaigned on behalf of a Russian Christian singer who was imprisoned for his religious activities.[72] Through such activities he began to work closely with David Alton, MP (later Lord Alton) on various human rights and justice issues, including Alton's Abortion Amendment Bill. He became actively involved with the Jubilee Campaign and also the Movement for Christian Democracy, of which he became vice-chairman. Later, he went on to establish a charity known as the Epiphany Trust, which works in parts of the UK, Eastern Europe, Asia and Africa to bring hope to deprived and often disabled young people, through construction projects, sponsorship and orphanage work.[73] In 2000, Bill Hampson's home town of Wigan recognised the value of his work and awarded him the freedom of the Borough.[74]

The conditions in Romania, following the overthrow of the Ceausescu regime in 1989, drew widespread concern in Britain and various charities took action, particularly in relation to the children in the country's orphanages. In addition to the work of Bill Hampson, other groups from IM churches gave help, including the Connexion's Christian Responsibility Committee which organised regular support visits to the Onesimus Brothers' Orphanage in Timisoara.

A project of a different nature was launched in 1991. Concern for homeless people led Walter Wilkinson, an IM minister from Spennymoor, Co. Durham, to work with young men and women living on the streets of North-East England. This began simply with gifts of food, taken directly to central Newcastle on Saturday evenings. Later, a suitably equipped mobile kitchen was provided, followed by a soup kitchen on church premises. Eventually, a charity was formed, known as 'North-East Help Link', which included several leading Independent Methodists as its trustees, with Walter

NORTH-EAST HELP-LINK TRUST

Feeding the
Homeless in
Newcastle

Housing the
Homeless at
Holly House,
Stockton

Then the King will say to those on His right hand, 'Come, you blessed of My Father, inherit the kingdom prepared for you from the foundation of the world: for I was hungry and you gave Me food: I was thirsty and you gave Me drink; I was a stranger and you took Me in, I was naked and you clothed Me; I was sick and you visited Me; I was in prison and you came to Me.

Matthew Chapter 25 vv 34-36

Advertisement for North East Help Link,
featuring its founder, Walter Wilkinson

Wilkinson as full time Director. The churches responded enthusiastically to the charity's appeals for help, with gifts of food and money. Some became volunteer helpers. In 1994 premises were leased in Stockton-on-Tees to provide a hostel, known as 'Holly House' for a small number of young men. This aspect of the work was discontinued for practical reasons, but the charity later purchased a double-decker bus which was adapted as a mobile centre for food provision, ministry and practical help. The whole project combined social action with evangelism and several young men and women came to faith as a result. The death of Walter Wilkinson in 2001 at only forty-nine years of age was a major setback to the work of North-East Help Link, but its work continues.[75]

Social concern also became a focus of individual churches, of which a few examples must suffice. The newly-formed Westy Christian Fellowship in Warrington set out from the beginning to work among deprived people in the surrounding community through practical help projects. Easington Lane Church, Sunderland, offered a different model, whereby church members pioneered activities in a former mining village and took their Christian service into the local community. Roman Road Church, Failsworth, Oldham, over several years developed an extensive community programme which met the needs of large numbers of people, including those with learning difficulties. Downall Green, Wigan, adapted its premises for community use and began to host a wide range of activities.

4.6. Ecumenical Developments

The early 1960s marked one of the most significant points on the time chart of British ecumenical history. Firstly, the Second Vatican Council set in motion a process that would profoundly affect relations between the Roman Catholic Church and other Christian communions. Secondly, the conversations between the Church of England and the Methodist Church looked likely to result in the union of the two bodies. Although this did not materialise, the whole process caused Christians of all denominations, including Independent Methodists, to look more closely than ever at issues such as ecclesiology, the sacraments and ministry. Thirdly, the 1964 Faith and Order Conference at Nottingham set a target date of Easter Day, 1980 for the unification of all Christians. Like the earlier unity schemes which began with the Lambeth Conference of bishops in the 1920s, it proposed an episcopal Church in which the Eucharist would be validated through its exercise by an episcopally ordained ministry.[76] Not surprisingly, the Independent Methodists envisaged an ecumenical bulldozer wiping them out and saw their only options as non-union or extinction.[77] As events transpired, they had nothing to fear, as the Nottingham proposals saw no visible outcome.

Nevertheless, attitudes were changing. Although Independent Methodists were in no position to take any ecumenical initiative, in view of the fact that their ministry was unrecognised by most other denominations, clergymen in the late twentieth century became generally more relaxed in their relationships with IM ministers who were increasingly included in pulpit exchanges and shared services. In a few places, IM churches were actually stronger than those of other denominations and could not be ignored. The co-operation which had long existed through pan-church movements such as Christian Endeavour, the Free Church Federal Council and the National Sunday School Union was gradually becoming something more. Easier relationships brought a reduced emphasis on denominational distinctives, which were the very *raison d'être* of the Independent Methodists. However, the greatest factor which drew Independent Methodists into closer relationships with other Christians was a sense of affinity with other evangelicals of all denominations. As they worked together locally on various campaigns and projects, denominational allegiances faded into the background. This was to affect Independent Methodism profoundly as its constituency became increasingly made up of people who were more interested in shared activity with other evangelicals than in the arcane politics of the denomination.

For Independent Methodists, one of the most significant events on the issue of ecumenism took the form of the 1964 Ministers' Conference, when the guest speaker was Rev. Rupert E. Davies, then a member of the

Anglican-Methodist Unity Commission and Vice-Principal of Didsbury College, Bristol. His addresses on 'Christian Unity – The General Situation' and 'Christian Unity – Particular Conversations (problems and prospects)' gave many Independent Methodists their first exposure to an informed treatment of the subject of Christian Unity and the opportunity to question a speaker of national standing. Many of the ministers present warmed to Davies' treatment of the subject and his sympathetic approach to the particular problems which unity schemes in general gave to the Independent Methodists. In discussion, it became clear that many ministers were less dogmatic than their forbears had been on the key issue of unpaid ministry. However, in the final session of the Conference, Dr. W.W. Kay, the Connexional President, gave an address on 'Christian Unity – The Independent Methodist position and views' in which he described the difficulties which the Independent Methodists would have in becoming part of a unified, Episcopal Church. It is perhaps indicative of the profile of Christian Unity in the minds of all churches at the time that the conference took a less cautious view than Kay, believing that the current movement was something which could not be ignored. A resolution was sent from the Conference to the ensuing Annual Meeting:

> That the Annual Meeting request the Connexional Committee to appoint a committee to examine our Statement of Faith and Practice and our polity in relation to the developing concept of the Universal Church and the movements towards Church Unity and bring our Churches into the stream of these movements by considering what, if any, approaches can be made to other sections of the church with a view to discussions on unity.[78]

In fact, the Ministers' Conference had acted *ultra vires*, having no authority to submit a resolution to the Annual Meeting. Nevertheless, in the light of views expressed at the Ministers' Conference and the report of William G. Burrows on the Faith and Order Conference, the Annual Meeting agreed to appoint a sub-committee to look at the Faith and Order proposals.[79] In the event, organic union remained an unrealised goal and the Independent Methodists settled back to more familiar levels of ecumenical activity. During the ensuing years, they maintained their involvement in the ecumenical movement through the British Council of Churches and the Free Church Federal Council. They attended representative gatherings, responded to consultation documents and supported such projects as the Nationwide Initiative in Evangelism. For a period of time, they participated in a small denominations' group known as the 'Evangelical Group for Fellowship', which included the Free Church of England, Countess of Huntingdon's Connexion, Wesleyan Reform Union and themselves, until this group was dissolved.

In 1984, in response to the World Council Churches' publication, *Baptism, Eucharist and Ministry*,[80] a weekend conference was held to enable the denomination's response to be formulated, while a series of articles in the magazine gave an IM view on each subject.[81] On the face of it, the process made little tangible difference to IM practice, but it served to develop an understanding of the issues as other denominations saw them and helped foster a sense of being part of the wider church.

1989 saw the completion of the process which saw the disbanding of the British Council of Churches, which was replaced by new ecumenical instruments – Churches Together in England and the Council of Churches for Britain and Ireland. The Independent Methodists therefore had to decide whether to join the new bodies. When the matter was debated at the Annual Meeting, there were clearly some doubts, based largely on the fears of conservative evangelicals that it would be detrimental to be aligned with more liberal churches. However, the decision to join was carried by sixty-seven votes to twenty-one and thus the Independent Methodist Connexion became a founder member of both new bodies.[82] During the years that followed, most IM Churches went on to become members of local Churches Together groups, taking an active part in their shared life.

4.7. The Covenant Partnership with the Baptist Union

As the Independent Methodists neared the end of the twentieth century, it became clear that the denomination was suffering from structure strain. Volunteer officers were harder to find in an age when numbers had fallen and capable people were often restricted by the 'long hours culture' which prevailed in the world of employment at the time. Government legislation increasingly impacted on the lives of churches, with the result that they now had to wrestle with issues such as health and safety, disabled provision and the implementation of child protection measures. This placed increased pressure on the leaders of smaller denominations as churches looked to them for help and guidance. For reasons such as these, thoughts began to turn to the possibility of pooling resources with one or more other denominations. Fraternal relationships were currently enjoyed with the Countess of Huntingdon's Connexion and the Wesleyan Reform Union, but with no definite agenda for amalgamation. Through this form of association, a number of shared events took place and the three denominations worked together to produce a handbook of services.[83] The Connexion had also developed links with the Baptist Union of Great Britain, mainly with the intention of finding assistance with representation to national ecumenical bodies.

David Coffey (left), General Secretary of the Baptist Union of Great Britain, and Bill Gabb, Independent Methodist General Secretary, sign the Covenant Partnership

As two sets of relationships existed, the Connexion undertook the process of presenting the possible implications of linkage with one party or the other, with the intention that the churches should indicate their wishes.[84] This entailed extensive consideration of issues which would prove potentially divisive. In the case of the two smaller denominations, the place of women ministers and the question of ecumenical involvement had to be considered; with the Baptists, the main question was the IM practice of infant baptism which was still widespread. In both cases, the IM pattern of ministry did not map easily on to the ministerial praxis of the other denominations.

The outcome of the process was a decision, taken by a referendum of the churches in 2002, to explore more fully the possibility of a form of integration with the Baptists. A team of Independent Methodists led by the Connexion's Ecumenical Officer, Geoff Lomas, undertook intensive talks with Baptist Union personnel, produced detailed reports and travelled around the churches to explain each stage of the developments. Eventually, a form of covenant partnership was devised and presented to the churches for their consideration, prior to the 2004 Annual Meeting, where it was accepted. The opening paragraphs read:

> The Baptist Union of Great Britain and the Independent Methodist Connexion, as two groups of churches holding a common understanding of ecclesiology including a congregational form of government, now commit themselves to share resources for the advancement of the Christian faith in accordance with the Declaration of Principle of BUGB and the Statement of Faith of the IM Churches, and to work towards full integration of the two groups by 31 December 2009 as outlined below.
>
> The Covenant Partnership will take effect on 1 January 2005, when all churches in membership of the Independent Methodist Connexion will be, for purposes of relating and resourcing, provisional Union Churches i.e. joint members of the Baptist Union of Great Britain, the relevant Baptist Associations and the Independent Methodist Connexion.[85]

This marked the start of a five year integration process, at the end of which each church could choose whether or not to become a fully-fledged Baptist Church or a 'Union' Church having dual membership in the Baptist Union and a continuing IM Connexion with only a skeleton structure. The issues of baptism and ministry continue to receive attention as the integration process develops.

The decisions taken throughout this process were the most momentous in the IM Connexion's history and they were not taken without much heartsearching and, indeed, some distress on the part of those who had a deep love for Independent Methodism. Others saw the current situation of the denomination as unsustainable in the long run and felt that this step offered a lifeline to the churches in terms of new support facilities and the strength of belonging to a much larger Christian body.

5. Conclusion

Certain aspects of Independent Methodism during this period are particularly worthy of note. Firstly, this was a period of increasing spiritual conviction which followed an era when social and political issues had been to the fore. The older generation of the 1960s could remember the days when the large chapels of mill town Lancashire were filled to capacity, but there was no memory of when they were growing or why they grew. Nostalgia for the past, with its built-in assumption that what had worked fifty years earlier should still work, often eclipsed any motivation to look to the future and kept churches bound to the customs and practices of a bygone era. A new generation questioned those assumptions, seeing only a situation of decline and churches which desperately needed a new infusion of spiritual life. Inevitably this resulted in the usual tension which comes where 'traditionalists' and 'progressives' pursue their respective agendas among the same people.

Theological change during this period amounted almost to a reversal of the process which had happened in the earlier part of the twentieth century. The doubts of previous generations gave way to a renewed emphasis on biblical authority and personal experience of Christ as Lord and Saviour. This standpoint was reinforced through the rise of strong evangelical scholarship which helped build confidence. Later, the charismatic movement (in some quarters) brought a new focus on gifts of revelation and belief in the miraculous. Some churches went on to flourish, particularly where they had strong leadership, community involvement, uplifting worship and a relevant presentation of the Christian message both from the pulpit and through outreach activities. However, they were the exceptions rather than the rule. Despite the deepening spiritual life which became apparent in most parts of the denomination, numerical decline continued. By the beginning of the twenty-first century, like many other Christians in the United Kingdom, Independent Methodists became increasingly conscious that they were fighting an uphill battle.

Secondly, the renewed social conscience which emerged during these years took Independent Methodism almost back to its roots as a body which began as a church of the poor, though this was by no means a peculiarly IM phenomenon. It has featured widely across many denominations, in some cases stimulated by the charismatic movement.[86] Among the Independent Methodists, concern for the poor and disadvantaged at home and overseas is seen in the two charities which Independent Methodists helped to establish, North-East Help Link and the Epiphany Trust, and also in the activities of churches which have consciously addressed the needs of their surrounding communities.

Thirdly, this was an era in which denominational matters diminished in significance as churches became increasingly composed of people whose priority lay in finding local churches which met their needs and aspirations, rather than churches of any specified denomination. Thus, the churches themselves found new identities which were shaped not so much by their denominational past as by their particular mixture of people. However, this did not necessarily make the Connexion as a body redundant, since churches still valued its facilities, worked together and retained a positive sense of belonging. Interdependence rather than independence was the defining characteristic. By contrast, the 'Methodist' part of the denomination's name began to look increasingly irrelevant as the Independent Methodists by this time resembled Methodism no more than any other denomination. The change of focus from IM distinctives to wider Christian values undoubtedly helped towards the momentous decision to link with the Baptist Union of Great Britain. The outcome of that process will be evaluated in the fullness of time.

Notes to Chapter Seven

1. O. Barclay, *Evangelicalism in Britain 1935-1995* (Leicester: IVP, 1997), 114ff. F. Schaeffer, *The Great Evangelical Disaster* (Westchester, Illinois: Crossway Books, 1984), 62.
2. See Chapter 6.
3. *IMMag.* 1962, 189.
4. *IMMag.*1963, 70.
5. *The Mission Band, No. 6* (Trimdon: 1963).
6. Information supplied by Jim Faulkner, a member of the Spennymoor Mission Band, 1960-66. See also *IMMag.* 1961, 143; *IMMag.* 1962, 125.
7. *IMYB* 1971, 24,
8. R.J. Goldman, *Readiness for Religion* (London: Routledge and Kegan Paul, 1965)
9. *IMYB* 1969, 30.
10. P.B. Cliff, *The Rise and Development of the Sunday School Movement in England 1780-1980* (Redhill, National Christian Education Council, 1986), 246.
11. *IMMag.* 1960, 123.
12. The Forward Movement (Wigan: Independent Methodist Churches, 1962), *passim.*
13. *IMYB* 1968, 54.
14. *IMYB* 1968, 42.
15. *IMYB* 1968, 67.
16. *IMYB* 1966, 56.
17. *IMYB* 1969, 73.
18. *IMYB* 1973, 69.
19. *IMYB* 1974, 23
20. J.D. Hill, 'Boulders or Blessings?' *IMMag.* September 1987, 1ff.
21. 'Macedonian Project Reaches People for Christ', *IMMag.* October 1987, 1f.
22. B.G. Worrall, *The Making of the Modern Church: Christianity in England since 1800* (London: SPCK, 1988), 274ff. The reservations held by IM leaders are reflected in the fact that the denominational magazine made no reference to the 1961 campaign.
23. 'Roker and Anfield: The Aftermath', *IMMag.* November 1984, 1ff.
24. *IMYB* 1969, 90
25. *ibid.*
26. *IMYB* 1971, 87.
27. C. Cleverly, *Church Planting: Our Future Hope* (London: Scripture Union, 1991), 11.
28. 'A New Church is opening at Warrington', *IMMag.* August 1987, 1f.
29. *IMMag.* September 1987, 2.
30. 'Annual Meeting welcomes . . . Bethel Fellowship', *IMMag.* September 1992, 1.
31. 'Connexion welcomes Two New Mission Churches', *IMMag.* September 2001, 2.
32. Summary accounts of the careers of the later IM missionaries can be found in W.A. Smith, 'A World to Win', *IMMag.* May 1983, 8ff; W.A. Smith, '100

Years of Worldwide Mission: A Secretary's View', *IMMag.* December 2004, 9; January 2005, 8.
33. *IMYB* 1969, 62.
34. *Independent Methodist Hymnal* (Wigan: Independent Methodist Bookroom, 1974)
35. 'Let's Celebrate', *IMMag.* February 1997, 1.
36. 'Connexion takes on a Theatre', *IMMag.* March 1997, 1.
37. 'Theatre Project to Conclude', *IMMag.* October 1998, 10
38. *IMMag.* 1965, 172.
39. See Chapter 6.
40. *IMMag.* 1960, 126
41. *IMYB* 1974, 60, 76.
42. *IMYB* 1976, 61.
43. *IMYB* 1977, 105ff.
44. D. W. Bebbington, *Evangelicalism in Modern Britain* (London: Unwin Hyman Ltd, 1989), 230.
45. 'Emmanuel School – Venture of Faith', *IMMag.* November 1988, 11.
46. Annual Meeting Business Handbook (Wigan: Independent Methodist Churches, 2001), 15.
47. 'Statements of Faith and Practice Approved', *IMMag.* September 1984, 14. See Appendix 7.
48. See Section 4.4. below for the changes in the Statement of Practice in relation to ministry.
49. *IMYB* 1968, 32.
50. See Appendix 6.
51. 'Obituary: Dr. W. W. Kay', *IMMag.* April 1980, 13.
52. 'Obituary: Dr. Tom Backhouse', *IMMag.* July 1998, 10.
53. See Chapter 3.
54. Statement of Practice (Independent Methodist Churches, 1984). See Appendix 8 for the Statement of Practice as amended in 2000.
55. 'Ministry Debate shows Polarised Attitudes', *IMMag.* September 1991, 1.
56. 'Ministry Debate sparks Lively Exchanges', *IMMag.* September 1994, 3.
57. 'Clause 4 Amended', *IMMag.* August 1995, 6.
58. Statement on Ministry (Independent Methodist Churches, 2000).
59. *IMYB* 1971, 38.
60. *IMYB* 1976, 34
61. Bebbington, *Evangelicalism*, 265.
62. 'Connexion joins Evangelical Alliance', *IMMag.* August 1995, 7.
63. *IMMag.* 1973, 74.
64. 'Child Pornography', *IMMag.* January 1978, 5.
65. 'Selling out on Sunday', *IMMag.* January 1986, 4f.
66. *IMMag.* 1972, 99.
67. 'Church Funds and Liverpool 8', *IMMag.* October 1981, 1f.
68. *IMMag.* 1973, 38.
69. *IMYB* 1977, 31.
70. 'To Poland with Love', *IMMag.* January, 1982, 1ff.
71. 'Free the Siberian Seven!' *IMMag.* August, 1981, 16.
72. 'Christian Musicians hounded in Russia', *IMMag.* February, 1985, 9.

73. www.epiphany.org.uk

74. 'Freemen of Wigan', *IMMag.* November, 2000, 2.

75. 'Obituary: Walter Wilkinson', *IMMag.* September, 2001, 12.

76. The full report of the conference is given in *Unity begins at Home. A report on the First British Conference on Faith and Order, Nottingham 1964* (London: SCM Press, 1964).

77. 'Christian Unity', *IMMag.* 1965, 5f.

78. *IMMag.* 1964, 102ff.

79. *IMMag.* 1964, 182.

80. *Baptism, Eucharist and Ministry* (Geneva: World Council of Churches, 1982).

81. *IMMag.* November 1984, 5; December 1984, 4; January 1985, 3; March 1985, 10.

82. 'Connexion says "Yes" to New Ecumenical Bodies,' *IMMag.* September 1989, 10.

83. *Together in the Lord. A Handbook of Services* (Trustees of the Countess of Huntingdon's Connexion, Independent Methodist Association Incorporated, Wesleyan Reform Union, 1997).

84. *IMYB* 2001, 7ff.

85. *IMYB* 2004, 4f.

86. N. Scotland, 'Evangelicalism and the Charismatic Movement' in C. Bartholomew et al, *The Futures of Evangelicalism* (Leicester: IVP, 2003), 271; D.L. Edwards, *The Futures of Christianity* (London: Hodder and Stoughton, 1987), 432.

Conclusion

With the exception of the mainstream of Methodism, represented by the Wesleyan Methodists until 1932 and thereafter by the Methodist Church, the Independent Methodists have had the longest history of all the Methodist divisions and will mark their 200th Annual Meeting in 2005.[1] The preceding chapters have shown why their peculiar characteristics ultimately kept them apart from other Methodists.

1. The journey from sectarianism to denominationalism

The middle of the nineteenth century saw a steady spread of free gospel ideas as various small sects and individual churches emerged, usually from Methodist discord, in different parts of the country. In most instances, they served the poorest of the poor, as witnessed by the comment of the Independent Methodist Church at Bromsgrove, Worcestershire: 'This is a free chapel . . . we have no pew rents, no paid minister that preaches in this chapel. The people are so very poor that attend this place of worship that they could not support a paid ministry.'[2] This church, and many others which used the name 'Independent Methodist', never even linked with the Independent Methodist Union, demonstrating the fact that that free gospel ideas were much more widespread than the actual membership of the IM Union of Churches suggested. Members of most such churches cared little about corporate identity and were content to find security and meaning within themselves, valuing localised freedom more than wider relationships. Yet, by the end of the nineteenth century, the Independent Methodists found themselves the only remaining Methodist-derived free gospel denomination. The Protestant Methodists (1836) and Minor Wesleyans (1838) had been subsumed into other branches of Methodism.[3] The Original Methodists, who had been stridently vociferous on free gospel ideas, had dispersed by 1867, mainly into the United Methodist Free Churches or Primitive Methodists.[4] The Christian Brethren had the same experience, with a small number joining the Independent Methodists.[5] Perhaps these groups were truer barometers than the Independent Methodists of Christian opinion on the free gospel system. As the Independent Methodists moved towards the new world of the twentieth century, they appeared like a remnant, upholding an ideology long abandoned by others. Three issues in particular now faced them:

1.1. The Issue of Identity: Methodist or Independent?

Of all Methodist offshoots, the Independent Methodists represented the greatest contrast in polity to the parent Wesleyan body. Nevertheless, in terms of doctrine and spirituality, they shadowed the rest of Methodism throughout the nineteenth century. When theological change came, they absorbed the same changes as other Methodist denominations. When Methodist ecumenism started, they were part of it. They were always followers of trends rather than initiators of them. In the 1890s when they decided to look for an agreed common name, the overwhelming majority of churches and people wished to include in it the word 'Methodist.' This appeared to prepare the ground for their gradual re-integration with other Methodists, but, in the event, for the Independent Methodists, the ideological price was too high. Their dalliance with Methodist unity effectively lasted from 1881 to 1904; their commitment to Methodist doctrine ended in 1927. Thereafter, their attachment to Methodism consisted largely of nominal identity and certain superficial resemblances such as circuit structures.

The inability of the Independent Methodists to join the United Methodist Church in 1907 was a defining point in their history. If joining carried a high price, so did staying apart. The cost of retaining their distinctive ideology was continued separatism which made them looked increasingly anachronistic in an ecumenical age. Their spiritual descendants a century later struggled to maintain the denomination's machinery with only a fraction of the 1907 membership.

1.2. The Issue of Definition: Preachers or Ministers?

Although the Independent Methodists dropped their strident 'anti-hireling' rhetoric towards the end of the nineteenth century, their fundamental views on ministry remained the same. This was a huge obstacle in their relationship with other Free Church denominations which held a transparently low view of IM preacher-ministers who were unordained, lacked any sense of *episkopē*, spent most of their time in secular employment and received greatly inferior training (or none at all until the 1890s). To the Independent Methodists, the fact that their prized, gratuitous ministry was not recognised by others, including their fellow nonconformists, rankled deeply. Rejection by bodies as different as the Evangelical Alliance[6] and the Bolton Burial Board[7] made them aware of how far out of step they were with the rest of the Christian Church and the expectations of society in general. To those looking at it from the outside,

Independent Methodism remained a 'lay' movement. However, those on the inside continued to see the people of God as one and found no use for the clergy-lay distinction. This ontological egalitarianism reflected a lingering element of Quakerism which posed the denomination's irresolvable dilemma. It wished to have a pattern of ministry which recognised no difference between ministers and members, but which also enjoyed parity with the ministries of the other Free Churches. Equality on one front was possible, but not on both. This ambivalence frequently led to a mismatch of expectations between ministers and congregations, while the resulting form of ministry defied the comprehension of other churches and local communities alike.

In practice, the Independent Methodists' peculiar system of ministry was to prove a two-edged sword, as they experienced neither the benefits nor the downfalls of pastoral change. Lacking the stimulus of new minds entering their situations, they often remained locked into established tradition. This was to prove the undoing of the large churches at Glasgow and Liverpool which thrived under their gifted leaders Alexander Denovan and William Sanderson respectively, but which declined dramatically after their deaths, when no internal successors of their stature could be found. Denovan's much-vaunted argument that each church should find pastors or elders from within its own ranks did not always work in practice. However, other large churches such as Nelson (Salem) and Oldham (Smith Street) were less focused on a single pastor and had a ready succession of able people from one generation to the next. Capable local leaders were not eclipsed by a single, full time pastor, and were able to develop their gifts, making their churches largely self-sufficient and stable through continuity well into the twentieth century.

1.3. The Issue of Cultural Transposition

Independent Methodism's pattern of ministry led to the formation of churches which genuinely reflected the communities which they served. Miners, agricultural workers and weavers ministered on Sundays to the people they worked alongside during the week. Poverty never proved a barrier to church membership nor did lack of education debar a preacher from the pulpit. A church which was made of working class people whose preachers addressed them in their own vernacular had an appeal to the poor, as John Furness noted, following a Preston Camp Meeting:

> I am more than ever convinced from today's proceedings, that God intends to make us a blessing to the poor: they at least can understand the speech of many of our brethren.[8]

Early Independent Methodism was, in this sense, a product of its age and catered for people who were not worried by the thought that their preachers were no more literate than themselves or that other denominations gave them no recognition. Their Sunday experience merely mirrored their everyday lives. This early pattern and outlook determined the areas where Independent Methodism would take root. By 1901, when the denomination was near the height of its strength with 153 churches and 8377 members,[9] the distribution of those churches across the country shows that the vast majority were still located in textile towns and mining villages.[10] The much smaller agricultural element was already dwindling as rural populations declined.

Throughout their formative years, the Independent Methodists undoubtedly found a niche and met a need, especially where deprivation was high and literacy was low. However, as educational levels rose and members' aspirations to better lives grew, the poor speech and low literacy of many preachers ceased to meet the changing situation. Far from addressing an entire congregation of indigent workers, the illiterate miner or weaver could now be facing shopkeepers, secretaries and even factory owners; they were no longer his fellow workmen. The social composition of congregations was changing and the pattern of fifty years earlier was now unsustainable. Moreover, middle-class chapel leaders at the end of the nineteenth century were no longer satisfied with leading localised sects of the poor. The opulent chapels they were building showed that poverty was no longer a potent argument for non-payment. The only way they could justify their continued rejection of paid ministry was to strengthen the ideological case for it without reference to poverty. Brimelow, Vickers and others rose to this challenge and were sufficiently persuasive to secure the ongoing commitment of the churches to free gospel ideas, thus ensuring the denomination's continued separate existence. Externally, they were less successful; despite their best efforts, the Christian public remained unimpressed and further expansion was minimal. The early nineteenth century cultural setting into which Independent Methodism was born had gone and its practices sat less easily with the new world of the twentieth century.

2. The Outcome of the Journey

By the 1920s, Independent Methodism had become a settled denomination which underwent no fundamental changes for the next sixty years, with a distinctive character which marked it out from other Free Churches. Individual churches remained independent in government, but tended to attach great importance to denominational principles which they observed tenaciously. Ministry had been carefully circumscribed by definitive statements which made clear what it *was not*, but which were less precise about what it *was*. Its churches, still predominantly working class in character, were very much part of their local communities, even if what they stood for was not widely understood. To the outward observer, Independent Methodism was a lay denomination of roughly Methodist character with a small geographical base.

However, when the process of decline which began after the First World War began to accelerate from the 1960s onwards, not only customs and traditions but foundational principles came under scrutiny. In a more ecumenical age, as with other denominations, Christians were more inclined to emphasise what they had in common than the issues that kept them apart. No-one filled the role of Brimelow or Vickers as an exponent of distinctive IM principles and practices. Some churches were simply preoccupied with survival, while those with a strong sense of mission had little interest in nineteenth century Methodist conflicts. This shift of emphasis paved the way for some of the changes which took place during the later years of the twentieth century.

Finally, the question must be asked: did Independent Methodism bring anything of value or significance to the Christian church as a whole? Certainly it never became a force in the nation, nor did it make a great contribution to major ecumenical developments. However, for much of its history, its churches and their preachers met a need in communities which could identify with their simplicity. As long as they were outgoing churches, with a particular concern for the poor, and churches which valued the ministries of people of all abilities, they had a role to fulfil locally if not nationally. Local autonomy and freedom from the financial burden of a paid ministry enabled them to fulfil that role. Those who ministered gratuitously often did so at great cost to themselves and their families, undertaking long journeys, often by foot, and devoting almost all of their non-working hours to the needs of their congregations. Many of them lacked learning, but their service was selfless and sacrificial.

At the beginning of the twenty-first century, the society into which Independent Methodism was born has gone and its churches find themselves in a very different situation, in a nation more prosperous than ever, but where broken families, social isolation and dysfunctional behaviour patterns have led to a new set of social problems. The positive values of Independent Methodism's heritage – a people's church with a sense of community, a mission-orientated church and a church caring for the needy and disadvantaged, all rooted in a high view of biblical teaching – transcend denominational identity. These values have much to offer British society in the twenty-first century and provide valuable signposts for the future not only for the Independent Methodists, but for churches of all traditions.

Notes to Conclusion

1. The Methodist New Connexion had an earlier date of origin (1797) than the Independent Methodists, but lasted only until 1907 when it became part of the United Methodist Church.
2. Home Office Papers HO 129: Ecclesiastical Returns, 1851, District 392.
3. See Chapter 3.
4. *Ibid.* The same was true of the Minor Wesleyans of Wales. See Chapter 3.
5. *Ibid.*
6. The Evangelical Alliance restricted membership to those who subscribed to nine points, the last of which was 'the Divine Institution of the Christian Ministry, and the obligation in perpetuity of the ordinances of Baptism and the Lord's Supper.' This excluded Quakers, Plymouth Brethren and Independent Methodists, none of whom interpreted ministry in terms of settled pastoral appointment. Peter Phillips, who by this time was the IM elder statesman, saw this as an unwarranted injustice, but supported the establishment of the Alliance in his home town. 'The Life and Labours of Peter Phillips', *ZT*, September 1855, 46.
7. See Chapter 4.
8. *IMMag.* 1852, 208
9. See Appendix 12.
10. See Fig. 3, page 193.

Appendix 1

The following statement, issued in 1815, is the first known official statement from an Independent Methodist Annual Meeting

(printed verbatim, including punctuation)

AN ADDRESS
TO THE
INDEPENDENT METHODIST CHURCHES

It is with heartfelt pleasure that, after the lapse of many years, and the prediction of many of our enemies, that we should fall and come to nothing, that we have to address you on the subject of *Independency* and inform you that beyond our most sanguine expectations we enjoy the greatest of early attainments, peace and prosperity in all our Churches; and that God is with us, is evident from the effects that are produced, for many of our people are becoming eminent for piety and virtue; and the great Lord of the Vineyard has raised many useful labourers, *men* of talent and ability, who are both able and willing to administer the word of life, without money and without price; men whose labours are, we have reason to trust, all owned of God; by great numbers being brought out of darkness into marvellous light; – in some places such numbers attend the preaching of the word, that we have need to cry out for more room, that our usefulness may be the more extended – that we may be the means of spreading Primitive and Apostolic Truth far and wide. We are convinced there is an open door before us, and that those truths received among us will bear down the tide of Infidelity and opposition before them and will be carried at some future day to earth' remotest bound!

From the diversity of opinion that prevails in the kingdom concerning us, we think it necessary at this time, briefly to state to the world what we mean by those peculiarities (so called) which are found amongst us; the first is that our preachers receive no salaries for preaching, and though it may appear strange at the present day, yet we consider it to be truly Apostolic and primitive: calculated to produce the best effects: for in the first place we have the example of Christ and His Apostles, who, according to the declaration of St. Paul, ministered both to their own necessities and also to those who were with them; – again we are fully persuaded that the money expended in support of hired ministers throughout the kingdom, might be employed to more useful purposes. We think if the money paid in this kingdom to such men, were divided into two parts, and one half of it appropriated for the use of the poor, the helpless, the fatherless, and the widow: and the other part employed in sending missionaries abroad, England might extend its labours and be the means of spreading the gospel from sea to sea and from shore to shore. Upon this plan men can have no motive to induce them to become preachers, but that they may present every man before God without spot or blemish; besides the great argument of infidelity, that men would cease to preach if their salaries were taken from them, is completely answered.

Again, the present state of things in England are so widely different from what they once were, that there is not the same necessity for men to be set apart for the ministry as when our countrymen were the subjects of ignorance, and superstition, when the number of Teachers were few, & when they were obliged to travel a great way to promulgate the Gospel. At present, things are very different, as there is hardly a town or a village in Britain, but they have preachers residing amongst them, who preach the gospel and labour with their hands for the bread that perisheth, whose preaching is both useful and acceptable to their brethren; after all, we have no objection to others doing as they think best in employing hired ministers; but, we consider our own plan as the bulwark of our liberty; for we acknowledge but one Master, even Christ, and we are all brethren in him.

The name of our Society as *Independent Methodists,* appears to have been misunderstood; the word *Independent* amongst us signifies no more than that each Church has the sole privilege of making its internal laws, independent of any canon laws, or of any Conference, or any other Church whatever of the same persuasion; the sole reason for our assembling together once a year as Churches is that the real state of each Church may be inquired into, and that they may be assisted if occasion require, that ministers may on proper occasions pay a friendly visit, from one church to another, and, if anything can be suggested for the good of the whole, well; but yet every Church is left to its own discretion, for none can say to another, why does thou so? The word Methodist with us, implies that we hold the same doctrine as the Wesleyan Methodists do, and that we use the same means of grace. It has been said, that as our ministers preach without salaries, that we have no need of Money, this is a gross mistake, for if we have no money, how is our chapels to be built? our poor relieved? or, other incidental expenses paid? but whatever it may cost us we have the pleasing reflection, that we know our money is expended in feeding the hungry, clothing the naked, and in spreading the glorious Kingdom of the greatest and best of Beings!!!

Now, brethren, we leave you to the care of that God whose eyes are ever watchful over the righteous, and whose ears are open to their prayers; who has said Lo! I am with you even to the end of the world.

Signed,

In and on behalf of the Independent Churches,

Peter Ashley, President
William Massey, Secretary

Appendix 2

RULES OF THE
INDEPENDENT METHODIST MISSIONARY SOCIETY,
1825

The following rules were established by a series of resolutions passed by the Annual Meeting 1825. In modified form they remained in force until 1876.

1. That for the purpose of establishing churches on the system of 'Independent Methodists', for promoting the prosperity of those already formed, and for the extension of the cause of Christ generally, this meeting deems it an imperious duty to form a General Missionary Society, to be supported by auxiliary societies formed by the churches in Union, as far as agreeable and expedient.

2. That the object of this society be to send missionaries to churches destitute of preachers, regularly; to those who have few preachers, at stated intervals; and to visit occasionally all the churches in the Union as far as expedient.

3. That to meet the unavoidable expenses of this measure the churches in Union be requested to form auxiliary societies, to be supported by regular contributions, donations and an annual sermon and collection at each place. The amount of which (after incidental expenses are paid) to be brought to the Annual Meeting every year; and this to be considered at the Parent Society.

4. That at every Annual Meeting a plan be formed for the supply of such churches as are thought necessitous, and others according to circumstances; and that such persons be appointed missionaries as can be spared from their avocations for one, two or three Sabbaths, and are disposed to labour to the utmost of their power for the good of the society to which they are sent.

5. That each church to be supplied by the missionaries be represented at the Annual Meeting and to be admitted on the Plan, according to the number of their preachers, and other circumstances, subject to the decision of the Missionary Committee to be appointed from time to time, and that no preacher stay at the same place above three Sabbath days at the same time; and that during their stay they shall, according to circumstances, form classes, visit the sick and absentees, and preach as often as possible in adjacent places.

6. That the amount of unavoidable expenses incurred be laid before the Annual Meeting by each church in behalf of their missionaries, and that the same be paid out of the General Fund, and regular accounts be kept of receipts and disbursements, as connected with this Society, each auxiliary society keeping its own accounts.

7. That no society be supplied regularly by the missionaries that is within 10 miles of another society having a number of preachers, but such be advised to join those societies in Union, and be supplied by their preachers; but that all others' societies situated at a greater distance be supplied subject resolutions the 5th and their situation as a society.

Appendix 3

Testimony and Principles of Union of the
United Free Gospel Churches
1855

Introduction

WHEREAS it being the will of the Lord Jesus Christ that his people should be united together and be one in Him, and that they should, in this union, be serviceable to each other, and lay themselves out for usefulness in the world, – it has long seemed good to the brethren composing the United Free Gospel Churches to co-operate with one another for these ends.

And whereas the better and more effectually to carry out such co-operation, and exhibit its basis and our principles at large, the Delegates who met from the respective Churches in June, 1852, issued a Document for the consideration of the whole united body; and whereas a few additions and alterations have since been brought under notice, – We, the Delegates assembled in Annual Meeting in May, 1855, with the full concurrence of the Churches we represent, in the fear of God, and we trust under the guidance of the Holy Ghost, do adopt the following

DECLARATION OF DOCTRINES AND CONSTITUTION,

In which the Leading Principles that we believe and are regulated by are set forth, that we may properly understand one another, and be all led to "speak the same thing, and be perfectly joined together in the same mind, and in the same judgment," standing "fast in one spirit, . . . striving together for the faith" and spread "of the gospel;" and that we may have a Document at hand by which we can give an answer to every man "who asketh a reason of the hope that is in us;" and, by referring to which, we may keep aloof from us those who profess Christianity, while they entertain opinions subversive of the truth as it is in Jesus. Luke i. 1-4; Amos iii. 3; 1Thess. v. 21; 1 Cor. i. 10; Phil. i. 27; 2 Tim. i. 13; 1 Peter iii. 13; Gal. v. 12; Jude 3 ver.; 2 John 10 ver.

Doctrines

Therefore we testify and declare that we believe,

I.   That there is One only living and true God, infinite, eternal, and unchangeable, and in all his attributes absolutely perfect. Deut. vi. 4. Jer. x. 10; John iv. 24; Job xi. 2; Ps. cxlvii. 5; Ps. xc. 2; James i. 17; Exod. iii. 14; Rev. iv. 8: xv. 4; Exod. xxxiv. 6, 7.

II.   That while some knowledge of God may be obtained by the works of creation and providence, it is especially necessary that recourse be had to the infallible guidance of the Eternal Spirit and the Holy Scriptures of the Old and New Testaments, that we and all others may be instructed and led by these, without the traditions and commandments of men, – giving no heed to any one, whatever his pretences may be, unless what he teaches be in accordance with the inspired volume. Ps. xix. 1, 2; Rom. i. 20: ii. 14, 15; Gen. vi. 3; Acts vii. 31: xiii. 2: xv. 28; 1 Cor. ii. 13: xii. 3 ; 2 Tim. iii. 16; John v. 39; Acts xvii. 11; Rev. ii. 2: iii. 8,10.

III.   That in the Godhead or Divine Unity there is a mysterious plurality of Three, commonly called persons, and distinctly named, the Father, and the Word or Son, and the Holy Ghost or Spirit; but these three are one God, equal and the same in all the perfections of Deity. Matt. iii. 11-17: xxviii. 19; 2 Cor. xiii. 14; John i. 1-14, 17-23; 1 Tim. iii. 16; 1 John v. 6-13; Rev. v. 13.

IV.   That God is the Creator, Preserver, and Governor of all things. Gen. i. 31; John i. 1,3; Heb. i. 3; Isaiah xxviii. 29; Ps. ciii. 19; Matt. x. 29.

V.   That he created angels holy and capable of doing his will, and continuing in happiness for ever; and yet at liberty to disobey, and bring upon themselves misery. Mark viii. 38; Ps. civ. 4; Heb. 1. 7; 2 Pet. ii. 4.

VI.   That, while some of these kept their first estate, and are therefore holy and happy angels of heaven, frequently ministering to those who shall be heirs of salvation, others having sinned, have become devils, and enemies of God and man; that for these hell has been prepared, and in it they are to suffer the punishment of everlasting fire. Jude 6; Luke ix. 26; Rev. v. 11; Heb. i. 13, 14; 2 Pet. ii. 4; Matt. xxv. 41.

VII.   That God created man, male and female, after his own image, in knowledge, righteousness, and holiness, with full ability to continue therein, but free to enter into temptation and sin. Gen. i. 27; Col. iii. 10; Eph. iv. 24; Gen. ii. 15-17.

VIII.   That our first parents, having sinned, fell from this exalted state, lost the image of God, became corrupt in their nature, and rendered themselves incapable of doing good or pleasing their Maker; that they also transmitted their corruption and inability to all their posterity, so that no mere man since the fall can of himself keep God's commandments, or do or suffer anything to merit or recover his favour. Gen. iii.; Eccl. vii. 29; Ps. li. 5; Rom. vii. 18: iii. 23; Eph. ii. 8, 9.

IX.   That God did not leave mankind to perish in this state of sin, but, in his love and mercy, provided for them an all-sufficient Redeemer; and through Him sent his Holy Spirit to enlighten, strengthen, and strive with men in order to save them. John iii. 16-17; Rom. v. 18-20; John. i. 9; Gen. vi. 3; John xvi. 7, 8; Rev. iii. 17-22; 1 Tim.i. 15: iv.10.

X.   That this Redeemer is the Lord Jesus Christ, who, although he was the Word in the beginning with God, and truly and properly was God, yet in the fulness of time was born of the Virgin Mary, and thus became man by taking upon himself a true body and a reasonable soul, but without sin; and having been found in fashion as a man, he died the just for the unjust-offering himself a real atoning sacrifice, and shedding his precious blood for the whole world; at the same time commending his spirit into the hands of his Father. 2 Cor. v. 18, 19; John i. 1-14; Matt. i. 18-25; Luke i. 26-35; 1 Tim. ii. 5, 6; Rom. ix. 5; Heb. ii. 14: vii. 26, 27; 1 John ii. 2; Luke xxiii. 46.

XI.   That on the third day after the Lord's crucifixion and burial, he rose from the dead; and having given the most satisfactory evidence of his resurrection, he ascended to heaven, and there lives the only Mediator between God and man. I Cor. xv. 3, 4; Acts i. 1-3; Mark xvi. 19; Acts. iv. 12; Heb. vii. 25; 1 Tim. ii. 5.

XII.   That, as our salvation is not of our works or sufferings, but is the gift of God, our justification, as sinners, is by faith alone. Rom. iii. 27-31: iv. 5.

XIII.   That, while we are saved by grace through faith, we are nevertheless required, and enabled by Divine power, to repent and turn from all iniquity, and be holy; that therefore those who are thus influenced, are "in the name of the Lord Jesus, and by the Spirit of our God," not only justified and have all their sins forgiven, but they are also sanctified and set apart to show forth from a renewed nature, "the praises of him who hath called them out of darkness into his marvellous light," and are "God's workmanship, created in Christ Jesus unto good works, which God hath before ordained that we should walk in them." Eph. ii. 8, 9; Jer. xxxi. 18, 19; Isaiah lv. 7; Luke xiii. 3; Acts xi. 18: ii. 37, 38: xiii. 38, 39; Rom. iv. 5-7; 1 Pet. i. 14-16; 1 Cor. vi. 11; Eph. iv. 23, 24; 1 Pet. ii. 9; Eph. ii. 10.

XIV.   That penitent, believing, holy persons, are adopted into the family of heaven, and are God's predestinated and elect people; and that as they had nothing naturally inherent in them more than their fellow-creatures to constitute them righteous, but "in time past were not a people, but are now the people of God; who had not obtained mercy, but have now obtained mercy," – so, to be united to them, all others are sincerely invited; and from their happy number none are excluded but those who, by their sin and unbelief, exclude themselves. John i. 12; Gal. iv. 4-7; Isaiah lxvi. 2; compare Rom. ix. 6-8, with iv. 16, 23-25, and x. 4, 11-13; Ps. iv. 3; Eph. i. 1-19: ii. 1-10; 1 Pet. i. 1-17: ii. 3-7; Prov. 1. 20-33; Isaiah xlv. 22: lv. 1-3, 6, 7; Matt. xxii. 9; 2 Cor. v. 19-21: vi. 1, 2; Rev. xxii. 17; Ezek. xxxiii. 11; Matt. xxiii. 37; John i. 11-13; Acts xiii. 38-46; Rom. xi. 19-23; Col. i. 21-23; Heb. iii. 5-19: iv. 1-11; 2 Pet. i. 5-11; Rev. xxii. 14, 18, 19.

XV.   That, consequently, such as are reprobates are those who, after having had gracious opportunities to obtain salvation, continue in, or backslide into, rebellion against God, by presumptuous sins or carelessness about their souls, whereby they either refuse or neglect the offers of mercy. Isaiah lix. 1, 2; Ezek. xviii.; Matt. xxii. 1-10; Heb. vi. 4-8; 2 Pet. ii. 6-22: iii. 5; Tit. i. 15, 16; Rom. ii.4-11; 1 Pet. iv. 18; Acts vii. 51; Heb. ii. 3; Rev. iii. 15, 16.

XVI. That man being possessed of an immortal spirit, at death the souls of the godly immediately pass into glory, and the souls of the ungodly go to the place of torment. Gen. ii. 7; Eccl. xii. 7; Matt. x. 28; Luke xxiii. 43; 2 Cor. v. 1-9; Phil. i. 23; Rev. vii. 13-17; Luke xvi. 19-31.

XVII. That there will be a judgment day, and a general resurrection of the dead, both of the good and bad, when all shall appear before the judgment-seat of Christ, to receive according to their deeds – the righteous being taken to heaven, and the unrighteous sent to hell. John v. 28, 29; Matt. xxv.; 2 Cor. v. 10; Rev. xx. 11-15.

XVIII. That these states of reward and punishment shall have no end, since the time of probation or trial is for ever terminated, and the Supreme King and Judge closes the whole by "saying to them on his right hand, Come ye blessed of my Father, inherit the kingdom prepared for you from the foundation of the world; and unto them on the left hand, Depart from me ye cursed, into *(aionion)* everlasting fire, prepared for the devil and his angels. And these shall go away into *(aionion)* everlasting punishment, but the righteous into life *(aionion)* eternal." Eccl. ix. 10; Matt. xxv. 46; Rev. xx. 10, 15.

Constitution

I. That Christ has established a Church on the earth, of which He is the only King and Head, and the alone High Priest. Matt. xvi. 18; Luke xix. 38; Rev. xix. 16; Col. i. 18; Heb. iii. 1: iv. 14.

II. That the Church is composed of Christ's disciples – "a royal priesthood, an holy nation, a peculiar people;" and that it embraces all His followers, however numerous, or scattered, or separated into distinct congregations. Eph. v. 25-27; 1 Pet. ii. 9; 1 Cor. x. 17; Eph. iii. 6: iv. 11, 12; Col. i. 18.

III. That as the Church is one as well as many, this oneness should be maintained under proper organisation; so that, as the Church is designated a house, a city, a nation, a people, everything may be rightly arranged, according to Holy Scripture, as in well regulated societies, that the smallest number, as well as the greatest, may experience good and shine forth examples of decency and order, and the united body may further, by all proper means, the work of God on the earth. 1 Pet. ii. 9; Isaiah lx. 14; Heb. xii. 22; 1 Tim. iii. 15; Heb. iii. 6: x. 21; Matt. v. 14; 1 Cor. xiv. 20; Luke xxiv. 47; Acts of the Apostles.

IV. That with such views of the Church of Christ, we agree to the following:-

   1. While we unite upon *principle* and not upon *name,* and therefore care little about any name, except what the early disciples of Jesus were called, yet to save confusion, and to give identity to ourselves by a designation exhibitive, in a short phrase, of our principles, especially connected with the ministry to which we adhere, – therefore the Name or Title of the whole Churches in union is and shall be, "The United Free Gospel Churches." But as the circumstances of a number of the churches may also require other designations, those now in union and such as shall be received hereafter, shall be at liberty to use their freedom as to other names in their different localities. Isaiah i. 26: xix. 23-26: xliv. 1-5: lxii. 1-4; Ezek. xxxvii. 15-19; Acts xi. 26. See also introductory verses of Paul's Epistles to the Romans, Corinthians, Galatians, Ephesians, Philippians, Colossians, and Thessalonians; James i. 1; 1 Pet. i. 1; and Note foot of pages 13 and 14 [i.e. of original publication].

   2. Each separate congregation of faithful persons, regularly assembling together, especially when organised under duly appointed office-bearers, shall be recognised as a Church; as the church in the house of Nymphas, at Laodicea,– Col. iv. 15, and the church in the house of Priscilla and Aquila, at Rome, – Rom. xvi. 3-5; Acts xiv. 23.

   3. When several such congregations or churches are at a convenient distance from each other, and can arrange that their ministers or other delegates shall occasionally meet to promote the good of the whole, it is recommended that they do so, and at convenient times and places, to be appointed when they come together, and that they consider themselves united and one; as was the case at Jerusalem – the Christians there being called "the church which was at Jerusalem," Acts viii. 1; although such multitudes belonged thereto as would require not a few places of moderate size to assemble in. Acts ii. 41: iv. 4: v. 14, 42. But they could all meet as one by representation, Acts xxi. 18-25. It was so likewise with the Corinthians, who were called "the church of God at Corinth," 1 Cor. i. 2, while they are written to in chap. xiv. 34, as "the churches." Acts ii. 42; iv. 4: v. 14-42. See also Rom. i. 7: xvi. 3-5, 10, 11, 14, 16; Acts xv.: xx. 28-31: xxi. 18-25.

   4. All the churches in the Union, however numerous, shall be considered as one. "There is one body"– Eph. iv. 4. Thus Christ prays "That they (believers) all may

be one"– John xvii. 20, 21; and he states that there "shall be one fold and one Shepherd"– John x. 16.

5. Every church shall have stated meetings, especially upon the Lord's Day, for Christian worship and edification; and this must be held requisite, even though full organisation has not taken place. Where such a lack is experienced, let the brethren faithfully do their duty. After having been in secret with God, attended to duties in their respective dwellings, and acquired all the knowledge in their power, let them meet together to wait upon the Lord – let them join with one another in praise and prayer – let them read the Scriptures, and if ability be afforded, drop a word, in truth and soberness, to edification, exhortation, and comfort; and let them be assured that He who hath seen them in secret, and searching after knowledge to the edifying of the church, shall reward them openly. In such circumstances did the first disciples draw near to God in the upper room at Jerusalem, comforting one another, and waiting for the descent of the Holy Ghost to lead them into all truth, – Acts i. 13, 14; and no doubt it was the same with the various companies who were first gathered by the apostles, evangelists, and others, and after some lapse of time, had the things that were wanting duly set in order among them. Acts xiv. 21-23; Tit. i. 5. "Having therefore, brethren, boldness (or liberty) to enter into the holiest by the blood of Jesus, let us draw near with a true heart, in full assurance of faith. Let us hold fast our profession of faith without wavering. . . . And let us consider one another, to provoke unto love and to good works: not forsaking the assembling of ourselves together, as the manner of some is, but exhorting one another; Heb. x. 19-26. See 2 Pet, i. 5; 1 Cor.xii.31: xiv. 1,12.

6. Regular office-bearers shall be appointed in each church as soon as properly qualified persons are found. These are presbyters or elders and deacons – the elders being also called overseers or bishops, and may be designated pastors: to such also, as is well known, the general name "ministers" is given. Acts xiv, 23: vi. 1-6: xx. 17, 28; Phil. i. 1; Eph. iv. 11.

   While the brethren are not to be excluded from what is required of them, as referred to in Nos. 5 and 9 hereof, it shall more especially be the duty of the pastors to teach, rule, baptise, administer the Lord's supper, and when sent for visit the sick of their charge; at the same time they are to watch for the souls of their flock as they who must give an account, and be careful that no one lead any of them astray, and that those who attempt to instruct them may do so with sound doctrine. 1 Tim. iii. 2, 5; Heb. xiii. 17; Mark xvi. 15, 16; 1 Cor. xl. 23; James v. 14; Acts xx. 28-31.

   To fulfil such an important trust, the presbyters or pastors must not be new converts, but experienced and well-tried persons, each being "blameless, vigilant, sober, of good behaviour (margin – "modest"); given to hospitality; not given to wine, no striker, not greedy of filthy lucre;[1] patient, not a brawler; one that ruleth well his own house, the husband of one wife, having faithful children, not accused of riot or unruly; (for if a main know not how to rule his own house, how shall he take care of the church of God?) Moreover, he must have a good report of them who are without," and be "holy, temperate, holding fast the faithful word as he hath been taught, (margin – "in teaching,") that he may be able by sound doctrine both to exhort and convince the gainsayers;" or if they will not be convinced, but will be unruly and vain talkers, that he may have authority to bring them under the discipline of the church, that their mouths may be stopped. 1 Tim. iii. 1-7: v. 22; Tit. i. 1-11; 2 Tim. ii. 2; Titus iii. 10; Gal. i. 8, 9; 2 John 9, 10.

Some of the elders, indeed, may not be so gifted as others, and their qualifications may not enable them to "labour in word and doctrine;" yet if they be otherwise competent as described, and be "apt to teach" in a more humble way, their services may be highly beneficial. Besides, their lack as speakers may be abundantly made up by helps – able exhorters and expounders of the word, whose circumstances otherwise hinder their being placed in the pastoral office.. The duties of these being arranged under the guidance of the elders, every one can serve in his own order, as it is written – "Having then gifts differing according to the grace given unto us, whether prophecy, let us prophesy according to the proportion of faith; or ministry, let us wait on our ministering; or he that teacheth on teaching, or he that exhorteth on exhortation, . . . he that ruleth with diligence." Rom. xii. 6-8. "And God hath set some in the church, . . . teachers, helps, governments." 1 Cor. xii. 28.

The deacons shall look after the temporal affairs of the church and the poor. "They must likewise be grave, not double-tongued, not given to much wine, not greedy of filthy lucre:[2] holding the mystery of the faith in a pure conscience, . . . husbands of one wife, ruling their children and their own houses well. And let these also [as well as the pastors before being put into office] first be proved; then let them use the office . . . being found blameless." 1 Tim. iii. 8-12; Acts vi. 1-6.

7. These officers, both pastors and deacons, having shown by their general deportment or transactions in business, before being called into office, that they were not "greedy of filthy lucre," nor covetous in their dealings,[3] must continue in the same spirit; and the pastors must make it manifest that they have taken "the oversight of the flock, not by constraint, but willingly; not for filthy lucre," – so as to make their position in the church subservient to worldly ends, – "but of a ready mind; neither as being lords over God's heritage, but being ensamples to the flock," – 1 Peter v. 1-3; and they are therefore required to maintain themselves and their families, according to the instructions given by Paul to bishops, in Acts xx. 17, 28, 33-35, and in Phil. i. 1, read with verses 17-19 of chap iii., and verse 9 of chap. iv.,[4] unless through affliction or old age they are unable to do so. In such circumstances of distress, "food and raiment" must be communicated to them – not as if they were paupers, but as fathers receiving that support which is their right from their children, when they require aid, agreeably to the following scripture, – " Let the elders that rule well be counted worthy of double honour" (1 Tim. v. 17), "honour" here signifying relief, and relief implying that the person that requires it is in need. Compare 1 Tim. v. 3 with v. 16. See also Gal. vi. 6, which compare with Heb. xiii. 16, and Phil. iv. 15-18.

8. Pastors having been thus duly appointed, should have the authority given them by Christ, through the choice made of them by the brethren, upheld and respected; their instructions listened to with seriousness and attention; and a cheerful obedience manifested to all they require according to the Scriptures. "And we beseech you, brethren, to know them who labour among you, and are over you in the Lord, and admonish you; and to esteem them very highly in love for their work's sake." "Obey them that have the rule over you (or guide you), and submit yourselves; for they watch for your souls as they that must give an account, that they may do it with joy, and not with grief." 1 Thess. v. 12, 13; Heb. xiii. 17.

9. Although the churches are organised and have able pastors placed over them, those not in office are still to remember that they have duties devolving upon them, both to the church and the world; and they should have their minds suitably affected

with .the consideration that, upon their faithfulness and improvement, under the blessing of God, a succession of Scriptural pastors depends. They must seek that "their love may abound more and more in knowledge and in all judgment," and as they acquire wisdom, lay themselves out for usefulness, in an orderly, humble, and faithful way. Having heard to the saving of their own souls, they are to say to those who are without – "Come." Being united to the body of Christ, they are to warn, exhort, and comfort one another. Once a week at least, in addition to the public services of God's house, let each church, therefore, meet expressly for worship and mutual instruction, either as a whole or in class or fellowship meetings, that all the brethren who can speak to edification, as well as the ministers, may one by one thus engage in their Master's work. Compare Heb. xiii. 17, with chap. v. 12; Rom. xii. 5-8, with. chap. xv. 14; Phil. i. 9; 1 Cor. xii. 31: xiv. 12, 40; 1 Tim. iii. 1,13; 1 Pet. v. 1-5; Rev. xxi. 17; Matt. v. 19; 1 Thess. iv. 18: v. 11, 14; Heb. iii. 13: x. 25; 1 Pet. iv. 10, 11.

10. Besides the members of each church endeavouring to further the cause in their own neighbourhood, and the gifted brethren being sent, when judged proper, or going voluntarily, if approved of, to promote the work at a distance, pious, faithful, wise, zealous, right-principled, well-tried men shall be appointed as Evangelists, to go from place to place preaching the gospel, and spreading the truth as it is in Jesus; to raise new churches and set them in order, and to visit, as they shall be able, the churches generally, especially those that are weak, – that they may guide and instruct all, both office-bearers and members, in their respective duties. And while thus engaged – having their time occupied like the apostles and original evangelists – they shall have liberty to "live of the gospel." Matt. v. 13-16, 19; Acts xi. 19-26: xviii. 27, 28: xiii. 1-5: xvi. 1-3; 2 Tim. iv. 2-5, 9-11; Tit. i. 5: iii. 12; 1 Cor. ix. 1-14, compared with Matt. x. 1-14, and Luke x. 1-8; Tit. iii. 13; 1 and 2 Tim. and Tit.[5]

11. All the members (including those in office) shall contribute conscientiously as the Lord hath prospered them, for the benefit of the cause in general, and for the help of the poor. Matt. xxvi. 6-13; Luke vii. 4-6: viii. 1-3; Tit. iii. 13; 3 John 5, 8; 1 Cor. xvi. 2; 2 Cor. viii., ix.; Acts xx. 28, 33-35.

12. Whilst, as churches, adhering to the principle, and adopting the practice of infant baptism, nevertheless, forbearance shall be exercised towards any member embracing other views of baptism: but it is expressly stipulated that such individual shall not be at liberty to disturb the churches by introducing his own sentiments relative to this ordinance. Acts ii. 38, 39: viii. 37, 38: xvi. 15, 33; 1 Cor. i. 14-17: ix. 19-23.

13. That while acknowledging the solemn obligation of every Christian to partake of the Lord's Supper, and the duty of every church, by its deacons, to provide for its due solemnization; yet the mode and frequency of administration shall be matters of forbearance – each church using its own discretion relative thereto. Matt. xxvi. 26-28; Luke xxii. 19, 20; Acts vi. 1-6; 1 Car. xi. 23-34.

14. Forbearance likewise shall be exercised about the order of discipline and matters of church business in the respective churches of the Union – whether carried on in a church capacity, or by means of those in office, or by a mixture of both, – the churches being free, in faithfulness and honesty, to follow their own convictions relative thereto. Gal. ii. 11-14; 1 Cor. v. 3, 4, 13; Gal. vi. 4, 5; 2 Tim. 11.2; Acts xx. 28-31: xv.; Heb. xiii. 17.

15. There shall be a meeting of Delegates from all the churches throughout the country, or within such a distance as its superintendence can reach, once a year, or whatever

time shall be agreed upon. Churches properly organised, and numbering less than one hundred members, are required to send one delegate each; churches numbering one hundred members and upwards may send two delegates each; and where there are, in any district, a number of meetings not organised as churches, they may unite together in sending a delegate, or have themselves represented by the delegate from a neighbouring church, whose ministers occasionally labour among them in word and doctrine. Acts xv.; Ephes. vi. 21, 22.

The representatives having assembled, shall choose from amongst themselves a President, who shall see that everything be conducted with decency and order; also a Secretary, to record proceedings. These shall hold their respective offices not only during the sittings of the assembly, but till their places are filled at the succeeding Annual Meeting; and of this meeting they, along with the Editor of the Union, and the representative of any special committee appointed by an Annual Meeting, shall, *ex-officio*, be members and qualified for re-election. Rom. xii. 8; 1 Cor. xii. 28: xiv. 40.

Besides engaging in a number of religious services for the benefit of the Church and also of "them that are without," this meeting shall receive reports from all the churches; investigate whether the doctrines most surely believed among us, and godly discipline are maintained; examine, appoint, and send out evangelists; and consider cases of appeal which the churches or district meetings may think proper to send for final decision. And all matters brought before this meeting shall be decided by a majority. Ephes. vi. 21, 22; Acts xxi. 17-26; 1 John iv. 1; Acts xvi. 1-3: xv.: xvi. 4.

16. Although persons, whose belief and practice are of such a nature as to entitle them to be judged as Christians, but who cannot fully assent to everything in the foregoing Doctrines and Constitution, may enjoy fellowship with any of the churches, it is hereby particularly stipulated that they shall not be at liberty to disturb the brethren by introducing their own views; and it is also stipulated that if any among us consider they have received some knowledge of doctrine or church order which we do not recognise, and they think it necessary that they should make known what has thus attracted their attention, they shall have the liberty of doing so, either personally or by letter to the Annual Meeting, which shall decide whether or not such an opinion should be laid before the churches for consideration. But it us fully understood that no one shall be allowed to abuse this liberty, by referring to any doctrine subversive of, or contrary to, the doctrines already agreed upon; or by calling attention to any church order that would infringe upon the prerogative of every church regulating its own internal affairs, agreeably to No.14 hereof. Rom. xiv. 1, 13, 19 ; Gal. ii. 1-9; Acts .xv. 2; 2 Tim. i. 1-3: iii.1-7; Titus i. 9-11.

Finally, it is required, whenever the brethren assemble, whether in smaller or greater numbers, about church affairs of any description, that they commence and conclude with Divine Worship. Philippians iv. 6-8.

Notes to Appendix Three

1. "Not one who earns money by base methods." So is this part rendered In J. Macknight's Translation; and he paraphrases and comments upon it thus :– A bishop must not be "one who gains money by sinful, or even by dishonourable occupations. As many of the brethren in the first age maintained themselves by their own labour, it might happen

that the occupations which they followed in their heathen state, and which they continued to follow after they became Christians, were not very reputable. Wherefore, to discourage trades of that sort, and especially to prevent the ministers of religion from gaining money by sinful and even by low methods, the apostle ordered that no one should be elected a bishop who was engaged in such occupations."

2. "Not persons who earn money by' base methods."– Macknight's Translation.

3. Macknight on 1 Tim. iii. 8, last word.

4. See also Acts xx. 28-31; Rom. xvi. 17, 18; 2 Thess.. ii. 6—15; Titus i. 10, 11.

5. *To put the churches in remembrance and for the information of others, the following is extracted from the Address in the Minutes of 1843: " It will be seen that, to give an identity to your Annual Meeting, we have judged it needful to add what is expressive of your peculiar principle of requiring those who minister the Gospel to you to do so freely, as they themselves have received freely of the Lord (that is, to designate ourselves the United Free Gospel Churches). This, you will observe, does not interfere with the names you go under in your local positions. It is a general phrase applicable to all the churches, whatever designations they bear. And it should also be particularly noticed, that this phrase must not be construed to mean more than the infinitely wise Jesus wished his people to understand when he said to his disciples, "Freely ye have received, freely give." It should never lead us to think that it authorises us to withhold help from a faithful pastor, who, by reason of old age or affliction, requires to be assisted; nor should we imagine that it relieves us from maintaining men of God who may be called to go throughout the country, or, it may be, Into all the world, to preach the unsearchable riches of Christ. Such have a right, if they choose, "to live of the Gospel." And we consider that, should brethren be evidently raised up by the Head of the Church for the work of Evangelists or Missionaries, they should not be limited to time – being sent out for a short period, and then necessitated to give up their work and return to their employment. In certain instances this, indeed, may be right, and some of our ministers may be qualified for such a work to accomplish a certain purpose, and may be incapable of doing more; but something else is required likewise: to make us New Testament churches, we should "pray the Lord of the harvest that he would send forth labourers into his harvest;" and when our prayers are answered, and labourers are sent forth, we should no more limit them now than the primitive church limited such men when "their sound went unto all the earth, and their words unto the ends of the world;" and we should consider ourselves as much bound to support men of this description among us, as Christians who attended to the will of God of old considered it their duty to support such in their day.*

There may, it is true, be a difficulty to understand who they are whom the Lord sends – and a thousand times rather have none than have those whom he does not send; but surely in this, as well as in everything else concerning spiritual matters, the wisdom coming from above is profitable to direct. Let us only attend to what is required of us, and pray for such workmen – holy, wise, prudent. loving, zealous, right principled men being sent forth – men who properly understand the New Testament system respecting the ministry, and who will be able, scripturally, to maintain it, but, at the same time, will, in meekness, make all proper allowances for the views of others – let us pray for this, and let us be willing and determined to countenance and encourage such men, and such men only, – and we need not fear but that, like the Ephesian church, we shall have discernment imparted to discover those who are liars and not sent of God. Rev. ii. 2.

Appendix 4

TEMPERANCE POLICY

On the establishment of the Connexion's Temperance Committee in 1900, a letter was sent to each District or Circuit Secretary, asking them to send the following list of points to all churches.

WE, the District Committee of the . . . . Circuit, respectfully recommend to your Church the great importance of –

1. Asking every Candidate for Church Membership, "Are you a total abstainer from all intoxicating liquors,"
2. Supporting a vigorous Band of Hope in connection with every Sunday School.
3. Arranging to devote the pulpit, at least one day every year, to Band of Hope and Christian Endeavour Work, making a Young People's Sunday.
4. Promoting Temperance Work among Adults, and devoting the pulpit at least one day every year to this purpose, and to the urgent need of legislation In the direction of the total prohibition of the liquor traffic.
5. Giving all possible support to the closing of public-houses on the Lord's Day.
6. Opposing the granting of new licenses, whether to public-houses, shops, or clubs.
7. Supporting legislative and all other efforts for reducing the number of public-houses, or restricting the hours for the sale of drink.

Appendix 5
METHODIST UNION
An Independent Methodist Response

**(produced for the Independent Methodist Connexional Committee
by William Brimelow and Arthur Watson)
Conference in London, November 13th, 1903.**

Present: Representatives of Methodist New Connexion, United Methodist Free Church, Bible Christians, Wesleyan Reform Union, and Independent Methodist Churches.

A Secretary was appointed for each Denomination. Mr. Brimelow was chosen for our body.

The Primitive Methodists were not represented, nor the Wesleyans. The Wesleyans have appointed a Committee to 'inquire' into Methodist Union apparently meaning the union of other bodies with themselves. The Primitive Methodists sympathise with Methodist Union but are not prepared to come into conference on the subject at present.

It was soon apparent that our representatives, together with the Wesleyan Reform Union representatives, occupied a position in the meeting differing considerably from the representatives of other bodies.

In the discussions repeated references were made to the 'three denominations.' There was no offence meant by this, and when pointed out as ignoring the Wesleyan Reformers and ourselves, it was apologised for.

But it was, in fact, simply language expressive of the actual situation.

The three bodies – Methodist New Connexion, United Methodist Free Church and Bible Christians – have been in negotiations for some time, and have held several meetings. As a result of correspondence and discussion the leaders have arrived at a basis of union for recommendation to their respective Conferences.

They have agreed upon their foundation, and are now gathering all materials necessary for the superstructure.

It is at this stage in the progress of the movement that we are invited to join. We are not asked to assist in finding a basis of union – that is already agreed upon.

What ourselves and the Wesleyan Reformers are invited to do is to come into the movement for union on the basis already adopted by the other three denominations.

We shall act wisely not to complain of this or make any grievance of it. Rather let us consider it is a friendly and graceful act that we are invited. Certainly nothing could exceed the cordiality of our welcome nor the courtesy with which we were listened to.

In reply to pointed inquiries as to our attitude on the question, we briefly explained that at our Annual Meetings warm sympathy had been expressed with the object in view and resolutions passed favourable to Methodist Union. But no basis of union had been considered either by our Executive or Assembly. The attitude of our representatives at that Conference would be to listen, and endeavour to ascertain if we could find ground on which to enter the proposed Union.

In reply to a remark that perhaps some of our Churches would be willing to join the proposed union if all did not, we ventured upon the assertion that we should be quite unanimous – one way or the other.

But the real point on which our attention should be directed is the basis of union agreed upon, and the object before us must be to consider whether we as an Executive Committee can recommend this basis of union, and whether it is likely our Churches will be willing to accept it.

Without enumerating all the seven conclusions already arrived at by the leaders of the three Denominations, the really fundamental conditions of this basis of Union agreed to may be stated as follows:

1. The Annual Conference of the bodies when united would consist of an equal number of Ministers and Laymen.
2. The Conference would have power to requisition funds from all Circuits for maintaining the Ministry and for all other Connexional Funds.
3. The Superintendent Minister would of right preside at Circuit, Church, Committee and Teachers' Meetings.

Now, are these such conditions as we can recommend and expect our Churches to accept?

We confess to a sense of some disappointment. We had hoped the question of Methodist Union might have been presented to us less unfavourably. The venerable William Arthur, speaking at Washington, 1901, said if Methodist Union was to come and be enduring it must involve no curtailment of liberty.

As regards the three denominations named above, their differences are so small that in uniting there is no sensible curtailment of liberty in any case.

But will this be so with us?

Will our Circuits accept the responsibility of providing funds for a maintained ministry, and will the Churches put themselves under fixed obligations to respond to the demands of the Circuits for these funds and for Ministers' Annuity and Ministers' Children Funds, also for College Funds, &c.

In stating the question in this way there is no wish whatever to throw cold water upon the movement. We merely desire to clearly realise the meaning of these proposals, and to have a plain statement before us on which to base an intelligent judgment. In what is here stated nothing is prejudiced.

If we are reasonably assured that our Churches will accept the three fundamental conditions enumerated above, then our representatives should have instructions to that effect for the next meeting of the Conference, which takes place on December 3rd.

But if our Churches are not likely to accept these bases of union, then the Connexional Committee should advise the representatives appointed by the Annual Meeting as to their future course of action. The issues may be stated thus:

1. Should our representatives withdraw from the Conference? And if so, on what grounds?
2. If not, then what directions should be given to them as to the purpose for which they must attend future meetings?

Virtually it comes to this: Do we consider our work as a separate Denomination finished? Can we for the future more effectually serve the Kingdom of God by uniting with other Methodist bodies? And is this the Divine opportunity for such Union?

We may be asked – What do *you* propose? Rather let us unite to discover what God proposes? Too often we look to *man* for a lead. In this grave issue – which we may be deciding for a generation – let all look to God for the lead.

To arrive at a sound and wise conclusion every one of us must lay aside our prejudices, and one and all earnestly, unitedly, and devoutly seek with open mind and heart the Divine impression, and be prepared to follow whithersoever it may lead.

We made one statement at the Conference in London which every member of the Connexional Committee will endorse, viz., that whether we can as a denomination join in the proposed union or not, our fervent prayers will ascend to God for the success of the movement for Methodist Union. Even if we cannot ourselves participate in the joy and blessing of it, we shall pray that as many Methodist Churches as possible may be one.

Appendix 6

STATEMENT
OF
FAITH AND PRACTICE[1]
(approved by the Annual Meeting, 1927)

PART ONE.

I.

There is One Living and True God, the Creator of the world and of man, Who is revealed to us as Father, Son, and Holy Spirit; Him alone we worship and adore.

II.

We believe that God so loved the world as to give His Son to be the Revealer of the Father, and the Redeemer of Mankind; that the Son of God, for us men and for our salvation, became man in Jesus Christ, Who, having lived on earth the perfect human life, died for our sins, rose again from the dead, and now is exalted Lord over all; and that the Holy Spirit, Who witnesses to us of Christ, makes the salvation which is in Him to be effective in our hearts and lives.

III.

We acknowledge that all men are sinful, and unable to deliver themselves from either the guilt or power of their sin; but we have received and rejoice in the Gospel of the grace of the Holy God, wherein all who truly turn from sin are freely forgiven through faith in our Lord Jesus Christ, and are called and enabled, through the Spirit dwelling and working within them, to live in fellowship with God and for His service; and in this new life, which is to be nurtured by the right use of the means of grace, we are to grow, daily dying unto sin and living more unto Him Who in His mercy has redeemed us.

IV.

We believe that the Catholic or Universal Church is the whole company of the redeemed in heaven and on earth, and we recognise as belonging to this holy fellowship all who are united to God through faith in Christ.

The Church on earth – which is One through the [Apostolic] Gospel and through the living union of all its true members with its one Head, even Christ, and which is Holy through the indwelling Holy Spirit Who sanctifies the Body and its members – is ordained to be the visible Body of Christ, to worship God through Him, to promote the fellowship of His people and the ends of His Kingdom, and to go into all the world and proclaim His Gospel for the salvation of men and the brotherhood of all mankind. Of this visible Church, and every branch thereof, the only Head is the Lord Jesus Christ; and in its faith, order, discipline and duty, it must be free to obey Him alone as it interprets His holy will.

V.

We receive, as [~~given by the Lord to His Church on earth, the Holy Scriptures, the Sacraments of the Gospel, and the Christian Ministry~~] *of Divine Authority*

(a) The Scriptures, delivered through men as moved by the Holy [~~Ghost~~] *Spirit, which* record and interpret the revelation of redemption, and contain the sure Word of God concerning our salvation and all things necessary thereto. Of this we are convinced by the witness of the Holy Spirit in the hearts of men [~~to and with the Word; and this Spirit, thus speaking from the Scriptures to believers and to the Church, is the supreme Authority by which all opinions in religion are finally to be judged~~] *speaking through the Scriptures to believers and to the Church.*

(b) The [~~Sacraments~~] *ordinances of* – Baptism and the Lord's Supper – [~~are instituted by Christ~~]. *We believe that* Christ [~~Who is~~] Himself *is* certainly and really present [~~in His own ordinances~~] *therein* (though not bodily in the elements thereof), [~~and are signs and seals of His Gospel not to be separated therefrom. They confirm the promises and gifts of salvation~~] and *that* when rightly used by believers with faith and prayer, they are, through the operation of the Holy Spirit, true means of grace.

(c) The Ministry as an office within the Church – not a sacerdotal order – instituted for the preaching of the Word, [~~the ministration of the Sacraments~~] and the care of souls. It is a vocation from God, upon which, therefore, no one is qualified to enter save through the call of the Holy Spirit in the heart; and this inward call is to be authenticated by the call of the Church, which is to be [~~followed by ordination~~] *confirmed by appointment* to the work of the Ministry in the name of the Church. [~~While thus maintaining the Ministry as an office, we do not limit the ministries of the New Testament to those who are ordained, but~~] *We also* affirm the *Scriptural teaching of the* priesthood of all believers and the obligation resting upon them to fulfil their vocation according to the gift bestowed upon them by the Holy Spirit.

VI.

We affirm the sovereign authority of our Lord Jesus Christ over every department of human life, and we hold that individuals and peoples are responsible to Him in their several spheres and are bound to render Him obedience and to seek always the furtherance of His Kingdom on earth, not, however, in any way constraining belief, imposing religious disabilities, or denying the rights of conscience.

VII.

In the assurance, given us in the Gospel, of the love of God our Father to each of us and to all men, and in the faith that Jesus Christ, Who died, overcame death and has passed into the heavens, the first fruits of them that sleep, we are made confident of the hope of Immortality, and trust to God our souls and the souls of the departed. We believe that the whole world must stand before the final Judgment of the Lord Jesus Christ, *and accept the solemn warning of Scripture: "He that believeth shall be saved, but he that believeth not shall be condemned."* And, with glad and solemn hearts, we look for the consummation and bliss of the life everlasting, wherein the people of God, freed for ever from sorrow and from sin, shall serve Him and see His face in the perfected communion of all saints in the Church triumphant.

These things, as all else in our Christian faith, we hold in reverent submission to the guidance and teaching of the *Scriptures and of the* Holy Spirit, Who is truth, *and leads into all truth*, and we shall ever seek of Him enlightenment and grace both to unlearn our errors and also more fully to learn the mind and will of God Whom to know is life eternal and to serve is perfect freedom.

And, being thus called of God unto the purpose of His redeeming love wherein He is delivering the world from sin and misery, and is reconciling all things to Himself in Christ Jesus, and being animated with faith in the final triumph of our Lord, we set before us as our end and aim to carry the Gospel to every creature and to serve and stablish, in our land and throughout the earth, His reign of righteousness, joy and peace.

Grace be with all those that love our Lord Jesus Christ in sincerity. and to God be the glory in the Church by Christ Jesus, throughout all ages, world without end. Amen.

PART TWO.

An abbreviated Statement of the Distinctive Features of the Principles and Polity of the Independent Methodist Churches.

I.   Doctrinal – as expressed in our Statement of Faith and Practice.
II.   Worship and Services – those usual among Methodist Societies.
III.   Every Church is self-governed, managing its own financial and other internal affairs.
IV.   There is equality of Christian fellowship, all members, men and women, sharing equally in the government of the Church, and all equally eligible for any office.
V.   Groups of Churches suitably situated are associated in Circuits or Districts for ministerial and other mutual advantages. All such united meetings are purely deliberative in character, and moral obligation only attaches to any decisions made.
VI.   A General Meeting of Representatives of the Churches and the Circuits, together with the Officers of the Connexion, is held annually in June.
VII.   The Ministry of the Churches is open and free, in harmony with the Scriptural teaching of the Priesthood of all Believers, and is purely voluntary and unpaid.
VIII. All Christians are called of God actively to labour in the work of His Kingdom, as God has gifted them, and their responsibility cannot be discharged by proxy.
IX   We do not recognise clerical titles or designations or distinctive ministerial dress, as these tend to accentuate distinctions between one servant of God and another.
X.   We have an Evangelistic agency, brethren being appointed to go from place to place, to conduct special missions, to visit weak and to plant new Churches; and whilst so engaged they may be maintained, Evangelists having "liberty to live of the Gospel." We are also represented in the Foreign Mission Field by Medical and other Missionaries.
XI.   A course of studies extending over several years is provided, which students for the preaching ministry are desired to undertake, under the guidance of suitable tutors. It is the common practice, when such candidates for the ministry are considered by any Church to be suitably prepared, and of a right spirit, to receive and recognise them as Ministers of the Church at a service held for this purpose.
XII.   We hold that in Doctrine, Church Government, and Ministry our belief and practice are in harmony with Scriptural teaching and the practice of the Church of the New Testament.

Note to Appendix Six

1. The Independent Methodists adapted the *Statement of Faith and Practice* of the Federal Council of the Evangelical Free Churches (1917) and used it to replace their earlier *Testimony and Principles of Union* (1855). Words of the *Statement* which they removed are shown thus – [Apostolic] and words which they added are shown in italics. Part Two is entirely of Independent Methodist origin.

Appendix 7

Statement of Faith
(Approved by the Annual Meeting 1984)

THE TRINITY
We believe in One Living and True God, Creator of all, eternal in three persons as Father, Son and Holy Spirit; Him alone we worship and adore.

GOD THE FATHER
We believe that God the Father Almighty, in holy love, gave His Son for the salvation of mankind.

GOD THE SON
We believe that the Lord Jesus Christ is God the Son. For our sake He became man, was truly human and truly divine, and lived a sinless human life.

We believe that He reveals the Father, that He died to atone for our sins, rose from the dead, ascended to heaven and was exalted. He is our Advocate, Mediator and Lord.

We believe that he will return personally in power and glory.

GOD THE HOLY SPIRIT
We believe that God the Holy Spirit convinces of sin, righteousness and judgement. He causes those who repent to be born anew and dwells within them, witnessing to their salvation and developing the fruit of a Godly life. He endows believers with gifts for the up building of the Church. He glorifies Jesus.

MANKIND
We believe that all people are sinful and are unable to deliver themselves from the guilt, penalty and power of their sin.

SALVATION
We believe that salvation from the guilt, penalty and power of sin to eternal life is a free gift of God. Salvation is His purpose for all mankind and is only possible through personal faith in the atoning work of the Lord Jesus Christ.

We believe that all must stand before the final judgement of Christ and that those who have refused His salvation will be separated eternally from God.

THE BIBLE
We believe that the Scriptures of the Old and New Testaments are the inspired Word of God and are the supreme authority in all matters of faith and conduct.

THE CHURCH

We believe that the Church is the whole company of the redeemed in heaven and on earth and consists of all who are united to God through faith in Christ.

We believe that Jesus Christ is the head of the Church, which is His body. The purpose of the Church is to worship God, to promote the fellowship of his people, to preach the Gospel and to make disciples of all nations.

THE SACRAMENTS

We believe that the sacraments of baptism and the Lord's supper are to be practised in obedience to the command of the Lord Jesus Christ.

We believe that in the observance of the Lord's supper, Christ is certainly and really present, though not bodily in the elements.

When used by believers with faith and prayer, the sacraments are, through the operation of the Holy Spirit, outward and visible signs of inward and spiritual grace.

THE CHRISTIAN LIFE

We believe in the priesthood of all believers, affirming that each believer has direct access to God through the Lord Jesus Christ. The individual believer is required to render obedience to Christ in every area of life, seeking always, under His direction, the advancement of His Kingdom.

Appendix 8

Statement of Practice
(Approved by the Annual Meeting 1984.
Printed as amended in 2000)

CHURCHES
Each Church is self-governing. Subject to the Church's trust deed, the members meeting is the final authority in all matters affecting the Church.

CIRCUITS
Groups of Churches are associated in Circuits for mutual benefit. The meetings of the Circuits are deliberative in character and recommendations can only be effective by the co-operation of each Church. The organisation of each Circuit is outlined in its rules.

CONNEXION
All member Churches constitute the Connexion of Independent Methodist Churches. The organisation of the Connexion is outlined in its constitution.

MINISTRIES
[a] Every believer is called to service in the Kingdom of God, there being no distinction between one believer and another beyond that of function. It is recognised that differing talents, spiritual gifts and ministries are bestowed on believers for the benefit of the church as a whole. Each church should, therefore, recognise and cultivate the talents, gifts and ministries of its members so that it may function as a ministering fellowship.

[b] To assist in church leadership, pastoral responsibility and the ministry of the Word and sacraments, the Connexion commissions to its ministry those who have been called to ministerial appointment in one or more of the Connexion's churches and who have met the qualifications laid down in the current statement on Ministry.

[c] To assist in the wider ministry of the Word, the Connexion commissions and accredits preachers who have been nominated by their church and Circuit and who have met the appropriate qualifications laid down in the current Statement on Ministry.

[d] The Connexion may, from time to time, provide training and accredit people to other specified ministries in the Connexion, such as Bible teachers, evangelists, missioners, missionaries and youth workers.

The Connexion makes no provision for the financial support of any personnel other than its central staff, evangelists and overseas missionaries.

MISSION
The Connexion is concerned with the spread of the Gospel at home and overseas. Where required, Churches and Missions are assisted and new Churches or Missions may be formed, using Connexional resources of finance and personnel

Appendix 9

Missionaries sent out during 1826

Preacher	Home Church	Areas covered	Dates
Joshua Jepson	Sheffield	Newcastle	early 1826
Hugh Kelly	North Shields	Driffield and York	early 1826
William Parker	Macclesfield	Driffield, Bridlington Pocklington, York, Leeds	early 1826 (17 days)
Joseph Woolstenholme	Bury	Central Scotland, based Glasgow	Feb-April, 1826
Joseph Woolstenholme	Bury	places en route to Scotland; Central Scotland	June-Oct, 1826
Joseph Woolstenholme	Bury	Dunfermline & Edinburgh places en route to Scotland; Edinburgh	Jan-Mar, 1827
John Eckersley	Lowton	Driffield	July 1826
Samuel Ashton with Thomas Jones	Macclesfield	Liverpool & St. Helens	July-Aug, 1826
	Macclesfield	Liverpool North Wales	Sept-Oct, 1826
William Yates	Stockton Heath	Bury, Rochdale, Oldham	June-Sep, 1826

Details of the missionaries and their journeys are found in *The Independent Methodist Magazine* for 1826 and 1827.

Appendix 10

Primitive Methodist Groups defecting to Free Gospelism
1830-1855

Group Name	Start	Locations/ preaching places
Indep Prim Meth	1832	Bingham (11 in 1839)
Prim Meth Revivalists	by 1833	Batley, Dewsbury (13 in 1833)
Gospel Pilgrims	1833	Leeds, Bradford (18 in 1834)
Gospel Pilgrims	by 1839	East Norfolk (18 in 1841)
Free Gospel Churches	1845	South Norfolk (10 in 1849)
Original Meth	1839	Selston & Ashbourne (21 in 1852)
Free Gospel Churches	1843	Oswestry & Ellesmere (8 in 1851)
Christian Brethren	1848	Bingley (1)
Free Gospel Churches	1851	Tiverton & Cox Bank (11 in 1852)
Free Gospel Church	by 1850	Preston, Ashmoor Street (1)
Non-Hireling Meth	1853	Barnsley (1)
Ranters	1850	Emley (1)
Christian Brethren	1851	Ossett (1)
Free Gospel Churches	1852	Wolverhampton (4 in 1852)
Free Gospel Churches	1851	Burnley (2 in 1852, others later)
Indep Meth Church	1851	Warrington (2)
Free Gospel Church	1853	Blackburn (1)

Abbreviations
Indep=Independent
Prim=Primitive
Meth=Methodist(s)

Appendix 11

Independent Methodist Day Schools

The following churches are known to have operated day schools:

Church School	founded	Outcome
Lowton Common[1]	1793	closed, c. 1863
Lowton Common resumed	1880	transferred to LEA, after 1912
King Street, Oldham	c1858	closed, 1888
Stockport	1864	not known
Pendleton, Salford	1868	not known
Folds Road, Bolton	1873	to School Board, 1882
Noble Street, Bolton	1874	to School Board, 1882
Cliviger, Burnley	1879	closed, 1895
Salem, Nelson	1881	to School Board, 1897
Horwich	1881	to LEA, 1905
Westhoughton[2]	1886	to LEA, 1915

Notes:

1. Lowton Common was Wesleyan Methodist until 1819
2. Westhoughton School operated jointly with other local free churches on I.M. premises

Appendix 12
Statistics 1871-2001

Year	Places of Worship	Members	Ministers	Sunday School scholars
1871	87	3,496	237	10,700
1881	109	4,589	261	14,399
1891	120	6,212	335	20,228
1901	153	8,377	372	26,194
1911	159	8,316	409	27,204
1921	159	8,398	374	24,852
1931	164	9,147	398	22,931
1941	160	8,044	379	13,514
1951	152	7,796	329	13,634
1961	152	7,486	294	10,306
1971	142	6,051	208	6,037
1981	121	4,399	150	3,601
1991	104	3,479	132	2,012
2001	94	2,354	102	898

Notes:

1. No statistics were recorded before 1865.
2. Before 1941, the term 'ministers' meant ministers or preachers recognised by their churches and circuits. After this date, the term meant those who were accredited by the Connexion.

BIBLIOGRAPHY

Primary Manuscript works and Unpublished Typescripts

(a) Independent Methodist Archives, Resource Centre, Pemberton, Wigan

Anon. History of Dukinfield Excelsior Mission.

Anon. History of the Independent Methodist Church, Gateshead Fell, c. 1824.

Anon. History of the Independent Methodist Church, Lymm.

Bark, A. The Foundation and Progress of Independent Methodism in the Village of Roe Green and its Daughter Church at Sindsley/Moorside in the 19th. Century. Unpublished essay, n.d.

Barnes, R. The History of Horden Independent Methodist Church. Unpublished essay, 1999.

Correspondence:

G.S. Barnes, Board of Trade, to Messrs. Taylor and Sons, Solicitors, 7 February, 1907.

W. Brimelow to G. Hunter, 5 October 1903.

W. Brimelow to E. Barker, 7 March 1904.

G. W. Collin to E. Barker, 30 September 1908.

W. Hamilton to A. Hamilton, 14 April 1842.

J.W. Johnson to A. Mounfield, 9 July 1908.

J.W. Johnson to E. Barker, 22 September 1908.

M. Kennedy to Evangelistic Committee, 19 June 1894.

M. Kennedy to W. Brimelow, 25 September 1894.

G. Packer to E. Barker, 9 May 1903.

G. Packer to E. Barker, 16 May 1904.

W.J. Skillen to A. Dalby, 18 May 1973.

Crumblehulme, C. Unpublished notes on the Crumblehulme family of Bolton.

Deeds of Parsonage Street Chapel, Macclesfield, 1808 (copy).

Denovan, D. and M. Smith, Unpublished notes on the Denovan Family of Glasgow.

Harrison, D. Unpublished notes on the Independent Primitive Methodists of Nottinghamshire.

Journal of the Independent Methodist Annual Meetings 1827-1882.

Minute Book, Charlestown Sunday School, Ashton-under-Lyne 1824-1857.

Minute Book, Independent Methodist Church, Glasgow, 1820-1840, together with statements of doctrine and other materials.

Minute Book, Warrington Independent Methodist Circuit, 1866-1923.

Minutes of Independent Methodist Connexional Committee 1860-1927.

Minutes of Independent Methodist Evangelistic Committee 1889-1924.

Minutes of the Independent Methodist Annual Meeting 1808-1927.

Minutes of the Minority Independent Methodist Churches 1854-60.

Naylor, R. Unpublished notes on the Beresford Family of Macclesfield.

Price, W. Notes on meeting between Connexional Representatives and the President of the Board of Trade, 1907.

Register of Baptisms, Folds Road Independent Methodist Church, Bolton, 1920-1970.

Roll Book of the Warrington Temperance Society, 1830-70.

Rules and Doctrines of the Christian Brethren Churches of the Holme Lane District, 1858.

Vickers, J. List of ministers eligible for military service, 1916.

(b) Other Collections and Sources

Bolton Borough Archives

The Correspondence of Thomas Bramwell, Shoemaker and Preacher of Bolton and Liverpool: Letter of William Parker to Thomas Bramwell, 14 August, 1840. (ZZ/7/4).

Borthwick Institute, York

Meeting House Licences, Primitive Methodist Revivalists, Yorkshire (DMH 1839/5, DMH 1839/6, DMH 1839/7, DMH 1839/8).

Chester Record Office

Burland Primitive Methodist Circuit Quarter Day Meeting Minutes, 1845-52 (EMC 2/11/2).

Burland Primitive Methodist Circuit Report 1852. (EMC 2/13/5).

Meeting House Licences, Independent Methodist and Free Gospel Churches, Cheshire(EDA 13/2/254 and EDA 13/2/148-212).

Cliviger Independent Methodist Church, Burnley

Walkmill School, Headteacher's Log Book, 1878-1895.

Friars Green Independent Methodist Church, Warrington

Register of Baptisms, 1801-2004.

Kirklees Borough Archives, Huddersfield

Barnsley Primitive Methodist Circuit Annual Report 1853 (GB NM/DD/CW 204).

Batley Providence Street Christian Brethren Chapel, Records 1845-1932 (GB NCB/B 204).

Liverpool City Archives

Journal of the Independent Methodist Church in Liverpool (287 IND 1/1/1)

Methodist Archives, John Rylands University Library of Manchester Correspondence:

Jabez Bunting to Richard Reece, 11 June, 18[03].

William Jenkins to Jabez Bunting, 29 January, 1806 (MAM PLP 61.24.4.).
MS Journals of Hugh Bourne (DDHB 3, folios 2-7).

Oldham Local Studies and Archives

Account Book of George Street Independent Methodist Church, Oldham, 1825-1863.
(C-M55).

The National Archives: Public Record Office, Kew

Ecclesiastical Census Returns, 1851 (HO129).

Sheffield City Archives

Baptismal Register, Scotland Street Methodist New Connexion Church and Bow Street
Independent Methodist Church, 1798-1835 (NR 299).
Minutes of the Wesleyan Protestant Methodist Society of Sheffield 1829-1839 (NR 1).

Primary Printed Works

(a) Independent Methodist Archives, Resource Centre, Pemberton, Wigan

A Statement of Facts and Observations relative to the late separation from the Methodist
Society in Manchester: affectionately addressed to members of that *body by their
preachers and leaders*. Manchester: S. Russell, 1806.
Christian Lay Churches, Preachers' Plan, Sunderland, February-May 1877.
Brimelow, W. *A Free Church and a Free Ministry*. London: Elliott Stock, 1883.
Brimelow, W. and A. Watson, *Notes on Methodist Union*. 25 November 1903.
Denovan, A. *An Appeal to the Christian World*. Glasgow: Bell and Bain, 1866.
Denovan, A. *Proposed Testimony and Bond of Union*. Glasgow, 1852.
Doctrines and Rules of the Independent Methodist Church Established July 1818 in
Liverpool. *Incorporation Proposals Explained*. Wigan, 1904.
Kelly, H. *A Rude Sketch or Good Days in Sarre Louis*. Newcastle, 1824.
Kelly, H. *The Stone cut out of the Mountain*. North Shields, 1821.
Moody, J.F. *Lecture delivered by the Rev. J.F. Moody on Free Gospelism at the* Wesleyan
Chapel, Prescot, on Tuesday evening, May 23, 1852.
Ministers' Assistance Fund belonging to the United Free Gospel Churches, 1874.
The Association for the Promotion of useful knowledge in connection with *Temperance*
(list of rules). Warrington, 1836.
Poster advertising the opening of the Independent Methodist Chapel, Gateshead Fell, 1823.
Poster, Independent Methodist Sunday School, Numbers Garth, Sunderland, 1822.
Proposed Independent Methodist Association (Incorporated), Notice of Objection,
Nov. 17, 1906.
Regulations for the Introduction and Acceptance of Candidates for the Ministry and
Recognition of Ministers. Wigan: Independent Methodist Churches, Ministers'
Committee, 1941.
Rules of the Bolton District of Independent Methodist Churches, 1879.
Rules of the Independent Methodist Churches in Durham and Northumberland, 1826.
Rules of the [name] *Independent Methodist Church,* Warrington, 1917.
Rules of the [name] *Independent Methodist Church,* Wigan, 1927.
Sanderson, W. *A Free Gospel Ministry proved to be most in accordance with the New
Testament*. Liverpool: W. Sanderson, 1860.
Sanderson, W. *The Life and Labours of William Sanderson*. Wigan: Independent Methodist

Bookroom, 1899.
Sanderson, W. and T. Sturges, *Is a Located Hired Ministry in direct opposition to the letter and spirit of the Scriptures, particularly the new Testament? A Discussion between William Sanderson and the Rev. Thomas Sturges.* Liverpool, 1852.
Scrapbook, Salem Church, Nelson.
Scrapbook, Salem Church, Pendleton.
Statement of Faith. Wigan: Independent Methodist Churches, 1984.
Statement of Practice. Wigan: Independent Methodist Churches, 2000.
Statement on Ministry. Wigan: Independent Methodist Churches, 2000.
The Forward Movement. Wigan: Independent Methodist Churches, 1962.
United Methodist Committee on Concerted Action amongst the Methodist Churches of Great Britain, 1903.

Magazines

Independent Methodist Magazine (under various titles) 1823-29 and 1847 to date.
Independent Methodist (Minority Churches) *Magazine* 1859-60.
Independent Quarterly 1927-1937.
The Mission Band. No. 6 (Trimdon: 1963).
Wingates Messenger. 1892-1945.
Zion's Trumpet 1853-58.

(b) Other Sources

Methodist Archives, John Rylands Library, Manchester

Address of the Preachers to the Methodist Societies. Leeds, 812.
Methodist Conference Minutes, 1797, 1803, 1812.
Methodist New Connexion Minutes, 1801, 1814.
Primitive Methodist Conference Minutes 1820, 1854.
Rules of the Independent Wesleyan Society established in Manchester. Manchester, 1825.
Committee on Religious Privileges: *'To the Societies in the Connexion Established by the late John Wesley, A.M.',* 12 November 1819.

Oldham Local Studies and Archives

Collection of Anniversary hymnsheets, George Street, Oldham, with Annual Reports of The Sunday School.

Preston Library, Lancashire

Preston Temperance Gazette, 1834-37.

Sheffield City Library

Doctrines, Church Government and Discipline considered by the Independant [*sic*] *Methodists to be consitent* [*sic*] *with the Word of God* (Sheffield, 1822).

Wakefield Local Studies Library, West Yorkshire Cryer Collection:

Bradford and Leeds Gospel Pilgrims Preachers' Plan, 1834.
Birstall Primitive Methodist Revivalists Preachers' Plans, 1833 and 1834.

Warrington Library

Hymnsheets for Friars Green and Stockton Heath Charity Sermons, 1821, 1827.

Wesley Studies Centre, Oxford

Wesleyan Methodist Association Assembly Minutes, 1838.
Wesleyan Protestant Methodist Yearly Meeting Minutes, 1831.

Newspapers

Bolton Journal, 13 June 1913.
Burnley Advertiser, 15 May 1878; July 27 1878.
Burnley Express, 13 July 1878.
Caernarvon and Denbigh Herald, 24 March 1838.
Durham County Advertiser and Chronicle, 22 September, 1933.
Liverpool Mercury, 13 January 1899.
Liverpool Review, 14 January 1899.
'Kaleidoscope', (Literary Supplement to Liverpool Mercury), Vol. 10 (1830).
Nelson Chronicle, 26 March 1891.
Newcastle Courant, 16 October 1819.
North Bristol Daily Mail, 16 October 1876.
Oldham Daily Standard, 23 June 1915.
Sunderland Daily Echo, 3 March 1877.
Sunderland Echo and Shipping Gazette, 15 January, 1945.

Secondary Works

(a)   Independent Methodist Sources

Banner, H.H. *The Three Freds and After.* London: Unevangelised Fields Mission, n.d.
'Barnoldswick Independent Methodist Church: A Brief History', in *Delegate's Handbook to Independent Methodist Annual Meeting,* 1926.
Brimelow, W. *Centenary Memorials of the Independent Methodist Church, Roe Green, Worsley.* Bolton, 1908.
Burrows, W. *Recollections.* St. Helens, 1975.
Burrows, W.G. *Independent Methodist Church, Thatto Heath, St. Helens, Centenary 1892-1992.* St. Helens, 1992.
Centenary History of King Street Independent Methodist Church, Oldham 1854-1954. Oldham, 1954.
Centenary History of the Independent Methodist Church and School, Greenough Street, Wigan. Wigan, 1930.
Centenary Souvenir of the Establishment of Independent Methodism in Oldham, 1916. Oldham, 1916.
Cooper, E. *Salem Independent Methodist Church, Pendleton, History of the Church and School,* 1955.
Dalby, A. *History of Waterside Chapel, Colne 1821-1951.* Colne, 1951.
Dolan, J.A. *From Barn to Chapel.* Warrington, 1989.
Dolan, J.A. *Peter's People.* Wigan: Independent Methodist Churches, 1996.
Dolan, J.A. *Two Hundred Years of Faith.* Warrington, 2001.
Durant, W. *The Story of Friars Green Church.* Warrington, 1951.
Denovan, A. *Election According to Holy Scripture.* Glasgow: Bell and Bain, 1832.
Foreman, A. *Christian History: A Free Church View.* Wigan: Independent Methodist Bookroom, 1932.
Foreman, A. *The Faith of a Christian.* Nelson: Independent Methodist Bookroom, 1925.

Higham, C. *Holme United Reformed Church, 1835-1985. A Short History.* Bradford, 1895.

Holt, J.R. 'The Zions of Prescot', *Methodist Magazine,* August 1934.

Howell, E. *Whispers of Wingates.* Bolton, 1984.

Independent Methodist Church, Easington Lane, Jubilee 1881-1931. Durham, 1931.

Independent Methodist Church and Schools, Lowton, Empire Bazaar Book, 1912.

Independent Methodist Church, Platt Bridge, Jubilee Celebrations. Wigan, 1916.

Jackson, R.A. *Greenacres Gleanings.* Oldham, 1987.

Jubilee History, Mount Zion Independent Methodist Church, Bristol, 1885-1935.

Kelly, H. *An Impartial History of Independent Methodism in the Counties of Durham and Northumberland.* Newcastle, Edward Walker, 1824.

Lister, T. *Memoirs of Thomas Lister, written by himself.* Bingley, n.d.

Matthews, I. 'Plans of Unusual Interest', *Cirplan Magazine,* Lent 1996.

Milburn, G.E. *The Christian Lay Churches and their Origins.* Sunderland, 1977.

Methodist Free Church, Buckley Street, Warrington, Centenary Booklet, 1952.

Mill Lane Independent Methodist Church, Wavertree 1840-1940. Liverpool, 1940.

Mounfield, A. *A Village Centenary.* Warrington, 1906.

Mounfield, A. *Brick Street Sunday School 1823-1923.* Warrington, 1923.

Mounfield, A. *Pictures of the Early Church.* Nelson: Independent Methodist Bookroom, n.d.

Mounfield, A. *The Beginnings of Total Abstinence.* Warrington, 1902.

Mounfield, A. *A Short History of Independent Methodism.* Independent Methodist Bookroom, 1905.

Murray, J. *Independent Methodist History 1905-1955.* Wigan: Independent Methodist Bookroom, 1955.

Peacock, S. *The Memorials of Gamaliel Swindells, Late of Stockport.* Stockport: Samuel Dodge, 1833.

Robinson, J. *Salem Independent Methodist Church, Nelson, Centenary Booklet.* Nelson, 1952.

Rothwell, S. *Memorials of Folds Road Independent Methodist Chapel, Bolton.* 2 vols. Bolton: Independent Methodist Bookroom, 1887, 1897.

Scholes, C. *History of Mount Zion Independent Methodist Church, Walkmill, Cliviger 1880-1980.* Burnley, 1980.

Simpson, E. *Miners and Saints in Sutton.* St. Helens, 1999.

Souvenir, Independent Methodist Church, New Seaham, Jubilee Celebrations 1877-*1927.* Sunderland, 1927.

Terry, G. *The Joint Celebration of the 150th Anniversary of the founding of Nook* Independent Methodist Church, Cleckheaton and 250 Years of Methodist *Preaching in Cleckheaton.* Cleckheaton, 1995.

Thirty Years in India. An Appreciation of the work of Edith Astley Bevan 1928-1958. Wigan: Independent Methodist Bookroom, 1958.

Tyldesley, H. L. *The Duke's Other Village.* Radcliffe: Neil Richardson, n.d.

Urmston Independent Methodist Church Centenary 1834-1934, souvenir pamphlet.

Vickers, J. *Horwich Independent Methodist Church and School, A Jubilee History 1862-1912.* Bolton, 1912.

Vickers, J. *Independent Methodism: Its Polity and Voluntary Ministry* (Wigan: Independent Methodist Bookroom, 1915)

Vickers, J. *History of Independent Methodism.* Wigan: Independent Methodist Bookroom, 1920.

Walker, A. *A. Souvenir History of the Independent Methodist Church and Sunday School, Smith Street, Oldham, 1837-1937*. Oldham, 1937.

Woods, F.E. and G. Rodgers, *History of Women's Auxiliary 1916-1966*.

150th. Anniversary: Brief History of the Independent Methodist Church, Barton Road, Stretford. *Stretford, 1970.*

(b) Other Sources

Addison, W.G. *Religious Equality in Modern England*. London: SPCK, 1944.

Anderson, O. 'Gladstone's Abolition of Compulsory Church Rates', *Journal of Ecclesiastical History, 25*. 1974.

A Short History of the Rise and Progress of the United Methodist Free Church, Surrey Street, Sheffield. Sheffield, 1855.

Ashworth, J. *The Life of the Venerable Hugh Bourne*. London: Joseph Toulson, 1888.

Baines, E. *History, Directory and Gazeteer of the County Palatine of Lancaster.* Liverpool: William Wales & Co., 1825.

Baptism, Eucharist and Ministry. Geneva: World Council of Churches, 1982.

Barbour, H. and J.W. Frost, *The Quakers*. Westport, Connecticut: Greenwood Press, 1988.

Barclay, O. *Evangelicalism in Britain 1935-1995*. Leicester: IVP, 1997.

Barker, J.T. (Ed.) *The Life of Joseph Barker, written by himself*. London: Hodder & Stoughton, 1880.

Barrett, C.K. *The First Epistle to the Corinthians*. London: A & C Black, 1968.

Batty, M. *Stages in the Development and Control of Wesleyan Lay Leadership, 1791-1878*. Peterborough: Methodist Publishing House, 1988.

Beamont, W. *Walks about Warrington*. Warrington, n.d.

Beare, F.W. *The Gospel According to St. Matthew*. Oxford: Basil Blackwell, 1981.

Bebbington, D.W. *Evangelicalism in Modern Britain*. London: Unwin Hyman Ltd., 1989.

Bebbington, D.W. 'Holiness in Nineteenth Century Methodism', in W.M. Jacob and N. Yates (eds.) *Crown and Mitre:Religion and Society in Europe since the Reformation*. Woodbridge, Suffolk: Boydell Press, 1993.

Bebbington, D.W. *The Nonconformist Conscience*. London: George Allen & Unwin, 1982.

Beckerlegge, O.A. *The United Methodist Free Churches*. London: Epworth, 1957.

Bettenson, H. *Documents of the Christian Church*. London: Oxford University Press, 1963.

Bourne, H. *History of the Primitive Methodists*. Bemersley, 1823.

Bowmer, J.C. *Pastor and People*. London: Epworth, 1975.

Brake, G.T. *Policy and Politics in British Methodism 1932-1982*. London: B. Edsall & Co. Ltd., 1984.

Brown, K. *A Social History of the Nonconformist Ministry in England and Wales 1800-1930*. Oxford: Clarendon, 1988.

Bunting, T.P. *The Life of Jabez Bunting, D.D., with Notices of Contemporary Persons and Events*. 2 vols. London, 1859.

Burleigh, J.S. *A Church History of Scotland*. London: Oxford University Press, 1960.

Butterworth, J. *History and Description of the Town and Parish of Ashton-under-Lyne*. Oldham, 1823.

Bythell, D. *The Handloom Weavers*. London: Cambridge University Press, 1969.

Careful Observer, *Sound Thoughts for Sound People,* n.d.

Carwardine, R. *Transatlantic Revivalism: Popular Evangelicalism in Britain and*

America 1790-1865. London: Greenwood Press, 1978.

Carter, H. *The English Temperance Movement: A Study in Objectives*. London: Epworth, 1933.

Chadwick, O. *The Victorian Church*. 2 vols. London: Adam and Charles Black, 3rd ed. 1971.

Church, R. *The History of the British Coal Industry*. 3 vols. Oxford: Clarendon Press, 1986.

Cleverly, C. *Church Planting: Our Future Hope*. London: Scripture Union, 1991.

Cliff, P.B. *The Rise and Development of the Sunday School Movement in England, 1780-1980*. Redhill: National Christian Education Council, 1986.

Coad, F.R. *A History of the Brethren Movement*. Exeter: Paternoster Press, 1968.

Coleman, L. *A Church without Prelate*. London: T. Ward & Co. 1844.

Crowther, J. *Thoughts upon the Finances or Temporal Affairs of the Methodist Connexion*. Leeds, 1817.

Cudworth, W. *Rambles around Horton*. Bradford: Thomas Brear & Co. Ltd., 1886.

Curnock, N. (ed.) *The Journal of John Wesley*. 8 vols. London: Epworth, 1931.

Currie, R. *Methodism Divided*. London: Faber, 1968.

Dale, A.W.W. *The Life of R. W. Dale of Birmingham*. London: Hodder & Stoughton, 1898.

Dale, P.N. *Many Mansions. The Growth of Religion in Bolton 1750-1850*. Bolton, 1985.

Dale, R.W. *A Manual of Congregational Principles*. London: Hodder & Stoughton, 1884.

Dale, R.W. *The Atonement*, London, 1897.

Davey, C.J. *The Methodist Story*. London: Epworth, 1955.

Davies, C. Stella, *History of Macclesfield*. Manchester: Manchester University Press, 1961.

Davies, H. *Worship and Theology in England*. 4 vols. Grand Rapids: Wm. B. Eerdmans Publishing Co. 1996 reprint.

Davies R.E. et al (eds.) *A History of the Methodist Church in Great Britain*. 4 vols. London: Epworth, 1965, 1978, 1983, 1988.

Denovan, A. *Observations in Relation to Mr. Fleming of Neilston's 'Critique in favour of Civil Establishments of Christianity in Two Discourses'*. Glasgow: George Gallie, 1834.

[Denovan] *Joshua Denovan*. Toronto: Standard Publishing Company, 1901.

Dews, D.C. 'Methodism in Leeds from 1791 to 1861.' M. Phil. thesis, University of Bradford, 1984.

Dews, D.C. *Ranters, Revivalists, Radicals and Reformers*. Leeds Methodist District, 1996.

Directory of Sheffield, *1833*.

Dow, L. *The Dealings of God, Man and the Devil as experienced in the Life, Experience and Travels of Lorenzo Dow*. Norwich, Connecticut: William Faulkner, 1833.

Drummond, A.L. and J. Bulloch, *The Scottish Church 1688-1843*. Edinburgh: The St. Andrew Press, 1973.

Edwards, D.L. *The Futures of Christianity*. London: Hodder & Stoughton, 1987.

Edwards, M. *After Wesley*. London: Epworth, 1935.

Edwards, M. *Methodism and England*. London: Epworth, 1943.

Ellens, J.P. *Religious Routes to Gladstonian Liberalism: The Church Rate Conflict in*

England and Wales 1832-1868. University Park, Pennsylvania: Pennsylvania State University Press, 1994.

[Entwistle] *Memoir of the Rev. Joseph Entwistle by his son.* Bristol, 1848.

Evans, E.J. *The Forging of the Modern State.* London: Longman, 1983.

Flew R.N. (ed.), *The Nature of the Church.* London: SCM, 1952.

Garlick, K.B. *Mr. Wesley's Preachers.* London: World Methodist Historical Society, 1977.

Gentleman's Magazine, November 1800.

Goldman, R.J. *Readiness for Religion.* London: Routledge and Kegan Paul, 1995.

Goold W.H. (ed.), *The Works of John Owen.* 24. vols. London: 1850-5.

Gowland, D.A. *Methodist Secessions.* Manchester: Chetham Society, 1979.

Gregory, B. *Sidelights on the Conflicts in Methodism 1827-52.* London: Cassell & Co. Ltd. 1899.

Grubb, E. *What is Quakerism?* London: George Allen & Unwin Ltd., 1917.

Grundy, D. 'The Original Methodists' in *Proceedings of the Wesley Historical Society,* 1966: Vol. 35, Parts 5, 6, 7, 8; 1967: Vol. 36, Parts 1, 2, 3; 1968: Vol. 36, Parts 4, 5, 6.

Guthrie, D. *The Pastoral Epistles.* London: Tyndale Press, 1957.

Hastings, A. *A History of English Christianity 1920-1990.* London: SCM Press, 1991.

Hempton, D. *Methodism and Politics in British Society 1750-1850.* London: Hutchinson & Co. 1984.

Henderson, W.O. *The Lancashire Cotton Famine, 1861-1865.* Manchester: University Press, 1934.

Henry, M. *A Commentary on the Holy Bible.* London: Hodder & Stoughton, 1884.

Herod, G. *Historical and Biographical Sketches, Forming a Compendium of the History of the Primitive Methodist Connexion up to the year 1823.* London, 1851.

Hewitson, A. *Our Churches and Chapels, by Atticus.* Preston, 1869.

Hill, C. *Religion and Politics in Seventeenth Century England.* Brighton: The Harvester Press Ltd. 1986.

History of Batley, Birstall and Heckmondwike. Batley: J. Fearnsides & Sons, 1860.

Holmes, J. *Religious Revivals in Britain and Ireland 1859-1905.* Dublin: Irish Academic Press, 2000.

Horton, R.F. 'The Congregational Church' in *Our Churches and Why we belong to them.* London: Service and Paton, 1898.

Hurt, J.S. *Elementary Schooling and the Working Classes 1860-1918.* London: Routledge and Kegan Paul, 1979.

Hylson-Smith, K. *The Churches in England from Elizabeth I to Elizabeth II, Vol. III, 1833-1998.* London: SCM Press, 1998.

Isichei, E. *Victorian Quakers.* London: Oxford University Press, 1970.

Jackson, T. (ed.) *The Works of John Wesley.* 14 vols. Kansas City: Beacon Hill, 1978.

James, J. *The History and Topography of Bradford.* London: Longman, Brown, Green and Longmans, 1861.

Jeremy, D.J. *Capitalists and Christians: Business Leaders and the Churches in Britain, 1900-1960.* Oxford: Oxford University Press, 1990.

Jones, C. et al, *The Study of Spirituality.* London: SPCK, 1986.

Jones, R.M. *The Later Periods of Quakerism.* London: Macmillan & Co. 1929.

Jones, W.H. *One is Your Master.* Sheffield: Wesleyan Reform Church House, n.d.

Jordan, E.K.H. *Free Church Unity.* London: Lutterworth, 1956.

Joyce, P. *Work, Society and Politics: The Culture of the Factory in Later Victorian England.* London: Methuen, 1982.

Keeble, S.E. *Industrial Daydreams.* London, 1896.

W. Kelly (Ed.) *The Collected Writings of J.N. Darby,* 34 vols. London: 1834.

Kendall, H.B. *The Origin and History of the Primitive Methodist Church.* 2 vols. London: Edwin Dalton, n.d.

Kent, J. *Holding the Fort: Studies in Victorian Revivalism.* London: Epworth, 1978.

Kent, J. *Jabez Bunting, The Last Wesleyan.* London: Epworth, 1955.

Kent, J. *The Age of Disunity.* London: Epworth, 1966.

Kilham, A. *The progress of liberty amongst the people called Methodists.* Alnwick, 1796.

Lander, J.K. *Itinerant Temples: Tent Methodism 1814-1832.* Carlisle: Paternoster, 2003.

Larsen, T. *The Friends of Religious Equality: Nonconformist Politics in Mid-Victorian England.* Woodbridge, Suffolk: Boydell Press, 1999.

Laqueur, T.W. *Religion and Respectability.* Yale, 1976.

Lister, W. *The Life of the Reverend and Venerable William Clowes.* London: William Garner, 1868.

Livesey, J. *Reminiscences of Early Teetotalism.* Preston and London, 1872.

Local Notes and Gleanings: Oldham and Neighbourhood in Bygone Times. Oldham: Express Office, 1887.

Lockley, W.H. *The Story of the Stockport Circuit of the United Methodist Church.* Stockport, 1909.

Lovegrove, D.W. (ed.) *The Rise of the Laity in Evangelical Protestantism.* London: Routledge, 2002.

Lysons, K. *A Little Primitive.* Buxton: Church in the Marketplace Publications, 2001.

McGrath, A. *Christian Theology.* Oxford: Blackwell, 1994.

McLachlan, H. 'The Christian Brethren', in *The Story of a Nonconformist Library.* Manchester: University Press, 1923.

Macpherson, J. *Henry Moorhouse, the English Evangelist.* London: Morgan and Scott Ltd, n.d.

Malmgreen, G. *Silk Town: Industry and Culture in Macclesfield.* Manchester: University Press, 1985.

Milburn, G.E. and M. Batty, *Workaday Preachers.* Peterborough: Methodist Publishing House, 1995.

Moore, R. *Pitmen, Preachers and Politics.* Cambridge University Press, 1974.

Munson, J. *The Nonconformists: In Search of a Lost Culture.* London: SPCK, 1991.

Nickalls, J.L. (Ed.) *The Journal of George Fox.* Cambridge University Press, 1952.

Niebuhr, H.R. *The Kingdom of God in America.* New York: Harper and Row, 1959 [orig. 1937].

Niebuhr, R. *The Social Sources of Denominationalism.* New York, Meridian, 1929.

Nightingale, J. *Portraiture of Methodism.* London, 1807.

Nuttall, G.F. *The Puritan Spirit.* London: Epworth, 1967.

Parkes, W. 'The Arminian Methodists 1832-1837 (the "Derby Faith"): a case study in Wesleyan Deviation.' M. Phil. thesis, University of Keele, 1994.

Peacock, A.J. *Bradford Chartism, 1838-40.* York: St. Anthony's Press, 1969.

Petty, J. *The History of the Primitive Methodist Connexion from its origin to the Conference of 1859.* London: Richard Davies, Conference Offices.

Pilkington, W. *The Makers of Preston Methodism and the Relation of Methodism to the Temperance Movement.* London, 1890.

Pollock, A. *Priestcraft, Priestcraft, Priestcraft.* Glasgow, 1876.

Pope, L. *Millhands and Preachers.* Yale University Press, 1942.

Primitive Methodist Magazine, 1820, 1830, 1833, 1861.

Proceedings of the Wesley Historical Society.

Rack, H. *How Primitive was Primitive Methodism?* Englesea Brook, 1996.

Rack, H. *The Magic Methodists.* Methodist Church Chapel Aid Association Ltd., 2001.

Rack, H. 'Survival, Revival: John Bennet, Methodism and the Old Dissent', *Studies in Church History 7: Protestant Evangelicalism: Britain, Ireland, Germany and America c. 1750- c.1950.* Oxford: Published for the Ecclesiastical Society by Basil Blackwell, 1990.

Ramsey, T. *The Picture of Sheffield.* 1824.

Richardson, W.F. *Preston Methodism's 200 Fascinating Years.* 1975.

Richey, R.E. 'Revivalism: In Search of a Definition', *Wesleyan Theological Journal Vol. 28*, 1993.

Ridyard, R. *Memories of Lowton.* 1935.

Rigg, J.H. *Congregational Independency and Wesleyan Connexionalism Contrasted.* London, 1851.

Robinson, J.R. *Notes on Early Methodism in Dewsbury, Birstal and Neighbourhood.* Batley: J. Fearnsides & Sons, n.d.

Rowdon, H.H. *The Origins of the Brethren 1825-1850.* London: Pickering and Inglis, 1967.

Royle, E. *Chartism.* London: Longman Group, 1980.

Schaeffer, F. *The Great Evangelical Disaster.* Westchester, Illinois: Crossway Books, 1994.

Scotland, N. 'Evangelicalism and the Charismatic Movement' in C. Bartholomew et al, *The Futures of Evangelicalism* (Leicester: IVP, 2003).

Sharp A. and J. O'Neill, *Not Forgetting Caythorpe.* Trent Valley Local History Group, 1992.

Sellers, C.C. *Lorenzo Dow, Bearer of the Word.* New York: Minton, Balch & Co., 1928.

Sellers, I. *Nineteenth Century Nonconformity.* London: Edward Arnold, 1977.

Semmel, B. *The Methodist Revolution.* London: Heinemann, 1973.

Sigston, J. *A Brief Memoir of Joseph Woolstenholme.* London: Wesleyan Methodist Association Bookroom, 1846.

Smith, B. *History of Methodism in Macclesfield.* London: Wesleyan Conference Office, 1875.

Smith, L. *Religion and the Rise of Labour.* Keele: Ryburn Publishing, 1993.

Snell, K.D.M. and P.S. Ell, *Rival Jerusalems.* Cambridge University Press, 2000.

Stephenson, W.H. *Address to the People of Gateshead.* Newcastle, 1821.

Stephenson, W.H. *The Loyalty of Methodist Preachers exemplified in the Persecution of their Brethren.* Newcastle, 1819.

Stephenson, W.H. *A Sermon Preached in the Independent Methodist Chapel, Newcastle, On the Nineteenth of July 1821, The day of the Coronation of His Majesty George IV.* Newcastle: John Marshall, 1821.

Stephenson, W.H. *A Sermon occasioned on the Death of Mr. John Dungett.* Newcastle, 1833.

Swift, W.F. *Methodism in Scotland. The First Hundred Years.* London: Epworth, 1947.

Telford, J. (ed.) *The Letters of the Reverend John Wesley, A. M.* London: Epworth, 1931.

The Methodist New Connexion in Sheffield 1797-1879, Local History Pamphlet vol. 74. no 7.

The Methodist Church, Shelford Road, Radcliffe-on-Trent 1883-1893. Nottingham, 1993.

'*The Rise and Progress of Methodism in Lancaster. Part 19:1822-25. The Secession of 1824*' in Lancaster Circuit Wesleyan Methodist Church Record, *February 1903*.

Thompson, D. *The Chartists*. London: Temple Smith, 1984.

Thompson, D.M. *Let Sects and Parties Fall: a Short History of the Churches of Christ in Great Britain and Ireland*. Birmingham: Berean Press, 1980.

Thompson, D.M. 'The Nonconformist Social Gospel', *Studies in Church History 7: Protestant Evangelicalism: Britain, Ireland, Germany and America c. 1750-c.1950*. Oxford: Published for the Ecclesiastical Society by Basil Blackwell, 1990.

Thompson, E.P. *The Making of the English Working Class*. London: Victor Gollancz Ltd., 1965.

Tidball, D. *Who are the Evangelicals?* London: Marshall Pickering, 1994.

Townsend, H. *The Claims of the Free Churches*. London: Hodder & Stoughton, 1949.

Townsend, W.J. et al, *A New History of Methodism*. 2 vols. London: Hodder and Stoughton, 1909.

Trevelyan, G.M. *English Social History*. London: Longmans, Green & Co Ltd, 3rd edition, 1946.

Troeltsch, E. *The Social Teaching of the Christian Churches*. 2 vols. New York: Harper and Row, 1960.

Trotter, W. *The Justice and Forbearance of the Methodist New Connexion, as they were illustrated in the case of W. Trotter*. London, 1841.

Turner, J.M. *Conflict and Reconciliation*. London: Epworth, 1985.

Turner, J.M. *Modern Methodism in England, 1932-1998*. Peterborough: Epworth, 1998.

United Methodist Free Churches Magazine, 1866.

Unity Begins at Home. A report on the First British Conference on Faith and Order, Nottingham 1964. London: SCM Press, 1964.

Valenze, D. *Prophetic Sons and Daughters*. Princeton University Press, 1985.

van Noppen, J.P. *Transforming Words. The Early Methodist Revival from a Discourse Perspective*. Bern et al: Peter Lang, 1999.

Vickers, J. (Ed.) *A Dictionary of Methodism in Britain and Ireland*. London: Epworth, 2000.

von Harnack, A. *What is Christianity?* 5th edition. London: Ernest Benn Ltd. 1958.

Walford, J. *Memoirs of the Life and Labours of the Late Venerable Hugh Bourne*. 2 vols. London: T. King and Burslem: R. Timmis, 1855.

Walker, R.B. 'The Growth of Wesleyan Methodism in Victorian England and Wales', *Journal of Ecclesiastical History* vol. 24, no 3, 1973.

Walker, W. *Builders of Zion*. London: Henry Hook, n.d.

Ward, W.R. *Religion and Society in England 1790-1850*. London: B. T. Batsford, 1972.

Ward, W.R. *The Early Correspondence of Jabez Bunting*. London: Royal Historical Society, 1972.

Ward, W.R. *The Protestant Evangelical Awakening*. Cambridge: Cambridge University Press, 1992.

Watts, M. *The Dissenters*, 2 vols. Oxford: Clarendon Press, 1978, 1995.

Webb, S.J. *The History of Liquor Licensing in England principally from 1700 to 1830*. London: Longmans & Co., 1903.

Weber, M. *The Sociology of Religion*, Ephraim Fischoff trans. Boston: Beacon, 1964.

Wellock, W. *Off the Beaten Track*. India: Sarva Seva Sangh Prakashan Varanashi, third edition, 1980.

Werner, J.S. *The Primitive Methodist Connexion, Its background and Early History.*

London: University of Wisconsin Press, 1984.

Wesleyan Methodist Magazine,*1827, 1835, 1840,*

Wesleyan Methodist Association Magazine, *1839*

Wesleyan Protestant Methodist Magazine, *1829, 1830*

White, W. *History, Gazetteer and Directory of Norfolk.* 1845.

Whittaker, G. *The Landless Family of Colne.* Colne, 1970.

Wilkes, A. and J. Lovatt, *Mow Cop and the Camp Meeting Movement.* Leominster: Orphans' Printing Press, 1942.

Willans, J. *Batley Past and Present.* Batley: J. Fearnsides, n.d.

Williams, A.H. *Welsh Wesleyan Methodism 1800-1858.* Wrexham, 1935.

Wilkinson, J.T. *Hugh Bourne 1772-1852.* London: Epworth, 1952.

Wilkinson, J.T. *William Clowes 1780-1851.* London: Epworth, 1951.

Wilson, B. *The Struggles of an Old Chartist.* Halifax, 1887.

Wilson, B.R. *Patterns of Sectarianism.* London: Heinemann, 1967.

Winskill, P.T. *The Comprehensive History of the Rise and Progress of the Temperance Reformation from the Earliest Period to September 1881.* 4 vols. Liverpool, 1881.

Wood, A. *Nineteenth Century Britain, 1815-1914.* Singapore: Longman Group 1982, 2nd edition.

Worrall, B.G. *The Making of the Modern Church. Christianity in England since 1800.* London: SPCK, 1988.

Zion Methodist Church, Legh Street, Souvenir. Warrington, 1954.

Websites

Epiphany Trust www.epiphany.org.uk © The Epiphany Trust

Family Search, www.familysearch.org © 1992-2002 Intellectual Reserve Inc.

Index

Accrington, 146
Agricultural labourers, 93, 141
Alcohol (*see* Temperance)
Allan, Thomas, 44-45
American Civil War, 118
Andrews, Thomas, 97
Anglesey, 86
Ashton, James, 52
Ashton, Samuel, 82-83
Ashton-on-Mersey, 134, 226-227, 243;
Heald Green, 243
Ashton-under-lyne, 57-58, 209
Australia: Adamstown, 140; Jamberoo, Kiama, 139

Backhouse, Thomas, 125
Backhouse, Dr. Tom, 224, 253
Baildon, 102
Baines, Edward, 184
Baldwin, Joseph, 219
Band of Hope (*see* Temperance)
Bandroom Methodists (*see* Manchester)
Banner, Horace and Eva, 208, 222, 243
Baptists, 6, 131, 225, 252
Baptist Union of Great Britain, 260-263
Barker, Ellis, 150, 169, 189, 219
Barker, Joseph, 98-105
Barkerite churches and teaching, 100, 103, 107
Barnoldswick, 118-119, 138, 162
Barnsley PM Circuit, 93
Barrett, Arthur, 221

Barrett, Henry, 211-212
Batley, 101-102, 118, 236
Beaumaris WM Circuit, 86-87
Belper PM Circuit, 91
Bennett, John, 15
Benton, John, 93
Beresford, John, 19, 31
Berry, Robert, 132, 134
Bevan, Edith, 141, 207-208, 223, 243, 253
Bible Christians, 60, 104, 148
Bingley, 102, 114
Birchall, Joseph, 133
Birkett, George Harrison, 61
Birkenshaw, 102
Birstall, 103
Blackburn, 35, 94
Blacko, 240
Blackpool, 134
Blythe, A. 213-214
Board of Trade, 154
Bocr War, 155
Bolt, Martin, 241, 243
Bolton, 5, 46, 47, 51, 56, 58, 100, 104, 126, 142-143, 202, 236, 240, 249; Beverley Road, 156; Bridge Street WM, 46-47; Burial Board, 142, 268; Chalfont Street, 126; Folds Road, 47, 62, 67, 118-119, 167, 173, 188, 236; High Street, 127; Noble Street, 126-127, 162, 186-188; Top'oth Brow, 212
Bookroom, 120, 122, 245, 246

Boote, William, 138
Booth, John, 16
Bourne, Hugh, 18, 28-32, 83, 91; *Remarks on the Ministry of Women*, 30
Bradford, 64, 97, 103-104; Holme Lane 100, 102-103; Little Horton, 64; PM Circuit, 91
Bramwell, Thomas, 67
Bramwell, William, 25-26, 82
Branfoot, William, 123, 128-129
Breakfasts, free children's 145, 205
Brethren, 6, 101, 192
Brierfield, 207
Bright, John, 177
Brimelow, Henry, 173
Brimelow, James, 171, 193
Brimelow, Richard, 193
Brimelow, William, 119-122, 130-132, 138, 147, 149-150, 154, 159, 171, 175, 177, 187-188, 192-194, 200, 215, 270
Bristol, 130, 225; Bedminster, 130, 220; St. John's Lane, 207
Broadhurst, John, 21, 24, 26, 31, 57, 67
Bromsgrove, 267
Brown, W. Cyril, 222-223
Brown, W. Drummond, 212, 240
Bryant, Thomas, 15, 20
Buck, Thomas, 127
Bunting, Jabez, 19, 22-24, 33, 49, 55
Burials Bill, 1880, 179-180
Burland PM Circuit, 94, 97-98
Burnley: Mereclough WM, 185; PM Circuit, 95; Walkmill School, 185, 188
Burnside Holiday Home, 159, 201, 212
Burrows, Edward, 219
Burrows, William, 155, 183
Burrows, Willam G., 245, 259
Burslem WM Circuit, 28
Butcher, Thomas, 185
Butler, Nanny, 143

Caernarvon WM Circuit, 86-87
Calvinistic Methodists, 88
Campbell-Bannerman, Sir H., 119
Camp Meeting(s) 26, 28-29, 31, 90, 92, 99, 202,
Camp Meeting Methodists, 28-30
Cantrell, Jack, 224, 226-227
Carthy, William, 91-92
Castro, Daniel and Gail, 243
Caven, Joan, 227
Chapel building, 136-138
Chartism (*see* Politics)
Cheshire, 27, 118
Chester, 132
Chirk, 82
Christian Brethren, 98-104, 106-107, 123, 267, 296; Doctrines, 15; *Christian Brethren's Journal and Investigator,* 103
Christian education: British Lessons Council, 239, 251; National Christian Education Council, 238-239 (see also Sunday Schools *and* Sunday School Union)
Christian Endeavour, 144, 159, 226, 242, 258
Christian Lay Churches, 123-124, 128-30, 140
Christian perfection (*see* Theology)
Christian Responsibility Committee (*see* Social Concern) 255-256
Christian Revivalists (*see* Macclesfield)
Church of England, 11, 13, 56, 59, 75, 176, 179-180, 183-187, 190, 217-219, 258
Church of Scotland, 75
Churches of Christ, 6, 114
Church Rates, 64, 78-79, 177-178
Civil War, American, 118
Clarke, Richard, 57, 72
Cleckheaton, 102, 107, 114
Cliff College, 252
Clifford, John, 184, 190
Clowes, William, 31, 33
Coal (*see* Mining)
Collin, Robert W., 128
Colne, 95, 97, 189; Primet Bridge (Bethel), 132, 240; Waterside, 214
Colne and Nelson Circuit, 185, 206, 240
Congregationalism, 6, 108, 123, 131, 153; Congregational Union, 184

Corn Laws, 42, 67
Cotton (*see* Textile industries)
Countess of Huntingdon's Connexion, 259-260
Crawfoot, James, 28-29, 32
Crewe, 126, 132, 214, 236
Crowther, Jonathan, 42-43
Crumblehulme, William, 177
Cullen, John W., 139-140

Dale, R. W., 184, 188
Darlington, 129, 207
Darlington, Matthew, 94
Daughtery, William, 103
Davenport, John W., 214
Day, John, 248, 255
Delamere Forest, 28-29
Denovan, Alexander, 74-82, 84-85, 105-108, 120-121, 123, 175, 200, 215, 252, 269
Dewsbury, 115; Thornhill Edge, 91
Diggins, Judith, 241, 243
Disraeli, Benjamin, 176
Doughty, William, 92
Dow, Lorenzo, 20, 26-30, 32, 37, 117
Dow, Peggy, 27
Downing, Dennis, 227-228, 237, 240
Driffield, 81
Duckers, Joseph, 97
Dukinfield, 204
Durant, William, 216
Dyson, Benjamin, 104

Eaton, Thomas, 40, 58, 61, 63
Eccleston, William, 214
Eckersley, John, 81-82
Ecumenism, 147-153, 194, 216-219, 245, 249, 258-262; British Council of Churches, 183, 216, 255, 259-260; Churches Together in England, 260; Council of Churches for Britain and Ireland, 260; Methodist Ecumenical Conferences, 147, 155, 192; World Council of Churches, 255, 260
Education, 53-60, 183-192, 194, 229; 1870 Act, 184-185, 191; 1902 Act, 190-192; Day Schools, 185-190, 297; School Boards, 189 (*see* also Christian education, Sunday Schools)
Edwards, John, 224, 253
Embleton, Margaret, 157
Entwisle, Joseph, 12
Entwistle, Robert, 122, 179
Entwistle, Thomas, 62
Epiphany Trust, 256, 263
Evangelical Alliance, 252, 255, 268
Evangelism/ evangelists, 84-85, 92, 104, 120, 124, 130-136, 143, 159, 211, 226-229, 241-242, 295

Factory Act 1833, 58
Factory Bill 1843, 183
Female preaching (*see* Ministry)
Fielden, Festus, 64
Film Unit, 226-227, 240
Finney, Charles, 117-118, 144
Finney, John and Elsie, 222-223
Fitzgerald, Samuel, 117
Fitzgerald, Sarah, 143
Ford, George, 219
Foreign Missions (*see* mission, overseas)
Foreman, Alfred, 212-214, 225
Foreman, William, 209
Forward Movement, 212, 240
Fox, George, 34
Framework knitters, 93
Free Churches, 151-152, 168, 190-192, 217-219, 251, 258-259
Free Church of England, 259
Free Gospel, 20, 28, 42, 85, 91, 93-98, 102, 123, 129, 134, 139
French Revolution, 11
Friends, Society of (*see* Quakers)
Frost, William, 91, 97
Furness, John, 269

Garner, James, 124
Gateshead, 50; Gateshead and Shields Union, 50; Gateshead Fell, 48, 59; WM Circuit, 48
Gladstone, William, 176-179
Glasgow, 74-80, 82, 84, 127, 177, 207, 269; Charlotte Street, 137; Church Presbyterians, 76; Low Green Street, 75
Gleave, Gordon, 243, 253
Golborne, 214

Good, A.J., 214
Gospel Outreach Team, 241
Gospel Pilgrims, 64, 91, 97, 102, 296
Graham, Billy, 226-227, 241
Greatham, 242
Green, Clara, 143, 207, 214
Greenhalgh, James, 131
Great Yarmouth, 127
Gregory, Thomas, 19
Grey, Charles, 219-220, 224, 242, 253
Grey, Tom, 205
Grundy, William, 219

Haggate, 207
Halifax, 64, 91, 99
Halliday, Jeremiah, 102
'Hallelujah Bands', 131
Hampson, Bill, 256
Handloom weavers, 42, 66, 93, 124
Hanley, Lane Delph, 52
Harrison, Miles and Iris, 243
Harvey, W.H., 213
Haslingden, 135, 215
Haydock, 125
Hebburn, 243
Herod, George, 93
Heyworth, Barrie and Maureen, 243
High Legh, 246
Hill, J. David, 227, 237, 240-241, 243
Hill, Thomas, 46-47
Hill, Walter, 224
Hilton, Richard, 126
Hindley, 134
Hindley, William, 199
Holgate, John, 67
Hook Gate, 114, 202
Horden, 204, 227
Horwich, 162, 177, 185-186, 188, 249
Howarth, Adam, 64
Howell, Arthur, 156, 209
Hull, 135, 207
Hunt, Henry, 47-48
Hunter, George, 173

Ince, Arthur, 206
Independent Methodist characteristics:
    Changes in character, 247-262;
    Congregational polity, 43, 80, 84,
    107; Connexionalism, 80, 105, 109;

Decline, 205-207; Egalitarianism,
46, 68, 269; Heterogeneity, 65,
247; Independence, 106, 108;
Influences which shaped, 32-34;
Migration of members, 66-67, 247;
Sociological perspective, 65 (*see
also* Free Gospel, Ministry)
Independent Methodist doctrines:
Statement of Faith and Practice,
170, 250, 252, 289-293; *Testimony
and Principles of Union,* 105-110,
132, 150, 168, 170, 276-284 *(*see
also *Theology)*
Independent Methodist institutions:
Annual Meeting, function of, 30, 35,
79, 83, 104-108, 112, 130, 154,
240, 244-245; Association Incorporated, 153-155, 159; Connexional
Committee, 121, 136, 154, 169-
170, 215, 221; Constitutions, local,
85; Corporate trusteeship, 153;
Hymn Book, 120, 122, 129, 243;
Magazine, 78-79, 120, 129, 169-
171, 175, 190, 192-193; Missionary
Committee (*see* Evangelists), Model
Deed, 120, 136, 138, 150, 236;
Model Rules, 204; Name of denom-
ination, 120, 123-124; Presidential
office, 120, 181; *Rules of the
Independent Methodist Mission,*
81, 275; Union of churches, 28, 80,
104, 267
Independent Methodist Minority
Churches 1854-1860, 109; Minority
Churches 1907-23, 154
Independent Methodist Missionary
Committee, 80-83, 86, 88, 104,
112, 121, 131-132
Independent Primitive Methodists, 90-
91, 97, 123, 129, 134, 296
Independent Quarterly, 201-202
Inman, Lunn W., 145
Ireland, 76, 178-179; Downpatrick, 76

Jenkins, William, 22
Johnson, 'Curly' James, 173
Johnson, John W., 128, 168-171, 174, 214
Johnson, Dr. Paul 16, 27, 30

Jones, Rufus M., 171
Jones, Thomas, 43, 82-83, 86-88

Kay, Dr. W.W., 224, 238, 251, 259
Kelly, Hugh, 49-50
Kendal, 88
Kennedy, Matthew, 135, 172-173, 175,
Kilham, Alexander, 13, 17-18, 20;
    Kilhamites (see Methodist New
    Connexion)
Kip Hill, 129
Knight, Richard, 172
Knowles, John, 121, 132-134

Lambeth Conference, 217
Lancashire, 27, 42, 51, 52, 66, 83, 104,
    118, 235, 237, 262
Lancaster, 44, 100, 132, 143, 207, 236;
    Buck Street PM Chapel, 100
Landless, John, 96, 143
Lee, Geoffrey, 224
Lee, Richard, 143
Leeds, 25-26, 28, 31, 55, 83-85;
    Kirkgate Screamers, 25; Organ
    dispute, 83
Leigh, 27, 32, 44, 65, 124, 133-134, 158,
    243; Astley, 173, 212; Atherton, 134;
    Bright Street (Westleigh), 134, 173;
    Croft, 243; Culcheth, 243; Mill Lane,
    134, 173; The Avenue, 134, 236;
    Tyldesley, 173, 250, 252
Libraries, 145, 167
Lister, Thomas, 102
Liverpool, 32, 42, 43, 80, 82-83, 88-
    89, 104, 119, 125-126, 132, 136,
    214, 225, 242, 269; Benns Gardens,
    53; Cochrane Street, 227; Elizabeth
    Street, 118, 184; Goodison Road,
    220; Kirkdale (Tetlow Street), 126,
    214-215, 220; Maghull, 126; Mill
    Lane, 252
Livesey, Joseph, 62
Lloyd George, David, 154
Lockley, W. Philip, 222-223, 247
Logan, William, 215
Lomas, Geoff, 261
Lomax, Thomas, 181
Londonderry, Marquis of, 179
Lord's Day, the, 205, 234

Loughborough, 127, 135, 227, 237
Lowton/ Lowton Common, 37, 44, 52,
    133, 180, 185-186, 201, 206
Lymm, 134

Macclesfield, 18-20, 22, 24, 26, 29-31,
    35, 53, 67, 82, 104; Christian
    Revivalists, 19, 26, 28, 33;
Providence Chapel, Parsonage St, 19
Magic Methodists, 28
Maiden, Bill, 227
Maiden, Eddie, 255
Manchester, 13, 21-22, 26, 28, 30, 45,
    53, 57, 104, 119, 126, 202, 204,
    225-227, 236, 241-242; Band Room
    Methodists, 21-24, 26, 31, 33, 35;
    Blackley, 134, 212; Hanover Street,
    119; North Street, 21, 23-24;
    Oldham Street WM, 21, 23; Varley
    Street, 220
Market Drayton, 236
Mason, Granville, 241
Matley, Joseph, 25
McDougall, Eliza, 189
Methodists, 11-14, 21-25, 28, 32, 44-45,
    66, 123, 219-220, 252, 258; Con-
    certed Action; Ecumenical Conf-
    erences, 147, 155, 192; MAYC, 227;
    Union, 147-151, 191, 286-288 (also
    the various branches of Methodism)
Methodist New Connexion 13-14, 17-
    21, 27-28, 31, 74, 85, 99, 103, 148
Miall, Edward, 184
Mining 124-126, 140-142, 179, 182,
    219, 235, 270
Ministry, 214-216, 218, 250-254, 258-
    259, 261, 268-270; accreditation,
    75, 139, 215; anticlericalism, 13, 68,
    99, 102; authority, 106-107; chap-
    laincy, 156, 215, 254; civil recog-
    nition, 157; clergy/laity, 34, 65, 90,
    123; conferences, 209; exemption
    from military service, 156, 216;
    female reaching/ministry, 30, 65;
    funerals, 142-143; lecture week-
    ends, 201; occupations, 141-143;
    ordination, 75; plural ministry, 75,
    82, 88; Students' Association, 201

Ministry: payment issues, 26, 34, 43, 50, 52, 65-66, 75, 77, 84-85, 89, 92, 94, 96, 99-100, 110, 127-128, 132, 134, 141-143, 148-153, 215, 249, 253-254
Ministers' Assistance Fund, 120
Ministers' Education Scheme, 120, 156, 168, 201, 212-213, 215, 250-251
Minor Wesleyans, 83, 86-88, 267
Mission, overseas: 140-141, 207-209, 222, 227, 244
Mission, overseas locations: Austria, 244; Brazil, 208-209, 222, 227; Cambodia, 244; China, 141; Costa Rica, 244; Colombia, 244; Cyprus 244; France, 244; Gambia, 244; India, 140-141, 207, 222-223, 244; Italy, 244; Ivory Coast, 244; Jordan, 244; Korea, 141; North Africa, 244; Pakistan, 244; Philippines, 244; Rwanda, 244; South Africa, 227; Thailand, 244; Uganda, 244.
Missionary societies: China Inland Mission, 141; Donald Frazer Mission Hospital, 227; Friends Foreign Missions Committee, 140-141, 222-223; Operation Mobilisation, 244; Overseas Missionary Fellowship, 244; Unevangelised Fields Mission, 208, 227; United Church of Canada, 223; Worldwide Evangelisation Crusade, 208
Moody, D. L., 131, 144
Moorhouse, Henry, 130
Morecambe, 135, 207
Mounfield, Arthur, 26, 61, 79, 140, 145, 149, 168-171, 193-194, 202
Mow Cop, 29
Murray, James, 210, 218
Murray, James D., 219-220, 224
Murton, 180
Mutual Improvement Societies, 145, 167, 182

Napoleonic Wars, 42, 70n
Nationwide Initiative in Evangelism, 259
Nelson, 95, 126, 138, 189, 206; Barkerhouse Road, 127, 207; Bradshaw Street, 250; Every Street, 207;

Nelson Church, 254; Salem, 95-96, 127, 143, 155, 157, 162, 173, 182, 188, 207, 269
Neston, 126
Newbury, 236
Newcastle-upon-Tyne, 50, 75, 78, 83, 88, 128, 256;
Town Moor, 47
Nield, John, 25
Nield, John (2nd), 63, 121
Nightingale, Joseph, 19, 33
Norfolk 91, 97
North East England, 49, 80, 125, 235, 237, 241-242
North East Help Link, 256-257, 253
Northern Counties Confederation, 129-130, 202, 225, 227, 241-242
North Shields, 47, 49
Northumberland, 207
North Walsham PM Circuit, 91
Northwich WM Circuit, 13, 15, 27-29
Nottinghamshire, 90-91, 134, 207; Bingham, 90; Bulwell, . 220; Lowdham, 91; Nottingham, 135-136, 214, 236

Okell, Joseph, 52
Oldham, 24-25, 28, 30, 50, 55, 63, 67, 79, 104, 127, 236; Broadway Street (Bethesda), 104, 145; Failsworth, 135, 257; George Street, 25, 158, 236; Grasscroft, 135; King Street, 63, 139, 145, 185; Lees, 64, 103; St. Mary's Street, 135; Smith Street, 145, 269; Waterhead Mill, 60; Whitehead Square, 25
Old Independents, 76
Openshaw, T. R., 153, 159, 174, 206, 209, 212, 216-217
Original Methodists, 91-93, 97, 267
Oswestry, 92
Owens, Owen, 87-88
Oxley, Thomas, 120
Oxley, William, 122, 138, 197n

Pacifism/ Peace, 51-52, 64-65, 99, 155-156, 201-202, 220, 225
Parker, William , 67, 81.104
Parkinson, John, Jr., 102

Parkinson, John, Sr., 91, 97, 104
Pastoral Office (*see* Wesleyan Methodism)
Peacock, Hannah (*see* Phillips, Hannah)
Pentecostal League of Prayer, 174
Persecution, 52-53
Peterloo Massacre 5, 9, 45-47
Phillips, Hannah, 16, 27
Phillips, Peter 16-17, 27, 30, 34, 44, 46, 51-52, 54, 63-64, 67, 107-108, 272
Pilter, Robert, 47-49
Pleasant Sunday Afternoon societies, 167
Plymouth Brethren, 101
Politics, 46-49, 64, 66, 68, 99, 174-183, 194-195, 224; Chartists 64-66, 99-100, 106, 144, 229; Democracy, 11, 144, 175; Industrial relations and employment, 182, 203, 205, 219; Labour Party, 173, 181-183, 202; League of Nations, 172, 202, 206; Liberal Party, 66, 119, 175-177, 181, 183, 186, 189-190, 224; Liberation Society, 176, 180; Members of Parliament, 181-182, 203, 219-220; Public office holders, 181; Movement for Christian Democracy, 256; Radical Reformers, 42, 44-57, 50-51, 58, 64, 66, 68, 78, 144; Tories/Conservatives, 177, 186;
Pollock, Archibald, 177-178
Poverty, 13, 16, 30, 42-45, 53-56, 58-61, 64-68, 76, 78, 90, 93, 118-119, 146, 160, 167, 181, 203, 269; Poor Law Unions, 119
Presbyterian (-ism), 75, 82, 84, 106
Prescott, Norman, 254
Prescott, Trevor, 248
Preston, 20, 31, 35, 62, 109, 269; Back Lane WM, 20; Lord Street MNC, 20; Vauxhall Road, 20
Price, Will, 158
Primitive Methodists, 51, 60, 64, 74, 100, 148, 191, 202, 204, 219, 267; Bookroom, 30; Conference, 98; day schools, 184; discipline, 94; finance,

92-93; free gospelism in, 93-94, 98, 296; origins, 26, 29, 31 preachers and leaders, 93-94; schisms, 90-98, 127, 130; view of itinerancy, 85
Primitive Methodist Revivalists, 91, 296
Protestant Methodists (*see* Wesleyan Protestant Methodists)
Pwllheli WM Circuit, 87

Quakers, 6, 16, 27-29, 34, 61, 66, 99, 127, 140, 145, 148, 153, 171, 192, 211, 218, 225, 229
Quaker Methodists, 15-17, 27-29

Radcliffe, 249
Radical Reformers (*see* Politics)
Ralphs, Edward, 144, 158, 168, 193-194, 200, 217
Rastrick, 35, 64, 91
Reform Act, 1867, 175-176
Resource Centre (*see* Bookroom)
Revivalism, 12, 18-25, 28, 30-31, 33-34, 52, 90, 98, 127
Revival of 1859, 117-118
Riding, Ward, 170
Rigby, Andrew, 245
Rimmer, Robert, 214
Ripley, Dorothy, 16
Roberts, John, 108-109
Robinson, David, Jenny, Mary, 243
Robinson, Joseph, 216, 219, 224
Robinson, Dr. and Mrs. Joseph, 140-141, 207
Robinson, Sir Thomas, 181, 219
Roe Green, 57, 59, 64, 162, 253
Rolfe, Hilda, 227
Roman Catholicism, 79, 179-180, 258
Roscoe, Alfred, 124
Rushton, Benjamin, 64
Sabbath (*see* Lord's Day)

St. Helens, 124, 183; Parr, 83; Sutton, 126, 173, 212; Thatto Heath, 125
Salford: Brighouse Street, 205, 225; Fitzwarren Street, 205, 220, 225; Salem, Pendleton, 119, 167, 185, 189, 202, 225; Weaste, 135, 225
Salisbury, Lord, 179
Sanderson, William, 34, 65, 89, 94-95,

97, 100, 102-108, 118-120, 122, 126, 132, 134, 147, 159, 166-167, 269
Sankey, Ira D., 161
Scientific enquiry, 168; evolution, 174
Scotland, 74, 79, 82, 177; Bothwell, Hamilton, Lanark, Paisley, 76 (and see Glasgow)
Scroggie, W. Graham, 174
Seaham Colliery, 126
Selstonites (see Original Methodists)
Shakespeare, J. H., 151
Sharples, Henry, 223
Shavington, 114
Sheffield 20, 31-32, 35, 48, 80-81, 83, 88, 104; Bow Street, 21, 85-86; Scotland Street MNC, 20-21
Shires, Ai, 216
Sidmouth, Lord, 44-45
Sigston, James, 21, 25, 30-31; Sigstonians, 25
Slack, James, 126
Smith, George, 20, 31, 88
Smith, Gypsy, 151
Smith, Rennie, 182, 202
Social concern, 203-204; Christian Responsibility Committee 255-256; Christian Social Council, 216; Jubilee Campaign, 256; social conscience, 254-256, 263; social provision, 204-205
Southport, 241
Spencer, Joseph, 107
Spennymoor, 129; Brandon, 207; Kelloe, 207; Metal Bridge, 207, 237; Mission Band, 237
Stanworth, Anne, 243-244
Starosta, Nona, 256
Stephenson, William H., 47-51
Stockport, 17-18, 28, 30, 53-54, 62, 104, 119, 185, 207
Stockton, 129
Stout, Ron and Betty, 227, 242
Stretford, 140, 181, 227, 243; Trafford, 243
Student Volunteer Movement, 140
Sunday Schools, 53-60, 201, 206, 220, 225-226, 238-240; Anniversaries,

145; Charity Sermons, 57, 145; Sedition, allegations of, 56; Writing, teaching of, 55-58
Sunday School Union, National, 56, 201, 251, 258
Sunderland, 50, 56, 127-130, 205, 209, 212, 242;
Bethany, 214, 220; Bethel, Thorney Close, 243; Boldon, 220; Easington Lane, 126, 237, 257; New Silksworth, 242, 250; PM Circuit, 127-128; Robert Street, 174, 214; Tatham Street PM Church, 127, 129
Swindells, Gamaliel, 17-18
Swinton, Moorside, 162, 207

Temperance, 60-65, 78, 99, 102-103, 146-147, 178, 203-205, 249, 255, 285; 'Jerry shops', 61-62; Licensing legislation, 60-61, 178, 203-204; Temperance Committee, 146, 203; Temperance organisations, 63, 146
Tent Methodists, 40.
Textile industries, 141-142, 270; Cotton famine, 65, 118-119; Cotton industry, 58, 95, 118-119, 124, 141, 160, 206; woollen industry, 124
Theatre Royal, 246-247
Theology, 105; Arianism, 43, 105-106; Arminian/Wesleyan, 5, 32, 43, 76-79, 106; Baptism, 211, 248, 261; Biblical authority, 168, 223-224, 263; Biblical criticism, 168, 192, 209; Calvinism, 76-79, 118, Charismatic movement, 249, 263; Christology, 209-210; Christian Perfection or entire sanctification, 5, 12, 18, 32, 118, 174, 214; Creeds, 106-107, 109, 172, 210; Ecclesiology, 107, 110, 124; Evangelicalism, 174, 209, 250, 258, 260; Heterodoxy, 109; Kingdom of God, 209-210; Liberal theology, 172, 174, 202, 214, 229, 251; Moral relativism, 224; Pelagianism, 77; Social gospel, 173-174, 194; Theological change, 166, 209-211, 228-229, 263; Universalism, 171, 210, 228
Thornton, Charles, 209-210

Trotter, William, 99-101
Turton, Dr. George, 31, 80-81, 86, 88
Twiss, Edward, 120

Tyneside, 42, 49, 86
Unitarian(ism) 79, 99-100, 104, 109
United Methodists, 104, 150, 219, 268
United Methodist Free Churches, 148, 152, 267
United Reformed Church, 252

Valenze, Deborah, 65-67
Vickers, James Jr., 156, 192-194, 270
Vickers, James Sr., 167-168

Wales, Welsh, 42-43, 80, 82, 86, 88; South Wales,
130; Talywain, 135; Trealaw, 135
Walker, Thomas, 135
Ward, Douglas, 241
Warrington, 17, 27-31, 44, 51, 61, 83, 93, 104, 108, 127, 32, 205, 240; Appleton, 243; Bank Street WM, 15, 16; Brick Street, 54, 57; Buckley Street, 205; Friars Green, 17, 54, 62, 184, 221; Grappenhall, 208; Kent Street, 242; Risley, 33; Stockton Heath, 40, 54-55, 57-58, 61, 145, 240, 243; Westy, 243, 257
Watson, Arthur, 148, 189, 199
Watts, Michael, 66
Weaver, Richard, 130
Wellock, Wilfred, 157, 173, 182
Welsh Wesleyan Methodists, 42-43, 86
Wedgwood, John, 93
Weir, Mark and Alison, 243
Wesley, John, 11, 32, 55, 77, 174
Wesleyan Methodist(s) 15, 24, 33, 58, 74, 80, 148, 152, 176, 204, 219, 267; Committee on Religious Privileges, 48; Conference, 12, 55, 58; Discipline, 87; Education Committee, 184-185; Home Missions Department, 131; Loyalty to the Crown, 45; Pastoral office, doctrine of, 24; Radical politics embargoed, 46; Working classes, loss of influence, 51, 68
Wesleyan Methodist Association 82-83,

88-89
Wesleyan Protestant Methodist(s), 20, 25, 31, 50, 82-86, 267
Wesleyan Reform Union, 147-149, 152-153, 158, 259-260
Westhoughton, 64; Dicconson Lane, 143;
Wingates, 45-46, 51, 57, 67, 144, 156, 186, 188, 207; *Wingates Messenger;* Wingates Temperance Band, 146
Westmorland, 127
Wigan, 56, 59, 104-105, 124, 126, 132; Downall Green, 257; Greenough Street, 220, 236, 245; Ince, 134; Lamberhead Green, 125, 245; Low Green (Platt Bridge), 125-126; New Springs, 125-126; Newtown, 201; Spring View, 134; Stubshaw Cross, 134, 145; Westwood, 125
Wilkes, Peter, 227-228
Wilkinson, Frederick, 188
Wilkinson, Walter, 256-257
Willington, 243
Wilmslow, 35
Women, ministry of (*see* Ministry)
Women's Auxiliary, 158, 202
Woods, R. B., 134, 158
Woollen industry, (*see* Textile industries)
Woolstenholme, Joseph, 38, 82, 88
World War I, 155-158, 171, 192, 200, 204-205, 216, 228; Conscientious objectors, 155, 157; Conscription Act, 156; Military Test Case, 156-157
World War II, 200, 204, 207, 211, 216, 219, 220-222, 225, 229
Worthington, Thomas, 132, 147, 154
Wrexham, 87, 236
Wyatt, Ken and Maureen, 243-244

Yates, Derek, 245
Yorkshire, 27, 64, 81, 103, 107, 236
Young Men's Fellowship, 158, 171, 202
Young people's activity, 225-228, 246; Children's Circle, 202; IMTAKS, 227, 237; Knock, 238; Quinta, 238 (*see also* Sunday Schools)

Printed in the United Kingdom
by Lightning Source UK Ltd.
104937UKS00001B/47-384

9 780227 679838